Musicology and Difference

Musicology and Difference

Gender and Sexuality in Music Scholarship

EDITED BY

Ruth A. Solie

UNIVERSITY OF CALIFORNIA PRESS
Berkeley   Los Angeles   London

University of California Press
Berkeley and Los Angeles, California

University of California Press, Ltd.
London, England

© 1993 by
The Regents of the University of California

Library of Congress Cataloging-in-Publication Data

Musicology and difference : gender and sexuality in music
scholarship / Ruth A. Solie.
    p.   cm.
Includes bibliographical references and index.
ISBN 0-520-07927-2 (alk. paper)
1. Sexuality in music.   2. Music—Psychological aspects.
3. Musicology.   I. Solie, Ruth A.
ML3838.M96   1993
780′.82—dc20   92-16317
                                                          CIP

Printed in the United States of America
9 8 7 6 5 4 3 2 1

For Marilyn and Susan

What is this "civilization" in which we find ourselves? What are these ceremonies and why should we take part in them?
Virginia Woolf, *Three Guineas*

Contents

INTERPRETIVE STRATEGIES

CRITICAL READINGS

Acknowledgments

The original idea for this book came from Judith Tick. I'm sure that a number of grand projects are first conceived over breakfast at musicology meetings, as this one was, but I doubt that many of them are so energetically godmothered afterwards. Although Judith was not able to serve as co-editor of the volume, as we had originally planned, it has profited immeasurably from her critical eye and her intellectual verve; I hope she will be glad that she mentioned it.

Doris Kretschmer, of the University of California Press, understood the importance of this project from the first and shepherded it through the long publication process with inexhaustible patience, tact, and good cheer.

The authors of the fifteen essays here must, of course, have the lion's share of thanks. They were a joy and a privilege to work with.

Introduction: On "Difference"

Ruth A. Solie

"Man that is born of a woman," says Job, "is of few days and full of trouble." But woman, alas for euphony, is also born of a woman—and if she is moved, unexpectedly, into the subject position in the verse, she disrupts its poetic duality. If we understand *man* here as a universal term for human beings, as commonsense exegesis suggests, we must nonetheless construe *woman* as particular and, thus, oppositional. Job's language indulges a habit long familiar in the discourses of the West: the everyday terms we use for human subjectivity (*one, he, everyone, mankind*) make universal claims but are nonetheless situated as male within cultural practice. The rhetorical opposition in Job's text is instructive: it invites us, as do all of the essays in the present volume, to ponder the generic and the specific, the universal and the particular. In short, it invites us to consider whether and in what circumstances the differences between and among people are worth taking seriously.

This is, to my knowledge, the first book about musicology and difference, and it was difficult to give a name to.[1] Perhaps a few words are in order about how to understand the title finally chosen. First and foremost, it is intended not to endorse the concept of *difference* but, rather, to interrogate it, as a comparative reading of the individual essays will make

This essay was written with considerably more than "a little help from my friends." For careful readings and many insightful and helpful suggestions—some rather stern—I am most grateful to Leyla Ezdinli, Marilyn Schuster, Elizabeth Spelman, Catharine Stimpson, Gary Tomlinson, and Elizabeth Wood. I have not always taken their advice, which is, of course, no responsibility of theirs.

1. An important collection dealing with many of the same issues, but not invoking this particular rubric, is Susan McClary's *Feminine Endings: Music, Gender, and Sexuality* (Minneapolis, 1991).

1

more than clear. Although all of the authors are concerned with matters that shelter under this rather broad umbrella, readers will find no obligatory or even consistent politics among them. Neither do we pretend to address all "differences" (interdisciplinary critical work presently has a great number of such categories under study); rather, while our title identifies the thematic focus of our volume, the subtitle makes clear its categorical limitations.

Invoking the notion of difference places us immediately upon the horns of a dilemma. As legal scholar Martha Minow has written, "When we identify one thing as like the others, we are not merely classifying the world; we are investing particular classifications with consequences and positioning ourselves in relation to those meanings. When we identify one thing as unlike the others, we are dividing the world; we use our language to exclude, to distinguish—to discriminate."[2] That is, on the one hand we confront the familiar danger of labeling some person or group as outside, inferior, or Other; but on the other hand we take the risk of demanding similarity or adherence to a norm whose valuation may be tacit.[3] Thus we may be caught between what Naomi Schor, in a memorable formulation, has dubbed "othering" and "saming."[4] What we need, Minow goes on to suggest, are ways of understanding when different treatment stigmatizes, and when similar treatment stigmatizes by disregarding difference.[5]

In various forms, this dilemma currently preoccupies a broad array of historical and critical disciplines. Whether the issue is gender, sexuality, race, social class, or a complex combination of these and other factors, interpretive controversies swirl around the legitimacy of labeling groups "different" from one another and, conversely, the legitimacy of claims of "difference" those same groups may make for their own purposes—for instance, to assert authority and control over their history or the interpretation of their own texts.[6] In either case, it is worth observing, a certain

2. Martha Minow, *Making All the Difference: Inclusion, Exclusion, and American Law* (Ithaca, 1990), p. 3.

3. On some musical ramifications of this last point, see Maynard Solomon, "Beethoven's Ninth Symphony: The Sense of an Ending," *Critical Inquiry* 17 (1991): 289–305.

4. Naomi Schor, "This Essentialism Which Is Not One: Coming to Grips with Irigaray," *differences* 1, no. 2 (1989): 38–58. For an anthropological view of the same phenomenon, see Johannes Fabian, "Presence and Representation: The Other and Anthropological Writing," *Critical Inquiry* 16 (1990): 753–72; I am grateful to Gary Tomlinson for this reference.

5. Minow, *Making All the Difference*, p. 20.

6. I offer as one example among many an anthology edited a few years ago by Henry Louis Gates, Jr., entitled *"Race," Writing, and Difference* (Chicago, 1986). The essays in the volume originally appeared in two issues of *Critical Inquiry*, 12, no. 1 (1985) and 13, no. 1 (1986). A similar debate on Afro-American literary theory occurred in *New Literary History* 18, no. 2 (1987).

amount of power accrues to whoever is in the position to decide what is "same" and what is "different."

My intent in this introduction is to chart the terrain of the difference debate.[7] I would like to explore the range of positions argued by an interdisciplinary array of scholars. (Musicologists have lately taken to deploring our customary methodological behindhandedness, but it does permit us to profit from a good deal of prior thought and exploration.) At the same time, I hope that such a survey can provide a context for reading and interpreting the essays that follow and for imagining inter-actions and confrontations of one with another. I want to make clear, though, that my illustrative references to these essays at apposite points in my discussion are by no means intended to stand as adequate sum-maries of their own arguments, or even to identify their central points as their authors see them.

To begin, I want to locate these issues of difference in the musicological sites where they come into play: that is, in the formulation of the most basic questions about what pieces of music can express or reflect of the people who make and use them, and thus of the differences between and among those people. These have not traditionally been central questions in musicology—a fact which bewilders many historians and critics in other fields—but only the most extreme formalist position (rare nowadays) can resist them altogether. Even advocates of that stance have customarily been able to speak, for instance, of "national styles," an acknowledged difference that may open the logical door to others. This example will serve to remind us that insofar as any matter of difference is taken to concern convention or the semiotic operation of a given musical lan-guage, it need not entail "essentialist" views (although, to be sure, it may accommodate them). Nonetheless, it is essentialism—which I will for the moment define as the doctrine that certain characteristics are essential and innate in certain groups (I intend to complicate the definition further on)[8]—that seems to be the sticking point in carrying such speculations further.

7. A good overview, from a scientific standpoint, is provided by Rachel T. Hare-Mustin and Jeanne Marecek in "The Meaning of Difference: Gender Theory, Postmodernism, and Psychology," *American Psychologist* 43 (1988): 455–64. Another, historical in orientation, is Joan W. Scott, "Deconstructing Equality-versus-Difference: Or, the Uses of Poststructuralist Theory for Feminism," *Feminist Studies* 14 (1988): 33–50.

8. Jean-François Lyotard defines essentialism in linguistic terms, as that which "con-ceives the referent of the name as if it were the referent of a definition" (*The Differend: Phrases in Dispute*, trans. Georges Van Den Abbeele, Theory and History of Literature 46 [Min-neapolis, 1988], p. 53).

Essentialism has a bad name. Both common sense and common decency incline us to reject the kinds of claims that have been used to legitimize the Holocaust, racist regimes, and the most vicious forms of homophobia and misogyny. And yet some theorists are now arguing that the *charge* of essentialism has itself become a mindless bludgeon wielded to stop conversation. "What revisionism . . . was to Marxism-Leninism, essentialism is to feminism: the prime idiom of intellectual terrorism and the privileged instrument of political orthodoxy. . . . The word essentialism has been endowed . . . with the power to reduce to silence, to excommunicate, to consign to oblivion."[9] Less dramatically but just as emphatically, another writer contends that few words in the critical vocabulary are "so little interrogated, and so predictably summoned as a term of infallible critique."[10] What prompts the heat of these objections? What interpretive loss are these critics identifying, serious enough to motivate the rehabilitation of a concept so provocative and with such a dubious past?

A theorist like Luce Irigaray would suggest that access to subjectivity is at stake, for whole categories of people; that, by claiming a special essence, women (or Blacks, or gays) resist the oppressive force of fictive universals like those Job invoked. French feminists have generally grounded their theories on the assumption of a feminine sexuality radically different from the masculine, a sexuality that is, in some versions, fundamentally bodily (though in others it is a matter of libidinal economy), and which produces a specific *écriture féminine*.[11] Such a notion, if credible and viable, would of course be of considerable heuristic use to musicologists; but it has, as Arleen Dallery has pointed out, "triggered an antiessentialist paranoia"[12] by virtue of the fact that it may be thought to invoke just the biological differences that led Freud to pontificate that "anatomy is destiny." The most sophisticated practititioners of French feminism insist, however, that even notions of radical female *altérité* may escape the charge of essentialism (still in the sense of biological deter-

9. Schor, "This Essentialism," p. 40.

10. Diana Fuss, *Essentially Speaking: Feminism, Nature, and Difference* (New York, 1989), p. xi.

11. My colleague Leyla Ezdinli has objected to this formulation and reminds me that the arguments of French feminism—subtle, playful, and grounded in somewhat unfamiliar philosophical traditions as they are—are all too easy for American scholars to misread. Although I take her point, I maintain that mine represents at least one possible reading of Irigaray, Hélène Cixous, and Julia Kristeva, and one that, rightly or wrongly, has been extremely influential in the development of American feminist thought. At the same time, it is worth noting that Cixous herself has applied the term *écriture féminine* to male writers.

12. Arleen Dallery, "The Politics of Writing (the) Body: *Écriture Féminine*," in Alison M. Jaggar and Susan R. Bordo, eds., *Gender/Body/Knowledge: Feminist Reconstructions of Being and Knowing* (New Brunswick, N.J., 1989), pp. 52–67.

minism) once it is understood that the body, too, is constituted and produced by culture, that "writing the body" is a performative activity.[13]

Some, however, are not concerned to escape the charge; they espouse biology and may explicitly embrace essentialism, which, as Gayatri Spivak has repeatedly argued, can be a powerful tool in the hands of the oppressed themselves.[14] To concerns that such a scheme merely reinvokes the mechanisms of oppression, these scholars respond that the risk is worth taking, that the practice of such an "identity politics" is an important strategy for reclaiming and valorizing the specific traits on account of which some group has already been defined as different and oppressed by others. This is a point of view with considerable historical familiarity, particularly to Britons and Americans; in both of those countries the campaigns for woman suffrage were largely based on such rhetoric, claiming that women's votes would "naturally" be cast for peace, family values, and various forms of moral rectitude.[15]

Like biology, psychology provides a ground for the invocation of strong forms of difference. Kaja Silverman, for instance, has based her remarkable work on cinema on such psychoanalytic concepts as castration anxiety, the infantile experience of the maternal voice, and the Oedipus complex, but she is adamant that her particular formulations avoid the hazards these ideas present in orthodox Freudian hands; she is unwilling "to suggest that female sexuality precedes language and symbolic structuration—to give it, in other words, an essential content."[16] The symbolic structuration is, of course, precisely what she wishes to study as it informs the conventions of filmmaking, and it is precisely the matter that could concern musical investigation as well. Somewhat similar assumptions have been used by Catherine Clément in

13. This assertion is of course counterintuitive. But see, for example, the essays collected in Catherine Gallagher and Thomas Laqueur, eds., *The Making of the Modern Body: Sexuality and Society in the Nineteenth Century* (Berkeley, 1987), as well as Laqueur's *Making Sex: Body and Gender from the Greeks to Freud* (Cambridge, Mass., 1990). See also Dallery, "The Politics of Writing (the) Body"; and Fuss, *Essentially Speaking*, chapter 4.

14. For instance, Spivak has claimed that "we have to look at where the group—the person, the persons, or the movement—is situated when we make claims for or against essentialism. A strategy suits a situation; a strategy is not a theory" (Gayatri Chakravorty Spivak with Ellen Rooney, "In a Word: Interview," *differences* 1, no. 2 [1989]: 127).

15. Essentialist beliefs were widely shared in late nineteenth- and early twentieth-century American culture—so that it made strategic sense, in Spivak's terms, for suffragists to invoke them—and the opposing viewpoint was much less visible than it has since become. Throughout her career, historian Mary Beard protested the essentialists' assumptions and, in consequence, felt the need to repudiate the term "feminist" altogether—an unfortunate irony, considering subsequent history.

16. Kaja Silverman, *The Acoustic Mirror: The Female Voice in Psychoanalysis and Cinema* (Bloomington, 1988), p. 123.

her *Opera, or the Undoing of Women*,[17] and there is no reason to suppose that the same symbolic operations cannot be examined in more detail within the sphere of musical sound alone.

Theories of difference, then, may operate independently of any commitment to essentialism, or even in repudiation of it. Their proponents point to the crucial importance, both political and epistemological, of such theories, and the politics of the debate are sometimes a little unexpected. It is, after all, the liberal intellectual who traditionally holds that the notion of difference is pernicious in any form, since from it prejudice and discrimination seem inevitably to follow. For American liberals in particular this argument has been undergirded by our heritage of "melting pot" imagery. But such a commitment remains problematic. It is not so far from an assumption of similarity to the demand for it, and it is not surprising that such demands, when they arise, come from those in charge. (White Anglo Protestants in the United States were hardly expected to "melt" into something resembling Eastern European or Asian immigrants; rather the reverse. By the same token, calls for "unity" are often decodable as demands for acquiescence.) If I can reasonably expect you to be the same as I am, then perhaps I am entitled to be outraged or simply incredulous if you insist upon behaving differently—if, for example, you do not hear a piece of music the way I do. We may offer competing accounts, but our disagreement takes on an explicitly political cast when your hearing arises from your experience within a marginalized and "different" community and mine from dominant cultural expectations. In that case I may feel justified in claiming that my version is simply "the way it goes."[18]

Politically, then, difference is about power. And, as we have seen, claiming one's own difference may be a form of resistance against subsumption into an undifferentiated universal subject. As Melissa Orlie puts it, "Difference . . . represents the subversive possibility of life and practices structured on alternative terms. The cultural knowledge and forms of resistance created by 'others,' by virtue of their marginalized and outcast character, may challenge the very presuppositions of given political and social relations."[19] In a similar vein, Biddy Martin speaks of the potential of a theorized lesbianism "as a position from which to read

17. Catherine Clément, *Opera, or the Undoing of Women*, trans. Betsy Wing (Minneapolis, 1988).

18. It seems clear that a claim of this sort underlies Pieter van den Toorn's critique of the work of Susan McClary. See his "Politics, Feminism, and Contemporary Music Theory," *Journal of Musicology* 9 (1991): 275–99.

19. Melissa A. Orlie, "What Difference Does Difference Make? The Politics of Identity in Feminist Discourse," *Critical Matrix* 2 (1986): 90.

against the grain of narratives of normal life course."[20] She suggests that energy may be gleaned from the insistence upon difference, an energy that may prompt insights and readings unavailable to those whose lives take the "normal" course. Just such readings are explored by Mitchell Morris, in the present volume, in his study of the interpretive community of opera queens. Morris's ethnography makes clear that this community constructs itself—that is, claims its difference—through taste, language, and behavior, which in turn construct its alternative readings of the opera repertory. His analysis is put forth explicitly to challenge or displace dominant readings, and this challenge requires a theoretical awareness and enumeration of what he calls the "mechanisms of interpretive enforcement" built into nineteenth-century opera as a genre. What may be particularly striking, in juxtaposition to recent feminist discussions of opera, is the way the sexual identification of this audience complicates the analytic notion of woman as spectacle, even as its adherents underline precisely that aspect of their experience.[21]

Philosophical broodings about difference present conundrums of their own. Since Descartes, Western thought has been accustomed to the assumption that subjectivity has universal properties against which to test the claims of truth and beauty, but as postmodern philosophy entertains the "discourses of difference" it posits instead a fragmented and radically decentered subject. One of these discourses, of course, is feminism, and it is in this very decentering that such theorists as Teresa de Lauretis find its "radical epistemological potential," by which she means

> the possibility, already emergent in feminist writings of the 1980s, to conceive of the social subject and the relations of subjectivity to sociality in another way: a subject constituted in gender, to be sure, though not by sexual difference alone, but rather across languages and cultural representations; a subject en-gendered in the experiencing of race and class, as well as sexual, relations; a subject, therefore, not unified but rather multiple, and not so much divided as contradicted.[22]

Indeed, difference has been an integral part of the whole "linguistic turn" of philosophy during this century, a turn that has questioned the foundations of metaphysics and certainty and has precipitated what Lyotard calls "the decline of universalist discourses."[23]

20. "Lesbian Identity and Autobiographical Difference(s)," in Bella Brodzki and Celeste Schenck, eds., Life/Lines: Theorizing Women's Autobiography (Ithaca, 1988), p. 79.

21. Carolyn Abbate's essay, discussed below, provides further complications to the same idea, from a different perspective.

22. Teresa de Lauretis, "The Technology of Gender," in Technologies of Gender: Essays on Theory, Film, and Fiction (Bloomington, 1987), p. 2.

23. Lyotard, The Differend, p. xiii.

If essences are putatively banished from these postmodern celebrations of difference and plurality, power is nonetheless still very much in circulation. Anthropologists in particular have been acutely aware of this situation, poised as they are between their desire to understand (to gain control of?) cultural difference and their reluctance to impose upon that difference the full weight of "universalist discourse."[24] The force of this dilemma is explored here by Ellen Koskoff, whose essay focuses on the body of Jewish laws known as *kol isha* (the voice of a woman) as they are understood and implemented in a particular Hasidic community. How can we understand a prohibition against hearing a (sexually unavailable) woman's voice in song? In the context of the present volume the question seems somehow particularly charged, circling as it does around questions of gender, sexuality, and the power of music. In approaching the question Koskoff draws a comparison between two possible ethnographies: one that takes differences at face value in order to obtain a coherent and seamless picture of the culture, the other revealing and playing upon inequities of difference that may be invisible to members of the community themselves. But, in a familiar irony, she recognizes that these same members may themselves appeal to difference in another sense, claiming the naturalness and rightness of different gender treatment within the group's tradition; she is able to show, ultimately, that all three of these positions have finally to do with the ways in which social power is perceived and exercised.

Let us, for the sake of argument, agree that few if any of the meaningful differences between groups of people are innate, but, rather, that they are constructed. Hester Eisenstein, noting that difference has been integral to feminist thought since Simone de Beauvoir, points out the irony of mass-media portrayals of the women's movement as a *threat* to difference: one might conclude that popular culture too sees gender difference as constructed and therefore as vulnerable to deformation. Certainly, she reminds us, such early second-wave feminists as Kate Millett and Elizabeth Janeway gave considerable attention to the extreme degree of social pressure necessary to produce such clear-cut differences.[25] Under such pressure, "construction" may turn out to be

24. Ramifications for historical musicology of the anthropological understanding of difference—and anthropologists' methodological approaches to otherness—are explored at some length in Gary Tomlinson's *Music in Renaissance Magic: Toward a Historiography of Others* (Chicago, 1993). Tomlinson has further suggested (in a personal communication) that traditional musical analysis is one of the most aggressively universalizing discourses still in common use.

25. See Hester Eisenstein, Introduction to Hester Eisenstein and Alice Jardine, eds., *The Future of Difference* (1980; rpt. New Brunswick, N.J., 1985), pp. xv–xvi.

more literal, and certainly more deforming of the individual, than we at first expect: Philip Brett's essay in this volume explores Benjamin Britten's operatic portrayals of the human devastation wrought by the internalization of social judgment. Britten's experience of his own homosexuality as what Brett describes as a "lifelong sense of . . . alienation" perhaps served as a kind of template for his various musical studies of the play of power among social groups and of the possibilities for human relationships. Brett traces the shifting focus of these concerns from the social "parables of oppression" of the 1940s, through the more ambiguous metaphysical stories of *The Turn of the Screw* and *Billy Budd*, to their most explicit statement in *Death in Venice*. It is in the "healing comedy" of *A Midsummer Night's Dream*, he suggests, that Britten could most fully imagine the carnivalesque release from everyday social constructions of identity.

For historians and cultural critics, the most interesting and potentially powerful questions arise just here. If differences are constructed, are products of nurture and culture, how and where does the process of construction occur? Conversely, how can we locate the sites at which (as we would expect) cultural forces permit or encourage resistance to the construction of difference? Theorists have concentrated mainly on three mechanisms: experience or "positionality," language, and representation.

Theorizing difference in terms of social positioning attempts to evade the entire question of essentialism by focusing either on subjective experience or on identity constructed in the fulfillment of a given role. This view of the matter has the great advantage of bringing history and culture crucially into play.[26] Thus Elaine Showalter formulated her "gynocriticism," an influential notion in American feminist literary criticism during the early 1980s, on a broad-based hypothesis about women's cultural environments and relationships.[27] Similarly, Christine Battersby has argued that aesthetic judgment must be gendered because what distinguishes a woman "is not her biology, but the way society categorises her and treats her because of her biology."[28] Art historian Griselda

---

26. Linda Alcoff has written a particularly cogent account of this position in "Cultural Feminism Versus Poststructuralism: The Identity Crisis in Feminist Theory," *Signs: Journal of Women in Culture and Society* 13 (1988): 405–36.

27. See in particular Showalter's "Feminist Criticism in the Wilderness," *Critical Inquiry* 8 (1981): 179–205, in which she also discusses critical invocations of the body, of language, and of psychology.

28. Christine Battersby, *Gender and Genius: Towards a Feminist Aesthetics* (Bloomington, 1989), p. 154. To put the same idea another way, sexual difference is "constitutive of one's sense [of the] possibilities of existence" (The Milan Women's Bookstore Collective, *Sexual Difference: A Theory of Social-Symbolic Practice*, trans. Teresa De Lauretis [Bloomington, 1990], p. 6).

Pollock too has written extensively about this understanding of identity categories:

> In this sense patriarchy does not refer to the static, oppressive domination by one sex over another, but to a web of psycho-social relationships which institute a socially significant difference on the axis of sex which is so deeply located in our very sense of lived, sexual, identity that it appears to us as natural and unalterable.[29]

These writers suggest that in the case of works actually created by those in the position of "difference," a critical conundrum results that is, perhaps, not unrelated to the civic one raised by Martha Minow: "Does equality mean treating everyone the same, even if this similar treatment affects people differently? Members of minorities may find that a neutral rule, applied equally to all, burdens them disproportionately."[30] Translated into the terms of criticism, the "neutral rule" may bring with it ineffectual interpretive strategies or, more troubling, inappropriate or even coercive standards of valuation.

Elizabeth Wood's study here of Ethel Smyth dismisses the neutral rule and instead takes for granted the availability of music as an alternative means to "tell the truth about life," one which may reveal or suggest what explicitly autobiographical texts seek to camouflage. The plots of Smyth's operas turn upon the vagaries of conventional heterosexual romance, but the story of her own lesbian experience—her difference—may be encoded in her instrumental music. The decoding of this identity requires a new and different interpretive strategy, a contrapuntal reading of musical and prose texts—but Wood suggests that the composer herself may have employed a similar strategy, using her books and her music not only to represent but to shape and make comprehensible her own experience in a culture that conveyed it only in hushed and veiled terms.

The question, then, is not "Is there difference?" or "What's the difference?" but, rather, "How do social life and culture construct the differences that all of us understand and enact in daily life?" For musicologists, as for other scholars of cultural phenomena, this particular line of reasoning may be of great importance: if identities are a matter of social role, we may be able to study the mechanisms—including musical ones—by which those roles are delineated, communicated, learned, and perhaps challenged. So it is particularly appropriate that Suzanne Cusick has called her contribution to this collection a "model" for the study of the intersection of gender with political power and musical expression. Her reading of Francesca Caccini's opera *La Liberazione di Ruggiero dall'isola d'Alcina*

29. Griselda Pollock, *Vision and Difference: Femininity, Feminism and Histories of Art* (London, 1988), p. 33.

30. Minow, *Making All the Difference*, p. 9.

rests on the paradox of the position occupied by its patron, the Arch-duchess Maria Maddalena: "A woman ruler is trapped by the contradic-tions inherent in the overlap between the gender system and the require-ments of monarchy." The composer, as Cusick shows us, provides a subtly nuanced interpretation of the opera's story by delineating both aspects of this predicament, both gender difference and the difference between two worldviews and the political philosophies toward which they incline. We may, then, understand the piece as "a musico-theatrical essay on women's ways of wielding power within a monarchy-affirming masterplot."

Lacan and Foucault, and the many scholars who have made use of their work, have examined the ways in which linguistic practices have consti-tuted subjects and positioned them within psychoanalytic and historical discourses, respectively. In general, *difference* in an encompassing sense has been at the center of one arena of linguistic study ever since struc-turalism proposed the notion that difference creates meaning. From this origin emerges the proposition that Western thought has been dominated by a series of tightly interconnected binary dualisms: good/evil, male/female, culture/nature, reason/emotion, self/other, and so forth. For the most part, their implications are preserved in the names cultural histo-rians have devised for oppositional styles or periods, such as Apollonian/Dionysian or classic/romantic. (It is also possible, as anthropologists have suggested, to sum them up as under control/out of control.) These linked pairings create long chains of associations, virtuosic in their ready ap-plicability, that exercise a strong and virtually subliminal influence on the ways we position and interpret groups of people, their behavior, and their works.[31] Furthermore, such habits of equation among categories of Other have also enabled familiar patterns of metaphor—for example, of the woman as (variously) darkness, nature, hysteria, or primitivity, or of the gay man as artistic sensibility.[32]

Revealing both the force and the protean nature of these associations, Judith Tick asks us in her essay to read Charles Ives's familiar sexual

31. These dualities are notoriously interchangeable in cultural discourse. For one ex-ample (among many) of their slippery traffic in meanings, see Andreas Huyssen, "Mass Culture as Woman: Modernism's Other," in Tania Modleski, ed., *Studies in Entertainment: Critical Approaches to Mass Culture* (Bloomington, 1986), pp. 189–207. It is possible that these linkages, in the form they have taken within the last century or so, have their origin in the structure and presuppositions of Victorian science. See Cynthia Eagle Russett, *Sexual Sci-ence: The Victorian Construction of Womanhood* (Cambridge, Mass., 1989), and Stephen Jay Gould, *The Mismeasure of Man* (New York, 1981).

32. See, for instance, Sander L. Gilman, *Difference and Pathology: Stereotypes of Sexuality, Race, and Madness* (Ithaca, 1985); and Stephen Heath, "Difference," *Screen* 19 (1978): 51–112. The latter characterization was the subject of Philip Brett's paper "Musicality: Innate Gift or Social Contract?" delivered at the 1990 American Musicological Society meeting in Oakland, California.

fulminations[33] a little against the grain, to see them as a pervasive and legible social discourse rather than (merely or primarily) as individual psychopathology. In turn-of-the-century America, a particular repertory of tropes of difference was used to define the relationship between gender and music; the same language persisted as this relationship, under challenge from the new musical roles women were undertaking as well as from changing musical styles, increasingly became a subject of dispute. Attending scrupulously to the historicity of this language, Tick teases out the process of metaphorization and the slippage of categories by which Ives's appeals to masculinity and virility may be decoded as a defense of modernism, concluding that Ives's project "was the emasculation of the cultural patriarchy."

These associations and dualities are continually reproduced and reinforced in representation, a process in which the arts are, of course, radically implicated. Susan McClary has elaborated an analysis of musical tonality as the representation of self and Other, and one all the more profoundly ideological because the terms of the system predetermine the outcome. Her essay here reads Brahms's Third Symphony as a gendered encounter that makes use of musical codes of publicly understood signification—understood because once associated with texted music before having been cut loose to carry their familiar meanings into the "absolute" realm. Her discussion invites the observation that the symphony orchestra must surely qualify as one of the "technologies of gender" by which, as Teresa de Lauretis says, "the construction of gender goes on today."[34] And in a maneuver with which we have by now become familiar, the symphonic female Other may transmogrify without much effort into a cultural Other—typically for the nineteenth century, an "oriental."

A question prompted by such analyses suggests further refinements to be considered: should we be concerned about the composer's—or the work's—attitude toward the representations created? Theorists interested in the construction of difference are quick to point out that representation must be taken, not merely to reflect or refer to some preexistent reality, but actually to produce that reality. "What is represented must be considered to be an effect of . . . the means of representation," argues Parveen Adams, warning that otherwise some form of essentialism, albeit a sophisticated form, will creep back in.[35] There is a kind of circular relationship between ideology and representation, in which each

33. Familiar especially from Maynard Solomon's discussion, "Charles Ives: Some Questions of Veracity," *Journal of the American Musicological Society* 40 (1987): 443–470. Many of the same passages are discussed in Leo Treitler's essay in the present volume.

34. De Lauretis, "The Technology of Gender," p. 18.

35. Parveen Adams, "A Note on the Distinction Between Sexual Division and Sexual Differences," *m/f* 3 (1979): 56, 51.

creates and reinforces the other. Scholars of the visual arts, theater, and film have paid particular attention to these operations. Thus, for example, Abigail Solomon-Godeau sets out to curate a photography exhibition on "Sexual Difference" with just such a theory in mind:

> Although it was a basic assumption of the exhibition that photography . . . normally functions to produce and reproduce dominant ideologies of gender, the photography selected for the show was chosen either because it specified or complicated those subject/object or viewing relations which are instrumental in reaffirming the status quo of gender, or, more militantly, actively attempted to intervene with them.[36]

It seems, then, that representation is not a one-way street. Not only can we not assume a particular reality preexisting its representation, but we cannot even assume a simple or direct transmission of ideology. Rather, we face a delicately complex situation in which works of art may also challenge, mock, or subvert reigning values. Interpretation becomes an ambiguous and difficult, but richly meaningful, activity.[37] Sometimes the ambiguity itself seems provocatively represented within a work, as is the case, Lawrence Kramer suggests here, with Schumann's *Carnaval*. There uncertainty and mobility of gender are at stake, as is appropriate to the traditional celebration of carnival festivities, and as also seems to have been characteristic of the composer himself. The disunity of the self, playfully indulged or naughtily flaunted in this topsy-turvy season, favors games of masquerade and cross-dressing, mirroring and mirage. Kramer shows us how Schumann's musical *scènes mignonnes* enact their representations of disunity and shape-shifting by means of stylized musical gestures and structural features, as well as by emphasis on feminine-identified paradigms such as the detail. He insists, too, on critical recognition of the subversive intent of carnival phenomena; to defuse that intent in formalist analysis is to denude the piece of the political power of its disruption of sexual difference.

The representation of gender and sexuality offers a piquant source of interest for scholars of music. The title Duke Ellington gave to his memoirs, *Music Is My Mistress*,[38] invokes a long-standing trope of European culture—one also famously articulated by Richard Wagner—in which music is understood to occupy a female position vis-à-vis the male com-

---

36. Abigail Solomon-Godeau, *Sexual Difference: Both Sides of the Camera*, exhibition catalogue, Miriam and Ira D. Wallach Art Gallery, Columbia University (New York, 1988), inside front cover.

37. Perhaps the most important and nuanced study of representation and its interpretation, and one that deals specifically with gender difference, is de Lauretis's "The Technology of Gender."

38. Duke Ellington, *Music Is My Mistress* (Garden City, N.Y., 1973).

poser. In Julia Kristeva's psychoanalysis, the voice (song, music, even sound in general) is identified with the maternal, with a state of being that precedes the symbolic realm of the father and is thus irrational, inarticulable—and marked female. Our volume offers two meditations upon this familiar conceit. Barbara Engh's study of Roland Barthes explores this gendering of music particularly as it has played a role in postmodern critical theory. Engh goes beyond Kristeva to point out the role, at once broader and more specific, that music plays for poststructuralist philosophy as the unrepresentable—in Barthes's words, "the degree zero of the system," "a primal state of pleasure." Music may stand for the unthought, may be a relic of the metaphysical (an ironic situation, perhaps, in the present professional context). Music is gendered feminine, that is, because of its difference. And, like woman and other Others, music finds itself freely metaphorized in these postmodern texts.

Echoing Barthes's assertion that music has been constituted an Other among social and intellectual discourses thought to be of more central importance, John Shepherd's cultural study of the same phenomenon offers a kind of origin story brought to bear upon a general social critique. Hypothesizing a primeval association of masculinity with the visual, femininity with the auditory (thus giving communal embodiment, so to speak, to Kristeva's sketch of primal individual experience), Shepherd examines "the situation of music in industrial capitalist societies" and finds it in important ways akin to the situation of "woman" as a construction. Assuming the originary privileging of visual power over oral, superior status will then flow to written language over spoken, to literature over music, in general to those realms of culture associated with the male over those associated with the female. But the Other is never successfully banished in this process; rather, it remains paradoxically present in the cultural gap between what Shepherd suggests is the self-sufficiency of vision and its inadequacy as a mode of experience. And music's power, Shepherd reminds us, rests (like women's?) upon our failure to recognize and understand it.

The debates I set out to map do not only concern questions about what "difference" is or where it originates. The case against it has also been energetically made, by critics who have come to the conclusion that theorizing difference, in any terms, does more harm than good. Borrowing a typical Victorian formulation from George Eliot, Nina Auerbach confesses: "I shun my 'precious specialty' and seek access to the larger, if tarnished, culture that dictates our own and others' differences."[39] Evidently she fears that no good can come of the reinvocation of oppressive

39. Nina Auerbach, "Engorging the Patriarchy," in Jerome J. McGann, ed., *Historical Studies and Literary Criticism* (Madison, Wis., 1985), p. 232.

categories, and she wishes, indeed, to be genuinely included within the compass of those universal or generic turns of phrase. Concern thus centers upon the activation of the old dualisms in expressly ideological form and the concomitant tendency for "Othered" groups to be defined solely in negative terms, as defective or deviant.[40]

This concern has special force for cultural critics who study the tendency of political ideology to operate by making "others"—in war, for example, or in colonization—and who particularly fear the importation of such operations into the intellectual realm. As Jonathan Dollimore has commented, "For a variety of complex reasons society needs its deviants," and Michel de Certeau has, more starkly, suggested that "theorizing always needs a Savage."[41] Better, these writers argue, to deconstruct the problematic categories of identity than to countenance the continuation of these processes. In his vigorous exposition of this position Leo Treitler offers a principled challenge to those who would risk essentialist attributions to musical works. Indeed, I have placed his essay first in this collection because it throws down precisely the gauntlet that this side of the debate always holds in readiness, and it does so through a provocative investigation of the ways in which difference as an interpretive scheme has already been pervasive in music history. For Treitler the ambiguities of this procedure rest partly on the familiar problem of what content we may attribute to music, but also on a strong distaste for essentialist politics. Treitler's essay ends, however (as I have proceeded here), with the recognition of a dilemma: how can we become sensitive to the real roles that sexuality and gender may play in music, without falling prey to the delusions of biological determinism?

Strong theories of difference—especially when essentialist—are often charged with the tendency to negate history, to hypostatize categories in such a way that change over time becomes invisible. But historical consciousness itself can turn the tables: the degree of specificity historians generally bring to their investigations proves very helpful in refining our understanding of difference as it has been constructed and as it has operated. Martha Minow has pointed out that "arrangements that assign the burden of 'differences' to some people while making others comfortable are historical artifacts."[42] She goes on to provide the specific

40. See Laura Mulvey, "Changes: Thoughts on Myth, Narrative, and Historical Experience," in her *Visual and Other Pleasures* (Bloomington, 1989), pp. 159–76.

41. Jonathan Dollimore, "Homophobia and Sexual Difference," *Oxford Literary Review* 8 (1986): 7; Michel de Certeau quoted in Josette Féral, "The Powers of Difference," in Eisenstein and Jardine, *The Future of Difference*, p. 88. On this general subject I particularly recommend Donna Haraway's remarkable *Primate Visions: Gender, Race, and Nature in the World of Modern Science* (New York, 1989).

42. Minow, *Making All the Difference*, p. 53.

understanding that historicizes and denaturalizes the asymmetries of binary systems along with the systems themselves. So, for example, Gretchen Wheelock explores the gendered rhetoric of eighteenth-century music theorists who, in attempting to match the simple duality of male/female with that of major/minor, ended by destabilizing both: the ambiguities of minor tonality as understood in their very theories produce a slippery and alarmingly androgynous result. Wheelock's careful attention to refinements of gender/mode attribution, as well as to its shifting signification in comic versus serious contexts, demonstrates in detail how the ascription of binary difference is its own reward: all too seldom is it unproblematically apt. In this musical universe we see again the linkage of femininity to the supernatural, the mutable, and the out-of-control; and when Wheelock draws attention to, for example, the repertory of Mozart arias in G Minor, we are perhaps less than surprised to discover in the company of their performers Osmin, the "oriental."[43]

We have been examining a variety of theoretical positions in the current debate about difference as a useful conceptual category for historical and critical scholarship. It is important to keep in mind, though, that the case "against difference" is twofold: that is, there are two distinct viewpoints that hold it in disfavor, and their critiques come from rather different political directions. One, as we have seen, makes the argument that difference leads to prejudice and discrimination. The other, however, protests that theories of essential difference offend as much by what they conflate as by what they segregate, that these essences are not different *enough* and simply shift oppressive assertions of sameness from "everyone" to all members of some illegitimately reified category—say, "all gays and lesbians." Advocates of this position, then, insist on a different definition of "essentialism," one that renders it much more difficult to dislodge from contemporary scholarly discourse. It is essentialist, they say, to assume any trait in common for a group of people—whether one is arguing for biological determinism or for cultural construction—irrespective of their membership at the same time in many other human groups.[44] Thus, for instance, the characteristics of white, middle-class

43. In another instance of the historicizing of difference, Kaja Silverman has found a useful theoretical tool for classic cinema—one which could also be provocative, it seems to me, for students of opera—in a chapter of the history of clothing in which, around 1750, "man abandoned his claim to be considered beautiful," with the resulting familiar hyper-specularization of the female during the nineteenth and twentieth centuries (Silverman, *Acoustic Mirror*, p. 25, quoting J. C. Flugel, *The Psychology of Clothes* [London, 1930]).

44. This is the central argument both of Martha Minow's book and of Elizabeth V. Spelman's *Inessential Woman: Problems of Exclusion in Feminist Thought* (Boston, 1988).

women academics in the twentieth-century United States must not be generalized to a hypothesis about "women."

Wrestling with this heuristic difficulty, critic Barbara Johnson has attempted to devise a strategy that avoids its pitfalls:

> The starting point is often a binary difference that is subsequently shown to be an illusion created by the workings of differences much harder to pin down. The differences *between* entities . . . are shown to be based on a repression of differences *within* entities.[45]

So, for example, the strong forms of sexual difference—those that are centered on an oppositional formulation of male/female and therefore may be identified as essentialist in our second sense—have the tendency to repress homosexuality; that is, the very tactic chosen to dislodge the universal human subject ends by positing a universal heterosexuality. The interpretive poverty of such analyses is demonstrated by Carol Robertson's essay here, which likens the ethnomusicological scholar to a midwife of musical and cultural perceptions. Robertson's field experience in cultures where gender boundaries are markedly fluid has sharpened her appreciation of the rigidity of those binarisms in the West, and difference, she maintains, has always been a primary ground for marginalization. She describes communities in which a gender identity may be deliberately taken on for its spiritual power and in which sexual orientation (as it is known to us) may be plural and situational. Here binary difference may be not only an "illusion," as Johnson suggests, but an artifact of Western expectations. In these cultural contexts Robertson finds—as have others of our authors—strong and suggestive links between sexuality, spirituality, and music, and she finds as well that those individuals for whom these connections are especially powerful are those who elude definition, who move between and among categories.

Binary views of sexual difference, whether they address gender or sexual orientation, may also have the effect of eliding both cultural and historical differences by taking into consideration only single aspects of people in isolation from the other characteristics that make up the specificity of their experience. From this point of view, essentialists of either stripe may be said to suffer from what Elizabeth V. Spelman has dubbed "plethoraphobia," or the fear of manyness[46]—the fear, for instance, that a gay musicologist cannot after all speak for gay experience in general, or that a feminist musicologist cannot rely on some transhistorical and transcultural "sisterhood" in every interpretive situation. And, of course,

45. Barbara Johnson, *The Critical Difference: Essays in the Contemporary Rhetoric of Reading* (Baltimore, 1980), p. x.
46. Spelman, *Inessential Woman*, pp. 2, 160.

they cannot. Essential difference thus fails to take into account the ways in which identity categories inflect one another. As Nancy Reich tells us in her study of nineteenth-century women composers, "To view them as one entity—by virtue of their being female—is misleading." Reich's research proves striking—even perhaps startling—because our received image of nineteenth-century Woman is so overwhelmingly determined by middle-class interests and preoccupations. Thus it may come as a surprise to learn of the opportunities for participation in professional life available to women of the artist-musician class, as opposed to the more sheltered amateur activities characteristic of the bourgeoise. Far from sharing the same experience or positionality as females, even within a common culture, the lives and careers of these women were strongly differentiated by socioeconomic class; an analysis limited to gender difference alone will produce a distorted picture.

The fragmenting and decentering tendencies of poststructuralist criticism can again be pressed into service; once invoked for the purpose of instating difference in place of an illegitimate universal, they may be pushed further to reveal fault lines inside the differential binary categories. To restate the dilemma:

> The cultural feminist response to Simone de Beauvoir's question, "Are there women?" is to answer yes and to define women by their activities and attributes in the present culture. The post-structuralist response is to answer no and attack the category and the concept of woman through problematizing subjectivity.[47]

No critic has been more energetic in this problematizing task than Judith Butler, who argues for a performative, rather than substantive, interpretation of identity categories. "There is no gender identity behind the expressions of gender," Butler says; "that identity is performatively constituted by the very 'expressions' that are said to be its results."[48]

In an essay making similarly powerful claims for the efficacy of performance, Carolyn Abbate tells us the tale of a "liberating confusion of subject that speaks and looks, and object silent and observed." It is a thoroughly postmodern confusion, a de-essentializing analysis of voice and authority in opera: both identity and subjectivity are seen as continually under threat from masquerade and transvestism, which them-

---

47. Alcoff, "Cultural Feminism Versus Poststructuralism," p. 407.

48. Judith Butler, *Gender Trouble: Feminism and the Subversion of Identity* (New York, 1990), p. 25. Butler's argument, audacious and philosophically sophisticated, comes full circle in feminist theorizing in its rejection of the distinction between sex and gender. Rather, Butler insists, the entire complex of subjectivity is performed.

selves recur in a variety of guises. In suggesting that the authorial subject in opera, traditionally taken to be the (male) composer, may be unmasked as in fact the (female) diva, Abbate borrows from Roland Barthes one of the quintessential poststructuralist moves: the unseating of a controlling authorial voice outside and prior to the text it seems to have produced, and its re-creation and dispersal among an array of voices within the text. Along with each voice comes one facet of a multiple and fractioned subjectivity, only partially (and insecurely) gendered and sexed.

Poststructuralism, then, "deconstructs" the dualisms, first by revealing that they are not in fact symmetrical, that within each pair dominance of the first over the second is embedded,[49] and then by entirely neutralizing the categories to which the pairs apply: gender, for instance. The implications of deconstructive philosophies for the committed scholarship of identity politics are perhaps not entirely clear: "A number of marginalized communities now face important questions about the possibility of reconceptualizing identity without abandoning it and its strategic deployment altogether."[50] Could it really be possible to ask such questions as "Are there women?" "Are there gays?" Do we fare better or worse if the answer is no?

The conversation among the essayists in this volume provides grounds for many possible critical stances. For myself, although I am mindful of the subtleties and complexities entailed, I believe it is nonetheless fruitful and important for disciplines involved in the interpretation of history and culture to take cognizance of systems and ideologies of difference that have prevailed, whether or not one's own politics admit them to an ideal polis or, indeed, to critical readings. There is still ample ground to be debated about the meaning of those systems and the means of their representation.

As the musicological disciplines in particular gradually reorient their focus of attention, their practitioners need to think about what discursive fields musics' semiotic codes can cover, in ways specific as to time and place. As part and parcel of that study, we will want to know what role musics play in the construction and reinforcement of ideologies of difference and, conversely, how they may challenge or resist those ideologies. One

49. See Deborah Cameron, "What Is the Nature of Women's Oppression in Language?" *Oxford Literary Review* 8 (1986): 79–87.

50. Martin, "Lesbian Identity," p. 79. There are, of course, strenuous objections to the deconstruction of binary categories, on the grounds that the generic subject that necessarily results is the familiar, dominant false-universal. For a particularly outspoken minority view, see Kathleen Barry, "The New Historical Synthesis: Women's Biography," *Journal of Women's History* 1 (1990): 75–105.

who has experienced a similar reorientation offers some personal testimony:

> I had no understanding of the limits that I lived within, nor of how much my memory and my experience of a safe place was based on places secured by omission, exclusions or violence, and on my submitting to the limits of that place.[51]

What is our investment in the "safe place" of art, of these privileged objects we have come to love? There is a good deal at stake here. Cultural artifacts and practices, works of art, are perhaps the most valuable belongings of a civilization, treasures to possess, share, and preserve. It matters to whom they belong and who is empowered to speak about them. It matters about whom *they* speak, and what they say.

51. Minnie Bruce Pratt, "Identity: Skin Blood Heart," in *Yours in Struggle: Three Feminist Perspectives on Anti-Semitism and Racism* (Brooklyn, 1984), pp. 23–26; quoted in Martin, "Lesbian Identity," p. 99.

Systems of Difference

Gender and Other Dualities of Music History

Leo Treitler

Music history is, among other things, a discourse of myth through which "Western civilization" contemplates and presents itself. This is said, not in order to question the truth value of music-historical narratives, but to emphasize their aspect as stories of traditional form that the culture tells in its desire to affirm its identity and values.

From early on music history has been guided by gender duality in its description, evaluation, and narrative form. Boethius, a principal conduit of ideas about music from antiquity to the Middle Ages, sounded a theme of lament in the midst of a music-historical narrative that would become typical in evaluations of "the present state of music":

> Ruder peoples delight in the harsher modes of the Thracians; civilized peoples, in more restrained modes; though in these days this almost never occurs. Since humanity is now lascivious and effeminate, it is wholly captivated by scenic and theatrical modes.[1]

As in this passage, gender typically plays its role in concert with dualities of ethnicity, nationality, or race—all dichotomies of self and Other that are linked as markers in the pathways and panoramas of understanding in our culture. The wording of my title hints at my sense of gender as the archetypal duality.

This interpretation arises from my experience with a particular collective discourse of music history—the story of medieval chant—and I shall try to give an account of how certain canonical beliefs about that subject have come to be formed, and what their broader associations are.

---

1. Boethius, "De institutione musica," trans. Oliver Strunk, *Source Readings in Music History* (New York, 1950), p. 81.

But there is a backdrop in "an ancient mythology that explains human consciousness as divided in two permanently antagonistic parts . . . a mythology in which reason and sensuality are mutually opposed, and that opposition is characterized as the duality of the masculine and the feminine."[2] The linkage of the duality of the rational and the sensual with that of the masculine and the feminine is a fact embedded in Western tradition. Here I shall be concerned to show how that linkage has been active in categories of music history and criticism.

Yet a third topic arises as underpinning for this central one. Gender duality, functioning as a structure of music-historical interpretation, depends on the—largely unreflected—identification of gender attributes in music. I want to consider such identification as it has been practiced historically, and to bring out the dilemma into which it leads as it is put into service in recent attempts to ground a feminist music criticism. The question of whether music can have an immanently masculine or feminine character that transcends history and culture brings forward anew—with highly specific ideological motifs and motives—already much-debated issues of aesthetic theory concerning what music conveys, expresses, and represents, and how one can know about such things. I shall ask whether, thus transformed, these issues merit the privileged status to which they seem to have been raised, and also whether their newly explicit ideological dimension exempts them from critical reflection, for that is the implication of some of the writings on the subject.

Finally, the issue of essentialism, which is raised by the practice of gender identification in music, points to the same issue with respect to race. The two modes of essentialist thinking have the same culture-historical background, they have played parallel and linked roles in the criticism and historical narrative of the arts, and they have functioned under the same ideological tenets.

The story that serves as my gateway may seem out of the way, to say the least: the modern reception-history of the liturgical chant of the medieval Western Church. I shall refer to it simply as "plainchant," following Jean-Jacques Rousseau, the writer with whom that history began.[3] Example 1 shows two stylistically different versions of an Introit antiphon, a chant that accompanied the entrance of the celebrant into the church and his procession to the altar to begin the Mass. The two versions belong to different medieval traditions. One, the Old Roman tradition, was sung only in Rome, and then only until it died out in the twelfth century. We

---

2. Leo Treitler, *Music and the Historical Imagination* (Cambridge, Mass., 1989), pp. 11–12.

3. Rousseau's *Dictionnaire de Musique* (Paris, 1768) includes an article entitled *Plain-Chant* (pp. 95–105).

EXAMPLE 1   From the Introit antiphon *Rorate caeli desuper*, in the Old Roman and
the Gregorian tradition.

Let the heavens precipitate from above

and let the clouds rain down the Just One.

Let the earth open

and sprout the Saviour

have the chant from notated manuscripts written in Rome in the eleventh
and twelfth centuries. The other version belongs to a tradition that was
transmitted in writing rather uniformly throughout most of Western
Europe and the British Isles from the tenth century on; it has come down
to us as Gregorian chant. There is no evidence that melodies of this

tradition were sung in Rome before the arrival there of some French chant
books in the twelfth century.

The Old Roman melody is quite recursive. It turns on itself repeatedly
in numerous circular figures which create an overall melismatic texture.
The melodic line shows an overall direction, but it is highly decorated.
The outlines of the Gregorian version are sharper. It, too, is ornamented,
but not as uniformly so. On the whole, whereas the decorative figures
determine the character of the Old Roman version, in the Gregorian
version it is the overall melodic shape and direction that stand out.

Students of medieval plainchant are in agreement that this difference
is characteristic of the two traditions. They are also in agreement that the
difference of style has something important to do with the origins of
plainchant and its early history in the Middle Ages. And since plainchant
is the earliest European music known to us, the questions raised by the
difference we have observed open out to nothing less than questions
about the origins and nature of European music. And the disagreements
that take over at this point—disagreements over how the style difference
came about, how to characterize it, whether either version can be identified as original and the other somehow derivative, and just what all this
can tell about the history as a whole—are argued out with a vigor that is
worthy of the rank to which this subject has now been elevated. I shall
sample some of the interpretations that have been offered and consider
what they portend for vital matters of cultural identity that are at the
center of my subject.[4]

Here is Bruno Stäblein, a preeminent German plainchant scholar,
writing about Old Roman chant: "Endless streams of melody that overflow the boundaries of textual divisions, . . . melodies that spread over
their texts like a chain of pearls or a voluptuous gown . . . soft, elegant,
charming and graceful, without sharp edges or corners."[5] Their style is
"naive, youthfully fresh, blossom-like, the expression of a general Italic,
folk-like feeling."[6] The Gregorian melodies, by contrast, are "disciplined
and ordered, a product of rational thinking." They are "clear, sculpted
configurations, systematically chiselled; a system of musical rhetoric
reigns in them." They display a "more perfect quality—*perfectior scientia*,
a wonderful expression that carries with it the thought of the thoroughly
systematic working-through of the musical language, accomplished with

---

4. An overview of the positions that have been taken is given by Helmut Hucke in
"Gregorian and Old Roman Chant," in *The New Grove Dictionary of Music and Musicians*, ed.
Stanley Sadie (London, 1980), vol. 7, pp. 693–97.

5. "Die Entstehung des gregorianischen Chorals," *Die Musikforschung* 27 (1974): 11.

6. *Die Gesänge des altrömischen Graduale Vat. lat. 5319, Monumenta Monodica Medii aevi II*
(Kassel, 1970) (= MMM II), p. 38*.

the highest intelligence."[7] Stäblein appends a list of attributes medieval writers had themselves found in Gregorian chant: *vis* (strength), *virtus* (manliness), *vigor, potestas* (power), *ratio* (reason).[8]

In Stäblein's view the Old Roman tradition is the older one, from which the Gregorian tradition was achieved by "stripping down and reshaping the unrestrained coloratura of the originals." This happened in Rome, whence the new melodies were carried, as the Cantus Romanus, to the major ecclesiastical and political centers of the Frankish North during the reigns of Pepin and the Emperor Charlemagne. Through this transformation, writes Stäblein, the provincial Roman melodies were raised to a higher, super-regional level as "melodies for a world power."[9] "Rome" is presented as two kinds of place: the provincial Italic home of a luxuriant Mediterranean singing practice, and the place where an efficient and economical model was fashioned for a European melodic style.

Clarity, system, understandability, strength, vigor, power, reason, manliness, on one side; on the other, softness, roundedness, elegance, charm, grace. It does not require much exegesis to recognize here, as the underlying principle, gender duality and its association with the duality of the rational and the sensual and with the concept of power.

An obvious alternative interpretation of the historical relationship of two such opposite melodic styles is that the Gregorian tradition is the older one, originating in Rome and diffused throughout the Empire in Carolingian times, as in the other story. The Old Roman tradition is a late survival representative of a local singing practice typical of the Mediterranean south, where Carolingian power and cultural influence were less decisive. Earlier Gregorian sources of Roman provenance were all lost. This interpretation is indeed represented in the modern literature, for example in the work of Hans Schmidt and Walther Lipphardt.[10] The difference is important for the view taken of the way things happened, but it is not great so far as critical assessment of the two styles is concerned. The one important difference is that this second interpretation picks up the concept of corruption, which had been an important part of this story from the beginning. That concept, too, is aligned on the female side of the duality.

In the *Dictionnaire de Musique* Rousseau wrote of plainchant as

> a noble relic, very much disfigured, but very precious, of [ancient] Greek music, which having passed through the hands of barbarians has not,

7. "Die Entstehung," pp. 13, 17. In the final citation Stäblein is quoting a ninth-century writer on ecclesiastical matters, Walafried Strabo (*De rebus ecclesiasticis* 22, published in Migne, *Patrologia latina* 114, p. 946).

8. "Die Entstehung," p. 14.

9. Ibid.

10. See the bibliography in Hucke's review.

however, been able to lose its natural beauties. There remains yet enough
of it to render it much preferable . . . to those effeminate and theatrical
pieces which in some churches are substituted in its place.[11]

The plainchant is, by implication, masculine, and the word with which
Rousseau labels its opposite—*efféminée*, literally, "effeminated"—carries
a sense of deterioration from what is by nature manly. This "dread of
corruption," as E. H. Gombrich has called it, was an obsession with writers
of the Enlightenment, and a fear they implanted deeply in the modern
unconscious.[12]

But as to the Old Roman–Gregorian question, we might well wonder
why, of all possible interpretations, it would enter someone's mind to
differentiate these two singing traditions as *masculine* and *feminine*. The
answer is surely that it was already in his mind, as a primary form of
cognition and therefore as "the very stuff" of a historical narrative that
transcends its apparent content.[13] What is displayed here is an underlying
mythic story that is told and retold with changing material. My hope is
that it may be the more boldly displayed because the very idea of medieval
chant traditions differentiated as masculine and feminine will strike us as
strange on the face of it. But the narrative of a cultural ascendance from
a feminine condition to a masculine one is readily transformed, in the
same mythology, into the parameters of other dualities.

In 1921 Peter Wagner, the most influential German writer on this
subject to date, used language similar to the language of Stäblein when
he characterized Gregorian Alleluia chants as "models of clear formal
structure and symmetrical organization, the work of aesthetic delib-
eration."[14] Thirteen years later Dom Paolo Ferretti, a writer just as in-

11. I quote from the English translation by William Waring: (London, 1779), pp. 64–65.
I think my interpolation of "ancient" before Greek is not problematic. Unlike his followers
John Hawkins and Charles Burney, Rousseau had no interest in bringing the Byzantine
Greeks into the story.

12. See E. H. Gombrich, *The Ideas of Progress and Their Impact on Art* (New York: The
Cooper Union School of Art and Architecture, 1971), pp. 12–34. Gombrich writes here
about Rousseau's forerunner and exact counterpart as historian of the figurative arts,
Johann Joachim Winckelmann, who set up a dualism virtually identical with Rousseau's:
"the noble simplicity," "purity," and "quiet grandeur of *Greek* statues" on one side, the
"corruption," "artificiality," "affectation," and "*effeminacy*" of the works of artists like Ber-
nini, on the other (*Thoughts on the Imitation of Greek Works in Painting and Sculpture* [Dresden,
1755; English edition, London, 1765], my emphases; Gombrich refers to this work as "the
famous manifesto of classicism"). "Corrupt" and "effeminate" are so closely associated in
this usage that they become virtually synonymous.

13. I take this phrase from the opening page of Hayden White's *The Content of the Form:
Narrative Discourse and Historical Representation* (Baltimore, 1989), p. ix. This is not the first
time I have found White's writing on historiography helpful.

14. *Einführung in die gregorianische Melodien, III. Gregorianische Formenlehre: Eine chora-
lische Stilkunde* (Leipzig, 1921), p. 398.

fluential for readers of Italian and French, characterized the composers of Gregorian chant as "artists," creating under the inspiration of their "personal genius" and the "logic" of musical principles. Their chants are "organic," "harmonious," "homogeneous," and "logical."[15] Wagner's language aimed at a contrast with an older layer of chants whose melodies were "unregulated and without plan." The difference is like that between a "skillfully laid-out flower bed" and a "luxuriantly proliferating growth." Those older melodies remind him of the "unregulated undulation of the melismatics of the Orient," whereas the later ones display "Latin, Roman traits."[16]

That these traits, which come down to matters of formal order and unity, are seen as epitomizing European music altogether comes out in one of the most extravagant-sounding bits of encomium in the whole story, a passage in Willi Apel's 1958 survey of Gregorian chant. Concluding an analysis of a group of Gradual chants, Apel wrote that "the perception of their structural properties greatly enhances their significance as unified works of art, no less so than in the case of a sonata by Beethoven."[17] This remark makes explicit what was implicit in the project all along: its task of qualifying Gregorian chants for their position at the headwaters of the main stream of European—as against Oriental—music by finding in them just those qualities that count as value and greatness in the culture that validated them in this way. At the same time the chants, by virtue of their historical authority as the beginning of European music, validated those qualities as *the* quintessential qualities of European music.[18]

By a stunning coincidence, this doctrine is displayed in almost identical form in a passage in Anton Webern's book legitimating "the new music."

15. *Estetica gregoriana, ossia Trattato delle forme musicali del canto gregoriano* (Rome, 1934), pp. vii–viii. That a treatise on musical forms would constitute the extension of the title "Gregorian aesthetic" is as significant as is the fact that a theory of form, in Wagner's title, would constitute a science of style. Regarding the influence of these aesthetic issues on the analysis of chant, see my essay "'Centonate' Chant: *Übles Flickwerk* or *E pluribus unus*," in *Journal of the American Musicological Society* 27 (1975): 1–23.

16. *Einführung in die gregorianische Melodien*, pp. 398, 403.

17. *Gregorian Chant* (Bloomington, 1958), p. 362.

18. I was myself once persuaded of the attractiveness of this way of thinking and have, regrettably, been a contributor to the mythology based on it. My essay "On the Structure of the Alleluia Melisma: A Western Tendency in Western Chant" (Harold Powers, ed., *Studies in Music History: Essays for Oliver Strunk* [Princeton, 1968], pp. 59–72) conveys in its very title the a priori idea that closure and unity of melodic structure and coherence of melodic syntax are essentially Western, as opposed to Oriental, features. Moreover, the interpretations of melody within the essay I now regard as too restrictive about what constitutes unity and coherence, even within the "Western" tradition. I would rather have my current understanding of that question be represented by the analysis of the Old Roman

Webern analyzed the form of a Gregorian Alleluia melody and exclaimed that it is "already the full structure of the large symphonic forms, expressed exactly as in the symphonies of Beethoven."[19] This time the demonstration drives in the opposite direction: the formal principles the new music has inherited from Beethoven are still more deeply rooted, lying in the most ancient European tradition.

But there is a difference between these accounts. In Apel's expression of this doctrine it is embedded in the duality of the European and the Oriental, which is not really an issue for Webern. No one has contributed more to our understanding of that duality as a structure of history than Edward Said, in his *Orientalism*. "Orientalism," writes Said, is

> a way of coming to terms with the Orient [the Near East] that is based on the Orient's special place in European Western experience. The Orient is not only adjacent to Europe; it is also the place of Europe's greatest and richest and oldest colonies, the source of its civilizations and languages, its cultural contestant, and one of its deepest and most recurring images of the Other. In addition, the Orient has helped to define Europe (or the West) as its contrasting image, idea, personality, experience [and as] a surrogate, underground self for the West.[20]

Later, in "Orientalism Reconsidered," Said wrote directly about the parallelism of the male-female and Europe-Orient dualities: "Orientalism is a praxis of the same sort . . . as male gender dominance, or patriarchy, in metropolitan societies: the Orient was routinely described as feminine, its riches as fertile, its main symbols the sensual woman, the harem, and the despotic—but curiously attractive—ruler."[21] I would take that one step further: the two are not only of the same sort, they are the same myth, differently peopled.

The similarity implies a psychological factor operating together with the ideological, political, and sociological factors that function to define our historical fields. It is the tendency to build an identity—individual or cultural—by positioning the self against a sharply defined Other that is contrasted with the self in essential ways. But what are regarded as the opposite traits of the Other are interpretable as the traits of a surro-

---

melody in my essay "The 'Unwritten' and 'Written Transmission' of Medieval Chant and the Start-up of Musical Notation," *Journal of Musicology* 10 (1992): 131–91. I offer that analysis, too, as counterexample to the characterizations of Old Roman and Gregorian chant that I have cited above. On its terms the Old Roman melody shown there is as coherent and unified as any Gregorian melody. It seems we are forever apt to allow ideology to command analytical methods, which then, of course, produce the accounts we desire.

19. *Der Weg zur neuen Musik* (Vienna, 1960), p. 23. I am grateful to Professor Anne Schreffler of the University of Chicago for pointing out this passage to me.

20. (New York, 1978), pp. 1–2.

21. *Cultural Critique* 1 (1985): 103.

gate, underground—we might as well say unconscious—self. The Other, in effect, is a projection of a suppressed and feared aspect of the self and consequently inspires deeply ambivalent attitudes in the acknowledged self.

Rousseau's influential article on plainchant in the *Dictionnaire de Musique* begins by characterizing the chant as "a noble relic, very much disfigured, but very precious, of [ancient] Greek music, which, having passed through the hands of Barbarians, has not, however, been able to lose all its natural beauties." Two related themes are set out here that are essential elements in the cultural self-portrait that was being drawn: the theme of the ancient Greek heritage of this founding tradition of European music—whence it derives its purity and perfection—and the "dread of corruption" (the dark side of the expectation of perfection in enlightenment historiography) at the hands of barbarians: Graecophilia and barbarophobia.[22]

Rousseau wrote as a participant in a major project in the forging of a European identity, which has been described by Martin Bernal in his *Black Athena*:

> [There are] two models of Greek history: one viewing Greece as essentially European or Aryan, the other seeing it as Levantine, on the periphery of the Egyptian and Semitic cultural area. I call them the "Aryan" and the "Ancient" models. The "Ancient Model" was the conventional view among Greeks in the Classical and Hellenistic ages. According to it, Greek culture had arisen as the result of colonization, around 1500 B.C., by Egyptians and Phoenicians who had civilized the native inhabitants.[23]

But under the paradigm of "races" that was applied to all human studies at the end of the eighteenth century,

> it became increasingly intolerable for Greece, which was seen not only as the epitome of Europe but also its pure childhood, to have been the result of the mixture of native Europeans and colonizing Africans and Semites.[24]

---

22. Beginning with Rousseau's article (pp. 66–67 of the English edition), the theme of corruption and the desire for the restoration of the pure tradition is concretized in a creation myth about Gregorian chant that has its origins in the ninth century and a transmission into the twentieth. See my essay "Homer and Gregory: The Transmission of Epic Poetry and Plainchant," in *Musical Quarterly* 60 (1974): 333–72.

Conrad Donakowski has interpreted the theme of the restoration of plainchant in the context of changes in European thought from the Enlightenment to the Romantic era: see *A Muse for the Masses: Ritual and Music in an Age of Democratic Revolution 1770–1870* (Chicago, 1972), chapter 5, "A Musical Return to the State of Nature."

23. *Black Athena: The Afroasiatic Roots of Classical Civilization.* Vol. 1: *The Fabrication of Ancient Greece 1785–1985* (New Brunswick, N.J, 1987), p. 1.

24. Ibid., p. 29.

Figure 1. *Musical Hall of Fame*, reproduced from *The Etude* magazine for December, 1911. The genre is that of the group portrait of artists in a sort of Parnassus, sacred to Apollo and the Muses. Composers shown, from left to right: Chopin, Handel, Gluck, Schumann, Weber, Bach (seated), Haydn, Mozart, Schubert, Beethoven, Mendelssohn, Wagner, Meyerbeer, Gounod, Verdi (seated), Liszt, Bruckner, Brahms, Grieg.

Bernal identifies this conception as "European chauvinism." The European-Oriental duality is itself entwined with the theme of Greek patrilineage. The two ideas reinforce one another.

> The Aryan Model, which most of us have been brought up to believe, developed only during the first half of the nineteenth century. In its earlier or "Broad" form, the new model denied the truth of the Egyptian settlements and questioned those of the Phoenicians. According to the Aryan Model, there had been an invasion from the north—unreported in ancient tradition—which had overwhelmed the local "Aegean" or "Pre-Hellenic" culture. Greek civilization is seen as the result of the mixture of the Indo-European-speaking Hellenes and their indigenous subjects. It is from the construction of this Aryan Model that I call this [first of three] volume[s] *The Fabrication of Ancient Greece 1785–1985*.[25]

There is nothing surprising in this legitimation of a conception and evaluation of the present through reference to the authority of origins. Nor is it a coincidence that the Greece that emerged through that process became at once the epitome of what counted as Western Civilization, the transcendent and timeless context for all our cultural achievements; that was the role for which it was created.

Figure 1, called *The Musical Hall of Fame*, is a vivid embodiment of that quality of timeless transcendence. When Willi Apel emerged from his analytical labors over Gregorian chants and proclaimed them to be as unified as a sonata by Beethoven, he was rescuing them from slipping into the Orient and assuring their place in this Graeco-European musical order presided over by Beethoven. The invention of Ancient Greece provided both a patrilineage for European culture and a model to contrast against the cultural Other. The two aspects work hand in hand.

The chauvinist/racist and sexist undertones of the historical and critical categories that underlie the modern reception of medieval chant were turned up to full volume in the culture-historical ideology published in the Germany of the 1920s and '30s. I refer first of all to work that was presented, not yet as Nazi propaganda, but as "scientific" research of a kind called *Rassenforschung*, heritage of a Romantic preoccupation with its roots in the late eighteenth century,[26] and productive of books with titles such as *Kunst und Rasse, Rasse und Stil, Rasse und Seele, Rassenkunde Europas, Die Rasse in den Geisteswissenschaften, Rassengeschichte des Hellenischen und des*

25. Ibid., pp. 1–2.

26. See George W. Stocking, *Race, Culture, and Evolution: Essays in the History of Anthropology* (Chicago, 1982), p. 44: "[The ramifications of] the nineteenth-century notion of race could—and should—be followed into various areas of social, historical, literary, philological, biological, and political thought, as well as into the 'external' reality of European expansion, slavery, nationalism, and all the manifold events and processes which help to define men's thinking regarding the problem of human differences."

Römischen Volkes, Rassenkunde des Jüdischen Volkes, Musik und Rasse. My
interest here is in the last of these, by Richard Eichenauer.[27]

Eichenauer displays exactly what Bernal describes as the racist dimension of the "Aryan theory" of Greek history: "Race research has demonstrated that Greek behavioral patterns as a whole show the picture of
a great ascent under Nordic influence followed by a decline brought
about by *Entnordung"* (de-Nordification, we might say; he also speaks of
Semitisierung).[28] Greek musical styles he characterizes with yet another
duality that has its own background of identification with the duality of
the rational and the sensual: that between the Apollonian, which is Nordic, and the Dionysian, which is Near Eastern, that is, Oriental/Semitic.[29]

The history of Gregorian chant begins in the latter cultural domain,
with the Jewish chant of the Near East. But with the spread of Christianity
it "wandered into the heartland of the Nordic race" where "the Germanic
musical feeling expressed itself ever more strongly." Peter Wagner is
criticized for having had all the facts in his *Einführung*, yet failing to draw
this clear conclusion. But Eichenauer did not fail to pick up the passage
in Wagner that I have already cited: "We recall that one of the strongest
Orientally flavored characteristics of ecclesiastical chant were the long
melismas. Wagner thus distinguishes an older, still purely Oriental group
from a younger group with Roman traits. He finds the difference in the
turn from unregulated up-and-down meandering [of the former] to the
clear structure [of the latter]."[30]

Then Eichenauer confronts the difficult problem of what is meant by
"Roman." He quotes Wagner again: "Systematic and design-wise melodic
process was ever the spiritual task of a strong side of the Roman genius";
and Heinrich Besseler, author of the influential *Musik des Mittelalters und
der Renaissance*: "In [the Gregorian Alleluia chants] rational control [his
word is the more violent *Bewältigung*] and the establishment of musical
form are felt most strongly as against the voluptuously proliferating [the
German *wuchernd* carries the pejorative sense of a decadent fleshiness]
Oriental melismatic style." According to Eichenauer, Besseler attributes
to the Roman cantors "a certain ideal of melodic cogency, terseness, and
clarity."[31] In all this Eichenauer sees a "racial influence." He writes: "If
it was really 'Roman genius' that was at work here, then it was surely the
ancient Roman-Nordic, still showing through in individual creative spirits" (this is Wagner's "Latin-Roman," as opposed to Stäblein's "old-Italic").
Eichenauer continues: "But for the period in question it is not impossible

27. (Munich, 1932). Bibliographic details for the other titles can be found in Eichenauer.
28. Ibid., p. 37.
29. Ibid.
30. Ibid., pp. 67, 87 note 1, 89.
31. Ibid., p. 89.

that a 'new-Roman' = Germanic genius ['Holy Roman'] is also speaking. In either case it would be the Nordic-strict constructive spirit that strives for the clear working-through of form."[32]

Since Beethoven there has been a tendency to compose European music history very much around that composer as the epitome of European music, in the sense that he is believed to epitomize the virtue of rational form that is held to be the defining quality of European music. He is the Apollo in the Parnassus depicted in *The Musical Hall of Fame*. Not far behind the scenes, however, is the implication that he epitomizes the essential masculinity of European music, given the history of the associations of the rational, formal, efficient, and so forth, with the masculine (the word *virtue* is chosen with care). It may be initially surprising that this identification should be made explicit in the new domain of feminist music criticism. I quote from Susan McClary:

> The tonality that underlies Western concert music is strongly informed by a specific sort of erotic imagery. . . . [M]usic after the Renaissance most frequently appeals to libidinal appetites: at the historical moment at which the legitimation of culture moved from the sacred to the secular realm, the "truth" that authorized musical culture became expressly tied to male-defined models of sexuality. . . . For most of the history of post-Renaissance Western music and in virtually all of its critical literature, the sexual dimensions of its mechanisms have been shamelessly exploited and yet consistently denied. The principle of building to climax three-quarters of the way through a piece is discussed in metaphors that almost always betray their underlying erotic assumptions, while at the same time the climax-principle (like the phallus of the classical Greek column) has been transcendentalized to the status of a value-free universal form.[33]

---

32. Ibid.
33. It is easy and common enough to decode Greek columns as phallic symbols. But in the recent *The Reign of the Phallus: Sexual Politics in Ancient Athens* (New York, 1985), the classicist Eva C. Keuls provides reason for caution. The book opens thus: "In the case of a society dominated by men who sequester their wives and daughters, denigrate the female role in reproduction, erect monuments to the male genitalia, have sex with the sons of their peers, sponsor public whorehouses, create a mythology of rape, and engage in rampant saber-rattling, it is not inappropriate to refer to a reign of the phallus. Classical Athens was such a society" (p. 1). Then to the point: "In speaking of 'the display of the phallus,' I am not referring, as Freudians do, to symbols that may remind us of the male organ, such as bananas, sticks, or Freud's own cigar [or architectural columns, we might add]. In Athens no such coding was necessary. . . . Athenian men habitually displayed their genitals, and their city was studded with statues of gods with phalluses happily erect" (p. 2). This raises a question about where the gender coding that is criticized in such writing as McClary's originates, whether in the artistic tradition itself or in the writing of the critic. I shall return to the question further on.

[The climax principle] is not even viewed as sexual (let alone masculine!) any longer—it is simply the way music is supposed to go. . . . The leading German encyclopedia of music, *Die Musik in Geschichte und Gegenwart*, goes so far as to define the dynamic of sonata form thus: "Two basic human principles are expressed in each of . . . two main themes: the thrusting, active masculine principle and the passive, feminine principle."[34]

This seems like a report made in outrage. But then McClary endorses the position herself, and all at once what promised to be a valuable piece of ideology-critique is derailed:

As if the thrusting impulse characteristic of tonality and the aggression characteristic of first themes were not enough, Beethoven's symphonies add two other dimensions to the history of style: assaultive pelvic pounding (for instance in the last movement of the Fifth Symphony and in all but the "passive" third movement of the Ninth) and sexual violence. The point of recapitulation in the first movement of the Ninth is one of the most horrifying moments in music, as the carefully prepared cadence is frustrated, damming up energy which finally explodes in the throttling, murderous rage of a rapist incapable of attaining release.[35]

There is a confusion here, as there is in the characterization of Greek columns as phallic, about where the gender-labeling is coming from. McClary writes about social constructions of gender, and these—for example, the gender-labeling of themes in writing about sonata form since the mid-nineteenth century—are at first the objects of her critique. She attacks the writers who do that labeling, and even the writers of modern textbooks and dictionary articles who transmit it. But then she also attacks the compositional traditions, and the composers operating within them, for purveying such gender constructions. In doing so she must assert, implicitly or explicitly, that instrumental music can and does embody or express those constructions. How she arrives at that premise, and at her particular decoding of the gender character of music, is problematic. In her most recent publication it is sometimes simply by direct assertion, sometimes by reference to semiotic codes she claims to be culturally understood, sometimes by appeal to contemporary witnesses.[36] She seems to work in parallel with literary critics who scrutinize the gender roles and relations in works of fiction, but in the absence of counterparts in musical works to the explicit embodiments of such constructions in texts about

34. "Getting Down Off the Beanstalk: The Presence of a Woman's Voice in Janika Vandervelde's *Genesis II*," *Minnesota Composers Forum Newsletter* (February 1987): unpaged; included, in an altered version, in her *Feminine Endings: Music, Gender, and Sexuality* (Minneapolis, 1991), pp. 112–31; see pp. 124–25, 130.

35. Ibid.

36. "Narrative Agendas in 'Absolute' Music: Identity and Difference in Brahms's Third Symphony," in the present volume.

men and women she must first herself construct them out of the musical materials. In doing so she adopts the very stereotypes that she has deplored, underscoring them by contrast with the feminine character that she describes in music composed by women. That ascription adds to the confusion, because then it is no longer gender-labeling itself to which she objects, but the male-dominated, gendered scenarios that have filled European music since the Renaissance.

The "woman's voice" in the composition identified in McClary's title sounds in "an alternative to the dominant discourse [that the composer had] internalized in the course of her training," displaying such qualities as these: "asymmetries of rhythm and pitch," "a sense of existence that is . . . timeless," "gentle ebb and flow," "non-directional model techniques that revel in the present moment, rhythms that are grounded in the physicality and repetitiveness of the dance."[37] That these are feminine traits is taken as self-evident.

Most of the composers shown in *The Musical Hall of Fame*, plus some others, were given a machismo rating by Charles Ives, as has been reported by Maynard Solomon: "Ives . . . wants to reject the sensuous in music, in sound, in life, to regard himself as a 'thinker,' a 'philosopher,' a 'rational' maker of music." The genius (for Ives) must fortify himself by "that self-restraint . . . which can control the emotional and intellectual impulses, as a 'man,' not a degenerate."[38]

These are Ives's assessments: Mozart, Mendelssohn, early Beethoven, Haydn, Tchaikovsky, Gounod, Massenet: all emasculated. "Richy Wagner is a soft-bodied sensualist = pussy." The three B's: "None of them 'as strong and great as Carl Ruggles . . . too much of the sugar-plum for the soft-ears.'"[39] Chopin: "One just naturally thinks of him with a skirt on." But Franck, D'Indy, and Elgar are praised for their wholesomeness, manliness, humility. Debussy: "Sensual sensuousness . . . better if he had hoed corn or sold newspapers for a living." Sibelius: "An emasculated cherry . . . yellow sap flowing from a stomach that had never had an idea."[40]

The genderization of music, of which Bruno Stäblein's and Charles Ives's utterances are but isolated instances, has been inescapably associ-

37. "Getting Down Off the Beanstalk."

38. "Charles Ives: Some Questions of Veracity," *Journal of the American Musicological Society* 40 (1987): 467. (See Judith Tick's essay in this volume for another discussion of these remarks by Ives—Ed.)

39. Ibid., pp. 452, 467, 453. An interesting coincidence: Ives makes an exception of one of McClary's exemplary masculine works, the Fifth Symphony, but on account of the philosophical character of the Fate Motive.

40. Ibid., p. 452.

ated with the pejoration and oppression of the feminine, however that is identified. Against that background the new gender characterizations from the feminist standpoint can appear initially liberating, in three senses at least. First, the preoccupation of music historians with the triumph of form as the main line of European music history—like the idea, since the eighteenth century, of the triumph of reason as the main line of history in general—is easily decoded as a celebration of the masculine (because it can be shown that excellence of form and the faculty of reason have been treated historically as masculine traits), and it is liberating to bring that into the open. Second, it is a kind of affirmative action. Said has written of "the right of formerly un- or mis-represented human groups to speak for and represent themselves in domains defined, politically and intellectually, as normally excluding them, usurping their signifying and representing functions, overriding their historical reality."[41] Here it would concern the right of women to speak themselves of the feminine in music and to judge the significance of such assessments. And, third, the mystical and mysterious categories of gender we encountered at the outset are replaced with what may be claimed to be demonstrable categories of gender difference, referred directly to immediate feelings and experiences of sexuality.

But these new claims about gender in music force open again a Pandora's box of questions about musical aesthetics that used to be fiercely debated without resolution and about which there has been, in the mainstream of musicological activity, tacit agreement to let them lie. I wonder whether we are really meant to stir them up anew. I am talking now about grand questions: whether music possesses a content beyond its purely musical syntax and structure (for example, the "erotic imagery" that informs "the tonality that underlies Western concert music"); or whether music imitates action or experience ("assaultive pelvic pounding"); or how music affects the listener ("music after the Renaissance . . . appeals to libidinal appetites"); or whether it expresses feeling (the "throttling, murderous rage of a rapist incapable of attaining release"). If we do not like to put it so grandiosely as that we can simply ask: What are the rules for playing the game that has been set up here? How, for instance, do we choose between McClary's language about the Ninth Symphony and Hermann Kretzschmar's ("The development unrolls the Faustian portrait still further: seeking and not attaining, rosy fantasies of future and past, . . . the fulfilled reality of a pain that now suddenly makes itself felt")?[42] Where is the context of agreement that is a condition for the conveyance of meaning? Will McClary's hermeneutic provoke another

41. "Orientalism Reconsidered," p. 91.
42. *Führer durch den Konzertsaal*, vol. 1 (Leipzig, 1932), p. 253.

round of formalist defenses, like the ones that Schenker threw up against Kretzschmar?[43] If I find a woman's composition assertive and thrusting (for example, Joan Tower's Concerto for Orchestra, 1991) and if a man's composition conveys to me a "sense of existence that is . . . timeless" (I have even thought that about the same Ninth Symphony of Beethoven)[44] am I bound to think that they are cross-dressing?

The rules of the game become ever more elusive. In another context McClary gives the principle of "building to climax three-quarters of the way through a piece" a different twist.[45] About the harmonic syntax of tonal music she writes: "This process is intensely teleological in that it draws its power from its ability to make the listener desire and finally experience the achievement—usually after much postponement of gratification—of predetermined goals." To this point we might still be in the neighborhood of sexuality, but then: "The social values it articulates are those held most dear by the middle class [of eighteenth- and nineteenth-century Europe]: belief in progress, in expansion, in the ability to attain ultimate goals through rational striving, in the ingenuity of the individual strategist operating both within and in defiance of the norm."[46] If these two interpretations of the "teleological principle" are taken literally, they combine to suggest that those social values are in some deep sense modeled on male sexuality and that history may be read as an advance toward a great, cosmic male orgasm—a big-bang theory of history, we might say. We are bound to wonder about the guidelines for choosing interpretations, and about the criteria of evaluation to which they might be subject.

Yet another assertion of McClary's about music and gender reaches us at second hand, by way of Rose Rosengard Subotnik. Writing about a passage in Chopin's Berceuse, op. 57, that evades resolution (mm. 47–53), Subotnik reports that McClary had "suggested a sexual interpretation. . . . Chopin's music, she noted, is often characterized as effeminate. Could this not be, in part, because its lingering sensuousness at such typical moments, in contrast to the masculine Beethovenian climax, evokes and affirms the quality and the rhythm conventionally associated with female sexuality?"[47] I would myself be inclined to doubt this explanation for the reputation of Chopin's music as "effeminate," not least because of my impression that this characterization has been largely

43. See my essay "History, Criticism, and Beethoven's Ninth Symphony," in *Music and the Historical Imagination* (Cambridge, Mass., 1987), especially pp. 28–29.
44. Ibid., pp. 19–20.
45. "The Blasphemy of Talking Politics During the Bach Year," in Richard Leppert and Susan McClary, eds. *Music and Society: The Politics of Composition, Performance, and Reception* (Cambridge, 1987), pp. 13–62.
46. Ibid., p. 22.
47. "On Grounding Chopin," in *Music and Society*, p. 127 note 20.

owing to men, in whose vocabulary this word is, after all, most at home, and who are mainly responsible for its association with "sensuousness," but whose authority regarding the quality and rhythm of female sexuality I am disinclined to trust (I am surprised to see these terms and their linking so valorized in this text). But beyond this question of convention, knowledge, and familiarity, the interpretation raises once again the question of guidelines, to which we may add the question of limits. Shall we say that the Mazurka, op. 7 no. 5, whose last written measure carries the notation *Dal segno* [end of m. 4] *senza fine*, is the ultimate "effeminate" work, since Chopin has set it up so as to prevent climax forever? But then I am confused, because the driving-motor rhythm of the piece could make me think of pelvic thrusting. Is this the frustrated masculine side of Chopin, unable, like Beethoven after all, to go the distance?

I miss the point of singling out those six measures of the Berceuse, since the piece breathes between the same two sonorities from beginning to end (who has not been struck by the circular and the evasive in Chopin's music, but within a psychological range of the greatest scope and the finest differentiation, which includes the most assertive, driving, teleological—if you must, "masculine"—expressions?). The sort of peasant music that Chopin heard in the Polish countryside every summer until he moved to Paris prominently displays just the sort of nonprogressive, nonclimactic, nonteleological back-and-forth movement between sonorities that commands both of the pieces we have just had before us.[48] We thus find ourselves having come full circle, linking the non-Western or the rustic with the feminine.

Introducing the enterprise of his book, Richard Eichenauer comments how limited music's representation is; it is never concrete but is confined to stirrings of the human soul and to moods and changes of mood. We can certainly agree with him about this important condition that sets music apart from the figurative and literary arts. But then he asks: "Are there nevertheless ways and means to read out of the disembodied lines of a musical work the face of a particular racial character [*Rassenseele*]?"[49] Of course he thinks there are, and the body of his book is given over to thumbnail racial characterizations of musical traditions and of the works of individual composers—an essentialism of race in music—framed in apposite historical narratives. I think I do not need to support with examples my impression of the low quality of

48. We now have the opportunity to hear such music, in the tape recording accompanying William H. Noll, "Peasant Music Ensembles in Poland: A Culture History," Ph.D. diss., University of Washington, 1986.

49. *Musik und Rasse*, p. 13.

these assessments.[50] But that is not to say that someone else would have made a better job of it. The problem is with the question itself, which deserves answers of such quality.

Is it now to be a task of gender studies in music to reinforce the long-practiced role of gender duality in critical and historical discourse by developing a more explicit essentialism of gender? Does it speak better for the quality of gender characterizations if they are referred directly to the character of sexual feelings and experiences? This makes me think of an anecdote that circulated when I was an undergraduate at the University of Chicago, where the great psychoanalyst Bruno Bettelheim taught. He is said to have interrupted a lecture to inform a woman student who was knitting in the front row that knitting is symbolic of masturbation, and she is said to have responded, "Professor Bettelheim, when I knit, I knit; when I masturbate, I masturbate." I cite this piece of mischief not in order to dismiss the idea of sexuality embodied in music—something about which we may surely have strong personal impressions and convictions—but to affirm that to transform such impressions into critical accounts and historical categories will require a hermeneutics of greater subtlety and power than we have encountered here in the gender characterizations of medieval chant, Beethoven symphonies, or Chopin piano music, or in Charles Ives's ranked lists of composers.[51] And it reminds us that communication requires a context of basic agreement about what will signify what.

In the first of her essays from which I have quoted, Susan McClary includes a poem by Adrienne Rich, "The Ninth Symphony Understood at Last as a Sexual Message":

> A man in terror of impotence
> or infertility, not knowing the difference
> a man trying to tell something
> howling from the climacteric
> music of the entirely
> isolated soul
> yelling at joy from the tunnel of the ego
> music without the ghost
> of another person in it, music

50. A summary is given by Warren Dwight Allen in *Philosophies of Music History* (New York, 1939), p. 165.

51. I count Ives's assessments as essentialist because underlying them must be an idea that there is some kind of musical quality that is essentially masculine, and that works by male composers would naturally embody it (that is, the old essentialism of the essentialist-nominalist debate). Music by male composers that does not display this musical masculinity is defective, emasculated (not effeminate). That Ives listed only male composers and evidently had no place for the feminine in his system is an acute sign of what I have already suggested, that until recently genderization has been essentially a masculine project.

> trying to tell something the man
> does not want to, would keep if he could
> gagged and bound and flogged with chords of joy
> where everything is silence and the
> beating of a bloody fist upon
> a splintered table.[52]

McClary writes of this intense poetic expression of a personal response to Beethoven's work that the poet has "arrived at a remarkably similar reading of the piece" to her own. But I find myself resisting the collapsing of a critic's "reading" of a work and a poet's sense of it into a single thing, yet without wanting to say those are entirely separate things. I think I know what McClary is responding to when she speaks of "the phallic violence lurking behind the 'value-free' conventions of classical form."[53] But I want to judge that phrase more as poetry than as criticism or history. Yet I don't mean by that to exclude personal feeling from criticism and history. That is what makes so difficult the question I have been raising in this conclusion—a question to which I do not by any means pretend to have an answer.

There is a third way of thinking about such a statement as the one just quoted: not as criticism or history, not as poetry, but as a speech-act in the context of the professionalization of a new discourse. Like the assertions about the gender character of Beethoven symphonies and about the social meaning of the harmonic syntax of tonal music, it is a way into an interpretation that can be interesting in itself and that can sometimes achieve insights as social commentary, despite the naive quality of the musical judgment that is its point of departure, despite the ambiguity over whose judgment it is, despite its failure to provide insights into the music itself, and despite the dubiousness of the claim that the social commentary is suggested by the music. In fact, as a speech-act it challenges the authority of the phrase "the music itself."

The effect of this way of thinking is to end criticism's subordination to its objects, to liberate it from its texts, to make it autonomous. It is a challenge not only to the authority of the idea of "the music itself" but to the authority of music and of composers, which (who) become demystified and reduced to occasions for criticism. It is predictable as a next step that *criticism* will replace music and composers as the occasions for criticism. Perhaps there will be talk of the death of the composer, as there has been about the death of the author. In the course of this process the critic rises into a newly privileged position, from which she can adopt the

52. *Diving into the Wreck: Poems, 1971–1972* (New York: Norton, 1973).
53. "Getting Down Off the Beanstalk."

accusatory and patronizing (irony intended) mode of McClary's comments about Beethoven, for example. There is a circularity in this: it is exactly from this privileged position that the critic can make such arbitrary statements about music, statements with which one can neither agree nor disagree—the kinds of statements that led me to ask earlier: "What are the rules for playing this game?" From this vantage point it is clear that no answer will be forthcoming, other than "Say what you need to say in order to get into the critical discourse that you want to run." It will seem maudlin in just this context to say that criticism will no longer proceed from the critic's response to music.

I have been guided in this description/prediction, because of the striking parallels, by published descriptions of what has happened in literary criticism, and especially by a new account by Brian McCrea.[54] There is one intriguing difference: the arcanum, the obscurantism, the neologisms of some literary-critical fashions, which have certainly had their counterparts as exclusionary empowering devices in analytical branches of music criticism and in some musicological discourses, have as their counterparts in this new feminist music criticism their opposites, cognitively speaking. There is nothing hard to understand in the discourse I have described. What is obscure is the set of criteria for selecting the things that are said. But that is a sufficient obscurity to challenge an old authority and establish a new one.

I do not know whether there are masculine and feminine voices to be heard in music or whether there is a music criticism that will be sensitive to such a difference. If criticism aims to help us understand the workings of the human imagination, then a feminist music criticism is something we may well hope for. In the texts I have reviewed here, however, I have not encountered any criticism that is sensitive to qualities that have their source in gender, but only varieties of adversarial exegesis in which, against some standard of how music should be, one voice is held up as exemplary and the other as defective. (In McClary's exegesis, Beethoven's Ninth is just as flawed by its defective gender parameter as are all those "endless streams of melody that overflow the boundaries of textual divisions" in Stäblein's account of Old Roman chant, and all that "emasculated" music in Ives's list.) That sort of exegesis cannot pass for criticism; it is, rather, an exploitation of the *idea* of gender difference in the service of political and ideological agendas for music history and criticism. When produced in the name of feminist criticism such a practice, I think, can only impede the development of the genuine article. But as I owe my own sensitivity to such exploitation initially to feminist writers, especially

54. *Addison and Steele Are Dead: The English Department, Its Canon, and the Professionalization of Literary Criticism* (Newark, Del., 1990).

on the history of philosophy and science,[55] I am struck by the range of what may be known as feminist theory and criticism.

The historical links between the essentialisms of race and gender are unmistakable. By virtue of their common roots in late eighteenth- and nineteenth-century social, cultural, and biological thought, the essentialist doctrines of race, ethnicity, and gender each constitute an aspect of the historical context of the others.[56] They developed simultaneously as scientific concepts with explanatory force and as ideological precepts supporting political will. As scientific concepts they have, on the whole, been discredited. We cannot read passages like the following, from one of the most influential treatises on music aesthetics of the nineteenth century, and think that anyone would say such things today:

> The cause of this ["why women . . . have not amounted to much as composers"] lies . . . in the plastic aspect of musical composing, which demands renunciation of subjectivity . . . while women are by nature preeminently dependent upon feeling . . . it is not feeling which composes music, but the specifically musical, artistically trained talent.

> The tyranny of the upper vocal part among the Italians has one main cause in the mental indolence of those people for whom the sustained penetration with which the northerner likes to follow an ingenious work of harmonic contrapuntal activity [is impossible].[57]

But without the ideological framework to which race and gender were subordinated as explanatory notions they would not have been linked, and we are not bound to link them now. We need to be aware of that history, because it has left its residue in our language and conceptual vocabulary. But we are not bound because of it to foreclose in advance the possibility of thinking about the role of sexuality in the musical imagination, or the possibility of developing a sensitivity to the voices of gender in music itself. The question would be whether those possibilities can remain open without giving over again to the idea that music and its history are ineluctably determined by a nature—whether of race or eth-

55. For example, Genevieve Lloyd, *The Man of Reason: "Male" and "Female" in Western Philosophy* (Minneapolis, 1984); Susan Bordo, "The Cartesian Masculinization of Thought," in Sandra Harding and Jean F. O'Barr, eds., *Sex and Scientific Inquiry* (Chicago, 1975), pp. 247–64; Evelyn Fox Keller, *Reflections on Gender and Science* (New Haven, 1985).

56. The background of the essentialism of race is given by Stocking. Literature regarding the history of the essentialism of gender is cited by Ruth Solie in her essay "Whose Life? The Gendered Self in Schumann's *Frauenliebe* Songs," in Steven Paul Scher, ed., *Music and Text: Critical Inquiries* (Cambridge, 1991), pp. 219–40. I am grateful to Professor Solie for providing me with a prepublication typescript of this essay.

57. Eduard Hanslick, *On the Musically Beautiful: A Contribution Toward the Revision of the Aesthetics of Music*, trans. and ed. Geoffrey Payzant (Indianapolis, 1986), pp. 46, 64.

nicity or gender—to which the artist is born and from which he or she cannot escape; the idea that it is the critic's and historian's task to enunciate the principles of that nature and to write exegetical and hermeneutic works of criticism and history based on them. Therein lies the dilemma to which I alluded near the beginning of this essay.

Whatever ways there may be out of this dilemma, I believe they will have to be guided by the recognition of what is evident from this study: that such supposed natures are not natural at all, but are constructions that have been responsive to personal and cultural needs and ideologies. As critics and historians we can exercise choice concerning these constructions, but in the end we remain responsible for our choices.

Difference and Power in Music

John Shepherd

Introduction

There are clearly many "differences" relevant to the study of music: national differences, stylistic differences, differences in genre, and so on. It is difficult to conceive of any form of difference not imbued in some way with balances and imbalances of power, but musicology has tended to recognize only a limited set of differences as being relevant to the study of music, and to examine them as though power were not necessarily implicated in them. In this essay I am concerned specifically with those differences in which power is unambiguously implicated, differences having to do with class, age, ethnicity, and, most important, gender.

As a discipline, musicology has paid scant attention to these kinds of difference: to the music of those cultures and groups who are located in a position of weakness in relation to those who have power and influence in society. Relations between social location and musical taste do not admit of easy, one-to-one correlations; nonetheless, it seems clear that certain kinds of music tend to be associated with and used by cultures and groups occupying certain social locations. The failure of musicology to deal seriously with difference thus indicates a desire to position and categorize the musics of other cultures and groups according to the preferred musical thinking of those with power and influence. As Joseph Kerman has admitted, "Musicology . . . has come to mean the study of the history of Western music in the high-art tradition." Musicologists, says Kerman, "come from the middle class; they are indeed likely to be moving up within its spectrum. It is middle-class values that they project and seek to protect."[1]

1. Joseph Kerman, *Contemplating Music: Challenges to Musicology* (Cambridge, Mass., 1985), pp. 11, 36.

Questions of musicology and difference cannot, however, be dealt with solely in terms of class. Power is distributed in societies along many lines, including those of class, ethnicity, age, and gender. These variables cannot legitimately be conflated. An examination of difference in terms of any one of them must be undertaken within a context constituted by the others. Questions of difference in music do, nonetheless, display a particular twist in how they are located within such contexts. This twist results from processes through which musical practices are grounded in particular usages of sound, and processes through which these usages have come to be understood and managed in heavily gendered ways. In this essay I will explore the conditions of this twist. My thesis is that it is impossible to understand the practice of music in modern Western societies without simultaneously exploring how the practice, understanding, and management of music have attracted a specific and powerful form of gendering.

This is not to suggest that music is essentially gendered. The processes explored here arise from the human construction of reality under particular historical and social circumstances. In being heavily gendered, they run through other variables such as class, ethnicity, and age that form the context for them and are significantly imbued by them. To contemplate the full ramifications of issues of gender and music, therefore, requires an examination that stretches beyond questions of power relations between genders in the world of music narrowly conceived. Indeed, these power relations as they affect music, and these relations in turn can be understood only in the context of the heavily gendered nature of the practice, understanding, and management of music.

If the constricted nature of what musicologists study and the class-bound position from which they study it are symptomatic of processes of gender, then a gender-sensitive account of such music will raise questions that musicologists are reluctant to address. Susan McClary has offered interpretations of operas that depart strikingly from conventional wisdom in pointing to the misogyny implicit in plots and music alike. Yet, as she tells us, she has been enjoined to exercise compassion, not toward those who are devalued through such works, but toward the established canon and *its* attendant values. Compassion is required because to analyze opera and other aspects of the established canon in the manner envisaged by McClary invokes notions of socially grounded criticism. Socially grounded criticism is threatening to many musicologists. Indeed, musicologists resist such criticism because it seems to compromise the aesthetic core of the established canon. As one "well-meaning, liberal musicologist" asked McClary, "'How is the work of art to survive the social critique? Is there a remedy that does not violate the work?'"[2]

A central issue is thus how music signifies: what does it mean, how does it have "affect" for people in different circumstances? This question is one that musicology has tended to avoid, even though liberal humanist musicology *has* deemed the question of affect important. "When the study of music history loses touch with the aesthetic core of music, which is the subject matter of criticism," says Kerman, "it can only too easily degenerate into a shallow exercise."[3] The problem is not that liberal humanist musicologists ignore questions of aesthetics and affect altogether; Kerman's point is in this sense well taken. My point is that this kind of musicology tends to ignore social context—the social location of creators, listeners, and users—in approaching questions of aesthetics and affect. As a consequence, the discourses liberal humanist musicologists construct around such questions tend not to be those constructed by "ordinary" listeners. Furthermore, the dominant discourses of musicology—positivistic and empirical rather than liberal humanist—result from "a pervasive institutional reluctance to address musical content at all."[4] In both cases, liberal humanist and positivistic empirical, what musicologists analyze is not what most people hear. As McClary continues:

> Most people care about music because it resonates with experiences that otherwise go unarticulated, whether it is the flood of cathartic release that occurs at the climax of a Tchaikowsky symphony or the groove that causes one's body to dance—that is, to experience itself in a new way. Yet our music theories and notational systems do everything possible to mask those dimensions of music that are related to physical human experience and focus instead on the orderly, the rational, the cerebral. The fact that the majority of listeners engage with music for more immediate purposes is frowned upon by our institutions.[5]

I will not discuss here how meaning or content in music occurs or how it can be understood legitimately only through a socially grounded criticism. I have addressed these issues extensively elsewhere.[6] I will instead raise gender-related questions fundamental to understanding music as the phenomenon described by McClary: a cultural form evocative of grounded, material realities, a cultural form through which power is

2. Susan McClary, "Towards a Feminist Criticism of Music," in John Shepherd, ed., *Alternative Musicologies, Canadian University Music Review* 10, no. 2 (1990): 11.

3. Kerman, *Contemplating Music*, p. 19.

4. McClary, "Towards a Feminist Criticism," p. 14.

5. Ibid.

6. See John Shepherd, *Music as Social Text* (Cambridge, 1991).

exercised in ways both empowering *and* diminishing for individuals, groups, and cultures.

Music has been conceptualized and positioned within modern societies in ways that have hidden from view its importance as a basis for the exercise of power. There has been a tendency to diminish music by categorizing it as "different," that is, by privileging other forms of human expression and activity as more important and more fundamental to social and individual existence. Paradoxically, the ability of music to position and empower individuals, groups, and cultures rests significantly on the limited extent to which that power is understood. Music, in its reception and analysis, tends not to encounter the kind of developed frameworks brought to bear in academic and commonsense settings on other forms of human expression and activity. Music has been constituted as an Other to dominant forms of intellectual discourse and social practice and has thereby been rendered more manipulable through them.

To explore ways in which processes of gender have militated against understanding music's material and corporeal realities, it becomes necessary to engage in an exercise that musicology has studiously avoided: as a prerequisite to theorizing music's power, we must problematize the nature of music itself. Do we, as musicologists, really know what we are talking about when we use this term? This problematization is undertaken in the following section as prelude to a brief theorization of music's affective power. It then becomes possible to explore how processes of gender have militated against an understanding of this power. It is necessary, in other words, to have some understanding of what is being avoided before we can attempt to understand the avoidance.

What Is "Music"?

The attempt to understand the power of different genres of "serious" and "popular" musics to affect people, together with some of the more critical work undertaken by ethnomusicologists and those who study "folk" and "traditional" musics, leads to the conclusion that many labels applied to the world's music are questionable. If music from various times and places can appeal to one individual located within a specific biography, it seems possible that there are processes at work that belie the principles according to which different traditions and genres of music are categorized. It is questionable, for example, whether there *are* "classical," "popular," "folk," and "traditional" musics. It seems more likely that there are *discourses* constructed around concrete musical practices, and that those discourses group such practices into categories that render the music amenable to various forms of social, political, and economic control. This raises the question of genre and category in music and, again, the troublesome question of the definition of music.

To say that traditional distinctions between "classical," "popular," "folk," and "traditional" musics are questionable does not imply that music the world over is "the same," a "universal language." The question "What is music?" is a complex one that cannot be addressed usefully in terms of the love affair with definitions that pervades the worlds of academic and commonsense knowledge. "Music" is a discursively constituted category. The meanings invested in it are not consistent but contested. As Line Grenier has observed, the term *music* is "highly polysemic."[7] Furthermore, in a number of other cultures the word is not found: the linguistic and epistemological category it invokes lies outside their landscapes and is not relevant to them. What, then, *is* what we call music? What *do* we mean by this linguistic and epistemological category? What do these issues have to do with the form of knowledge to which music gives rise and the particular power it exercises over people in their daily lives?

One statement can be made about music that is unlikely to be seen as contentious: it is a cultural or artistic phenomenon that implicates sound in its manner of expression in ways significantly different from the implication of sound in language. Those cultures that have the term *music* seem to have little difficulty, in the contexts of academic and everyday life, in distinguishing between music and language, even when the relations between the two are evident and close. In order to throw some light on the apparent ease with which people distinguish between music and language, it is useful to observe that sound displays three potentials to act as a ground and pathway for the generation of meaning and significance.

First, sound can imitate and thus "refer" to other sounds. That is, the sound of evocation and the sound of reference have related inherent sonic qualities. That is to say, their relationship is not arbitrary and must, to a certain degree, be homologous. Second, sound can act as a homologous means of signification in relation to phenomena which themselves are not comprised of sound. This particular use of sound is discussed in the following section in examining the relation of sound in music to the human body as a site of social and cultural mediation. These first two potentials together provide the basis for the phenomena that have come to be discursively constituted as music.

Third, sound can act as a purely arbitrary means of signification in relation to the phenomena evoked. That is, the relationship between the sound and the phenomenon is established and determined purely by convention and tradition. This is the potential of sound that has given rise

7. Line Grenier, "The Construction of Music as a Social Phenomenon: Implications for Deconstruction," in *Alternative Musicologies*, p. 28.

to language in human societies. It is a crucial condition of language (as it, too, has come to be discursively constituted) that there need not be— although there frequently is in practice, as in the case of onomatopoeia— any necessary relationship between the characteristics of the sounds utilized and the characteristics of the phenomena referred to.

This clean break between sound and meaning has permitted a distinction between thought and the world on which thought operates, and so permitted the open-ended and, in recent history, spectacular development of massive, extended social structures and their attendant and facilitating technologies. However, although it is useful to think of music and language in terms of the discursive tendency to conceptualize them, one through the homologous, the other through the arbitrary, potential of sound, such discursive constitution is seldom unproblematic or uncontested. In practice, music is no more exclusively constituted through the homologous than is language through the arbitrary, a point to be taken up later.

Music as Power

The processes that have made possible the development of extended social structures and spectacular technologies (traceable in modern times to the European Renaissance of the fifteenth and sixteenth centuries) have mystified and hidden from view the importance of music as the basis for the exercise of a particular kind of power. Music, as the downside of "educated language," has come to be trivialized and marginalized. This trivialization and marginalization has compromised an awareness of the unquestioned ability of music to structure and shape individual awareness, individual subjectivity, and social and cultural formations. Within the contemporary industrialized world, music is conceptualized and managed either as cultural capital, the property of those with power and influence, or as leisure and entertainment, a diversion and distraction for those without power. Contrary to these traditional functions and understandings, however, music has power—exceptional power—precisely to the extent to which, through its discursive construction and formation in various categories and genres, people have been persuaded that it *is* peripheral and marginal, of little consequence to the important social and political concerns of the day.

As discursively constituted, music can evoke and refer to, give life to, our corporeal existence. Our internal states are physiologically coded, physiologically manifest; that is how we come to be aware of ourselves. These internal states—structured, textured, visceral, concrete—occur in dialectical tension with the external social world. We feel as we do overwhelmingly because of our relations to other people, to the world outside.

Yet the world is the way it is because of the manner in which we collectively intervene in it and present ourselves symbolically in the face of the meanings we assume the world has for us. One inescapable feature of human, and therefore social, existence is that internal human awareness is ultimately the seat of all social and cultural reproduction. Music is ideally suited to coding homologously, and therefore to evoking powerfully yet symbolically, the structures, rhythms, and textures of the inner life of the individual; the structures, rhythms, and textures of the external social world; and the order of relations between them. Sound, the basis of music as discursively constituted, reflects and articulates the internal physical properties, the movements, and the surface textures of the bodies that generate it. As it goes out into the world, it is further shaped by the structures, movements, and surface textures of the physical objects that reflect it. Sound is shaped and shaping, structured and structuring. In connecting these aspects of the external and internal physical worlds it can act, homologously and symbolically, as a code, a concrete ground and pathway, for the evocation of the relationships between the inner and outer social worlds.

Because music can enter, grip, and position us symbolically, it can act powerfully to structure and mediate individual awareness as the ultimate seat of social and cultural reproduction. That is why, in European post-Renaissance societies and those cultures over which such societies have held colonial and imperial sway, music has come to pose a problem. In some societies the power of a certain form of language (rational, arbitrary, isolated) and a certain form of linguistically encoded thought to manipulate and control the world unilaterally has, at various times in history, become so seductive as to result in attempts to exclude from awareness all other forms of experience. In such societies the power of music to remind people of their inalienable and inevitable connectedness to themselves, to others, and to the material and natural worlds has come to constitute a challenge to dominant forms of social, political, and economic control. In order to understand this challenge and how it has been met, it is necessary to consider the complex relations among gender, vision, language, and music as these have been implicated in the paradoxical and contradictory processes through which industrial capitalism continues to reproduce itself.

Gender and Vision

The material and symbolic aspects of human social reproduction are inseparably linked. Neither the processes of material reproduction nor the processes of social reproduction within which they are embedded and which they serve to sustain could occur independently of the symbolic systems that preserve and reproduce human awareness of them. This unbreakable linkage should not, however, obscure the fact that the mental and cultural constructs through which societies organize themselves and manipulate the material environment are distinct, as phenomena, from the material processes through which the constructs are put into operation and find expression. Mental and cultural constructs are abstract. They take on a life in a society only when they find expression through some material process, or, to put it a different way, when they are mapped or notated.

The form of notation fundamental to the development of human societies has been that provided by verbal language. However, as a form of communication speech has two disadvantages. First, the aspect of the material environment it invokes, the molecules of a medium (usually air), give rise to a perception—sound—that is ephemeral and insubstantial. Second, the abstract patterns of sound created need not, as we have seen, bear any intrinsic relation to the mental and cultural constructs with which they are conventionally associated, and a language can therefore to a significant degree develop independently of the world in which it exists. Once the sound and the mental and cultural construct have come together to form an apparently seamless sign, that sign can influence people's perceptions of the external world as much as it is itself formed and influenced by those perceptions. Verbal language is thus slippery and potentially capricious.

Although the worlds of culture and nature are inextricably linked through processes of social interaction, this linkage should not hide from view the mapping or notational function of the material world, whether natural or people-made. In societies without writing, the most reliable notational base for cultural concepts remains the material environment itself. In the material world, one difference in terms of which people can map or notate opposed cultural categories is human biological difference, a difference which in many cultures has been discursively (and thus socially) constituted as "female" versus "male." Societies frequently reproduce themselves through the coming together of opposed and frequently incommensurable cultural categories. This fertile and reproductive coming together is mapped in many societies, including those of industrial capitalism, through the coming together of women and men at the level of biology. Modes of biological reproduction come to stand for modes of cultural reproduction.

Gender roles in processes of biological and cultural reproduction do not, however, seem equally distributed. Through gestation and breastfeeding, women are involved in a more intensive and lengthy manner than men in the biological reproduction of the human species. As a consequence there might be said to exist a *predisposition* for men to feel distanced from or peripheral to one of the processes essential to the reproduction of human societies. This *perceived* status of marginality might be said to result in a *tendency* for men to attempt not only to compensate by controlling processes of cultural reproduction but also to control modes of biological or sexual relatedness at second hand through the processes of cultural reproduction that are mapped onto them. And since cultural processes are mapped onto *material* processes, at no point is this control more effectively exercised than on the mapping or notational procedures that facilitate and constrain processes of cultural reproduction.

This tendency seems to have received increased expression as human societies ceased to be nomadic, developed various forms of agricultural technology, and so established a significant, people-made *material* substratum for human existence. Be that as it may, a feature of this form of male control is that it is *visual* in character. Where environmental circumstances allow (rain forests, for example, usually allow for visual identification of prey only moments before the kill) vision reveals more quickly, precisely, and effectively than hearing the location of objects in time and space. The process of precisely defining and manipulating objects is one that thus depends more on vision than hearing. As the sensory channel fundamental to processes of material reproduction, vision facilitates control of abstract cultural constructs through control of the material substratum on which they are mapped or notated. Such control encourages, ultimately, an item-centered rather than a relational or structural understanding of the world. Consequently, men seem to have a tendency to understand people, objects, and concrete ideas, not as expressions and symptoms of the relational and interactive forces that give life to and reproduce societies and individuals, but, rather, as entities that in themselves demarcate, delineate, and put into motion the very social, cultural, and environmental relationships in which they are embedded.

This predisposition seems to be strengthened by the centrality of language to the development of human societies. The ability to manipulate discrete objects in the environment—an ability that is ultimately grounded in the power of visual conceptualization—is aided by the arbitrary relationship between sound and object, by the possibility of separating the inherent characteristics of sounds from those of the objects in the world on which those sounds operate. If the sounds of an utterance are not homologously bound or limited in their configurations by the inherent configurations of the objects to which they refer, then they can be open-endedly manipulated in relation to those objects and more easily prescribe their future manipulation in time and space. Indeed, the inherent characteristics of the *sounds* of language can have no necessary relationship with the inherent characteristics of such objects as *visually* defined. The arbitrary quality of language (which cannot be exclusive in its verbal forms) is guaranteed through verbal language's "cross-sensory" operations.

However, this further expression of the desire of men to control culture seems to have been held in check in traditional nonliterate societies through the inherent characteristics of sound as the inalienable medium of linguistic communication. Although language, in its verbal or literate forms, is essential to the item-centered ability to manipulate the material environment and so to create human societies, the sound of verbal language in nonliterate societies serves to remind people of their relatedness to themselves, their society, and the environment. Sound not only gives rise to a sense of integration, coexistence, and interaction. As given life through the voice, it serves also to emphasize that all communication through verbal language in nonliterate societies takes place in face-to-face situations. The orality of face-to-face communication cannot help but emphasize the social relatedness of individual and cultural existence.

This balance of individual and cultural sensoria is changed significantly with the advent of literacy, and phonetic literacy in particular. Phonetic literacy, as opposed to ideographic literacy, encodes visually the sounds people make in speaking. Furthermore, *analytic* phonetic literacy encodes visually *all* the sounds essential to meaning. This does not mean that visual signs encode all the sounds that people actually make in speaking. It means that visual signs encode all the sounds that people typically select and recognize as being essential to the generation of meaning. As a system of visual signs that are again quite arbitrary in their cross-sensory relation to the sounds they represent, analytic phonetic literacy can, in principle, take on a life of its own in relation to the sounds of the language it notates. A secure knowledge of the conventional relationship of these visual signs to the sounds of the language encoded obviates the need to refer back to the life of the spoken language to check meanings. All the information required for the creation and transmission of meaning—as grounded ultimately in the life of the spoken language— is contained within the system of visual signs. Sound—ephemeral, evanescent, slippery, and challenging—ceases to be the central presence in language. It is replaced increasingly by the safety, permanence, immutability, silence, and isolation of vision. Vision becomes in principle self-sufficient in its ability to manipulate and develop a material world as visually identified.

The development of literacy thus gave freer rein to a predisposition on the part of men to attempt to control culture through an item-centered hold on the material world. The new technology of writing quickly became the preserve of scribal elites, *male* elites. The ability of analytic phonetic literacy to act as a central point of definition and control for the management and dissemination of knowledge received an important additional emphasis during the Renaissance with the invention of movable-type printing. This invention made possible not only the mass-production and dissemination of books but also the complete self-sufficiency of vision in manipulating and developing a material world as visually identified. The bumpy texture of the medieval manuscript— handwritten, idiosyncratic in every instance, frequently a palimpsest that required considerable and concentrated decoding—was replaced by the uniform and easy ride of the repeatably printed page. It is perhaps not coincidental that it was the period after the Renaissance that witnessed the spectacular technological developments that have come to characterize industrial capitalist societies and that until recently have paid reduced attention to the cultural, social, and environmental contexts within which they have occurred. The history of industrial capitalist societies has been characterized by an exponential growth of technologies and material wealth pursued for their own sake by men. What has been absent is the influence of sound as an inalienable, inescapable, and centrally important medium of communication capable of interrogating and balancing the strongly visual bias of such growth. Sound— textured, circumjacent, and circumambient, "a way of touching at a distance"[8]—ceases to be a mediating presence. Visual language— smooth, silent, cerebral, rational, isolated—thus hides from view its doubly arbitrary nature, its strongly negotiable character, and creates the myth that there is no myth, that truth can be known and the world controlled.

Music as Paradox

The development of industrial capitalism has given rise to irresistible social and economic forces that now reach to every corner of society. Few people remain untouched by a social system that takes for granted the necessity for economic growth, the inevitability of competition, and the ability of all individuals to succeed on the basis of their own merits. Yet, massive and powerful though it is, industrial capitalism as a social form has rested upon a central paradox. It is a paradox that has made possible impressive technological feats while condemning a substantial proportion of the population to lives of poverty and misery. It is a paradox that has given rise to exciting and vibrant forms of cultural expression while creating social problems of very considerable dimensions. It is a paradox

8. R. Murray Shafer, *The Tuning of the World* (New York, 1977), p. 11.

evident in the contrasts that can typically be drawn between the lives of men and women, the middle classes and the working classes, and Anglo-Americans and other ethnic groups. It is a paradox whose roots lie at the very foundation of human sociality: the ability of people on the one hand to manipulate the material environment through symbolic processes that are in a certain sense independent of the world on which they operate while, on the other, remaining indissolubly linked to that world. It is a paradox highlighted inalienably by music as music has come to be discursively constituted in the modern world.

The tension between the inalienable potential for artifice and the inescapability of the material is one that is evidenced in the development and reproduction of any society. Yet it is a tension that those who developed industrial capitalism have attempted to disguise. The attempt has been to ignore certain aspects of the world's materiality as vision became self-sufficient as a mode of cerebral apprehension and manipulation of that world. Yet vision remained inadequate (as would any of the senses) as an exclusive mode of experience. This gap between self-sufficiency and inadequacy was significantly reduced by ensuring that the characteristics of mental and cultural constructs were, as far as possible, rendered amenable to forms of material expression that were themselves conceived in a visual manner. If the cultural was reduced to the material as visually conceived, then the actualities of the material world would not pose a threat to the dominance of a culture as visually conceived.

The attempt, in essence, was to eliminate the tension between artifice and the material by conceiving reality as a cerebral construct independent of the material world on which it rested and from which it drew sustenance. Since the overwhelming majority of those who have engaged in this attempt have been men, it is an attempt that has been centrally and inescapably gendered, with massive consequences for women. For example, in their conventional roles as emotional nurturers and principal providers of children's early social life (roles that have been socially constructed as a part and consequence of the attempt to eliminate the tension between artifice and the material), women came to symbolize the very process—that is, social interaction—through which people and societies are created and reproduced. Men, by contrast, have attempted to control social and cultural processes by mapping them onto aspects of the material world as divorced from the ecology that sustains them. Since women present one such aspect, men have tended to attempt a conceptual control of women as the providers of a material ground on which processes of social interaction are symbolized and mapped.

Men's desire to control women therefore derives from their desire to control the social world as something external to them, something with which they are not essentially engaged. This desire for control has led men to manipulate women as isolated objects. Social relatedness implies negotiability of political power. The conceptualization of people as objects decontextualized from social relations, by contrast, implies the possibility of uncontested, unilateral control. The objectification of women by men thus became a crucial step in the mystification of social relatedness. If men assume that women symbolize the social interactions that are the source of people's being, and if sexual relatedness provides a biological code for these same processes, then men tend to equate women with sexuality. It is of course one thing for men to attempt this identification and quite another for women to subscribe to it in just the way men think they do, but it nonetheless seems reasonable to conclude that power relations as mediated through processes of gender and sexuality in the modern world have been characterized by a certain stereotypic imaging of women.

In industrial capitalist societies the processes of biological reproduction, in which men figure only momentarily, come to be controlled conceptually through an objectification of the processes of cultural reproduction that are mapped onto them. That is, culture as controlled by men is projected onto the material world so that women as objects come to be equated with a material world susceptible to unilateral control by men. By pinning down the discrete material phenomena onto which the cultural constructs essential to social life are mapped, men preserve themselves as paradoxically independent and in control of the social relations that in fact produce them.

However, the reality that underlies this paradoxical attempt at conceptual control of the world is that ultimately, because men have a very real need of material and social relations, they simply *cannot* deny them. This situation guarantees that the processes of social control, alienation, and ideology which constitute such powerful presences in the social life of industrial capitalism can never become totalities. The essential paradox on which industrial capitalism rests ensures that within its complex and extended processes runs a constant and inevitable playing out of contradictions and inconsistencies. This playing out provides individuals, groups, and entire cultures with opportunities to assert their presence in the face of more powerful forces. Indeed, it is through the containment and assimilation of such assertions that industrial capitalism continues to develop, adapt, and reproduce itself.

An understanding of these contradictions and inconsistencies does much to explain the situation of music in industrial capitalist societies. On the one hand, the special ability of music to encapsulate the related processes of the internal and external worlds has always posed a problem for scribal elites. Confucius, Plato, and Saint Augustine, for example, all uttered warnings against the sensuous and seductive appeal of music. On the other hand, the existence and power of music, together with the world it represents, cannot simply be denied.

The response to this tension within industrial capitalist societies has been twofold. First, music has been categorized as an unimportant mode of human expression—unimportant, that is, to processes regarded as central to the continued life of society. However, it does not follow from this categorization that music *is* marginal to social processes. In this way music comes to represent the central paradox on which industrial capitalism rests: through the appeal of various genres to individual and collective realities, music serves to reproduce the life of capitalism, yet this very function is implicitly denied through the ways in which music is understood and institutionalized in various cultural and educational processes. In this sense music occupies contradictory positions in the social structures of industrial capitalism that are parallel to those of women: music reaffirms the flux and concreteness of the social world at the same time that, through its categorization and packaging, it denies them.

Second, those with power and influence in industrial capitalist societies have valued certain genres of music over others. Genres that are valued tend to have stylistic characteristics regarded as less challenging to the established social and moral order, because those characteristics have emerged from and are consequently more amenable to dominant modes of visual and technological control. However, within industrial capitalist societies are musical genres whose stylistic characteristics have emerged in other ways, permitting the genres to betray more graphically the power of music to evoke directly and concretely the related processes of the internal and external social worlds. These genres have, as a consequence, been regarded as more of a challenge to the established social and moral order. Musical genres whose social qualities cannot easily be denied appear to contradict the notion that music in itself is of little consequence to the continued life of society.

It is in this way that the range of musical genres within industrial capitalist societies marks out the consequences of the central, gendered paradox on which such societies rest, and so understanding this paradox is fundamental to comprehending the functioning of industrial capitalism. It is also crucial for an understanding of the positions and meanings of the many different genres of music that have existed within the structures of industrial capitalism, positions and meanings which in turn have served to reproduce the central, gendered paradox from which such structures flow. It is to the question of genre and category as discursively constituted, gendered means for the control of music that I now turn.

Music as Discursive Formations

The dominant, hegemonic tendencies through which preferred notions of language and music have come to be constituted, together with preferred formulations of "classical," "popular," and "folk" as categories in which to confine music, resonate strongly with the dynamics of strategies through which men have attempted to eliminate the tension between artifice and the material. As discursively constituted, preferred notions of language, music, the classical, and the folk have been, in various ways, cleansed, rendered "silent" in their capacity to articulate the inconsistencies and contradictions of life. This is in itself a contradictory process, because such silencing can never in actuality be achieved. It is the popular that has become the sole repository for the contradictory and corporeal realities of life, a repository which for these reasons has been treated pejoratively. This process is yet again contradictory, because the popular has itself on many occasions served to hide the tension between artifice and the material. The contradictions implicit in the discursive formations of language, music, the classical, the folk, and the popular serve, indeed, to highlight their discursive nature and to point to a necessary distinction between discursive formations and the material reality of the cultural practices on which they rest.

No language, not even the most arid of academic language, is completely and purely arbitrary, with no allusion or reference to sound's homologous potentials. All language, to be evocative, employs rhythms and textural properties, the more so when it seems monotonous and flat. Similarly, no music—not even the most rhythmic, the most textural, on the one hand, or the most abstract, the most "syntactical,"[9] on the other— is without a range of meanings that have become conventional, traditional, and to a certain degree arbitrary in relation to the homologous potentials and possibilities of the sounds through which it receives articulation and life.

All human societies use sounds to communicate, and they use sounds— in a variety of social and cultural contexts—in ways that draw in different degrees and combinations on the various signifying potentials of sound as a physical phenomenon. These different and complex modes of sonically based signification and communication then come to be grasped and

9. For the distinction between the "syntactical" and other dimensions of music such as the "sensuous," see Leonard B. Meyer, "Some Remarks on Value and Greatness in Music," *Journal of Aesthetics and Art Criticism* 17 (1959): 486–500.

categorized in various cultures in relation both to the immanent characteristics of these modes as socially and culturally constructed and in relation to the linguistic and epistemological categories that come to be discursively constituted in relation to them. "Music" does not have to be "homologous" any more than "language" has to be "purely arbitrary." Indeed, the ability of music to go beyond the homologous potentials of sound in constituting itself as a performance event through words, images, and movement has its counterpart in the ability of language to go beyond the arbitrary potentials of sound in constituting itself as a performance event through the paralinguistics of rhythm, inflection, image, and movement. It is no coincidence that those forms of music and language that draw attention to their multimedia constitution and so to the lived, concrete, and messy realities they evoke (for example, various forms of popular and traditional musics, and various "dialects" of English such as black English) are devalued precisely in terms of their difference from "good music" and "proper English."

There exist, in other words, both concrete practices of sonically grounded human signification and communication, and an understanding and categorization of these practices in terms of the ways a society or culture may reflect on them through an extension of these same practices. That understanding is itself created within a society or culture through the application of the practices themselves. These practices and their discursive categorization and formulation are powerfully and indissolubly linked because they emanate from the same, interconnected modes of communication and metacommunication. However, in acting on practices to render them susceptible to the exercise of power, discourses are in a sense distinct from the practices themselves. As Richard Middleton has observed concerning the study of popular music, it is essential to understand how knowledge is discursively constituted, controlled, and established as a basis for the exercise of power. "Much recent historical work, notably Michel Foucault's," says Middleton,

> has stressed the importance of investigating the discursive formations through which knowledge is organized. If we do not try to grasp the relations between popular music discourses and the material musical practices to which they refer, and at the same time the necessary distinctness of level between these, we are unlikely to break through the structures of power which, as Foucault makes clear, discursive authority erects.[10]

It is essential to develop such understandings, because discursive formations render the world as "natural" and unexceptional, given rather than constructed. However, neither language nor music is given *as such*

---

10. Richard Middleton, *Studying Popular Music* (Milton Keynes, 1990), p. 7.

in reality. That is to say, no such things or processes as "language" and "music" exist, at least not if existence is taken to mean that sets of cultural practices exist in the objective, social world that may be consistently and uncontestedly subsumed under these categories. Although the practices that these discursively constituted categories gather up and present to us as "natural" are, indeed, given in the sense that they constitute a very important aspect of the constructed objective reality of the external social world, the way in which they are *discursively* formulated is not. Rather, the categories "language" and "music" have come into being at particular points in history and have since then been used to exercise a certain, albeit contested, kind of political power.

Within the context of European post-Renaissance societies and the cultures that these societies have come to control or influence, a discursively constituted notion of language, and of a certain form of language at that (rational, arbitrary, isolated), has come to be regarded as being of fundamental importance to the development, management, and perpetuation of a world mediated through increasingly spectacular technologies and increasingly dependent on sophisticated industrial and information networks. Within this world, music has had to be managed very carefully. Whereas the constitution of dominant and controlling forms of language has pushed it as far as possible toward the arbitrary and away from the homologous signifying potentials of sound, music has been pushed as far as possible toward the homologous and away from the arbitrary. But this constitution maximizes the homologous in a way that plays down sound's rhythmic and textural possibilities, those possibilities most potently evocative of the concrete relations between individuals and cultures. The music of the established Western canon has, through the technical musical parameters it foregrounds—those of pitch and duration, of abstract relations *between* sounds, of the "syntactical"—played down as far as possible the importance sound's inherent characteristics have in concrete musical practices. While remaining *structurally* homologous and therefore quintessentially "musical," this music has at the same time approached as closely as possible to the preferred condition of "language" by involving the inherent characteristics of sound as little as possible in processes of constructing meaning.

This particular discursive constitution of the dominant and preferred condition of music within European post-Renaissance societies and the cultures they have influenced was challenged by the development of so-called popular musics, which began approximately at the end of the eighteenth and the beginning of the nineteenth century. However, the development of popular musics had as much to do with the discursive constitution of "the popular" as it did with the development of distinctive musical practices. There has always been popular music—that is, music that has lain outside the immediate and effective control of those with power and influence and that has spoken to the everyday lives and realities of "ordinary" people. As long as such music posed no threat to the dominance of the preferred tradition, those with power and influence saw no need to take notice of it. However, within the European societies of the late eighteenth and the early nineteenth century changes in the social and cultural formation increased the political and social consequence of various forms of working-class and lower-middle-class musics—a degree of consequence made more startling through this music's increasing commodification in the form of sheet music and the mass dissemination such commodification made possible.

These events instigated the development of the popular as a discursively constituted cultural construct. The popular, as a condition of mass industrial society, drew attention to this very sociality, to its relevance to the everyday lives of people. And it was this very relevance to the everyday world of a developing industrial society that denied it value as an "authentic" cultural or artistic phenomenon. This particular form of "contaminated," everyday, industrialized sociality drove the social and the everyday (*social* and *everyday*, that is, to the aristocracy and the upwardly mobile middle classes) out of the discursive construction of "high" culture. "High culture," along with "serious" or "classical" music, became good and valuable to the extent that they were as far as possible removed from present times and present places and instead addressed the mysteries of the universe. It is against this development in the discursive constitution of high-culture music that we can understand the propensity of musicology (itself a creature of related developments in the nineteenth century) to ignore the power of music as a special form of individual, social, and cultural knowledge and to act, rather, as an apologist for high-culture music or to engage in extended taxonomical categorizations of the world's musics.

Against this development we can also comprehend the construction of "the folk" and of "traditional" music as the music that subsequently became the favored concern of folklorists and ethnomusicologists. The folk can be understood in relation to the discursive constitution of the popular: the folk became what had been the popular before the popular was commodified and disseminated on a mass basis. In contrast to the social "contamination" that typified the popular, the folk became sanitized. If the folk and folk music were social, as was self-evidently and undeniably the case, then the social had to be reconstructed in a state of purity, a state of grace. The folk were pulled out of actual social relations—contradictory, messy, implicated with morally dubious political practices—and placed in a false world of mutually organic, egalitarian, and just social relations. The folk were discursively constructed, as was high-culture music during the nineteenth century, as a basis for critiquing musical developments that, through their increasing commodification and mass dissemination, could profile *more publicly* than before the corporeal, the material, the social, the rhythmic, and the textural in music. Middleton is uncompromising, and justifiably so, in his critique of the politics of the "folk":

> The politics of "folk" centre, through all interpretative nuance, on the "authenticity" of the music. Its value—particularly when set against other, less favoured kinds of music—is guaranteed by its provenance in a certain sort of culture with certain characteristic processes of cultural production. Thus the supposed "purity" of folk society . . . goes hand in hand with the "authenticity" of the music . . . both are myths. Culturally they originate in the romantic critique of industrial society; politically they derive from the bourgeoisie's attempt to make such critique comfortable, providing an ideologically functioning fantasy which can be used to counter the threat of real workers' culture. The judgement of "authenticity" is always directed at the practice of someone else. Either it removes this practice from its own mode of existence and annexes it to the system of an imperialist cultural morality, or it scapegoats undesirable ("inauthentic") practices and casts them beyond the pale.[11]

The tendency to buy into this fantasy has significantly characterized the practice of both folklore and ethnomusicology. Despite the origins of the latter in the pioneering work of Charles Seeger and his experience of social conditions in the United States during the 1930s, its dominant trend has been that constituted by "area studies." Such studies, replicating in large measure the dominance of empiricism and positivism within historical musicology, have been based, if only implicitly, on the philosophy that the traditional musics of the world should be gathered up and preserved before they are eradicated through the destructive advance of industrial capitalism and its attendant cultural forms.

Conclusion

The discursive constitution of preferred notions of language and music, together with the idealization of classical music and the sanitization of folk music, can all be read as an attempt by male culture to control musical culture by eradicating the tensions between artifice and the material. Preferred notions of language and of classical and folk music have attempted to cleanse the cultural practices on which they are based and so to enter these practices into a masculine discourse. Notions of popular music, in contrast, have entered the cultural practices on which they are

11. Ibid., p. 139.

based into a discourse of the feminine (a discourse nonetheless over-whelmingly constituted and controlled by men). Questions of music and gender thus go deeper than the difference in power that women and men typically experience in relation to the world of music. To raise concerns of music and gender is to raise concerns having to do with the socially grounded affect of music: the ability of *all* music to speak powerfully, directly, and in different ways to the concrete and contradictory realities of those whose specific biographies are symptomatic of different and particular social locations. As McClary has observed, feminist musicolo-gists "cannot afford to focus solely on obvious instances of gender—to be one-issue critics. . . . [They] must also be alert to the politics of race, of class, of subjectivity, of popular culture: those elements that traditionally have been relegated to the 'feminine' slagheap."[12]

An awareness of the gendered "difference" of music requires a dis-mantling of the discursive authority that maintains such difference. Only through such dismantling will those situated "differently"—including women—be able to recuperate music as a cultural practice of power and consequence. What is required is not a politics of opposition, resistance, and negation. Music is not a sanctified icon requiring protection from the hostile forces of industrial capitalism. As Simon Frith has observed:

> The flaw in this argument is the suggestion that music is the starting point of the industrial process—the raw material over which everyone fights—when it is, in fact, the final product. The "industrialization of music" can't be understood as something that happens *to* music but describes a process in which music itself is made—a process, that is, which fuses (and confuses) capital, technical, and musical arguments.[13]

What is required, rather, is a politics of articulation, a politics based on understandings of those fused and confused, messy, paradoxical, and contradictory cultural practices that have come to be discursively consti-tuted as different genres of music. Such understandings will allow indi-viduals, groups, and cultures to intervene in these practices that are of consequence to their future trajectories. The development of such un-derstandings should surely be the business of contemporary musicology and ethnomusicology.

12. "Towards a Feminist Criticism," p. 15.
13. Simon Frith, "The Industrialization of Popular Music," in James Lull, ed., *Popular Music and Communication* (Newbury Park, Calif., 1987), p. 54.

Loving It: Music and Criticism in Roland Barthes

Barbara Engh

The writings of Roland Barthes are well known in literary and cultural studies, where they have been found to be of inestimable importance. And, as one of the most prominent of French postwar intellectuals, whose name is associated closely with structuralism and poststructuralism, Barthes has been influential in feminist studies, where "French theory" has transformed the debates concerning the construction of gender.[1] However, Barthes's work has not been influential in musicology, which has resisted, more so than the other disciplines, interdisciplinary approaches to the study of culture. Music itself has a special status in Barthes's work: when he is at work as a semiotician, as an ideology critic, music is absent from his considerations. When he moves to a critique of those practices, music emerges as a privileged discourse. It is that neglect of music on the one hand and its valorization on the other that this essay will explore. Although it will proceed chronologically through Barthes's writings, it should not be read as a developmental narrative. Barthes's phases exist synchronously. The older Barthes, the lover of music, returns us with a difference to the younger Barthes, the mythologist.

"a few difficulties, in feeling if not in method"

The moment of publication of Barthes's *Mythologies* (published in 1957), which subjects quotidian aspects of French culture to a semiological critique, might be described as the moment at which ethnography came home—the moment at which, in other words, European intellectuals

1. See, for example, Alice A. Jardine, *Gynesis: Configurations of Woman and Modernity* (Ithaca, 1985).

began to scrutinize the practices and the assumptions of European culture in the thoroughgoing and detached manner that had been reserved for European study of the non-West. Edward Said, whose *Orientalism* is concerned to show that the "Orient" is a construction of Western academic discourse that is fully implicated in Western imperialism, supplied the blurb on the back cover of the 1988 printing. "Each of the little essays," he remarks without regret, "wrenches a definition out of a common but constructed object, making the object speak." Bourgeois culture seems to have become the object of the violence of its own methodologies. There is a brio in Barthes's writing, and he later spoke of his pleasure in "outplaying" the codes. Nevertheless, by the book's end he has discovered a pervasive sort of pain, and he writes that the mythologist may have "a few difficulties, in feeling if not in method."[2] He has no qualms about the project's political necessity:

> Holding as a principle that man in a bourgeois society is at every turn plunged into a false Nature, it [mythology] attempts to find again under the assumed innocence of the most unsophisticated relationships, the profound alienation which this innocence is meant to make one accept. The unveiling which it carries out is therefore a political act. . . . Mythology *harmonizes* with the world, not as it is, but as it wants to create itself.[3]

This musical metaphor names the very goal of the politics of mythology, but it also names the pain of the mythologist. Harmonization can only be effected at a distance, of course—that is a condition of harmony—and the mythologist feels excluded, from a clear-cut efficacy (it is not "revolutionary action"), from the community whose "very humanity" myths represent, and even from history: "The havoc which he wreaks in the language of the community is absolute for him."[4] There is no going back, no present payment, nor can he allow himself the luxury of imagining the future in the name of which he struggles. Finally, he is excluded from reality itself: "condemned to metalanguage," the mythologist is condemned to ideologism. He cannot "speak the object":

> We constantly drift between the object and its demystification, powerless to render its wholeness. For if we penetrate the object, we liberate it but we destroy it; and if we acknowledge its full weight, we respect it, but we restore it to a state which is still mystified.[5]

We are presented with a choice: we may ideologize or we may poetize; we may either demonstrate that "reality is entirely permeable to history" or

2. *Mythologies*, trans. Annette Lavers (New York, 1972), p. 156.
3. Ibid., p. 156 (emphasis in original).
4. Ibid., p. 157.
5. Ibid., p. 159.

"search for the inalienable meaning of things." The choice is clear, Barthes declares: we must ideologize, and forgo the luxury of essence, because "essence" is precisely what bourgeois culture deploys to naturalize its history. "And yet," he closes, "this is what we must seek: a reconciliation between reality and men." The "feelings" produced by these contradictions persist.[6]

Music, interestingly, is excluded from *Mythologies'* otherwise thoroughgoing consideration of the various manifestations of bourgeois culture. There are places where one might expect its mention—for example, in a discussion of mathematical and poetic discourse, which have so protected themselves against interpretation that myth does not invade them, it goes around them, and "takes [them] away en bloc."[7] But music, despite its long-standing connections to both poetic and mathematical discourse, is not mentioned. In defining myth, whose only grounding is history itself, Barthes writes:

> not only written discourse, but also photography, cinema, reporting, sports, shows, publicity, all these can serve as a support to mythical speech. Myth can be defined neither by its object nor by its material, for any material can be arbitrarily endowed with meaning.[8]

Absent from this enumeration of cultural practices which wants to suggest exhaustive scope is music. Present (and we will shortly be noting the same presence/absence oscillation in another context) is an assertion regarding the suitability of "any material" for myth.

There *is* one brief discussion of music, in "The Bourgeois Art of Song" (collected in *The Eiffel Tower* from the French *Mythologies*). It reveals the paradoxical significance of music's absence: it is presence itself, the presence of inalienable essence that Barthes had renounced by his commitment to ideology critique. He writes that the bourgeois art of song imposes "a parasitical intellectual order" of interpretive practice on the "sensual truth of music, a sufficient truth." There are performers who avoid interpretation—some amateurs, Panzéra, Lipati. "They trust in the immediately definitive substance of music."[9] Poetry seems to be at hand in music, a circumstance that should justify—according to the terms of the project as it is deployed in every other instance—the utmost suspicion on the part of the mythologist, who recognizes that the ideological operates most effectively precisely under the guise of the natural, the "immediately

6. Ibid., pp. 158–59.
7. Ibid., p. 132.
8. Ibid., p. 110.
9. Barthes, *The Eiffel Tower and Other Mythologies*, trans. Richard Howard (New York, 1979), pp. 120, 121.

definitive." But music, with its unique affinity for the feelings, is reserved as a refuge for the alienated mythologist, who is feeling bad.

Nine years later, in the "Introduction to the Structural Analysis of Narratives," Barthes proposes a study of narrative whose explanatory power would be as far-reaching as that claimed for the study of myth:

> Narrative is first and foremost a prodigious variety of genres, themselves distributed amongst different substances—as though any material were fit to receive man's stories. Able to be carried by articulated language, spoken or written, fixed or moving images, gestures . . . ; narrative is present in myth, legend, fable, tale, novella, epic, history, tragedy, drama, comedy, mime, painting, . . . stained glass windows, cinema, comics, news item[s], conversation. . . . Narrative is international, transhistorical, transcultural: it is simply there, like life itself.[10]

Again the conspicuous absence of musical practices (why?), and an assertion regarding the serviceability of "any material" in a discourse that appears unwilling to delimit itself in any way. Unwilling, that is, until the final sentences of the essay, which speculate on the origin of narrative: "Narrative is contemporaneous with monologue, a creation seemingly posterior to that of dialogue. . . . The little human invents at once sentence, narrative, and the Oedipus." This "ending" quietly yet radically delimits the universalizing aspirations of the structuralist project, characterizing the object whose universality was to have authorized its scope— and by extension, those aspirations themselves—as monological, oedipal, and gendered. Narrative, Barthes writes, is "a form which has vanquished repetition and instituted the model of a process of becoming."[11] In narrative he locates the developmental triumph of mind over matter, and what this involves is a silencing of *mater*. The institution of oedipal monologue displaces preoedipal dialogue or—to get at the question of the silence around music—preoedipal polyphony. The silence of the Other's voice(s) enables the little inventor to announce: I am international, transhistorical, transcultural; simply here. I have invented, I speak, life itself.

Consider the ever-popular myth of Orpheus: does not Euridice's silence, or death, provide the enabling condition of his musical accomplishment? Even at the price of "a few difficulties, in feeling if not in method." For Barthes, Orpheus is the "eponymous hero . . . of theory" because of the reflexive gaze: "a discourse that looks back on itself is thereby a theoretical discourse."[12] Barthes does not discuss the slippage between woman and theory in his appropriation of that myth. Orpheus

---

10. In *Image-Music-Text*, trans. Stephen Heath (New York, 1977), p. 79.

11. Ibid., p. 124.

12. *The Grain of the Voice: Interviews 1962–1980*, trans. Linda Coverdale (New York, 1985), p. 144.

looks back responsibly to Euridice, defying the law that has prohibited that gaze. The same law that it is his responsibility to transgress demands in retribution her repeated death, but ideologize we must. There is in consolation the "orphic prerogative": the ability to animate dumb matter with song, with myth, with narrative.

"plunging into the matter of the text"

Barthes later spoke of "a very definite break" in his work after "Introduction to the Structural Analysis of Narratives."[13] In numerous contexts he expresses dissatisfaction with the ideology critique proposed in *Mythologies*, because it had itself become mythology, a "second-nature" functioning not as critique but as the neurotic and repetitive discourse of stereotype and doxa. As for literary structuralism, for Barthes it founders methodologically on the difference between science and literature, between a "paternal" and "terroristic" discourse that instrumentalizes language and the domain where that discourse is eluded and defied.[14] Again he poses the problem as a critical choice and responsibility, but whereas the earlier Barthes would mournfully have prescribed the necessity of science against literature, at the price of the alienation of both, this later Barthes understands the problem differently. The transformation effected by the move "From Work to Text" will make possible, and even necessary, Barthes's considerations of music. Before I turn to those essays I need briefly to discuss what is at stake in this notion of "text."

Barthes's demand is on the one hand that we "change the object itself," and on the other that critical practice make itself "homogeneous to its object." This field, where neither the subject nor the object of knowledge can remain untransformed, is that of the text. "We must somehow immerse ourselves in the signifier, plunging far away from the signified into the matter of the text."[15] In a 1970 interview he states:

> The struggle must be taken further now, it is not signs that must be cracked wide open—signifiers on one side, signifieds on the other—but the very idea of the sign. . . . It is Western discourse as such, in its foundations and elementary forms, that we must now try to break apart. . . . In the West . . . we must wage a deadly serious and historic battle with the signified.[16]

13. Ibid., p. 129.
14. "From Science to Literature," in his *The Rustle of Language*, trans. Richard Howard (Berkeley, 1989), pp. 3–10.
15. "Change the Object Itself: Mythology Today," in *Image-Music-Text*, pp. 165–69; "From Science to Literature," in *The Rustle of Language*, p. 10; *The Grain of the Voice*, p. 125.
16. Ibid., p. 85.

The signifier, usually understood as simply the material partner of the signified, is more importantly its most effective adversary. This locution is uncharacteristically aggressive, but it is interesting for that: partaking of the language of aggression, it announces a battle which Barthes will wage in entirely other terms, from the field of the signifier's play, the text. He argues that the West's regime of meaning is monotheistic and monological—always underpinned by God or one of his hypostases: Man, Reason, Science, Law. To wage the war against the signified as a militant action aimed at killing that father would be to remain obedient to the oedipal prescription, and to an ethics of violence. Barthes states that "violence is something that must be directed toward well-defined tactical ends, not adopted as a permanent ethical attitude."[17] The move to the field of the signifier is not to be understood, as it so frequently is in critiques of poststructuralism, as a valorization of nonmeaning against meaning. Nonmeaning is for Barthes "the worst meaning."[18] Rather, he wants to loosen the fixity of meaning, to pluralize it.

The concept of signification takes meaning to be a product held in repository, the withdrawal and circulation of which are the task of interpretive practice. By contrast, "the text is a process of demonstration," and the operative notion in the field of the text which names that process is not signification but *signifiance*. (To translate this as "significance" is to name precisely what it is not.) The text is not an object, Barthes stresses; rather, it *"is experienced only in an activity of production."*[19] *Signifiance* (a notion Barthes takes from Kristeva), is "a labour outside exchange, inaccessible to 'calculation.'"[20] It is

> not the work by which the subject (intact and external) might try to master the language . . . but that radical work (which leaves nothing intact) through which the subject explores how language works him and undoes him as soon as he stops observing it and enters it.[21]

Barthes admits that the text is a luxury item, but he persists in its "impossible science" to the end. He appears to withdraw from his earlier commitment to ideology critique and to immerse himself in an individual *jouissance* which is not even induced by respectably populist means. To defend himself he summons Brecht, who insisted that pleasure and criticism coexist, and he even invokes Marx and Lenin, who were attentive to the problem of pleasure, he argues, if they had "historically . . . to

17. Ibid., p. 152.
18. Ibid., p. 211.
19. *Image-Music-Text*, p. 157 (emphasis in original).
20. "Theory of the Text," in Robert Young, ed., *Untying the Text: A Poststructuralist Reader* (London, 1981), p. 40.
21. Ibid., p. 38.

resolve problems of need."[22] For most of the world the problem of need has been in no way resolved, and Barthes has been often and justly criticized from this standpoint.

However, as Paul Smith writes in a discussion of the later Barthes, "What this trajectory constitutes is, I think, something profoundly uneasy to *judge*. That is, there is a certain impossibility in bringing to bear upon that work . . . all the doxical manners which the work has effectively denounced."[23] Indeed, we confront a figure who, on the prestigious occasion of his assuming the chair of semiology at the Collège de France, presents his work as "the comings and goings of a child playing beside his mother, leaving her, returning to bring her a pebble, a piece of string, and thereby tracing around a calm center a whole locus of play."[24] In Barthes's later works, to quote Smith, "the place of the mother has been espied as the very locus of resistance."[25] Here we might protest at the mother's silence, her stillness, her provision of a harmony, a distance without separation. But how and why object to this historic moment? The methods of the child, for whom "the pebble, the string come to matter less than the enthusiastic giving of them" are taken up by the mature intellectual as he commits himself to "loosening, baffling" the lockstep relations of discourse and power.[26] One of the philosopher-kings of the Western world has forsaken the fathers to join the women and children in the realm of the vulnerable. What the privileges of his class and gender seem to lead him to believe, however, is that life in that realm is an endless round of *plaisir et jouissance*.

"I love it"

"What is there to say about what one loves except: I love it, and to keep on saying it?"[27] If one wanted to conduct a musical analysis of Barthes's texts on music—that is, to treat those texts as music and to bring to bear upon them the methods of traditional music theory—then this declaration "I love it" would be enlisted to constitute the motif from which the opus generates, is generated. One would demonstrate its repetitions, transpositions, configurations . . . dissect the Barthesian/musical bodies . . . determine in stasis relations which technically do not exist in stasis . . . and present these abstractions (*abstrahere*: to drag away) with their armature of numbers: music theory.

22. *The Grain of the Voice*, pp. 162–63.
23. *Discerning the Subject* (Minneapolis, 1988), p. 113.
24. "Lecture," *October* 8 (Spring 1979): 15.
25. *Discerning the Subject*, p. 113.
26. "Lecture," p. 15.
27. "The Romantic Song," in his *The Responsibility of Forms: Critical Essays on Music, Art, and Representation*, trans. Richard Howard (New York, 1985), p. 286.

Again and again Barthes, who seemed to observe a sort of taboo on music in his early, semiological work, turns to it as the unrepresentable figure par excellence of the text: "By music we better understand the Text as signifying [*signifiance*]. . . . Listening potentially releases the metaphor best suited to the 'textual': orchestration, . . . counterpoint, stereophony."[28] He also begins to write about music itself, and seven of these essays are collected in *The Responsibility of Forms* under the heading "Music's Body." In none of them is Barthes concerned with what in music can be systematically analyzed, with what musicology has always taken as its object. "Let the first semiology manage, if it can, with the system of notes, scales, tones, chords, and rhythms; what we want to perceive and follow is the effervescence of the beats." This would comprise what he calls "a second semiology, that of the body in a state of music."[29]

Traditional musical analysis usually proceeds as if music were nonreferential. Implicitly (positivism's silent idealist partner), beyond itself, beyond its formal systems, music has been imagined to refer to something like the soul or the spirit, to the very essence of the divine or the human mind, so that, paradoxically, what matters most (valuable entities, these) literally "doesn't matter." Barthes outmaneuvers all of these debates with the simple insight that music's referent is the body. He writes that because music is "a field of *signifying* [*signifiance*] and not a system of signs, the referent . . . is the body. The body passes into music without any relay but the signifier."[30]

I want to pursue this question of music's referentiality by way of Barthes's final book, *Camera Lucida*. He described it as a modest meditation on the phenomenology of photography, but that is the pretext (albeit a commissioned one) for his real preoccupation, the recent death of his mother. He searches for her in photographs, for an image of (in his words) her essence, genius, truth. In a photograph of her as a child, a five-year-old he never knew, he writes, "I . . . at last rediscovered my mother."[31] Barthes acknowledges that he is susceptible to a psychoanalytic critique, but he refuses in this instance to accept the terms of an analysis in which the mother and the family are institutions. He writes: "Thus I could understand my generality; but having understood it, invincibly I escaped from it. In the Mother, there was a radiant, irreducible core: my mother."[32] To express the particularity of that truth he turns to the music of Schumann—to the first of the *Gesang der Frühe*—but

28. "Rasch," in his *The Responsibility of Forms*, p. 312; "The Third Meaning," in his *The Responsibility of Forms*, p. 42, footnote.

29. "Rasch," p. 312.

30. Ibid., p. 308.

31. *Camera Lucida: Reflections on Photography*, trans. Richard Howard (New York, 1981), p. 69.

32. Ibid., pp. 74–75.

he does not explain. Like the photograph of the five-year-old, this particular music presents him with something unanalyzable which might enter language only inadequately, through "an infinite series of adjectives." These artifacts provide the evidence "utopically, *for the impossible science of the unique being.*"[33]

It is in the quality of an image that expresses something that is in excess of any merely analogical likeness that Barthes locates "the essence of photography." Although the questions this essence prompts are the "romantic" ones, the "metaphysical" ones—questions of love, death, presence, being, time[34]—it is itself material, by virtue of a privileged relation to the referent, to which language in its fictionality has no immediate access:

> The photograph is literally an emanation of the referent. From a real body, which was there, proceed radiations which ultimately touch me, who am here. . . . A sort of umbilical cord links the body of the photographed thing to my gaze: light, though impalpable, is here a carnal medium, a skin I share with anyone who has been photographed.[35]

Likewise music is an emanation of the referent, a carnal medium, a shared skin. It is "radiant"—more like an image than a language. The essay "Rasch" is a rhapsody on the body in Schumann's *Kreisleriana*: "I hear what beats in the body, what beats the body, or better: I hear this body that beats."[36] In "Loving Schumann" he writes on music's "umbilical" relation: "This is a music at once dispersed and unary, continually taking refuge in the luminous shadow of the Mother (the lied, copious in Schumann's work, is, I believe, the expression of this maternal unity)."[37]

It is important to note that none of Barthes's essays concerns music in general. He explains:

> About music, no discourse can be sustained but that of difference—of evaluation. As soon as someone speaks about music—or a specific music—as a value *in itself*, or on the contrary—though this is the same thing—as a value *for everyone*—i.e., as soon as we are told we must love all music—we feel a kind of ideological cope falling over the most precious substance of evaluation, music: this is "commentary." Because commentary is unendurable, we see that music compels us to evaluation, imposes difference upon us.[38]

Music, he insists, derives from "a lover's discourse."[39]

33. Ibid., pp. 70–71 (emphasis in original).
34. Ibid., pp. 73, 85.
35. Ibid., pp. 80–81.
36. "Rasch," pp. 301–2, 299.
37. "Loving Schumann," in his *The Responsibility of Forms*, p. 298.
38. "Music, Voice, Language," in his *The Responsibility of Forms*, p. 279.
39. Ibid., p. 284.

Accordingly, the pieces on music each undertake "the impossible science of the unique being," a science, Barthes claims, which is "without method."[40] There *is* a methodology at work here, however, different from that systematic deployment of generalizations that is usually taken to constitute a "method" and the integrity of a science. This other method can be located in the attention to particularity, to specificity, to idiosyncrasy and detail. It might be called a maternal methodology or, in Barthes's term, a lover's discourse. It might also be a methodology that music can teach. In an aphorism titled "One must learn to love," Nietzsche begins:

> This is what happens to us in music: First one has to *learn to hear* a figure and melody at all, to detect and distinguish it, to isolate it and delimit it as a separate life. Then it requires some exertion and good will to *tolerate* it in spite of its strangeness, to be patient with its appearance and expression, and kindhearted about its oddity. Finally there comes a moment when we are *used* to it, when we wait for it, when we sense that we should miss it if it were missing . . .
> That is how we have *learned to love* all things that we now love.[41]

The figure of the amateur (from the Latin *amator* = lover) embodies this practice for Barthes. He was an amateur musician, and all of the musics in his writings were those he loved. Their particular qualities are maddeningly inaccessible to the interested reader (however educated in music), who cannot become a consumer of them, who is left to her own devices to experience the grain of the voice, or the body that beats. Of course, in pursuit of the grain we may purchase recordings of Fischer-Dieskau and Panzéra, the heuristic comparison of which allows Barthes to explore the *signifiance* Panzéra's song opens to his experience and to attempt "the impossible account of an individual thrill."[42] But the importance of the notion of amateurism (as of *signifiance*) is that it is an activity of production. At a theoretical level, Barthes says that a "completely de-alienated" society would be a society of amateurs:

> The great figure of a liberated civilization would be the amateur. . . . The amateur is not a consumer. Contact between the amateur's body and his art is very close, imbued with presence. . . . [But] we are a consumer society, and not at all a society of amateurs.[43]

40. *Camera Lucida*, pp. 71, 80.
41. Friedrich Nietzsche, *The Gay Science*, trans. Walter Kaufmann (New York, 1974), p. 262.
42. "The Grain of the Voice," in his *Image-Music-Text*, p. 181.
43. *The Grain of the Voice*, pp. 204, 217.

In "Musica Practica," Barthes considers the question of Beethoven, and of composition, in relation to that of amateurism. He argues that there is in Beethoven "the powerful germ of a disturbance in civilization," that Beethoven marks a historical moment in which music is being taken out of the hands of amateurs and placed in the hands of experts—a moment of transition from the "practical music" that is played to a music that is passively received, heard in the "soul" and not the body.[44] Because Beethoven occupies an undecidable moment in that transition, Barthes writes that there is something inaudible in Beethoven, and that what that inaudibility designates is a "tangible intelligibility"—that which cannot be apprehended through notions of the old aesthetics, through abstraction or interiority, but only through an activity of "reading." This reading "does not consist in receiving, in knowing, or in feeling this text, but in writing it anew." Barthes poses the following question: "What is the use of composing if it is to confine the product within the precinct of the concert or the solitude of listening to the radio? To compose, at least by propensity, is to *give to do*, not to give to hear but to give to write."[45]

a "devious dialectic"

In what was probably the last text he wrote, left unrevised and published as "One Always Fails in Speaking of What One Loves," Barthes seems to be moving toward a critique of the shared status of music, woman, and the foreign in his work, all of which seem to offer access to a domain in which one can be exempted from the "social military service" of meaning. The essay is about Stendhal, in love with Italy, but the disguise is thin. "I once knew someone who loved Japan [that] way," Barthes writes sympathetically, of himself.[46]

A decade earlier he had written a book "on" Japan, *Empire of Signs*. At a glance it appears to be a Japanese *Mythologies*—but Barthes's first move is to dispel this assumption: the importance of the other culture is not that it provides new and different reading material, "to be compared and contrasted historically, philosophically, culturally, politically." Rather, Japan presents Barthes with "the possibility of a difference," of the "unheard-of." The foreign allows the subject "to descend into the untranslatable, to experience its shock without ever muffling it, until everything Occidental in us totters and the rights of the 'father tongue' vacillate." Neither is one subject to the alienations of the mother tongue, to its marking of the differences within, of class, ethnicity, social position.

44. "Musica Practica," in his *Image-Music-Text*, p. 150.
45. Ibid., p. 153 (emphasis in original).
46. "One Always Fails in Speaking of What One Loves," in his *The Rustle of Language*, p. 297.

Freed of familial politics altogether, one is "without words," enveloped in a protective "auditory film" of *signifiance*, in a state of music.[47]

But in the essay on Stendhal Barthes has located a problem: "In the love of a foreign country there is a kind of reverse racism: one is delighted by difference, one is tired of the Same, one exalts the Other."[48] This racist love of a foreign country is linked in Stendhal to women and to music:

> In Stendhal's Italian system, Music has a privileged place because it can replace everything else: it is the degree zero of this system: according to the needs of enthusiasm, it replaces and signifies journeys, Women, the other arts, and in a general manner any sensation. Its signifying status, precious above all others, is to produce effects without our having to inquire as to their causes, since these causes are inaccessible. Music constitutes a kind of *primal state* of pleasure: it produces a pleasure one always tries to recapture but never to explain; hence, it is the site of a pure effect, . . . an effect severed from and somehow purified of any explicative reason, i.e., ultimately, of any *responsible* reason.[49]

Barthes says that in Italy, as neither a tourist nor a native, Stendhal was "voluptuously delivered from the responsibility of the *citizen*; . . . he need merely harvest the brilliant effects of a civilization for which he is not responsible." Barthes adds, "I have been able to experience the convenience of this devious dialectic myself." The state of irresponsibility and the "dialectic of extreme love and difficult expression resembles what the very young child experiences—still *infans*, deprived of adult speech." Indeed, Stendhal's travel journals are a "fiasco of style": repetitious platitudes, inadequate adjectives. "One always fails in speaking of what one loves." But in *writing*, twenty years after the journals, Stendhal achieves a developmental triumph, "a kind of miraculous harmony . . . the effect described finally coincides with the effect produced." How? "Stendhal . . . has abandoned sensation, a vivid but inconstruable fragment, to undertake that great mediating form which is Narrative, or better still Myth."[50]

Immanent, at least, in this last work are the elements of a critique: the dawning recognition of a certain privileged irresponsibility enjoyed in the realm of the Other, and of the zero-degree status of music when it goes uninterrogated by ideology critique, by that "first semiology" which Barthes had earlier dismissed. These final words in his opus implicitly return us to the early writings. Without dismissing or renouncing the insights and critical lessons of the second semiology, the necessity of the first

47. *Empire of Signs*, trans. Richard Howard (New York, 1982), pp. 3, 6, 9.
48. "One Always Fails in Speaking of What One Loves," p. 297.
49. Ibid., p. 299.
50. Ibid., pp. 303, 304.

semiology is invoked. Musicology is only beginning to elaborate that first semiology, to understand the ways that music's systems operate in relation to power and the social, and to analyze musics in their specific historical and discursive conditions. Neither will these analyses suffice without the second semiology, which understands, in a way that the generalizing discourses of ideology and history cannot, what is at the heart of the matter when we repeat "I love it."

We have seen how the musical object itself is transformed by the terms of Barthes's critique. But what might it mean to meet his second demand: that we not only change the object itself but also make critical practice homogeneous to the object? What would it mean to understand music not as the *object* of critique, but as its very practice?

In the essay "Brecht and Discourse: A Contribution to the Study of Discursivity," Barthes shows how the amateur's practice of music-making can be deployed destructively, how the methods of the lover approach ideology critique. "All that we read and hear," he writes, "covers us like a layer, surrounds and envelops us like a medium: the logosphere." Recall the musical "auditory film" which had provided the foreigner such pleasure. No longer without words but with them, Barthes becomes the responsible citizen. He writes of Brecht: "His critical art is one which opens a crisis: which lacerates, which crackles the smooth surface, . . . one which discontinues the textures of words, distances representation without annulling it." This distancing, he explains, "is merely a reading which detaches the sign from its effect." Recall the discussion of music in the Stendhal essay: "Its signifying status, precious above all others, is to produce effects without our having to inquire as to their causes." Now we are being given a demonstration on how to produce these severed effects. Barthes likens Brecht's art to the practice of Japanese dressmakers, who use pins that have tiny bells; when the garment is finished the pins cannot be forgotten, because they make noise, little shocks. Brecht uses these pins and leaves them in: "Thus, when we hear a certain language, we never forget where it comes from, how it was made."[51]

> Brecht gives us a reading exercise. . . . What is astonishing, at the endurable limit of the paradox, is that this refined practice is applied by Brecht to the reading of a hateful text. The destruction of monstrous discourse is here conducted according to an erotic technique; it mobilizes not the reductive weapons of demystification but rather the caresses, the amplifications, the ancestral subtleties of a literary mandarinate . . . as if it were natural to take pleasure in the truth.[52]

51. "Brecht and Discourse: A Contribution to the Study of Discursivity," in his *The Rustle of Language*, pp. 213–14.
52. Ibid., pp. 215–16.

The reader is to read the text of a Nazi speech softly aloud, rehearsing and repeating the text like the amateur playing music alone. "Because they are concatenated, Brecht says, errors produce an illusion of truth. . . . The first attack is therefore to make it discontinuous—to discontinue it: literally to dismember the erroneous text is a polemical act." In the spaces produced the reader adds to the text "by intercalating between its sentences the critical complement which demystifies each one of them. . . . The critique does not diminish, does not suppress, it adds."[53] The text is thereby

> deprived of what in music is called the Zeigarnik effect (when the final resolution of a musical sequence retroactively gives it its meaning). Discontinuity of discourse keeps the final meaning from "taking": critical production does not wait, it is instantaneous and repeated.[54]

If music, like the foreign, provides one with "a descent into untranslatability," producing effects that are singular, inexpressible, then here the very qualities that make music so very resistant to critique are being deployed as critique, aimed at rendering its object untranslatable, unable to reproduce its effects. And if we think about the qualities of this critical practice—repetitive, persistent, patient, attentive—and remember the mother at the "calm center" of Barthes's critical practice . . . we find her disturbed, displaced, noisy, activated, put into discourse, critical.

53. Ibid., pp. 216, 215.
54. Ibid., p. 217.

Cultural Contexts of Difference

Charles Ives and Gender Ideology

Judith Tick

A leopard went around his cage from one side back to the other side; he stopped only when the keeper came around with meat; A boy who had been there three hours began to wonder, "Is life anything like that?"
Charles Ives, "The Cage"

Among twentieth-century American male composers, Charles Ives stands out as the prime example of an artist who ascribed a masculine ideal to music. His famous description of the birth of music—how "it's going to be a boy—some time!"[1] typifies the emotional investment he had in that ideal. Many people who knew Ives remembered his destructive bursts of anger, his redundant harangues on a few themes; many of us who read the *Memos* feel under the volcano.[2] Ives's various writings about music present the most extraordinary use of gendered aesthetics in the public testimony of an American composer.

How are we to understand Ives's language of prejudice? What is its function and meaning in his musical thought? In the last fifteen years, some answers have been suggested by biographers and psychoanalytically oriented historians and critics; those interpretations will be briefly surveyed here. My own goal, however, is to try to understand Ives by exploring the context of his language within the framework of gender scholarship: historically, by discussing the literature on American women and music from the period, and theoretically, by using gender as an analytic prism through which other ideas and values are refracted.[3] Like

I wish to thank a number of people who read earlier versions of this essay: Stuart Feder, H. Wiley Hitchcock, Ellen Koskoff, Lawrence Kramer, Maynard Solomon, and Catherine Smith. I am especially grateful for the advice and criticism offered by Adrienne Fried Block, Carol J. Oja, Wayne Shirley, Mark Tucker, and Elizabeth Wood.

1. Charles E. Ives, *Memos*, ed. John Kirkpatrick (New York, 1972), p. 30.

2. This phrase borrows the title of a novel by Malcolm Lowry. For one such harangue from Ives, see the Lehman Engel interview in Vivian Perlis, *Charles Ives Remembered* (New York, 1967), p. 195; for another, see John Kirkpatrick's comments in Ives, *Memos*, p. 280.

3. An excellent overview of the current theoretical literature on music and gender is Ellen Koskoff, "An Introduction to Women, Music, and Culture," in Ellen Koskoff, ed.,

the concepts of race and class, that of gender can encompass multiple meanings, not only "the social relationships based on perceived differences between the sexes" but also a "primary way of signifying relationships of power."[4] I hope to show, first, that Ives inherited both a social grammar of prejudice and an ideology of gender differences in art;[5] and, second, that through these Ives expressed other kinds of meanings and values.

The earliest and perhaps still the most influential interpretation is that offered by Frank Rossiter, Ives's third biographer.[6] Rossiter argues that "the connotation of effeminacy that art music had for Americans in the nineteenth century . . . is a crucially important means of approaching Charles Ives as a composer."[7] At the time (the mid 1970s) this analysis was not only provocative but brave. For one thing, with women's studies still in the early stages of development, few academics acknowledged gender as a viable historical variable, whereas Rossiter structured the argument of his book around it.[8] For another, Rossiter was exploring a darker side

---

Women and Music in Cross-Cultural Perspective (Westport, Conn., 1987), pp. 1–24. See also Susan McClary, *Feminine Endings: Music, Gender, and Sexuality* (Minneapolis, 1991).

4. Joan W. Scott, "Gender: A Useful Category of Historical Analysis," *American Historical Review* 91 (1986): 1067.

5. The concept of a "social grammar of prejudice," to be distinguished from ideology as a belief system, is developed by sociologists Gertrude J. Selznick and Stephen Steinberg: "As has been frequently remarked, people become prejudiced not by becoming acquainted with Jews, but by becoming acquainted with the prejudiced beliefs current in their environment. From the perspective of linguistics, prejudice is a social grammar. Every language has rules, most of them implicit, for the use of adjectives. A man is handsome, a woman beautiful; rooms are long and narrow, people tall and thin. Any prejudice, including anti-Semitism, can similarly be viewed as a set of implicit rules specifying which adjectives are relevant or appropriately applied to which groups: Negroes are lazy, Irish are drunkards, Scots are stingy. . . . It would be a mistaken view of prejudice, and its viability, to define only a false ascription as prejudice. Above all else, a prejudiced ascription is a differential ascription: the same trait may be as applicable to one group as to another, yet it is applied only to one." (*The Tenacity of Prejudice: Anti-Semitism in Contemporary America* [New York 1969], p. 20.) The notion of "gender ideology" is defined in Koskoff, "An Introduction," p. 5.

6. Frank R. Rossiter, *Charles Ives and His America* (New York, 1975); this book was based on Rossiter's dissertation, "Charles Ives and American Culture: The Process of Development, 1874–1921," Princeton University, 1970. The first biography was Henry Cowell and Sidney Cowell, *Charles Ives and His Music* (New York, 1955), and the second David Wooldridge, *From the Steeples and Mountains: A Study of Charles Ives* (New York, 1974).

7. Rossiter, *Charles Ives and His America*, p. 24.

8. This point about the structure of Rossiter's argument is made by Betty E. M. Chmaj in "'Reality Is on Our Side': Research on Gender in American Music," *Sonneck Society Bulletin* 16 (1990): 53–58. See also her observation about the "lack of recognition . . . of the role of [Ives's] wife" in Rossiter's biography ("Sonata for American Studies: Perspectives on Charles Ives," in Jack Salzman, ed., *Prospects: An Annual of American Cultural Studies* 4 [1979], p. 52 n. 7).

of this composer who was celebrated—perhaps even glorified—for his Emersonian transcendentalism.

Some of Rossiter's evidence comes from *Essays Before a Sonata* and the "Postscript to the 114 Songs," both published in 1921. For example, in the *Essays* the connection between Substance as masculine and Manner as effeminate is made explicit in an attack on the Liberace-like deportment of virtuoso pianists, with "their cissy-like postures over the piano keys."[9] Other citations in the dissertation draw, from the then-unpublished *Memos*, a set of caricatures of classical-music critics, such as "Rollo" and "Aunty," and a shocking level of invective based on sexual stereotypes:

> Rollos—resting all their nice lives on, and now hiding behind, their silk skirts—too soft-eared and [-]minded to find anything out for themselves. Their old aunt (for her old aunt had told her) told Nattie when he was youthful: "This is a masterpiece—this is a great artist"—it has the same effect on their heads that customs stamps have on their trunks. Every thing *that* man did is "great" because they were *told* so when young and grew up with it hanging around their nice necks, and every thing *this* man did is "no good"—whether or not they have ever seen any of his pictures has nothing to do with it—Aunt put the bangle on his vest and it sticks there as a cobweb sticks to the pigsty window.
>
> It has never entered their pretty heads—or even to sit down near the bangle for twenty, thirty, or fifty years or so, and hear anything out themselves, or think anything hard and long—it has never occurred to them—and how cross they would get, and scold and caper around peevish-like in their columns, if anyone should happen to say that music has always been an emasculated art—at least too much—say 88⅔%.
>
> Even those considered the greatest (Bach, Beethoven, Brahms, etc.) have too much of it, though less [than] the other rubber-stamp great men. They couldn't exactly help it—life with them was such that they had to live at least part of the time by the ladies' smiles—they had to please the ladies or die. And that is the reason—through their influence—that no one can prove (not even the ladies) that there has been [any] great music ever composed—that is, in this world. And this is not [so much] criticising or running down or under-appreciating Beethoven, Bach, et al, as it [is] a respect and wonder that they didn't do worse under the circumstances.[10]

9. "The pose of self-absorption which some men in the advertising business (and incidentally in the recital and composing business) put into their photographs or the portraits of themselves, while all dolled up in their purple-dressing-gowns, in their twofold wealth of golden hair, in their cissy-like postures over the piano keys—this pose of 'manner' sometimes sounds out so loud that the more their music is played, the less it is heard." (Charles Ives, *Essays Before a Sonata and Other Writings*, ed. Howard Boatwright [New York, 1970], p. 78.)

10. This excerpt appears in Rossiter's dissertation, "Charles Ives and American Culture," pp. 59–60; it is taken from the *Memos*, p. 30. However, Rossiter's biography does

The emotional affect of Ives's prose was so intense, and the metaphors so sexual, that if Ives had been female Rossiter might have diagnosed him as hysterical. Perhaps Ives's "mercurial excitability," as John Kirkpatrick has called it,[11] impelled Rossiter to the second, more speculative, stage of his argument. According to Rossiter, Ives divided music into two great opposing camps. One, the cultivated tradition, was "effeminate, aristocratic, pretentious, easy on the ears, commercial and lacking in ideals in spite of its pretensions, only rarely breaking its bondage to women"; the other, the vernacular tradition, Ives saw as "masculine, democratic, down to earth, fervent, speaking to men of the substance of their daily lives." In Ives's writings Rossiter hears "the outcries of wounded manhood against an effeminate musical culture in which he feared he had become entangled."[12]

After citing various historians on the important role of women in American musical life, and the implications of effeminacy attached to the arts, Rossiter moves from "effeminacy" to "emasculation," as if these were synonyms. To take but two examples, he declares that Charles's father, George Ives, was "emasculated" in front of his son by two music teachers in Danbury who neglected to give George credit for helping them arrange a concert for the YMCA; and that Charles "had his own emasculation to worry about as well . . . when he was compelled . . . to venture into a field dominated by women." For instance, "when he was twelve, he appeared in a recital, [performing] a tarantella by Heller on a program that also included Lange's 'Chirping Crickets' and Behr's 'Fire-Balls' Mazurka."[13]

Building on such extravagant interpretations, Rossiter proposes a theory of emotive displacement as the first cause of Ives's modernism:

> Instead of his having first rejected cultivated-tradition music on aesthetic and moral grounds . . . and then having attached connotations of effeminacy to what he had already rejected, it appears that the actual process was just the reverse: he first rejected such music for its sociosexual implications of effeminacy, and only then did he develop an aesthetic and moral rationale for that rejection. Only in this way can the underlying paranoia about masculinity and femininity in his writings about music be adequately explained.[14]

---

not quote the source in full, probably because the *Memos* had by then become available. Rossiter's dissertation is more extreme in its use of what might be called the "feminization theory" than his book, which I take to represent his more considered views.

11. *Memos*, Appendix 19, p. 280.
12. Rossiter, *Charles Ives and His America*, pp. 42, 162.
13. Ibid., pp. 28, 29.
14. Ibid., pp. 36–37.

In Rossiter's view, Ives's rejection of "cultivated music" was validated by his youthful experiences with female musicians, who symbolized the larger fact of musical feminization. In effect, he accepts Ives's philosophical dualism as social reality. Who "wounded" our first modernist musical frontiersman, forcing him into the double existence of artist and businessman that Rossiter deplores? The Victorian lady musician.

Stuart Feder's work, which has recently culminated in a powerful and distinguished biography of Ives, uses psychoanalysis to analyze Ives's creative dynamic through his relationship to his father.[15] As in his previous work, Feder postulates a central fantasy of the rich affective life of men living and working together (as for instance in the march) and their creative life.[16] Absent from this fantasy are women, for, according to Feder, Ives defined the processes of creation as the province of men, a definition that flowed out of Ives's idealization of his father. Feder does mention Ives's conflicts regarding sexual identity and the threat of homosexuality, but these are not the focus of his study, "except insofar as they participate in characterological uniqueness, innovation, and creativity. For pathology is never the whole story." Although Feder criticizes the reductionist simplicity of Rossiter's assertion that music represents effeminacy and that other activities, say sports and business, represent the masculine, he accepts Rossiter's characterization of nineteenth-century American musical life as feminized, that is to say, as dominated by women.[17]

If Rossiter's emphasis on the role of women in the genteel tradition exaggerates their cultural power, the primacy of Feder's interest in the father-son relationship leaves virtually no place for them. In a sense, a recent interpretation by Maynard Solomon mediates between these two positions. In his controversial article about Ives's "veracity" as documenter of his own life and work, Solomon points out that the main objects of Ives's attacks were "effeminate" men. Solomon links Ives's compensatory "heroic pose of strength and masculinity" to the fact that his

> extreme prudery, his fear of intimacy, his morbid aversion to the nude female body . . . connects to his preoccupation with emasculation, his incessant ranting against "effeminacy" in music, and his quite pathological

15. Stuart Feder, *Charles Ives: "My Father's Song"—a Psychoanalytic Biography* (New Haven, 1992).

16. Stuart Feder, "Charles and George Ives: The Veneration of Boyhood," in Stuart Feder, M.D., Richard L. Karmel, Ph.D., and George H. Pollock, M.D., Ph.D., eds., *Psychoanalytic Explorations in Music* (Madison, Conn., 1990), esp. pp. 152–54; cf. Feder's "Decoration Day: A Boyhood Memory of Charles Ives," *Musical Quarterly* 65 (1980): 234–61.

17. Feder, "Charles and George Ives," p. 125. See also Feder, *Charles Ives: "My Father's Song,"* p. 95.

aversion to homosexuals, whom he variously derogated as "pansys," "lily-pads," "old ladies," and "pussy-boys."[18]

Solomon catalogues Ives's opinions of many great masters:

> He thought Ravel and Stravinsky "morbid and monotonous." . . . Debussy's music was permeated by a "sensual sensuousness." . . . He praised Franck, d'Indy, Elgar for their "wholesomeness, manliness . . . and deep spiritual . . . feeling"; but he frankly condemned as "emasculated" works by Mozart, Mendelssohn, early Beethoven, Haydn, Massenet, Tchaikovsky, Gounod, Wagner, and Chopin. . . . Elsewhere he writes approvingly of the three B's—though, in an afterthought, he strikes Brahms's name altogether and finds none of them "as strong and great as Carl Ruggles . . . because [they] have too much of the sugar-plum for the soft-ears."[19]

Solomon concludes that Ives "wants to reject the sensuous in music, in sound, in life, to regard himself as a 'thinker,' a 'philosopher,' a 'rational' maker of music."[20] Yet this summary judgment does not really allow room for Ives's admiration for Scriabin, whose spiritual ambitions were not incompatible with a sensuous surface in his music, and whose resemblance to Chopin caused the Russian composer Cui to describe his style as "bits filched from the trousseau of Chopin," the sexual innuendoes simultaneously hitting both Chopin and Scriabin.[21]

Pushing the debate beyond Ives's psychology, Solomon widens the context for Ives's attitudes by pointing out affinities between Ives's war against "the indecent," the "decadent," and the "degenerate" and that being waged by some of the most anti-modernist critics of the period, such as Irving Babbitt and Daniel Gregory Mason. Thus Ives's gender discourse is both seen as the working out of psychosexual problems (a "pathological aversion to homosexuals") and ascribed to his intellectual reactionary tendencies. (How ironic that Mason—who wrote an essay on "Dissonance and Evil," who disparaged American music from 1914 to

18. Maynard Solomon, "Charles Ives: Some Questions of Veracity," *Journal of the American Musicological Society* 40 (1987): 466.

19. Ibid., pp. 451–53.

20. Ibid., p. 467.

21. Rossiter says that "Ives did become a patron of Miss Heyman's Scriabin activities" (*Charles Ives and His America*, p. 205). Katherine Heyman was a pianist and head of the Scriabin Society in New York. On 9 September 1927 Ives wrote to Heyman when she was in Europe giving concerts of Scriabin's piano music: "We wish you success in your 'Adventure,' not the success you deserve but that Scriabin does. You can't object to this." (Correspondence located in the Ives Collection, Beinecke Library, Yale University, and cited here with permission.) The comment from Cui is cited in an essay by Paul Rosenfeld, "Scriabin Again," in *Discoveries of a Music Critic* (New York, 1936), p. 160.

1928 as the "Music of Indigestion," and whom Henry Cowell, Ives's great champion, called "the enemy"—is shown to be Ives's comrade-in-arms.)[22]

Solomon's conclusion is a variation on Rossiter's theme that Ives was ashamed of all art music. Ives has "the misfortune to believe that music and its composers are often—even usually—embodiments" of this decadence and degeneracy. By bringing Ives's attitudes toward homosexuality into the foreground, both Feder and Solomon have made explicit issues that Rossiter left latent.[23] Neither, however, concerned himself much with women's history or gender scholarship.

Yet concepts of gender roles—whether of masculinity, femininity, heterosexuality, or homosexuality—are interrelated through their historical constructions.[24] To take but one example, one of the critics cited by Solomon as a warrior against "decadence and degeneracy" also wrote that the "predominance of the feminine over the masculine virtues . . . has been the main cause of the corruption of literature and the arts during the past century."[25] With respect to Feder, his biography enriches and deepens our understanding of Ives. Nevertheless, a psychoanalytic perspective masks the power of society to transmit gendered views of culture, rife with prejudice and viable precisely because issues other than sexuality are engaged through tropes of masculinity and femininity.[26] "In the absence of countervailing forces, prejudice is as

22. MacDonald Smith Moore discusses Mason's essay on dissonance in *Yankee Blues: Musical Culture and American Identity* (Bloomington, 1985), pp. 53–55. Moore sees many parallels between Mason and Ives as Yankee composers. For the indigestibility of American music, see Daniel Gregory Mason, *The Dilemma of American Music and Other Essays* (New York, 1928), p. 12. Cowell's comment is in a letter to Charles Ives, 16 May 1933, cited in Rita Mead, *Henry Cowell's New Music 1925–1936: The Society, the Music Editions, and the Recordings* (Ann Arbor, 1981), p. 241.

23. Solomon, "Charles Ives," p. 469. The history of the link between "effeminacy" and music in American thought remains to be documented. In a recent paper Philip Brett has referred to Ives's "homophobic panic" in the context of new approaches to the issue of "essentialism" in music ("Musicality: Innate Gift or Social Contract?" paper read at the national meeting of the American Musicological Society, Oakland, 1990). One starting point for American historians that seems potentially relevant to Ives is Philip Greven, *The Protestant Temperament: Patterns of Child-Rearing, Religious Experience, and the Self in Early America* (New York, 1977), particularly the section entitled "'The Choice of Hercules': Manliness or Effeminacy?" (pp. 243–50). I wish to thank Adrienne Fried Block for this reference.

24. This point is astutely discussed by Linda K. Kerber in "Separate Spheres, Female Worlds, Woman's Place: The Rhetoric of Women's History," *Journal of American History* 75 (1988): 9–39. The present essay is indebted to many of Kerber's observations about the distinctions between ideology and society, and the intellectual consequences of accepting the dualism implied by the trope of "separate spheres."

25. Irving Babbitt, *Representative Writings*, ed. George A. Panichas (Lincoln, Neb., 1981), p. 86.

26. Barbara Melosh discusses how "image makers used images of manhood and womanhood as tropes in a political rhetoric directed to issues other than gender," in her

easily acquired as language itself."[27] In my view, Ives used aspects of the gender ideology of music to discuss not just sexuality but power and entitlement. He held and used misogynist and homophobic beliefs partly because he had learned them (that is to say, they had a cognitive component) and partly because he needed them (that is to say, they had an emotive component.)[28] Obvious though it may seem, it is worth pointing out that how well we can distinguish between what he learned and what he needed—that is, between the social context of his prejudice and the functions that it served—depends partly on how well we understand the cultural sources of his beliefs with respect to women.[29]

Between 1890 and 1930 the American literature discussing gender and music reflects the extraordinary changes of that period in both American musical life and the socioeconomic status of American women. The growth in institutions of classical music (such as orchestras and conservatories), combined with the movement of women out of the home and into the work force, challenged the old ideologies defining music as a feminine "accomplishment" confined to the parlor. This is not the place to review that history in great detail. It will suffice merely to remind the reader of fairly recent documentation of the high proportion of female students in American conservatories; the entrance of women into the occupation of "music and music teaching," as the U.S. census called it; their "emergence as the chief promoters of culture"; and the appearance of the first generation of female composers of American classical music.[30]

Engendering Culture: Manhood and Womanhood in New Deal Public Art and Theater (Washington, D.C., 1991), p. 4.

27. Selznick and Steinberg, *The Tenacity of Prejudice*, p. 20.

28. Selznick and Steinberg distinguish between the emotive and the cognitive components of prejudice. (*The Tenacity of Prejudice*, pp. 135–37.)

29. This essay is primarily concerned with women's history, and that limitation is duly noted. It does not discuss effeminacy as a concept or the implications of Ives's language with respect to homosexuality. That work remains to be done.

30. A selective list of titles includes: Judith Tick, "Women as Professional Musicians in the United States, 1870–1910," *Yearbook of Inter-American Research* (1973), revised as "Passed Away Is the Piano Girl: Changes in American Musical Life, 1870–1910," in Jane Bowers and Judith Tick, eds., *Women Making Music: The Western Art Tradition, 1150–1950* (Urbana, 1986); Adrienne Fried Block and Carol Neuls-Bates, eds., *Women in American Music: A Bibliography of Music and Literature* (Westport, Conn.,1979); Christine Ammer, *Unsung: A History of Women in American Music* (Westport, Conn., 1980); Block, "Why Amy Beach Succeeded as a Composer: The Early Years," *Current Musicology* 36 (1983): 41–60, and "Arthur P. Schmidt, Music Publisher and Champion of American Women Composers," in Judith Lang Zaimont, ed., *The Musical Woman: An International Perspective*, vol. 2, 1984–85 (Westport, Conn., 1987): 145–76; Laurine Elkins-Marlow, "Music at Every Meeting: The Role of Music in the General Federation of Women's Clubs and the National League of

Such changes help explain the sheer quantity of literature discussing gender and music, as well as its wide range of themes and its controversial nature. Writ large over this diverse literature are tensions and disputes generated by shifts in power and gender roles.[31] Further muddying its waters is the debate over biological determinism. Themes and values in the literature include identity and commitment (the process of becoming a composer), professionalization (the socioeconomic choice of occupation), and aesthetics (the relationship between gender and musical content—touching on styles, genres and composers, and performance).

Ives's musical environment was far more complex and the gender ideology that supported it far more diffuse and contradictory than past interpretations of the "feminization" of American musical life have implied. Without doubt, "music," at its most general level of meaning, was regarded in the nineteenth century as a female accomplishment.[32] But it therefore occupied domestic space, in the parlor. And even then, the function of such "accomplishment" was to encourage music-making by women, not to prohibit men from taking it up. Public music-making by professionals was never sex-typed as female, a distinction reflected in the 1910 census, which divides the occupation into the two categories of "musician" and "music teacher." As Henry J. Harris stated in his pioneering sociological study published in 1915, "The great majority of musicians are men while the great majority of the teachers of music are women."[33] In 1910 it was also the case that a slightly larger number of native-born than of foreign-born men were musicians.

During the period in which Ives came of age as a composer (ca. 1890–1910), the assertion was widely made that women were innately incapable of composing in the "higher forms," that is, symphonic music

---

American Pen Women," paper delivered at the Sonneck Society annual meeting, April 1990. The phrase in quotation is from Linda Whitesitt, "The Role of Women Impresarios in American Concert Life, 1871–1933," *American Music* 7 (1989): 159.

31. Catherine Parsons Smith discusses this literature in "On Feminism and American Music," paper delivered at the national meeting of the American Musicological Society, Austin, 1989. It will appear as "On Feminism and American Art Music" in Susan Cook and Judith Tsou, eds., *Cecilia: Feminist Perspectives on Women and Music* (University of Illinois Press, forthcoming). Linda Kerber notes that "the ideology of separate spheres—like all ideology—is not frozen in time but is in a constant state of refinement until it fits reality so badly that a paradigm shift in conceptualization is unavoidable." ("Separate Spheres," p. 27.)

32. "Accomplishment" was a nineteenth-century term that included amateur musical education. Its use in the literature on gender and music, and the kinds of education in female academies and seminaries of the period that were associated with it, are discussed at length in Tick, *American Women Composers Before 1870* (Ann Arbor, 1983).

33. Henry J. Harris, "The Occupation of Musician in the United States," *Musical Quarterly* 1 (1915): 303. The figures are given in Table II (p. 302): 39,163 of 54,848 musicians are men; 68,783 of 84,452 teachers of music are women.

and opera. Although women were encouraged to study and perform music, the language of creative musical achievement was patriarchal.[34] In the extensive debate that surrounded the first generation of American women composers, who emerged at the turn of the century—should or could they compose?—Rupert Hughes typifies a general position: perhaps "art knows no sex," but women writing in what he called "mantone"—symphonic or operatic genres—were "seeking after virility."[35] A contemporary of Ives, the composer Mary Carr Moore (1873–1957), expressed the central problem of her generation:

> But of all the difficulties I encountered, perhaps the greatest has been in the fact that I am an American and a woman. That combination, I assure you, has been the most discouraging obstacle of all! So long as a woman contents herself with writing graceful little songs about springtime and the birdies, no one resents it or thinks her presumptuous; but woe be unto her if she dares attempt the larger forms! The prejudice may die eventually, but it will be a hard and slow death.[36]

By 1910 we find in place assertions of male creative superiority on many levels. The psychologist Havelock Ellis analyzed biologically determined limits to the creative potential of women.[37] Critics and journalists such as George Upton and Lawrence Gilman drew on nineteenth-century aesthetics of music to perpetuate the masculine/feminine dichotomy through "das ewig-weibliche" or the "eternal feminine" in music.[38] Other late nineteenth- and early twentieth-century writers tracked

34. See, for example, Edith Brower, "Is the Musical Idea Masculine?" *Atlantic Monthly* (March 1894): 332–39.

35. Rupert Hughes, *Contemporary American Composers* (Boston, 1900), pp. 425, 438. The Boston composer Mabel Daniels grew up with this ideology and retained its core throughout her life. She "[did] not believe women are able to compose a long list of symphonies, operas, string quartets and all kinds of concerted music, for the sole reason that they do not have the physical stamina of a man." ("Music After College—as a Profession," *Radcliffe Quarterly* [May 1957]: 11. I am indebted to Sara Jobin for this source.)

36. Quoted in Catherine Parsons Smith and Cynthia S. Richardson, *Mary Carr Moore, American Composer* (Ann Arbor, 1987), p. 173.

37. Cited by Huntington Cairns in "The Woman of Genius," in Samuel D. Schmalhausen and V. F. Calverton, eds., *Woman's Coming of Age* (New York, 1931), p. 391.

38. George P. Upton, *Woman in Music* (Chicago, 1880), pp. 23 ff.; Lawrence Gilman, "Women and Modern Music," in his *Phases of Modern Music* (New York 1904): 93–101. See also T. L. Krebs, who writes about vocal music as the essence of "das ewig-weibliche" because it appeals more directly to the heart ("Women as Musicians," *Sewanee Review* 2 [1893]: 77), and Fanny Bloomfield-Zeisler, who insists that she is not an apostle of "Woman's Emancipation" and claims that there are "many fields of intellectual activity upon which women never do or can trespass without sacrificing their more delicate and sensitive nature, the 'ewig weibliche.'" Rather, "what we need now is not to imitate man and try to become great in a field in which he has achieved success, but to develop those qualities which specifically belong to woman," that is, beautiful melodies ("Woman in Music," *American Art Journal* 58

composers by style, for example, labeling Chopin and Mendelssohn as feminine, Beethoven and Wagner as masculine.[39] Basically, this ideology reflects what historian Rosalind Rosenberg has described as "the Victorian faith in sexual polarity—from the doctrine that women are by nature emotional and passive, to the dogma that men are by nature rational and assertive."[40]

In many respects Ives's attitudes reflect that Victorian perspective. Yet it would be a mistake to think that gender ideology in music disappeared during his later years and that his *Memos* mirror only a distant past. American society had changed dramatically in his lifetime, but the literature on gender and music changed far less. The feminization of music remained a viable tenet of gender ideology throughout the 1920s. It found itself, however, increasingly mired in contradictions, for after 1910 significant shifts took place in the labor force that constituted "music and music teaching" in the United States. For the first time since 1870, in the 1920s the gender proportions of the profession reversed: census data for 1930 showed that men outnumbered women in the field.[41] In an article entitled "The Feminization of Music," a faculty member from the Peabody Conservatory catalogued every associated ill, from the lack of men in the conservatories to the sentimentalization of style: "Is it not that the women have required it of us that we have come to gush and sentimentalize to the extent we do now?" he asked the 1922 convention of the Music Teachers National Association. He continued: "I believe the male has naturally a finer sense of rhythm and proportion than his mate. . . . The man's composers are Bach, Beethoven, and Brahms, with ninety per cent of [women] preferring Chopin."[42] In his article for Harold Stearns's *Civilization in the United States*, Deems Taylor claimed that "women constitute ninety per cent of those who support music in this country. . . . This well-nigh feminization of music is bad for it. . . . Their predominance in our musical life aggravates our already exaggerated tendency to demand that art be edifying. . . . The feminine influence

[17 October 1891]: 1, 3). For a recent critical study of this concept and its relationship to nineteenth-century music, see Lawrence Kramer, "Liszt, Goethe, and the Discourse of Gender," in his *Music as Cultural Practice, 1800–1900* (Berkeley, 1990), pp. 102–34.

39. James Huneker claimed that women could never play Beethoven as well as men. ("The Eternal Feminine," in *Overtones: A Book of Temperaments* [New York, 1904], pp. 277–306.)

40. Rosalind Rosenberg, *Beyond Separate Spheres: Intellectual Roots of Modern Feminism* (New Haven, 1982), p. xiv.

41. Sophonisba P. Breckinridge cites the figures of 85,517 men and 79,611 women in the occupations of music and music teaching as indicating a "real decline" for women. (*Women in the Twentieth Century: A Study of Their Political, Social, and Economic Activities* [New York, 1933], pp. 188, 202.)

42. Harold Randolph, "The Feminization of Music," *Papers and Proceedings of the Music Teachers National Association, 1922* (Hartford, 1923), p. 198.

helps to increase the insularity of our musicians."[43] Mary Herron DuPree claims that "direct reference to America's 'manliness complex'" was "rather rare" in the 1920s, suggesting that perhaps the perception of music as "women's work" was abating; she cites an interview with Russian pianist Mischa Levitzki, who claimed it was a widespread problem, but an editorial rebuttal appeared soon after.[44]

The literature on women and music rode the tide of interest in the "new woman" of the 1920s. One article queried, "Now that women vote like men, why shouldn't they play the piano like men?"[45] A young composer, who had been hailed as a "flapper genius," voiced her resentment about the condescension that greeted her work, "either in a too facile praise . . . or in a wholesale condemnation."[46] This small sampling of the literature proves her point: "Women are naturally mechanical, therefore no woman is really musical."[47] The "emotional life of Woman" is "antagonistic to the creative process in music." "Today there are many feminine composers to constitute a rebuttal to the statement that women are incapable of composing great music." "To me there is a certain queerness in the interpretation of a man's work by a woman." A survey asks, "Are Men Better Musicians Than Women?"[48]

43. Deems Taylor, "Music," in Harold E. Stearns, ed., *Civilization in the United States: An Inquiry by Thirty Americans* (New York, 1922), p. 205. This anthology is a blistering attack on American culture edited by a "lost generation" writer who in his introduction deplores the feminization of American culture as a whole. For the cultural placement of this book, see Richard H. Pells, *Radical Visions and American Dreams: Culture and Social Thought in the Depression Years* (Middletown, Conn., 1973), p. 23.

44. DuPree discusses the issue of women and music and the "manliness complex" in "The Failure of American Music: The Critical View from the 1920s," *Journal of Musicology* 2 (1983): 311–12. The interview is Henrietta Malkiel, "Levitzki Holds the Musical Mirror Up to America," *Musical America* (26 January 1924): 5; the rebuttal, Editorial, "Music and Manliness," *Musical America* (2 February 1924): 20.

45. "Here and There," *Musical Leader* (29 September 1921): 301.

46. Margaret Starr McLain, "Women as Composers," *Musical Leader* (5 November 1931): 7.

47. "Lecturer Declares Women Not Really Musical," *Musical Leader* (28 July 1921): 100, reporting on a talk by J. Swinburne before the Royal Musical Association in London. Swinburne's talk was published in the proceedings a few months later and duly reported in an article by D. C. Parker, "Is Woman a Failure as a Musician?" for *Musical America* (10 December 1921): 45.

48. R. M. Knerr, "Noted Feminist Defends Women's Place in Music," *Musical America* (21 January 1922): 5. This article reported on a speech by W. L. George, whom the writer describes as a "noted English writer and feminist" who "defends Woman as Man's Intellectual Equal in Literature But Makes Suggestions Concerning Her Restricted Prowess in Music." M. T. Reilly, "Women in Music," *Musical Leader* (16 April 1925): 387, 414. Carlos Salzedo, "Personality and Interpretation," *Aeolian Review* 3 (1924): 8. Esther Waite, "Are Men Better Musicians Than Women?" *Musical Digest* 13 (1928): 26, 54, 61. Waite's subtitle, "Both the Affirmative and Negative Sides Are Heard on This Absorbing Subject," was the lead for a survey of opinions by contemporary performers of both sexes.

The prevailing aesthetic discourse that equated masculine or virile with vital and original received a different gloss from some Modernist critics. Catherine Smith believes that "anti-feminism was as fundamental to American musical modernism as it was to literary modernism," citing among others this critic for *Modern Music*, who in 1929 wrote that

> one begins to sense a distinctively American quality in some of the American music that has been written recently. One senses in it a distinguishing virility—the virility with which it so constantly seeks to express its ideas and feelings. This characteristic was absent before. The older American music was a labored and generally weary reiteration of thoroughly alien forms and styles.[49]

When Ruth Crawford's Sonata for Violin and Piano was premiered in 1927, the critic for the *New York Herald Tribune* described it as "the most masculine in quality that the afternoon brought forth."[50] And the leading modernist critic of the twenties, Paul Rosenfeld, linked effeminacy to Edward MacDowell's musical weaknesses in terms resembling Ives's. Rosenfeld condemned MacDowell's "sentimentality":

> The feelings entertained about life by him seem to have remained uncertain; and while fumbling for them he seems regularly to have succumbed to "nice" and "respectable" emotions, conventional, accepted by and welcome to, the best people. . . . Where his great romantic brethren, Brahms, Wagner, and Debussy, are direct and sensitive, clearly and tellingly expressive, MacDowell minces and simpers, maidenly, and ruffled. He is nothing if not a daughter of the American Revolution.[51]

Thus gender ideology could be used to praise and contain the achievements of a woman by explicitly or implicitly describing her as "writing like a man," and to reproach a man for writing like a woman.

From aesthetics to sociological observation, engendered views of culture provided a contemporary rhetoric for controversies that had little to do with gender. Attitudes toward patronage are a case in point. In the 1920s the power of patronage when wielded by upper-class women made a progressive group of women particularly vulnerable to social criticism as women rather than as members of a wealthy leisured class. A common attitude was "that the patronage of women assured the continued weakness of American composition."[52] It did not matter much what kind of

49. Irving Weill, "The American Scene Changes," *Modern Music* 6, no. 4 (1929): 7–8, cited in Smith, "On Feminism and American Art Music."

50. "Music by Six Young Americans Is Heard by a Large Audience. Composers' League Has Program for Native Writers with Works for Piano, String and Voice Given," *New York Herald Tribune*, 14 February 1927, p. 10.

51. Paul Rosenfeld, *An Hour with American Music* (Philadelphia, 1929), p. 46.

52. DuPree, "The Failure of American Music," p. 305.

music they supported. Consider the reasons offered for the life and death of the New York–based and short-lived National Symphony, founded by Edgard Varèse in 1919. Walter Damrosch called the birth of the orchestra—which played the new music he deplored—the mistake of a susceptible patron, Gertrude Payne Whitney, who had been taken in by a "young handsome European composer" (Varèse).[53] After a single, disastrous season the orchestra failed, and Paul Rosenfeld blamed its death on women as well—"but one of the innumerable consequences of the fact that in America musical organizations have patronesses more often than they have patrons." In fact, New York women such as Blanche Walton and Claire Reis sustained the activities of new music in New York; as Carol Oja has documented, women were criticized by some as *too* supportive of modern music in the 1920s.[54] The virulent attack by a modern biographer of Ives on one of the most important patrons of the period, Elizabeth Sprague Coolidge, shows how tenacious such scapegoating attitudes are.[55]

In sum, gender ideology in Ives's culture covered a spectrum of beliefs, some far more noxious than others. Its relationship to social realities was dynamic rather than static, characteristically lagging behind social change. At its crudest it stigmatized classical music as "effeminate" and simultaneously defined its highest achievements as masculine. At its most fundamental level, it continued to promote Victorian dichotomies of biologically determined sexual difference. Its viability cut across stylistic and political divisions, resonating in the attitudes of conservatives and progressives, Victorians and modernists, men and women. And so the terms *masculine* and *feminine*, or *effeminate* and *feminized*, were used similarly by people of highly disparate musical orientations and taste.

Although gender ideology largely reflected the inequalities and asymmetries in American society,[56] depending on one's point of view men or

53. Walter Damrosch was the conductor of the New York Symphony and a major establishment figure in New York's musical life. For his ambivalence about women, see the chapter on "Women in Musical Affairs" in his *My Musical Life*, 2d ed. (New York, 1930), pp. 323–32.

54. Paul Rosenfeld, "Musical Chronicle: The New or National Symphony Orchestra," *The Dial* (December 1920): 670. I am indebted to Carol J. Oja for this reference. The issue of female patronage of modern music is documented in Oja, "Women Patrons and Promoters of New York's New Music During the 1920s," paper read at the national meeting of the American Musicological Society, Chicago, 1991.

55. "The Elizabeth Sprague Coolidges of this world are a perennial curiosity." Their fathers make their fortunes, and then they "beget daughters who inherit (a) their money, and (b) a vague, uncomprehending awareness of who rather than what their ancestors have been—*viz.* 'artists.' That, plus daddy's money, gives them a sense of power: wealth *plus* art = 'culture.' They will never become patrons of the arts." (Wooldridge, *From the Steeples and Mountains*, p. 172.) I am grateful to Wayne Shirley for this reference.

56. Koskoff, "An Introduction," p. 9.

women could be and indeed were viewed alternately as its victims or its benefactors.[57] To put this in terms of feminist theory: like most gender ideologies, ours has had the potential to be both instrumental and prescriptive for both male and female musicians.[58] That is to say, the rhetoric of music as a female sphere on the one hand sanctioned female musicality through sexual difference, and on the other rejected the possibility of creative equality with men. The parallel for men is that they could be harmed by the identification of music with feminization and/or effeminacy, or they could be empowered by their dominant role in music history.[59] Small wonder, then, that it is possible for contemporary historians to tap this literature to document the effects of prejudice on both men and women.

The writings of Charles Ives thus hold up a mirror that both reflects and distorts the world around him.[60] Those of his prejudices that were more or less routine should be distinguished from the hostile beliefs that mark his extremism. In some respects he simply conformed to his culture. Rather conventionally, he confessed to "feeling partially ashamed" of his musical interests as a boy, "an entirely wrong feeling but one typical of boys in small towns"; similarly, throughout his lifetime he assumed men and male achievement to be at the center of any discussion of musical genius or, indeed, of high culture in general. Chivalrous and sentimental about women in the family, a Victorian gentleman in mores,[61] he was condescending in his artistic judgments. He was "skeptical and impatient about any music written by a woman," according to Sidney Cowell, who co-authored the first biography of Ives,[62] yet his deeds could transcend his own limits. For example, when Henry Cowell proposed Ruth Crawford's *String Quartet 1931* as the first recording of the New Music series

57. Kerber, "Separate Spheres," p. 18.
58. Ibid., p. 26.
59. Whitesitt, "The Role of Women Impresarios," cites both kinds of perspectives in the past and present literature.
60. For two recent discussions of Ives and gender, see Nora M. Beck, "An Examination of Gender in Selected Writings and Music of Charles Ives," and Lawrence Kramer, "Ives's Misogyny and Post-Reconstruction America." Both papers were delivered at the conference on Feminist Theory and Music: Toward a Common Language, Minneapolis, June 1991. I wish to thank both authors for sharing drafts of these papers with me, and Beck for her references to my work as well.
61. Vivian Perlis points out that "one of the paradoxes in Ives is that he could be both ultra-modern and terribly old-fashioned, way ahead of his time and far behind it." She cites John Kirkpatrick's opinion of Ives and his wife Harmony as "very old-fashioned." ("Charles Ives: Victorian Gentleman or American Folk Hero?" in William Ferris and Mary L. Hart, eds., *Folk Music and Modern Sound* [Jackson, Miss., 1982], pp. 141–42, 144.)
62. Personal interview with Sidney Robertson Cowell, 15 January 1988. Quoted by permission.

in 1931, Ives questioned the decision—would Crawford be "mansized enough?"—but after hearing Cowell's spirited defense of the work, went on to fund the project.[63] It is telling that when Ives published his *114 Songs* he adopted a female persona as a composer. As if he were a Victorian lady amateur, Ives postscripted a note to this publication addressed to the "gentle borrower" of his music, describing this unusual act of private publication as "cleaning house." Perhaps such humility was supposed to disarm the receiver of his music and to counterbalance the radical content of the musical items "left out on the clothes line."[64]

Despite the common ground between Ives and his environment, it must not be forgotten that he was an extremist about effeminacy. That attitude is marked perhaps more by what he did not say than by what he did. That is to say, Ives was reticent on most of the standard issues of the literature on gender and music. Having chosen to remove himself from the profession as such, he was not concerned about the sex-distribution within the musical labor force. Nor did he participate in the Victorian debate over the potential of the woman composer, or marshal its substantial literature in support of his arguments about the essentially masculine nature of music. Unlike modernist male writers waging "the war of the words," he did not "define his artistic integrity in opposition to the musical incompetence of women"[65] or to the older tradition of music as feminine accomplishment.[66] Female musicians were on the periphery of Ives's universe, and there is no mention of any professional female musician—either composer or performer—in the *Memos*.[67]

Ives was playing for bigger stakes. As Linda Kerber has written, "We live in a world in which authority has traditionally validated itself by its distance from the feminine and from what is understood to be

---

63. Cowell wanted to record music by Henry Brant and Ruth Crawford. Ives writes, "I know nothing about Brant's or Crawford's music, except what you . . . & others have told me—which is that 'in time & a nice tide' they may get mansized (even Miss C.)." This incident is discussed in Rita Mead, *Henry Cowell's New Music 1925–1936: The Society, the Music Editions, and the Recordings* (Ann Arbor, 1981), p. 256.

64. Ives, "Postface to *114 Songs*," reprinted in *Essays Before a Sonata and Other Writings*, p. 130.

65. This is the thesis of Sandra M. Gilbert and Susan Gubar, *No Man's Land: The Place of the Woman Writer in the Twentieth Century*, 2 vols. (New Haven, 1988), vol. 1, p. 157, which has been applied to American music by Smith, "Feminism and American Art Music." Some of the composers she cites seem to fit the model much better than Ives.

66. "Younger American men apparently believed they had to make the public distance between this older notion of the place of art music [as feminine accomplishment] and their own aesthetic posture as wide as possible." (Smith and Richardson, *Mary Carr Moore*, p. 173.)

67. "Although Ives often mentioned ladies metaphorically in his Memos, real women received little attention. In fact, only a dozen-odd of women are mentioned by name." (Nora M. Beck, "An Examination of Gender in Selected Writings and Music of Charles Ives," unpublished paper, p. 21, cited here with permission of the author.)

effeminate."[68] In my view, Ives's most vituperative outbursts of sexist prejudice derive from that search for validation and from his turbulent confrontation with the authority of the great tradition of European classical music.

In considering the nature of this confrontation, we need to distinguish questions of stylistic influence and indebtedness from questions of artistic status and patterns of recognition. With respect to style, like "every major composer of his era," whether neoclassic or progressive, Ives "used material from the past to establish a relationship with the past . . . [invoking] the past in order to reinterpret it."[69] Perhaps as a corrective to the emphasis on Ives's extraordinary powers of reimagining the vernacular past in his music, some recent scholarship has focused on reconnecting him to the classical mainstream, on demonstrating the extent to which he absorbed technique and vision from any number of European composers, both past and contemporary.[70] Perhaps it is in the nature of artistic gratitude to be ambivalent about one's debts. Ives's ambivalence is so loaded with hostility that it has led J. Peter Burkholder to conclude that Ives "set out to disinherit himself from European music" in order to deny the influence of the past; and, further, that his name-calling of European composers was a way of effecting the rupture.[71]

Certainly, Ives's statements about effeminacy and music, which do not appear until after 1905, seem to be correlated with the evolution of his radical experimental style, which crystallized around the same time.[72] Ives presented some of these compositions as declarations of stylistic independence and dissent. The Piano Study no. 20 (1907–1909) has a note burlesquing Rachmaninoff as "Rachnotmanenough."[73] Another burlesque exercise was a "Take-off" on the Andante of Haydn's "Surprise" symphony (1909?) with the following marginal notes: "All this G string had to be made after getting back from the K. . . . . .Q concert in winter '09 (nothing but triads. . . .)."[74] He travesties the Haydn Quartet as "nice little easy sugar plum sounds for the soft ears' pocketbooks," "perfumed sounds for the Dress Circle cushion chair ears," "velvet pocketbooks," "nice sweety silk bonnet melodies," "nice sweety jellycake har-

68. Kerber, "Separate Spheres," p. 39.

69. Joseph N. Straus, *Remaking the Past: Musical Modernism and the Influence of the Tonal Tradition* (Cambridge, Mass., 1990), pp. 2, 1.

70. For one example, see J. Peter Burkholder, "'Quotation' and Paraphrase in Ives's Second Symphony," *19th-Century Music* 11 (1987): 3–25.

71. J. Peter Burkholder, "Charles Ives and His Fathers: A Response to Maynard Solomon," *Newsletter of the Institute for Studies in American Music* 18 (1988): 10.

72. Ives says this stage in his evolution came in about 1908 (*Memos*, p. 74).

73. Rossiter, *Charles Ives and His America*, p. 36.

74. John Kirkpatrick, ed., *A Temporary Mimeographed Catalogue of the Music Manuscripts of Charles Edward Ives* (1960; rpt. New Haven, 1973), p. 221.

monies."[75] In the margin of a manuscript of the Second String Quartet Ives wrote "This is music for men to play—not the Lady Bird K. . . . .Q."[76] With its expression mark of "Andante Emasculata" in the second movement, the quartet savages both tonal music and its status as a commodity for "conspicuous consumption"[77] by a leisure class. In the *Memos* Ives embellishes his account of this concert even further, damning it with his favorite epithet of "nice":

> mellifluous sounds, perfect cadences, perfect ladies, perfect programs, and not a dissonant cuss word to stop the anemia and beauty during the whole evening. . . . I got to feel, at a Kneisel Quartet concert, finally that I was resting my ears on a parfumed sofa-cushion—so got out![78]

Other works are described as opposition or reaction. The chamber piece "In Re Con Moto et.Al" was intended to be "a piece that no permanent-wave conductor of those days could conduct."[79] The Third Sonata for Violin and Piano was "to make a nice piece for the nice ladies" after a "famous German Virtuoso violinist" had said his first sonata "bore no resemblance to music."[80]

As an artist, then, Ives used and absorbed the great tradition of Europe, while at the same time he chafed under the confines of what Charles Seeger used to call "the prison of good music."[81] Ives once wrote that Bach, Beethoven, and Brahms may be the "best music we know" but—invoking the image of a cage—it was "too cooped up."[82]

Yet the issues of style and compositional indebtedness do not, in my view, suffice as explanations for the ways gender ideology served Ives. His profound hostility is not just ingratitude run amok. Ives's other writings, particularly in the *Memos*, move beyond style to social context. Implicated as well as (if not even more than) composers are performers, critics, and their upper-class constituency of patrons and listeners—in short, what was once fashionably called "the establishment." As Lehman Engel, who met Ives in the early 1930s, observed, "He was constantly throwing out

75. Rossiter gives the complete marginal note, only the first few words of which are printed in the Kirkpatrick catalogue. ("Charles Ives and American Culture," p. 308.)

76. Marginal notes to the score, printed in Kirkpatrick, ed., *A Temporary Mimeographed Catalogue*, p. 60.

77. This famous phrase comes from Thorstein Veblen, *The Theory of the Leisure Class: An Economic Study of Institutions* (New York, 1899).

78. *Memos*, p. 73.

79. Ibid., p. 100.

80. Kirkpatrick, ed., *A Temporary Mimeographed Catalogue*, p. 79.

81. Charles Seeger to Ruth Crawford, 11 November 1930, Seeger Estate, private collection, quoted by permission.

82. *Memos*, p. 100.

venom about the musical establishment of his day."[83] His name-calling of composers belongs to a larger cultural dissent.

In America early twentieth-century composers were forced to compete as never before with music from a great past that lived through orchestral performances and the advocacy of great conductors. American composers carried a double burden. Although in some senses they shared in the family tradition as "Western" composers, they were its stepchildren, having to prove their status by developing a national identity or school. The famous literary critic Van Wyck Brooks described the interplay between the past and the present in late-nineteenth-century Boston in a tone that throws some light on Ives's own attitudes. The cultural life of Boston had become

> higher and dryer than ever. Having become a religion, it was dying as culture; and it regarded with a glassy eye the poor little efforts of poets who struggled beneath it. It identified itself with Dante, Browning, with Matthew Arnold, Ruskin, Walter Pater, and felt that because it somehow knew these authors it was entitled to regard with scorn the ingenuous beings who also tried to write. Did they think they could write as well as Browning? What nonsense, then, to try to write at all.[84]

With similar bitterness, Ives forged links between the sanctification of the past and the intolerance for modernity that marked the reception of his music. American composers had to work in the vacuum of an extended tradition of classical music. "To try to write at all" was an act that often provoked comparisons with the European masters. To write as a radical modernist exceeded that point of comparison and therefore the boundaries of what was permitted. Ives used gender ideology to articulate his own resentments at and frustrations with his critics and to retaliate for the condescension and rejection he found so hard to endure.

One need only pick up the opening of the *Memos* with its caricatures of music critics (quoted above) to see the extent to which Ives's hatred of conventional tonal style is inseparable from his hatred of institutions (including establishment critics) and of the overbearing presence of music from the past. Some of that fury must have come from the *Memos*' having been written so close in time to one of Ives's great disappointments: the critical rejection of his music at the Pan American concerts conducted by

83. Engel writes, "He hadn't approved of it, probably largely because they hadn't approved of him, hadn't accepted him in any possible way." (Quoted in Perlis, "Charles Ives," p. 197.)

84. Van Wyck Brooks, *New England: Indian Summer 1865–1915* (New York, 1940), p. 442.

Nicolas Slonimsky in Berlin and Paris.[85] But even in an earlier letter to Slonimsky, discussing commercial media, Ives trumpeted the same theme:

> Radio: Art and business all hitched up together. 91⅜% (I like to be precise) of all radio and phonograph records—are "sebaceous cysts," and soft ones at that—and they sell—though if a 3-year-old is always fed candy for breakfast he will always be a 3-year-old—and the oatmeal market will die. The letter from the Victor Co.—"all commitments are made by themselves"—unnecessary statement!—just look at them, g—d—soft-headed lists! 95⅝% "ta ta" stuff.[86]

The covenant between the European past and the upper classes is a main theme in the *Memos*. Two illustrative excerpts, which need full quotation, reveal Ives's politics, in which taste, class, and power are conjoined. First:

> A stronger use of the mind and ear would mean less people (usually ladies) whose greatest interest and pleasure in art, in music, and in all nice things, is to get their names down among the Directors and Patrons of Rollo's friends, and in giving dinners to European artists, conductors, etc., with more reputation than anything else (that is, artists and conductors, not dinners)—letting themselves become dumb tools of a monopoly, kowtowing to everything the monopolists tell them about America being an unmusical country, and creating a kind of American Music inferiority complex. These commercial monopolists, whether prima donna conductors, violinists or singers, have so long fostered and held their monopolies (for just about a hundred years in this country) that as a result too much of the American ear has become a Soft-Static Co. (Limited) and the Gabrilowitsches et al. have got the money and coll[ected] the ladies' smiles.[87]

That world is captured in the frontispiece photograph for Daniel Gregory Mason's autobiography. Together are the symbols of Ivesian resentment: the virtuoso (Josef Hoffman) and his patron (Edward De Coppet, the most famous New York pre–World War I melomane) in elegant dress.[88]

Ives's fulminations against his own situation as a scorned modernist occasionally transcended the personal element to become broader protests against what recent historians have called the "commodification of

85. In his preface to *A Temporary Mimeographed Catalogue* Kirkpatrick makes this clear, framing the opening sections of the *Memos* for the reader by giving details of Slonimsky's concerts and the critical reception (pp. 12–16).

86. Charles Ives to Nicolas Slonimsky, 26 December 1930. Reprinted in Nicolas Slonimsky, ed., *Music Since 1900*, 4th ed. (New York, 1971), p. 1325.

87. *Memos*, p. 41.

88. Daniel Gregory Mason, *Music in My Time and Other Reminiscences* (New York, 1938). Mason devotes a chapter of his book to another Ives villain, Ossip Gabrilowitsch.

culture."[89] Although this concept has generally been applied to popular music, Ives was not alone in suggesting that classical music from the past was being "commercialized," that, to sustain profits in the marketplace, listeners were conditioned to accept only those works as "good music." The notion that appears in the previous excerpt, that art is controlled by a cultural "monopoly," occurs in a later statement in a context that is even more revealing than his reaction to the Kneisel Quartet:

> (Sep 4 [5], '34)—in London. . . . The music on the boats and Green Park didn't bring it home to me more strongly and hopelessly surely, than sitting there for an hour or so and hearing those groove-made chewed-cuds (those sound-sequences tied to the same old nice apron-strings, which have become greasy in the process,)—that music (and all art, like all life), must be part of the great organic flow, onwards and always upwards, or become soft in muscles and spirit, and die! I was never more conscious of the vapidity of the human minds that accept anything, round, soft, fat, or bazoota, which somebody else with a nicer silk hat than theirs hands them—commercial silk hatters—music conservatories (the better known the worse)—the paid newspaper critics—the prima donna monopolists—and perhaps the lowest of all, the publishing, the broadcasting, and recording for profit. The Valse Triste (as brown-sugar-coddle as it is) is bigger than what we heard last night—for the first is a nice lollipop, and it doesn't try to be something else—but these symphonies, overtures etc. are worse because they give out the strut of a little music making believe it's big. Every phrase, line, and chord, and beat went over and over the way you'd exactly expect them to go . . . trite, tiresome awnings of platitudes, all a nice mixture of Grieg, Wagner and Tchaikovsky (et al, ladies). But the worst part—a thing hinting that music might some day die, like an emasculated cherry, dead but dishonored—was to see those young people standing downstairs, seriously eating that yellow sap flowing from a stomach that had never had an idea. And some of them are probably composing, and you can see them going home, copying down those slimy grooves and thinking that they are creating something—helping music decline—dying—dying dead.[90]

For Ives the Proms concert evening precipitated his worst nightmare, an apocalyptic vision of the Death of Music in surrealistic imagery: round, soft minds melting like clocks in a Dali painting, yellow sap flowing from a stomach—is this poisoned mother's milk? And the ultimate dishonor: music as an "emasculated cherry"—cherry here indicating not a hymen but, probably, a homosexual. This entire jeremiad is informed by political

89. Charles Hamm, "The Periodization of North American Music," paper delivered at the meeting of the American Musicological Society, Oakland, 1990, uses the work of Jacques Attali to suggest that "commodification" be the general descriptive term applied to the culture that accompanied the "rise of an American brand of capitalism."

90. *Memos*, pp. 135–36.

reaction that uses gender as a way to talk about the realities of the marketplace.

The politics of culture makes strange bedfellows. Ives's indictment of a commercialized repertory of classical music is echoed in some writings by Daniel Gregory Mason, who excoriated Toscanini concerts as "museums of the past" servicing "fashion-enslaved, prestige-hypnotized minds."[91] Both Mason and Ives, who once called Toscanini "Toss a Ninny," foreshadow the crusade against Toscanini undertaken by Virgil Thomson and spurred by his distaste for the rigidity of a repertory commercializing the great masterpieces and the "greatest symphonies" of the past.[92] Ives's denouncement of "the business-man-musician-European . . . the commercialists . . . always (most always) on the side of the conventional and so sellable," occasionally gendered as the "Prostitution of Art," can also be compared to Theodor Adorno's criticism of "Capitalist Monopolies."[93]

Other ultramodern composers were equally belligerent about performers. Carl Ruggles is alleged to have ranted privately about

> Juilliard, leaving his millions to music and they spend it all teaching good-for-nothing fiddlers and pianists. Nothing for the composer. That fathead of a John Erskine sitting at the head of it, and Ernest Hutcheson, emasculated moron. Toscanini? Third rate conductor. A damn swine.[94]

And Varèse is reported to have

> felt a resentment toward the great virtuosi who all without exception performed the same works of old masters—and only a limited few of those—over and over again, ignoring completely contemporary composers who wrote in a new idiom, unfamiliar and unpopular. "They don't give a [shit] about music," he said, "only their 'careers'—their 'interpretations.' They still think I'm a circus freak."[95]

Ives used the *Memos* to strike back. The purpose of Ives's militant gender ideology was to weaken his adversaries by inverting gender discourse, rendering the patrimony—the heritage of male achievement—suspect on its own terms. By denying the Great Masters the authority of what might be called "the Eternal Masculine" he made his own bid for the reordering of power and artistic entitlement. If "they"—the Eurocentric conglomerate of performers, promoters, and critics—defined conso-

---

91. Mason is quoted in Joseph Horowitz, *Understanding Toscanini* (New York, 1987), p. 238.
92. Ibid., p. 244.
93. *Memos*, p. 94. Adorno is cited by Horowitz, *Understanding Toscanini*, pp. 236–40.
94. This comment is quoted by Ruth Crawford in an unpublished memoir, ca. 1930, Seeger Estate, Library of Congress.
95. Quoted in Louise Varèse, *Varèse: A Looking-Glass Diary* (New York, 1972), p. 195.

nance as natural, he redefined it as effeminate and therefore unnatural. If new music was pilloried by snobbish comparisons to the Old Masters (as it often was), then Ives desecrated the false idols. If Bach, Beethoven, and Brahms were ranked as hard and masculine, then he suggested that they were instead soft and tainted with effeminacy. In this sense his name-calling was purposeful. His project was the emasculation of the cultural patriarchy.

That he undermined his own cause by relying on the language of gender prejudice is only one of the ironies attending the life and works of this great composer. Let me remind the reader that the literature about gender and music in American culture has not been surveyed here as an apology for Ives but, rather, to demythologize his anger and to confront our own cultural legacies. "In isolation, anger is privatized and neutralized, unrecognizable," its political implications suppressed.[96] Thus the "manner" of Ivesian polemics has to some extent undone its "substance," not only diminishing his historical stature as an American paradigm but obfuscating the political content of his dissent. Given our post-Freudian habit of reading sexuality into every context, it is all the harder to read it out where it misleads. Given our cultural addiction to the music of the past, we have been uncomfortable confronting Ives's apostatic treatment of the canon. In our gender ideology of music the "masculinization" of high art has been no less powerful and pervasive than the "feminization" of musical "accomplishment," these associations retaining some resonance even today. Unless we distance ourselves from this legacy, we run the risk of cementing the orthodoxies of "separate spheres" into our own interpretations, rather than recognizing the continuum of possible adaptations and resistances between individuals and society and between men and women who, as composers and musicians, are bound together as much as torn apart by the ideology surrounding music and gender.

It is beyond the scope of this essay to do more than acknowledge the complexity of the larger relationship between Ives's rhetoric and his music. To paraphrase a historian of science, "Just as music—always more abundant than its representations—inevitably transcends our laws, so the practice of composition—always more abundant than its ideology—transcends its own prescriptions."[97] It is open to question whether Ives's "music issues from a contest between opposing aspects of his own nature" or whether "the Ives who talked about the emasculation of music is not

96. Marianne Hirsch, *The Mother/Daughter Plot: Narrative, Psychoanalysis, Feminism* (Bloomington, 1989), p. 193.

97. "Just as nature—always more abundant than its representations—inevitably transcends our laws, so the practice of science—always more abundant than its ideology— transcends its own prescriptions." (Evelyn Fox Keller, *Reflections on Gender and Science* [New Haven, 1985], p. 136.)

the Ives who wrote the music."[98] The "Ives who talked" learned the social grammar of his culture; the "Ives who wrote" used its related ideology as a defense against rejection, an important element in his modernist dissent and his presentation of himself as an artist—a way, that is, to distance himself from the inherited patrimony on his own terms.

Women—either as "Woman" or as real women—were only a small part of this polemic. The ultimate misogyny in Ives's aesthetic is its total devaluation of feminine values, the despoiling of difference as it was understood then. Like the boy who watched the leopard in the cage, we witness Ives's turbulent intellect pace between his false antinomies, his words and music offering up the challenge of his unanswered question: "Is life anything like that?"

98. The first quotation is from Solomon, "Charles Ives," p. 467, the second from J. Peter Burkholder, quoted in ibid.

The Ethnomusicologist as Midwife

Carol E. Robertson

The themes of this essay revolve around midwifery as a metaphor for the translation of information from one set of cultural realities to another. I will focus on Mapuche and Hawaiian concepts of self-knowledge and cultural identity that directly impinge on the transmission and articulation of music.[1] These concepts being brought into our midst demand changes in some of our most basic assumptions about the nature of musical knowledge and the role of the performer in society. Thus, the task undertaken here is to give safe passage to musical perceptions that might easily be dismissed simply because they do not fit our habits of thought and interpretation.

Midwifery also involves bringing something—a child, a tradition, a belief, a "different" human being—from the periphery of awareness to the center of attention. Many human communities, be they socially or intellectually based, tend to relegate to the edges of a community those who do not conform to a common denominator of thought, behavior, or physical presentation. Difference, in other words, is the most common

An earlier version of this essay was presented in 1988 in Berlin at the symposium on Music in the Dialogue of Cultures, sponsored by the International Institute for Comparative Music Studies and Documentation. The presentations from that event have been published in Max Peter Baumann, ed., *Music in the Dialogue of Cultures: Traditional Music and Cultural Policy*, Intercultural Music Studies, vol. 2 (Berlin, 1991).

1. The Mapuche today inhabit the southern Andean areas of Chile and Argentina. My concern here is with the groups in Argentina that were first conquered by the Chilean Mapuche and, at the turn of the twentieth century, by the Argentine army. The research on these Mapuche was conducted in 1972–1973, 1978, and 1981–1982 with funding from the Ford Foundation, Indiana University, Columbia University, and the University of Maryland. Research in Hawai'i was undertaken in 1987–1988, under the auspices of the National Research Council.

criterion for marginalization. Mapuche and Hawaiian attitudes toward difference often allow the individual who has been relegated to (or has chosen) the periphery of social life to travel to the center of tradition. When the boundaries of a society remain so fluid, individuals who can travel between the center and the periphery hold a special kind of power inaccessible to persons who are "fixed" in the center.

Travel between center and periphery also calls for midwifery. Mapuche healers/chanters and Hawaiian performers who travel freely between the center and the periphery give birth to concepts, behaviors, and musical perceptions, and these are often unique to this process of translation and movement. They bring with them views, chants, and insights that simply cannot be seen from the center—the status quo of the tradition.

I want to approach these issues by looking at the relationships between what we have valued in scholarship as *mainstream* and as *marginal*, and by examining the ever-shifting relationship between the *center* and the *periphery*. I choose these notions because they can also be applied to ethnomusicology as a culture and to the ways that we project ourselves into the cultures we study. I will focus on the domains of gender and spirituality because these two aspects of experience can teach us a great deal about the dynamics of the center and the periphery in the arena of performance.

I will repeatedly emphasize the fluidity of these categories, because what we are able to perceive or apprehend of them depends on where we stand in relation to the periphery, to the center, to notions of gender, and to the practice of spirituality. The traditions of Western linear thought often make such fluidity difficult. Whereas most of the cultures in which I have done field research perceive time and human relationships as having a spiraling, circular, or elliptical trajectory, academic convention has pressed me to write about them in ways that align me with the mainstream styles of rationalism and linear thought.

Mapuche Healers: Chanting the Periphery into the Center

> *When we pull this [chant] out of our bodies we create and change ourselves. We bring the ancestors and all the forces that move the universe into this open space. This is how we give birth to our spirit. And you, if you sit in our circle with a pure heart, are one of the midwives.*[2]

2. Carolina Milliapi, Malleo reservation, Neuquén, Argentina, 1972. This statement was made during a wake in which all the women present were performing or "pulling out" the lineage chants (*tayil*) of the deceased.

When I returned to Argentina in 1971, after six years of study in Mexico and the United States, I saw myself as an ethnomusicologist prepared to observe contemporary Mapuche life and engender explanations that would render that culture accessible to my colleagues. It was not until 1978 that I realized that the healer in whose work I had become intimately involved saw me not as a "teacher" or a "student of music in culture," but as an apprentice. At first this realization terrified me, for it implied a level of social interaction, chanting expertise, and spiritual responsibility for which I did not feel prepared. The most unnerving aspect of this shift in perception was that the way in which I was being "midwifed" into the community profoundly altered the ways that I was able to internalize my own experience of spiritual and social realities.

Carolina Milliapi and her mentor, the late Kushé Papai, were the midwives for my own perceptual transformation. They were also central in teaching me how to dispel the protective mantle I had learned to call by the self-justifying, magical names of *objectivity* and *scientific distance*. As ethnomusicologists we assume that learning to perform competently in the musical traditions we study increases our grasp of performance dynamics. In the same way, learning about healing deepens our grounding in the dynamics of ease and dis-ease. Both forms of performance competence require that we drink deeply of the cultural and spiritual realities that make music and healing effective in their goals.

One of the most remarkable facets of Mapuche healing has arisen from the cultural discontinuity wrought by the defeat and genocide of the late-nineteenth-century Argentine-Mapuche wars. Mapuche oral history tells us that by the beginning of this century the Argentine authorities had mounted a massive campaign to discredit and eliminate the Mapuche shamanic practitioners, who are known as *machi*.

Although the *machi* have usually been women, I know of a few healers who were identified biologically as men and spiritually as women. During their training and sometimes before, they donned the garb, vocal textures, and responsibilities of women. They worked to perfect their female spirit and energy so that the gods would see them as "life givers" rather than as "life takers." They underwent female initiation rites, celebrated symbolic monthly menstrual cycles, and mastered the lineage-based vocal repertoires that are the exclusive domain of women.

All *machi* were powerful spiritually in that they were able to harness the transformational forces of female energy. Their clairvoyance made them extremely powerful politically as well: in their ability to see the many layers of the present, they were often able to move their people to action. Their ability to predict hostile attacks, their power to mold public opinion, and their ability to strengthen defeated warriors through chant made the *machi* a serious threat to the Argentine military.[3]

By the time Carolina Milliapi reached adolescence, in the 1930s, the practice of shamanism had gone so far underground that no woman would have thought of identifying herself as a *machi*. A few women used the term that designated their role as drummers and chanters in annual rites of increase: *witakultruntufe* (the woman carrying the drum). Only a few had ever attended *machitún* rites, where *machi* healed one another through sound and summoned their shared powers to restore the land. In fact, some present-day Mapuche, fearful of being associated with these forbidden ancestral practices, refer to *machitún* gatherings as *salamancas*, the medieval Spanish term for witches' covens.

Thus, when Carolina started hearing disembodied chanting and having the dreams, visions, and seizures that are the trademarks of the *machi*'s calling, she had no role models in her community to whom she could turn for guidance and training. Mapuche women still draw on kinship structures in the process of socialization, seeking out their grandparents and their mothers' brothers for sustenance and knowledge, and Carolina found refuge in her paternal grandmother, whose son had been a great seer and warrior-chief, a man whose visions while imprisoned by the Argentine army had reformulated ritual practice among his people. By the time of her menarche, Carolina would often be overtaken by a vision or seizure in the sheep pens; she would regain consciousness to find herself covered with dung and haunted by voices and images. Her grandmother would clean her up and reassure her that what seemed to be the curse of witchcraft could be transformed into a blessing. Carolina's grandmother was not a practicing healer, yet she would often comfort her with chants that no other women in the community seemed to know.

By Carolina's teen years, Mapuche communities, broken and demoralized by their brutal defeat, had entered a period of spiritual shock and massive cultural denial. Had there been a *machi* practicing openly in her

3. The persecution these women endured is comparable to that suffered by the female healers of Europe and New England, whom the authorities of the Enlightenment put to death as witches and heretics or as practitioners of the Old Religion. This pattern of repression of women in medicine has marginalized even the traditional midwife, a role that in many areas of Latin America has been taken over by the *partero*, or "midhusband." For discussions of the marginalization of women in European and North American traditions, see Jeanne Achterberg, *Imagery in Healing: Shamanism and Modern Medicine* (Boston, 1985); Mary Daly, *Gyn/Ecology: The Metaethics of Radical Feminism* (Boston, 1978); Arthur Evans, *Witchcraft and the Gay Counterculture: A Radical View of Western Civilization and Some of the People It Has Tried to Destroy* (Boston, 1978); and Starhawk, *Dreaming the Dark: Magic, Sex, and Politics* (Boston, 1982). In many Western communities, as in the Andes, women's medicine entered an underground wherein marginalization offered some protection from regulation by the male-dominated allopathic tradition.

niche of the Andes, Carolina could have undertaken her own healing under supervision. As it was, her choices were to be shunned as crazy or cursed, to hope that the seizures and voices would stop spontaneously, or to begin a solitary pilgrimage that would give birth to some inner clarity. Although it was not an established practice among her people, she chose to embark on a vision quest.

At the age of eighteen, Carolina began a four-year journey. She wandered over the peaks and through the valleys of Andean Patagonia collecting roots, herbs, and seeds, which she combined in proportions given to her in dreams. It was during this time that she became an experimental scientist, using the many micro-ecologies of the mountains as her laboratory and herself as the guinea pig. She has spoken of the mixed faith and uncertainty of those years:

> In those days I had no understanding of what this was all leading to. Sometimes I was dreaming and a figure in blue was coming towards me . . . "You must be going to this leaf and pulling out its spirit song so that it will know why you need to use it. Each plant can be for a different way, but if you have the song, you can use it." Sometimes the dream would give me the same song for different things, but the will that you put into it is different. Sometimes I had no dreams for a long time; but when I was coming to a new ingredient, the knowledge would just drain into my head, and I could feel my heart [pointing to her solar plexus] saying that this is right.[4]

Central to Carolina's medical education was the mastery of the chants that unlock the healing properties of specific herbs, roots, barks, and fungi. In addition, through complex initiations presented to her by spirits Carolina was given the song-codes of rivers, clouds, mountains, and other natural phenomena. Every substance is encoded with a wealth of information of medical and spiritual significance, and its song-code, a combination of tones, durations, and magical texts, releases that information. Since the body and the soul are seen as two different emanations of matter, one significantly denser than the other, body and soul can be treated by some of the same elements.

Carolina has commented that some of the musical structures for the chants she received during her pilgrimage were first sung to her by her grandmother, as she comforted her during or after seizures. Many healers who have been able to recreate their vanishing traditions have given accounts of having been in a particular place in the mountains and there having received a flood of information from the past. Some have found an object, usually a rock in the shape of a double heart, left in their path by healers of old so that the sacred knowledge would not be lost. Infor-

4. Carolina Milliapi, Huilquimenuco, 1981.

mation can be coded into power objects so that it can be retrieved only by the person for whom it was intended. Since Mapuche time is cyclical rather than sequential, Mapuche healing is not limited by the assumptions of linear time, and knowledge can travel across the boundaries of realities ordinarily perceived by Westerners. This cultural fact forces us to look beyond commonly accepted notions of oral transmission to a kind of communication that challenges some of our fundamental assumptions about time and place. Because we have no vocabulary for this kind of transmission, known in many cultures outside our own, we have simply ignored it in most of the ethnographic literatures to which we have given birth.

Carolina chose to open her reality to the evidence offered by her experience. Her assimilation of learning was based on Mapuche notions of what we call empiricism, involving the space and time parameters of Mapuche reality. The knowledge she gained in this way was confirmed in her fourth year of pilgrimage, when she was led by her spirit guides to the dwelling of Kushé Papai, one of the greatest healers and leaders of the Andes. Kushé Papai, who already knew of Carolina's quest through her own dreams and visions, readily accepted her for a brief time as an apprentice. The elder shaman had been practicing in secret for three decades. She was the only female chief in the province of Neuquén, and she commanded such respect that no gathering of chiefs could commence without her. Toward the end of her life she was recognized as a paramount decision-maker and spiritual force among the indigenous peoples of Patagonia.

I have heard many versions of the first meeting of these two women, and all point to a profound and mutual recognition. For Carolina, this encounter was evidence that, although she remained at the periphery of contemporary Mapuche society, she was not alone. For Kushé Papai, the meeting showed that her efforts to keep the healing sciences alive and to dream herself into the minds of those who could be taught the Great Mysteries were being rewarded. Moreover, Carolina's presence proved that what had survived on the margins of culture took its power from the center of belief and that the power of women to heal could not be excised by the patriarchal and misogynist policies of the Argentine Republic.

What amazed Carolina most about Kushé Papai was that she knew of the visions Carolina's father had experienced toward the end of his imprisonment in Fort Azul, in southern Buenos Aires. In 1890 Milliapi, a respected Mapuche war chief, had been staked to the ground in the fort courtyard and left to die. To keep his spirit from leaving his body prematurely, he continually sifted sand through his fingers as a libation to Ñuke Mapu, Mother Earth. On his fourth day of anguish, a blue vision appeared to him and instructed him in a new way of doing animal sacrifices and dances for the annual rite of increase (*ŋillipún*). He was told in the vision that if he agreed to follow these instructions he would be freed. He was released and sent back to western Argentina four days after this vision.

Kushé Papai was able to describe the vision to Carolina, even though the chief had shared this information only with his intimates. Carolina has told me that Kushé Papai was able to recall even the smallest details of how people in Carolina's community, on the Malleo reservation, celebrate the *ŋillipún* ritual cycle. Kushé Papai said, "You do not see me, but I am always there, standing on the edge [periphery?] of the ritual circle."[5] When Carolina returned to her home in Malleo, she was initially cautious about acknowledging her healing skills. She practiced quietly among members of her own family, but news of her expertise slowly filtered out into the neighboring regions of Aucapán, Atreuco, and Huilquimenuco, which is now her home. Her skill made her known as an *entendida*, one who holds and understands deep things. Eventually, non-Mapuche patients began to call on her or request her services in the towns of Junín de los Andes and Zapala. At the same time, she continued to enlarge her resources, learning tarot divination from a Swiss rancher and the tea-leaf oracle from a family of gypsies, and expanding her herbal apothecary, adding remedies suggested by urban homeopathic doctors. Even when confronted with a totally new herbal infusion, Carolina continues to sit silently with the substance until a chant emerges in which the medicinal code of the substance is revealed.

To this day, her position of knowledge within her community is still one of both centrality and marginality. She wields great power in the *ŋillipún* fertility ceremony, both as the senior daughter of the chief who revised the rites and as the woman responsible for protocol and for the performance of all lineage songs. She sets the ritual calendar, confronts community members over misuses of authority, and mediates cases of sorcery. She is also a vital counselor to her brother-in-law, the current chief. Although her role as a truthsayer is central to the ongoing dynamics of reservation life, her words and the power behind them are feared by many. Because she runs a successful healing practice and has inherited one of the few fertile strips of land in the area, she is often the brunt of envy and gossip. Those Mapuche who have adopted the views and values of the Chilean-based pentecostal movement decry her as a "witch of the Antichrist" and have repeatedly killed her sheep at times that she was away on a shamanic mission.

5. This quote was consistently given by Carolina Milliapi in this way throughout 1972–1982.

In the larger context, through many centuries of warfare Mapuche women have become accustomed to independence and isolation. Absentee husbands and sons, who a century ago would have been on the battlefield, now seek employment on ranches and road-construction crews. This household pattern of absenteeism, combined with rampant alcoholism among men, continues to shift authority to the hands of women. However, the models of authority that exist in the larger, Spanish-speaking world are overwhelmingly male-centered, as was the code of the Mapuche battleground. When men return to their reservation families, they often feel and create confusion and tension over authority and decision-making. Even so, women continue to play a central role in ritual, for only they may perform the sacred vocal repertoires that link the living to the ancestors and spirits. Carolina counsels many local families and treats alcoholism by means of herbal potions and shamanic intervention. Still, she is aware of her isolation. She leads women and men in the performance of ritual, but her unique and powerful (and, to some, dangerous) skills as a healer and chanter single her out as different; and her ability to see into people's lives and through their pretenses can make her unwelcome in some homes.

The story of Carolina Milliapi is a paradigm of what art historian Josephine Withers calls "commuting between the center and the periphery."[6] Like her mentor, Kushé Papai, Carolina has managed to move a tradition that had fallen by the wayside back to a position of dignity and centrality among many contemporary Mapuche. Even though the practice of shamanic healing again has a place at the center of reservation life, however, the healer remains on the periphery, a character whose marginality and uniqueness give her access to many scenes in the drama of shifting beliefs and values. She is a powerful actor who is able both to challenge and to comply with change, and who is more comfortable sharing the paradox of her life with an outsider than with an insider.

Since I am that outsider, let me reestablish my position within this circle. Although I am an Andean person, my European ancestry and ability to move in and out of this mountain area establish my marginal status. When I was first gathering data for a dissertation I sought those individuals who would best epitomize Mapuche culture. Such persons represented my illusion of a norm, and I thought that they would provide my key to what Clifford Geertz has termed "thick description."[7] Instead I found that each individual I met stood at a different point on a continuum of inner conflict resolution and outward cultural adaptation. The

6. Josephine Withers, "Commuting Between the Center and the Periphery," paper presented at the Women's Caucus for Art, Boston, 1987.

7. Clifford Geertz, "Thick Description: Toward an Interpretive Theory of Culture," in his *The Interpretation of Cultures: Selected Essays* (New York, 1973).

Mapuche axiom that "if a question can't be argued in four different ways, it's not worth asking" gives great latitude for individuality. But my own training was not quite that flexible. It took me a long time to realize that the persons who would become instrumental in defining a Mapuche identity were those at the periphery—the nonconformists, the defiers of categories, the tricksters, the survivors of defeat.

Carolina's movement between the center and the periphery occurs on both a social and a spiritual plane. One of the characteristics of the shaman is the ability to move, often with the aid of sound, fluidly between different realities. In maintaining such fluidity the shaman often stands outside the modes of classification with which the inside culture and the alien ethnographer may be most familiar. The significance of this stance will become clearer as we turn our concerns toward a particular kind of performer in Polynesia who defies our Western, bi-polar notions of gender.

Hawaiian Performers: Mediating the Polarization of Gender

If [a māhū child] is given to your family, you try to raise it with pride, so that it can see that it too has a gift to bring to the community. That used to be a good life for the māhū—*the best of both worlds. But today people judge more, and that child might have a hard time. Usually we take such a child into the hula family, because there the special creative gifts they have can be put to good use.*[8]

Whereas among the Mapuche a *machi* these days might appear once among four hundred individuals, one *māhū*, or mixed-gender individual, in Hawai'i might be found for every nine others, especially on the island of Moloka'i. These differences in the frequency of occurrence of *machi* and *māhū* mandate diverse methods of research and styles of presentation. Since being a *māhū* creates controversies, much discretion must be exercised in discussing individuals whom Westerners tend to lump into a monolithic category based on presumed sexual orientation. Initially I defined the *māhū* as androgynous. However, the astounding variety of gender manifestations throughout Hawai'i has led me to replace androgyny with the broader notion of mixed gender. This mix occurs in permutations that defy some of the most basic Western assumptions about gender.

Field research in Hawai'i has yielded many emic terms for persons of mixed and indeterminate gender as well as evidence that, in many areas of Polynesia, these individuals play an ancient role that has survived missionization and the polarized view of gender introduced by Western-

8. Georgina Shito, Maui, 1988. Georgina is a respected musician who was raised on the island of Moloka'i with Auntie Moana (discussed below).

ers. Through examples drawn from this research I wish to show that the role of the *māhū* is to commute between the center and the periphery. The vehicles most often used for this commute are music and dance.

Western views of the Pacific have been molded by the moral judgments and sexual attitudes of nineteenth-century missionaries and Victorian ethnographers. The missionary element that invaded Polynesia—especially Tahiti, Hawai'i, and Samoa—has been described by Alan Moorehead as "the most primitive, inflexible end of the range of eighteenth century Calvinism."[9] Although many early ethnographers of the Pacific focused on various forms of *kapu* (tabu) and restrictions governing social transactions and ritual conventions, they were blind to their own cultural tabus.

Fortunately, contemporary ethnographers of the Pacific have begun to set aside some of the more profound Victorian prejudices. In *Women of Polynesia*, Tui Terrence Barrow includes a significant section entitled "The Intermediate Sex." Therein he describes this phenomenon quite clearly:

> Sex is to the Polynesians a very down-to-earth thing which need not be too much thought about and is certainly not repressed. Sometimes Mother Nature cannot make up her mind whether to make a man or a woman, even in Polynesia, so she mixes up a little of the male with some of the female element. In Polynesia transvestites in whom male and female are not clearly differentiated, either at the physical or the psychic level[,] are called the *māhū* who, although physically speaking more men than women, prefer to dress and act as women.[10]

My own field research shows that in Hawai'i even transvestism is only one point on a broad continuum of gender-blending. Several elderly men have told me that after their parents had begotten many sons and no daughters, they had made the decision to raise their youngest son as a girl. This way of compensating for gender imbalance in the family provides additional labor for female tasks and insures a creative presence that otherwise might not surface in a homocentric household. (I use the term *homocentric*—as opposed to *heterocentric*—to indicate a situation focused only on one gender.)

Some of these men raised as women eventually choose to marry women and embrace a male procreative role, but most of them accept the mixed-gender, *māhū* role for life, whether or not they have children. What this information shows us is that, contrary to the stereotype propounded by ethnographers who have focused their observations on the Hawai'i of

9. Alan Moorehead, *The Fatal Impact: The Invasion of the South Pacific, 1767–1840* (New York, 1987), p. 98.
10. T. Barrow, *Women of Polynesia* (Wellington, New Zealand, 1967), p. 76.

male war gods and human sacrifices, women were highly valued in Hawai'i.

A study of Hawaiian religion confirms the importance of women. Despite the male homocentric literature concerning the islands, we have ample evidence that women had their own spiritual and social practices, which centered on goddesses. The male gods (Ku, Kane, Kanaloa, Lono) and their male advocates focused on warfare, gender-restricted *heiaus* (temples), and the authority of chiefs and priests. These gods have all been abandoned now. Lono, however, as the god of agriculture and fishing, was an exception to this concentration on blood, and to this day Lono is revered by fishermen and farmers. The goddesses, by contrast, were all linked to phenomena in nature. Because these elements of the natural world still govern the lives of many Hawaiians, the relationship of humans with the goddesses persists. Paramount among these beings are Pele, goddess of volcanoes and genealogical ancestor of many families in the Puna and Ka'u districts; Hi'iaka, junior sister of Pele (or one of her many personae), linked to regeneration of the land and the birth of *hula*; Hina, the moon goddess and mother of the island of Moloka'i as well as of the demi-god Maui, the trickster; and Laka, goddess of the *hula*. Many modern Hawaiians see Laka as an androgynous deity. On Moloka'i, Laka is sometimes seen as the female element associated with healing, and Kapo is seen as the male element that fosters sorcery. The dual nature of Laka/Kapo is especially important to the *hula*, which attracts more mixed-gender performers than any other activity.

Further evidence of the importance of women in Hawaiian culture can be seen in the vocal tradition known as *leo ki'eki'e* or *pu'ukane nahenahe* (sweet voices). Derived from the *himeni* (hymn) style introduced by missionaries combined with the yodeling techniques of Spanish-speaking cowboys (*paniolo*, for *español*), this vocal style employs what in the West we call falsetto, even though there is nothing false about singing in this register. This type of singing became extremely popular among men in the nineteenth century, who often had to sing without female companions. The quality of female voices was so greatly prized that many men chose this sharp contrast between registers as a way of bringing aesthetic balance into homocentric performance. Today, the Ho'opi'i brothers, the Cazimero brothers, Ledward Ka'apana, Sam Bernard, and Kekua Fernandes are among the finest practitioners of this art. Indeed, this style has been so popular in this century that today many virtuosic women have taken up the *leo ki'eki'e* style. In other words, we now have "women imitating men who are imitating women."[11]

11. This description is used by ethnomusicologist Ricardo Trimillos in the Robert Muggee film *Hawaiian Rainbow*, 1988.

The abandonment of male war gods and the persistence of nature goddesses, the aesthetic preferences expressed in falsetto singing, and the practice of raising some boys as girls together challenge Valerio Valeri's claim that women were marginal to Hawaiian ritual and social systems. In a way, they were marginal to the male homocentric system—just as males were marginal to women's menstruation huts and birthing rites. The fatal flaw in Valeri's analysis is that he never questions his polarization of gender.[12] Thus, he translates the notion of *kapu* as a connotation of male sacredness and the notion of *noa* as female defilement and impurity. A closer look at the complexity of Hawaiian semantics shows that *kapu* could be seen as representing the laws and boundaries erected by men, who identify themselves with their gods and temples, and *noa* could be interpreted as the dissolution of those boundaries by female power, which requires no temple other than those provided by nature. The ritual fear of *noa* in the male system could then be seen as a recognition that women can *transform* male power into ordinary terms through demystification.

Yet another challenge to Valeri's polarization of gender is the respected presence of the *māhū* in all performance traditions. Still another is expressed in the *mana'o* (opinion, vision) of Mary Kawena Pukui, one of Hawai'i's greatest cultural authorities:

> The hermaphrodites—also referred to as *māhū*—said to have landed at Waikiki were respected men; talented priests of healing and the *hula*. Whether this is history or legend, it reflects attitudes of approval and admiration. . . . "And," says Mrs. Pukui, "Hawaiians always knew we had in us something feminine and masculine."[13]

Today, the term *māhū* can designate men and women who procreate and raise children, hermaphrodites with male genitals and noticeable breasts, women who dress and work as men, men who wear trousers as well as long hair and earrings, men who dress "festively," women who present themselves fully as women but have same-gender relationships, men and women who present themselves as female-centered but have no sexual relationships, individuals who present themselves as sexually uninterested in both genders, men who dress as women and seek additional ways to seem feminine, and men who undergo hormone treatments and those who eventually have their sex altered surgically. These are but a few of the most noticeable permutations of gender in Hawaiian life. Performance offers an arena wherein gender can be mediated and wherein the

12. Valerio Valeri, *Kingship and Sacrifice: Ritual and Society in Ancient Hawaii*, trans. Paula Wissing (Chicago, 1985).

13. Mary Kawena Pukui, E. W. Haertig, and Catherine A. Lee, *Nana I Ke Kumu*, vol. 2 (Honolulu, 1972), p. 110. Although Pukui is in fact the primary author, the book presents her as a source cited by the white authors.

polarized attitudes of maleness and femaleness introduced by the missionaries can be challenged and softened. Almost every imaginable combination of gender identities can be found in the *hula* performance contexts, except for women who dress and work as men. *Hula*, after all, is an art form that since the reign of King David Kalakaua (1883–1891) has been associated with femaleness. It was not until 1973 that male *hula* schools reemerged and dance became an accepted career for young men.

Many of those *māhū* whose presentation of self defies gender classifications are characterized by a corpulence that harks back to ancient Hawai'i, where physical bulk was equated with high status. Marshall Sahlins, who tells us that in old Hawai'i "famous ruling chiefs were bisexual," goes on to say:

> The ideal beauty of the chief is counterpart of his or her ideal potency—
> and we are speaking, of course, of ideals. The high chief is "divine," as we
> should say ourselves: huge, fattened, skin lightened by protection from
> the sun, body glistening with perfumed oil, bedecked in the dazzling feather
> cape that is the treasure of his kingdom. Any why not generate a king-
> dom on such a fundament? Existing only in the eye of the beholder,
> beauty is necessarily a social relationship. . . . In Hawaii, beauty is placed as
> it were at the center of society, as a main principle of its organization.[14]

Many *māhū* literally embody this aesthetic. Their corpulence bespeaks their *mana* or spiritual power. But modern city life has made the practice of fattening hazardous to the health. Persons who in the sixteenth to the eighteenth century would have offset their four to seven hundred pounds with surfing and other activities today live a sedentary life of motor transportation, food additives, and too little fish and *taro* root. Most *māhū* of massive size who are involved in the *hula* tradition serve as teachers, drummers, and chanters—in Hawaiian, *ho'opa'a*, the ones who "memorize" and remain "fixed," as opposed to the dancers, or *'olapa*, who are "movable." Mixed-gender masters of the *hula* who have received acclaim are seen as role models by other mixed-gender individuals who might otherwise fear ridicule or rejection in some communities. To amplify our view of this role, I will mention a handful of such teachers and performers.

Darrell Lupenui, who died in August 1987 from illnesses related to obesity (heart and kidney failure) channeled his several hundred pounds of *mana* (spiritual power) into changing the face of the *hula*. He pioneered in developing a strong, aggressive male style in his *halau* (dance school) known as the Men of Waimapuna. He won titles at the Merrie Monarch Festival with both his male and female dancers in 1978, 1979, 1980, and 1986. In that year his group of male dancers performed at the festival clad only in scanty loincloths that left the buttocks exposed and drove the

---

14. Marshall Sahlins, *Islands of History* (Chicago, 1985), pp. 10, 17.

audience into a frenzy of approval. He holds the perpetual trophy for *Kane Hula* (male *hula*). Lupenui, who taught some of Hawai'i's finest musicians, worked closely with his mother, Muriel, who was one of his main sources of knowledge and inspiration. On 21 September 1987, his death was mourned and celebrated in a concert featuring some of the dancers and musicians he had taught, challenged, and motivated. Both the stage and the audience on that night were filled with persons of every gender permutation imaginable, for it was one of their own who was being venerated.

At that concert Sam Bernard, one of Hawai'i's most gifted falsetto singers, in Lupenui's honor did a *hula*, after many years of not dancing because of his size. His agility and humor brought him a standing ovation. Bernard took Lupenui's death as a danger signal for himself, and has since been trying to reduce his weight to four hundred pounds. He is especially concerned because he has "hanai'd" (adopted) a little girl to whom he is devoted. Bernard, a gentle and compassionate individual, is greatly loved in the music community. He sings with the Sam Bernard Trio, which also includes *kuma hula* Kaulana Kasparovich. Kasparovich's greatest success has been in the children's *hula* movement (*keiki hula*), which now has its own annual competition. He introduces the little girls in his Lehua Dance Company to his mid-gendered persona by telling them they must think of him as their "festive uncle." He aspires to create a line of young male dancers that will embody his particular vision of physical beauty in movement.

One of the most beautiful performers and teachers of *hula* on Oahu is the svelte and elegant Leina'ala Paleka Mattos, whose women have performed to great acclaim throughout the history of the Merrie Monarch Festival. She graces the stage as a paragon of womanhood even though, according to Western norms, she was born male. Clearly the identity to which she has adhered over the years is more important to her community than is the sexual equipment with which she was born. During the 1988 event I sat next to a young *māhū* who, bedecked in flowing purple gown, a crown of flowers, and a necklace of dog's teeth, wept to see Leina'ala recognized as a legitimate member of *wahine hula* (women's *hula*).

One of the most influential mixed-gender performers in the traditional Hawaiian community today is Auntie Moana, who lives on Moloka'i. Auntie Moana's original name was Maurice. As a youth active in oratory and performance in the Catholic church of Wailua, Maurice became known as Butchie, for he reminded his family of a "butch" (masculine) girl. He excelled in school and played on his high school football team. In the ninth grade he began studying *hula* with Auntie Harriet Ne, and he went through his *uniki* (*hula* graduation) ceremony when he was in the twelfth grade. At the time of his *uniki*, he requested that he not have to dance bare-chested, as a man; so his teacher designed a special leaf costume to hide his breasts. It was around this time that Butchie began the transformation to the persona now known as Moana— "Auntie Moana" to *her* students of *hula*. Today Moana dresses in shorts, T-shirts, and earrings during the day, when she drives the school bus and directs the school transportation system for the whole island. At night she dons flowing silk overblouses that soften her quarterback physique, tapered black slacks, and makeup, and becomes the head waitress at the Hotel Moloka'i. There, truly in her element, she often performs with her students and with the *māhū* in her family. Many years ago she adopted (through the *hanai* system) a young boy who took the name Raquel, who is now her assistant in the girl's *hula* school. Moana is one of the few people on Moloka'i who do not drink or smoke (the island has a staggeringly high rate of alcoholism). She is also the main source of AIDS counseling in her community and often intercedes in families where child abuse is taking place. Most people on Moloka'i would agree that if you want something done on this island you must go to the *māhū* community, for they have managed to create a bridge of hope in a situation ravaged by unemployment and cultural depression.

Through my work with Moana I learned that, at least in this setting, the lesson of the *māhū* is one of compassion. She has made her own kind visible, acceptable, and indispensable to the island. She has also proven that the true spirit of *aloha* is acceptance of diversity, and that a position on the periphery can be a sacred gift that can transport what might seem marginal to the center of cultural discourse.

Midwifery Revisited: Birthing a New Attitude Toward Gender

These brief biographical data may help to underline the rigidity of gender as we have interpreted it in the West and to emphasize the astounding variety of gender as it exists in human experience. The literatures of mainstream anthropology and feminist scholarship do not help us internalize the diversity of gender, for they insist on questionable bipolar models that ignore the existence of the *māhū* in Hawai'i and Tahiti, the *fa'a fafine* and *fa'a tama* of Samoa, the *bissu* of Indonesia, the *hijras* of India, the *kokalaka* and *wintke* among the Lakota, the *lhamana* among the Zuni, and countless other mixed-gender identities throughout the world. Exceptions to the exclusion of those who might be perceived as marginal are found in works that espouse interdisciplinary, cross-cultural approaches to the study of gender.[15] Ivan Illich has shown that in the West Christianity transformed the concept of gender into that of sex. His approach to gender as a political and economic issue may eventually lead musicologists and ethnomusicologists to reexamine the theocratic roots of our academic biases.[16]

Rather than putting the male/female dichotomy at the center of our models, let us experiment with putting the *māhū* or mixed gender at the center and the polarization of gender at the periphery. For if, as Mary Pukui says, "Hawaiians always knew we had in us something feminine and masculine," then the *māhū* stands as the embodiment of an ancient cultural ideal of integration. There is of course in the West at least a tentative vocabulary for this idea of spiritual and psychological completeness: Carl Jung's terminology of *anima* and *animus*. In fact, a Jungian might explain the *māhū* as part of a universal continuum of anima and animus integration.

The Hawaiian *māhū* commutes between the center and the periphery through the medium of performance. The Andean *machi* also lives on the margins of everyday gender expectation, for by virtue of her ritual responsibilities she lives in a gray area between male and female. Her femaleness qualifies her to speak directly with the spirit world; but her spiritual discourse puts her outside the normal gender categories and behaviors of her community.

The cultural bias surrounding the topics of gender, spirituality, and marginality makes our responsibility in giving birth to a literature of ethnomusicology all the more staggering. If we want to provide a true picture of musical life in our host communities, we must make visible those whose modes of self-expression may embarrass us or threaten the boundaries that make us feel safe and give supremacy to our version of reality. We will understand these unfamiliar roles and the reasons why performance often attracts or requires gender variance only by bringing these individuals into cross-cultural dialogue. We must realize, too, that

15. For example, Peggy Reeves Sanday, *Female Power and Male Dominance: On the Origins of Sexual Inequality* (Cambridge, 1981); Paula Gunn Allen, *The Sacred Hoop: Recovering the Feminine in American Indian Traditions* (Boston, 1986); Caroline Walker Bynum, Stevan Harrell, and Paula Richman, eds., *Gender and Religion: On the Complexity of Symbols* (Boston, 1986); Walter L. Williams, *The Spirit and the Flesh: Sexual Diversity in American Indian Culture* (Boston, 1986); Judith Lynne Hanna, "Patterns of Dominance: Men, Women, and Homosexuality in Dance," *Drama Review* 31 (1987): 22–47; Robert I. Levy, *The Tahitians: Mind and Experience in the Society Islands* (Chicago, 1973); Gilbert H. Herdt, ed., *Ritualized Homosexuality in Melanesia* (Berkeley, 1984); June Singer, *Androgyny: Toward a New Theory of Sexuality* (Garden City, N.Y., 1977); Wendy Doniger O'Flaherty, *Women, Androgynes, and Other Mythical Beasts* (Chicago, 1980).

16. Ivan Illich, *Gender* (New York, 1982).

commuting between the center and the periphery can require great courage. The Polynesian *māhū* and the Mapuche *machi* merit our respect, for they are the individuals within their communities who, in daring to be themselves at a very dear price, become the truthsayers.

The ethnomusicologist is often engaged in a dance of midwifery. She can coach or nurse the tradition she studies into public perception, but she may not excise its limbs when they do not move to the rhythms of the scholarly world. She is not the parent of the tradition; she is merely the facilitator. Yet how she brings the tradition into the light may determine its survival and its acceptance. This is an awesome responsibility. Here, the birthing technique of the midwife is negotiated through her own cultural politics and through her willingness to address central cultural issues that have been rendered invisible by the theocratic codes of our disciplines.

Western study of music has been guided primarily by a doctrine of aesthetics that judges composition and performance in terms of culture-bound attitudes toward structure and significance. The inclusion of particular repertoires and traditions in music research and performance hinges on criteria that emerge out of a complex struggle in academia to define which musical traditions are worthy of mainstream status and which are peripheral to our deeper understanding of musical processes. On the whole, mainstream creations in some way mirror the power structures and personalities that govern the discipline of musicology. That is to say, the attitude seems to be that a glimpse of my own reflection in the music is what makes it worthy of study. I have no quarrel with this consistent and subjective mode of assigning value; it seems inherent in the habits of our species. I object, rather, to the assumption that if something does *not* reflect my image it is *unworthy* of study—and to the belief that if an altogether different reflection emerges, it poses a threat to the status quo of the discipline. This mode of selection and research gives us a musical mainstream that mirrors images of white men who aspire to identification with a cultural and social elite. The power structure of musicology reflects the power structures imposed by many centuries of colonialism. But as we approach the twenty-first century a turning of the tables is occurring, with difference no longer a state to be ignored. Rather, we are faced with an urgent need to expand the parameters of our musical knowledge by including scholars cut from other fabrics and ideas about music born in other cultural settings. Those traditions and views relegated to the periphery are now moving to the center to redefine the very essence of music research. Such movement from the periphery to the center, again, is accomplished through a kind of midwifery, wherein ideas from a variety of sources are infused with life and guided into new patterns of growth.

Cultural synergy may rest in the hands of those who are willing to wear many masks, play many roles, and defy the stasis of the mainstream. Change, when seen as a constant in any living tradition, always seems to yield a fool or trickster who embodies the paradox of experience and who transforms the perception of truths in order to open discourse between the center and the periphery.

Women as Musicians:
A Question of Class

Nancy B. Reich

Now that the women musicians of nineteenth-century Europe are becoming visible,[1] it is time to look at them closely and question some previously held assumptions about women in musical life. But to view them as being one entity by virtue of their all being female is misleading. Although I believe that all women musicians, particularly composers, suffered from certain restrictions because of their gender, the question of class also plays a large part in nineteenth-century European music history and must be addressed.

The professional woman musician was a member of a class that definitely existed but has not been adequately defined. Descriptions of class divisions can be treacherous; in the 1860s, Émile Zola made such an attempt, dividing French society into five worlds. His final category, "*un monde à part* consisting of whores, murderers, priests, and artists,"[2] obviously will not do here. For want of a better term, I will refer to professional musicians as members of an artist-musician class, a category which includes actors, artists, artisans, dancers, writers, and practitioners of allied professions. They had in common an artistic output and a low economic level. Above all, they depended on their work for a livelihood.[3]

1. With thanks to Renate Bridenthal, Claudia Koonz, and Susan Stuard, eds., *Becoming Visible: Women in European History*, 2d ed. (Boston, 1987).

2. Peter Gay, *The Bourgeois Experience: Victoria to Freud*. Vol. 1: *Education of the Senses* (New York, 1984), pp. 21–22.

3. The soprano Clara Kathleen Rogers (Clara Doria), daughter of John Barnett, English voice teacher and composer, recalled an incident from her childhood when other children were separated from the Barnett girls at a beach "because [the Barnetts] are not gentlefolks like you; their father's only a music-master and he works for his living!" (*Memories of a Musical Career* [Boston, 1919], p. 26.) Rogers also describes a select girls' school where she and her sister were the only pupils whose father was a "bread winner" (p. 85).

Professional women musicians were working women but did not belong to the working class. Most were married to men who accepted, even encouraged, their participation in the workplace.[4] Many were mothers who had to deal with pregnancies in the midst of careers and arrange for the care of their children. Almost all professional women musicians were born into families in which members worked together to earn a living and had done so for more than one generation. In these families, the participation of women in professional life was taken for granted.[5] Of thirty-six working musicians studied, twenty-seven were from the artist-musician class; the other nine had parents who were ardent music lovers and encouraged their daughters' professional involvement in music. Of the thirty-one who were married, four retired from public musical life at marriage (but two returned) and five modified their careers at marriage. Twenty-one are known to have had children, one as many as ten (see Table 1). These women competed, as the men did, for the honors and rewards of a musician's life.

The nonprofessional musicians, women from aristocratic families or from what has been called "the bourgeois aristocracy,"[6] were gifted, highly educated, skilled—and at a disadvantage compared to professional women musicians. Henriette Voigt, Fanny Hensel, Livia Frege, and Elisabeth von Herzogenberg, for example, composed, sang, played instruments, conducted, instructed, and judged on a professional level. But their participation in musical life was private: they neither performed in public nor published their work. Because they did not undergo the scrutiny of reviewers and compete for the attention and money of audiences, they did not grow artistically and sharpen their skills as the

4. Soon after her marriage in April 1831 to Camille Pleyel, composer and piano manufacturer, Marie Moke Pleyel wrote to a friend that her husband "has willingly consented to my continuing to give lessons; you know that I am very attached to my independence." (Rita Benton, "Pleyel," *The New Grove Dictionary of Music and Musicians*, ed. Stanley Sadie [London, 1980], vol. 15, p. 11.)

5. Throughout the eighteenth century, women had been employed in court musical establishments; most were singers but there were instrumentalists among them as well. Josepha Müllner (1769–1843), court harpist in Vienna, was harp soloist in the orchestra and harp teacher of the archduchesses. Caroline (Schleicher) Krähmer (1794–ca. 1850), clarinetist and violinist, took over her father's duties as a town musician at his death but left when she was offered a position in the orchestra of the Duke of Baden. Women from the artist-musician class who carried on the family tradition over several generations included the Benda-Reichardts, the Garcia-Malibran-Viardots, the Tromlitz-Wiecks, and the Wurm-Vernes.

6. "These men could now live in a style which resembled that of the nobility closely enough that they became part of the cities' high society. In fact, it became common in the three capitals [London, Paris, Berlin] to refer to a 'bourgeois aristocracy,' a 'financial nobility,' or a 'second high society.'" (William Weber, *Music and the Middle Class: The Social Structure of Concert Life in London, Paris and Vienna* [New York, 1975], p. 8.)

TABLE 1 Class and Marital Status of Thirty-six Professional Women
Musicians of the Nineteenth Century

Professional Name	Artist-Musician Class[a]	Married	Children[b]
Louise Reichardt, 1779–1826 (composer, choral director)	Yes	No	None
Dorette Spohr, 1787–1834 (harpist)	Yes	Yes	4
Maria Szymanowska, 1789–1831 (composer, pianist)	No	Yes	3
Lucy Anderson, 1790–1878 (pianist)	Yes	Yes	?
Caroline Krähmer, 1794–ca. 1850 (clarinetist, violinist)	Yes	Yes	10 (most did not survive infancy)
Margarethe Stockhausen, 1803–1877 (singer)	No	Yes	6
Wilhelmine Schröder-Devrient, 1804–1860 (singer)	Yes	Yes	4
Louise Farrenc, 1804–1875 (composer, pianist)	Yes (artists)	Yes	1
Henriette Sontag, 1805–1854 (singer)[c]	Yes	Yes	Yes
Louise Bertin, 1805–1877 (composer)	Yes (journalists)	No	?
Maria Malibran, 1808–1836 (singer, composer)	Yes	Yes	2
Anna de Belleville-Oury, 1808–1880 (pianist)	Yes	Yes	Yes
Marie (Camille) Pleyel, 1811–1875 (pianist)	Yes	Yes	Yes
Léopoldine Blahetka, 1809–1885 (composer, pianist)	Yes	No	?
Josephine Lang, 1815–1880 (composer, pianist)	Yes	Yes	6
Clara Novello, 1818–1908 (singer)[d]	Yes	Yes	4
Clara Schumann, 1819–1896 (pianist, composer)	Yes	Yes	8 (7 survived infancy)

(continued)

TABLE 1 *(continued)*

Professional Name	Artist-Musician Class[a]	Married	Children[b]
Rowena Laidlaw, 1819–1901 (pianist)[e]	Yes	Yes	?
Jenny Lind, 1820–1887 (singer)	No	Yes	3
Pauline Viardot, 1821–1910 (singer, composer, pianist)[f]	Yes	Yes	5
Teresa Milanollo, 1827–1904 (violinist)[g]	No	Yes	?
Wilhelmine Clauss-Szarvady, 1834–1907 (pianist)[h]	No	Yes	?
Arabella Goddard, 1836–1922 (pianist)	No	Yes	2
Wilma Neruda (Lady Hallé), 1838–1911 (violinist)	Yes	Yes	?
Amalie Joachim, 1839–1898 (singer)[i]	No	Yes	6
Ingeborg von Bronsart, 1840–1913 (pianist, composer)[j]	Yes	Yes	?
Camilla Urso, 1842–1902 (violinist)	Yes	Yes	None
Adelina Patti, 1843–1919 (singer)[k]	Yes	Yes	?
Clara Kathleen Rogers, 1844–1931 (composer, singer)[l]	Yes	Yes	None
Sophie Menter, 1846–1918 (pianist)	Yes	Yes	Yes
Agathe Backer-Grøndahl, 1847–1907 (composer, pianist)	Yes	Yes	4
Luise Adolpha Le Beau, 1850–1927 (composer)	No	No	None
Teresa Carreño, 1853–1917 (pianist, composer)[m]	No	Yes	6
Mary Wurm, 1860–1938 (pianist)[n]	Yes	No	?

(continued)

TABLE 1   *(continued)*

Professional Name	Artist-Musician Class[a]	Married	Children[b]
Marie Soldat-Röger, 1863–1955 (violinist)	Yes	Yes	?
Ilona Eibenschütz, 1873–1967 (pianist)[o]	Yes	Yes	Yes

SOURCE: Modeled after Table 3 in Marcia J. Citron, "Women and the Lied, 1775–1850," in Jane Bowers and Judith Tick, eds., *Women Making Music: The Western Art Tradition, 1150–1950* (Urbana, 1986), p. 229.

[a]In each case in which a musician was from a class other than the artist-musician, she had parents who were skilled amateurs and supported the musical education and career of their daughter.

[b]Numbers given here may be understatements: many children died in infancy; some artists kept the existence of their children secret.

[c]Retired from career at marriage in 1830 but returned in 1848.

[d]Retired from career at marriage in 1843 but returned in 1850.

[e]Retired from career at marriage in 1855.

[f]Younger sister of Maria Malibran; see above. Daughter, Louise Héritte-Viardot, 1841–1918, was also a professional musician.

[g]Retired from career at marriage in 1857.

[h]Made few appearances after marriage.

[i]Retired from opera at marriage in 1855 but continued career as singer.

[j]Left concert stage at marriage in 1862 and turned to composition.

[k]Sister, Carlotta Patti (1835–1889), was also a professional musician.

[l]Left concert stage at marriage in 1878 but continued career as a teacher.

[m]Grandfather a musician.

[n]Younger sisters, Mathilde (1865–1936) and Adele Verne (1877–1952), were also professional musicians.

[o]Retired from career at marriage in 1902 but made some recordings thereafter.

professionals did. Some, such as Fanny Hensel and Livia Frege, diverted their talents into home musicales somewhat in the tradition of the political and literary salons of the eighteenth and early nineteenth centuries.[7] There were some rare spirits from the ranks of the aristocracy or the bourgeois aristocracy, such as the Vicomtesse Marie de Grandval and Ethel Smyth, who did turn professional. For most well-to-do women, however, family background hindered aspirations.

Throughout the nineteenth century and well into the twentieth, then, we see women musicians on two tracks: on the one hand the composers whose listeners were restricted to friends and family, on the other hand

7. See Carolyn C. Lougee, *Le Paradis des Femmes: Women, Salons, and Social Stratification in Seventeenth-Century France* (Princeton, 1976); Deborah Hertz, *Jewish High Society in Old Regime Berlin* (New Haven, 1988); and Hilde Spiel, *Fanny von Arnstein oder die Emanzipation: Ein Frauenleben an der Zeitwende 1758–1819* (Frankfurt, 1962).

women whose published works were performed in public auditoriums and reviewed in widely read periodicals; on the one hand women who sang and played only in the privacy of their own homes, on the other hand women who appeared on concert and opera stages in London, Paris, Vienna, Berlin, and St. Petersburg; on the one hand women who taught young ladies in genteel parlors and did not get paid for their work, on the other hand women who held positions in the great conservatories and trained potential concert artists; on the one hand women whose musical lives were limited to their own homes and their immediate community, on the other hand women who left home and family to tour, sometimes for as long as three years at a stretch, in America, India, Australia, and Africa.

As a result of the congruence of the French Revolution, the economic and technological changes introduced by industrialization and capitalism, the growth of a prosperous middle class, and the ideologies of the romantic movement, the distinction between the professional and the non-professional woman musician was drawn more sharply in the nineteenth century than it had been in earlier periods. Moreover, the nineteenth century brought to women musicians problems, handicaps, and strains they had not faced earlier.

After the French Revolution, musical life increasingly became the province of the middle class,[8] but this circumstance was not necessarily an advantage for women musicians. It is true that the founding of new institutions by the bourgeoisie created more employment opportunities for musicians, both male and female.[9] But it must be remembered that in the world of music, whether controlled by the court aristocrats or the urban middle class, power and authority were still exerted by the male members of society. Men held the important posts in music education and publishing, formed the committees making decisions for concert organizations and festivals, conducted the orchestras, hired the players, and determined the fees.

Furthermore, women were specifically excluded from the freedoms and rights in the new codes that extended the civil and legal rights of middle-class males. Bonnie Anderson and Judith Zinsser point out that

8. Weber points out that "after the end of the Napoleonic wars a new era began in the history of the concert world, one in which the middle class began taking on dramatic new roles" (*Music and the Middle Class*, p. 6).

9. These new institutions included music festivals and concert organizations, concert halls, new and expanded music publishing companies, a growing piano-building industry, musical journals and dictionaries of music (of which several were especially designed for women), and, above all, educational institutions to which talented students, both male and female, were admitted.

"women *lost* power, both relatively and absolutely." The small group of (mainly married) women of the bourgeois and aristocratic classes who had previously possessed some legal and economic privileges were now deprived of them.[10] The primary role of the female in the postrevolutionary world became that of nurturer of the young: "Women: Do you want to be republicans? Love, obey, and teach the laws that remind your husbands and children to exercise their rights."[11] Persuaded by such statements as "it is horrible, it is contrary to all the laws of nature for a woman to want to make herself a man," the revolutionary Paris government barred women from its sessions in 1793,[12] and in the same year the French government outlawed all women's political activity.[13] In the English Reform Act of 1832 the word *male* was for the first time inserted in franchise requirements. Legal codes such as the Allgemeines Landrecht (1794) and the Napoleonic Code (1804) limited the property rights of women and even legislated such functions as breast feeding.[14] Family laws regarding marriage, children, property, and divorce that discriminated against women did not begin to be changed until the final decades of the nineteenth century.[15]

And although working and middle-class women (as well as some intellectual aristocrats) took an active part in the revolution, many undoubtedly hoping for advances in political and legal status, the postrevolutionary emphasis on home and family, stability, and property destroyed these hopes. In the reaction to the dramatic events of the revolution—and this not only in France, but throughout Europe— women of all classes were considered to be the property of their hus-

10. Bonnie S. Anderson and Judith P. Zinsser, *A History of Their Own: Women in Europe from Prehistory to the Present*, 2 vols. (New York, 1988), vol. 2, pp. 148, 149. My emphasis.

11. Quoted from Paule-Marie Duhet, *Les femmes et la révolution 1789–1794*, in Bonnie G. Smith, *Changing Lives: Women in European History Since 1700* (Lexington, Mass., 1989), p. 130.

12. A French legislator, quoted in Anderson and Zinsser, *A History of Their Own*, vol. 2, p. 148.

13. Ibid., p. 147. For documentary evidence of women's action and society's reaction between 1789 and 1795, see Darline Gay Levy, Harriet Branson Applewhite, and Mary Durham Johnson, eds., *Women in Revolutionary Paris, 1789–1795: Selected Documents, Translated with Notes and Commentary* (Urbana, 1980).

14. Anderson and Zinsser, *A History of Their Own*, vol. 2, p. 147. Also see Susan Groag Bell and Karen M. Offen, eds., *Women, the Family, and Freedom: The Debate in Documents*, 2 vols. (Stanford, 1985), vol. 1, pp. 38–40, for excerpts from the Allgemeines Landrecht and the Napoleonic Code on marriage and the respective rights and duties of husband and wife.

15. See Anderson and Zinsser, *A History of Their Own*, vol. 2, pp. 149–51; and Gay, *Education of the Senses*, p. 174, where he writes, "Throughout much of the bourgeois century, all across the Western world, women remained virtual chattels in the hands of their fathers and, later, of their husbands."

bands, and motherhood was elevated to a position of sainthood. The situation has been described in this way:

> Running *parallel* to the liberation of man as a "citizen" whose whole exis-
> tence and energies are devoted to "society" and its daily economic, political,
> and social struggles, is the commitment of woman and her whole being to
> her house and family, and the utilization of the family as "refuge" from daily
> struggles.[16]

The emphasis on the home as the proper sphere of woman and the subsequent "cult of domesticity" that developed during the first half of the nineteenth century must have caused considerable conflict for and perhaps even embarrassment to professional women musicians, but for them earning money was a real necessity, and so they continued to leave home and work.

Artistically gifted women of the growing middle class in the new patriarchal capitalist economy may also have experienced frustration. They now had the leisure to study drawing and music, skills formerly available only to royalty and the aristocracy. Some distinct talents emerged from the musical training intended merely to provide enter-tainment and pave the way to better marriages, but pressure from male family members and society thwarted full development of these talents and discouraged even the most gifted from taking music too seriously. The upwardly-mobile middle-class male may well have feared that ac-cepting money for work performed by the women of his family would weaken his control of the household and reflect on his ability to provide. Worse than this possible disgrace, however, was the shadow of unre-spectability (a suggestion of exhibitionism in the public display of talents and even of one's body) that still clung to the world of theater and, by extension, to music. The appearance of a woman on the concert stage could undermine the hard-won social status of her bourgeois family; consequently, even the most gifted were expected to confine their musical activities to the home.

Those professionals who married into the bourgeoisie or aristocracy were expected to abandon their careers and cross over into the ranks of the nonprofessionals, thus gaining social status and respectability but relinquishing earning power. Clara Novello (1818–1908) and Henriette Sontag (1805–1854) both duly crossed over, but each returned to her professional career when her husband suffered financial reverses. Sontag was the daughter of a comedian and an actress and, at eighteen, the

16. Herbert Marcuse, "Autorität und Familie in der deutschen Soziologie bis 1933," quoted by Renate Möhrmann, "The Reading Habits of Women in the Vormärz," in John C. Fout, ed., *German Women in the Nineteenth Century: A Social History* (New York, 1984), p. 108.

soprano soloist in the first performance of Beethoven's Ninth Symphony. She married Count Rossi, an Italian diplomat who, one critic wrote, "did not publicly announce the marriage until after his wife . . . had made a very lucrative concert tour."[17] When, some eighteen years later, the count had financial troubles, he resigned his diplomatic position so that his wife could resume her career and support the family. Countess Rossi, however, was declared déclassé because of her return to professional singing. Novello had a similar experience.[18]

Romantic attitudes toward gender also played a significant part in separating the professional from the nonprofessional musician. Jean-Jacques Rousseau's pronouncements on the duties and education of females had a long-lasting influence on opinions about women and their place in society[19]—a place which was, as Abraham Mendelssohn firmly told his musician-daughter Fanny, as a housewife in the home.[20] As early as 1777, Johann Bernhard Basedow and Joachim Heinrich Campe, pedagogues in the tradition of Rousseau, specifically singled out women who worked in the musical or dramatic arts as bad wives, housekeepers, and mothers.[21]

Furthermore, the romantic ethos idolized the male artist-creator who incorporated in his art such typically "feminine" traits as deep feelings, tenderness, and sensitivity, which were regarded by the romantics as a sign of genius in males.[22] Conversely, woman was idealized; her function was to serve as a muse for the creator, to inspire and guide his talent. Wilhelm von Humboldt's view of creative power as an aggressive, spon-

17. H. Sutherland Edwards, *The Prima Donna: Her History and Surroundings from the Seventeenth to the Nineteenth Century*, 2 vols. (1888; rpt. New York, 1978), vol. 1, p. 237.

18. Clara Novello, of the English music-publishing family, married Count Gigliucci, retired from singing, and settled into the leisured life of the Italian aristocracy. When her husband lost his land and money because of his political activities, Novello made a comeback to provide for the family. See Averil Mackenzie-Grieve, *Clara Novello 1818–1908* (London, 1955).

19. For such Rousseau dicta as "woman was specifically made to please man," or "she must be modest, devoted, reserved and she should exhibit to the world as to her own conscience testimony to her virtue," or "thus the whole education of women ought to be relative to men," see Bell and Offen, eds., *Women, the Family, and Freedom*, vol. 1, pp. 44, 46, 49.

20. "Du musst Dich ernster und emsiger zu Deinem eigentlichen Beruf, zum *einzigen* Beruf eines Mädchens, zur Hausfrau, bilden." (Abraham Mendelssohn to his twenty-three-year-old daughter in Sebastian Hensel, *Die Familie Mendelssohn. 1729–1847*, 2 vols., 2d ed. [Berlin, 1880], vol. 1, p. 99.)

21. "Die erste Virtuosinn, die beste Sängerinn und die belesenste, fertigste Künstlerinn eine schlechte Gattin, eine schlechte Hausfrau und eine schlechte Mutter sei." (Quoted by Annemarie Krille in *Beiträge zur Geschichte der Musikerziehung und Musikübung der deutschen Frau (von 1750 bis 1820)* [Berlin, 1938], p. 94.)

22. See Alan Richardson, "Romanticism and the Colonization of the Feminine," in Anne K. Mellor, ed., *Romanticism and Feminism* (Bloomington, 1988), pp. 13–25.

taneous male force opposed to the passive receptivity of the female was widely accepted.[23] Consequently, the nineteenth-century woman who defied convention by attempting creative work was presumed to be "un-womanly." Fanny Mendelssohn Hensel, upper-class and a composer, expressed her anger at this dilemma in a letter to a male friend: "That every day, at every step in life, one is reminded of her miserable feminine nature by the lords of creation is something that could put one into a fury. But the anger would destroy one's womanliness and make the wrong even worse."[24]

The concept of home as "refuge," the new domestic roles for women, the legalization of their disenfranchisement, and the prevailing romantic ethos affected all women, but most particularly the professional woman musician of the artist-musician class. The prescriptive ideology was especially hard on creative women. This may explain why such a gifted composer as Clara Schumann could make the pronouncement that women should not compose and (incorrectly) state that none had ever done so.

It has been assumed that the conservatories established in the early nineteenth century widened opportunities for females and created a pool of professional women musicians. The question is frequently asked why women graduates of these institutions did not become, if not great composers, at least known *Kleinmeisterinnen*. An examination of conservatory education may provide some answers. To begin with, many women from upper- or middle-class homes attended and graduated from the schools but generally left the musical world when they married. Attending the conservatory was "a nice thing for a girl to do," but turning professional was not. Women who used their conservatory diploma to join the profession were most often from the artist-musician class—women who came from families traditionally in music or theater and who would have entered that world with or without a conservatory education.

Second, although the European conservatories did not bar women (who were obliged to meet the same entrance requirements as men), their education was separate and not equal to that of the male students. The Paris Conservatoire, which provided the model followed by most European music schools, admitted women singers and instrumentalists in

23. Wilhelm von Humboldt, "Über den Geschlechtsunterschied und dessen Einfluss auf die organische Natur," quoted in Bell and Offen, eds., *Women, the Family, and Freedom*, vol. 1, pp. 68–70. Humboldt, a linguist and statesman (brother of Alexander, the scientist), served as Prussian minister of education for only one year (1809–1810) but his educational reforms lasted until 1933, according to Hajo Holborn, *A History of Modern Germany 1648–1840* (New York, 1967), p. 474.

24. Hensel, *Familie Mendelssohn*, vol. 1, p. 197. My translation.

1795, its founding year. The London Royal Academy of Music accepted an equal number of boys and girls at its opening in London in 1823. Conservatories in Milan, Vienna, Brussels, Leipzig, Cologne, Dresden, Bern, Berlin, Naples, and Frankfurt—to name only a few—all admitted female students. In each of these schools, separation of the sexes was a prime concern.[25] Classes were often housed in separate quarters (in Paris, boys and girls used separate staircases and entrances)[26] and taught on alternate days (in Brussels, Mondays, Wednesdays, and Fridays were reserved for the girls; Tuesdays, Thursdays, and Saturdays for the boys).[27] Such classes as declamation, pedagogical techniques, and, of course, mixed chorus were coeducational.

Nominally, in most schools, women could study any subject, but in fact for a good part of the century they were limited to voice, piano, and harp. The author of the history of the Bern Conservatory, which was founded to train orchestral players, wrote, "The appeal for students [for the new music school] was made only to boys; girls were not even considered, because at that time [1857], the idea of females participating in a public concert was quite unthinkable. According to the point of view of the time, only singing and piano-playing were fit subjects for girls and women; violin and certainly the cello, much less a wind instrument, were quite unsuitable for them."[28] When women did begin to study violin, huge controversies erupted over their presence in orchestra classes (see Appendix at the end of this essay).

In almost every musical institution women were required to study harmony, but their course of study differed from that of the male students. In Leipzig, a three-year course in theory was required for men, whereas the women took a two-year course: "For the female students there is a separate class in harmony organized for their needs."[29] In 1859, the Paris Conservatoire offered to male students two classes in written harmony as well as two in keyboard harmony and accompaniment; women were of-

25. "Les classes d'élèves de chaque sexe sont séparées" (*Règlements* of the Paris Conservatoire, 1800, in M. Lassabathie, *Histoire du Conservatoire impérial de musique et de déclamation suivie de documents recueillis et mis en ordre* [Paris, 1860], p. 250); and "Der Unterricht der Schülerinnen ist von dem der Schüler völlig getrennt" (*Das Conservatorium der Musik in Leipzig* [Leipzig, 1843], p. 6).

26. In his memoirs, Berlioz describes having unwittingly used the entrance reserved for the girls and having been brought to account by none other than the director, Cherubini. See *The Memoirs of Hector Berlioz*, trans. David Cairns (New York, 1969), pp. 60–61. My thanks to M. Elizabeth C. Bartlet for pointing out this incident.

27. *Annuaire du Conservatoire Royal de Musique de Bruxelles* (Brussels, 1876), pp. 57–59.

28. Werner Juker, *Musikschule und Konservatorium für Musik in Bern 1858–1958* (Bern, 1958), p. 10. My translation.

29. "Für die Schülerinnen besteht eine besondere für Ihre Bedürfnisse eingerichtete Classe der Harmonielehre" (*Das Conservatorium der Musik in Leipzig*, p. 6).

fered only the practical courses in keyboard harmony and accompaniment and were not permitted to study written harmony until 1879.[30]

Few schools offered composition classes for women. The Paris *Réglements* of 1822 decreed that harmony, counterpoint, and fugue were "for men." Composition was specifically "for men only."[31] Not until late in the century do we see women studying such "intellectual" subjects as counterpoint and score-reading.[32] There were as always, however, some exceptions: in the Brussels Conservatoire Royal, beginning in 1833, Director François-Joseph Fétis personally gave composition lessons to female students from three to five on Wednesday afternoons, and this tradition continued for many years.[33] Clara Barnett Rogers, who entered the Leipzig Conservatory in 1856 (under a special dispensation, since she was only twelve), rather naively explains, "There was no composition class for my sex, no woman composer having yet appeared on the musical horizon with the exception of Mendelssohn's sister, Fanny Hensel, who showed some talent in that direction, and also Clara Schumann. None of the girl students in the Conservatorium, however, had ever shown any bent for composition, therefore a composition class seemed to be superfluous." But in 1859, after the administration heard her string quartet (composed when she was thirteen), a composition class for girls was created.[34]

Despite all the circumscriptions, the women were not deterred: a conservatory diploma was a prize that could be an asset in the marriage market, attested to competence, and afforded entry to the musical world and to professional status if it were desired. The numbers of female

30. Lassabathie, *Histoire du Conservatoire impérial*, p. 323, describes the course of study. For the date 1879, see Bea Friedland, *Louise Farrenc, 1804–1875: Composer, Performer, Scholar* (Ann Arbor, 1980), p. 36.

31. "Classe d'harmonie pour les hommes . . . Classe de contre-point et de fugue pour les hommes . . . Classe de composition et style de tous genres pour les hommes seulement." (Lassabathie, *Histoire du Conservatoire impérial*, p. 284.)

32. In 1883, several female students at the Hoch Conservatory in Frankfurt listed counterpoint, composition, and score-reading as major studies, but in Munich no woman was admitted to the class in score-reading until 1902. See Mabel Daniels's description of her studies in Munich in Carol Neuls-Bates, ed., *Women in Music: An Anthology of Source Readings from the Middle Ages to the Present* (New York, 1982), pp. 219–22.

33. See *Annuaire*, pp. 57–60. Fétis, director of the Brussels Conservatory from 1833 to 1871, had many prejudices but evidently did not include one against women as composers among them. He had taught composition to Louise Bertin in Paris before he went to the Brussels Conservatoire, and his *Biographie Universelle des Musiciens* (1833–1844; 2d ed., 1860–1865) gives information (unfortunately, often erroneous) about many women musicians.

34. Rogers, *Memories*, pp. 108, 177. See also her description of the performance of the quartet, which was arranged by fellow-student Arthur Seymour Sullivan (pp. 165–67).

students increased steadily. At its opening in 1843, the Leipzig Conservatory had thirty-three male and eleven female students. When the Hoch Conservatory in Frankfurt was established in 1878, the ratio of males to females had nearly reversed: there were ninety-seven females and forty-two males.

What happened to all the talented, highly educated females? Those from upper-class families used their skills and education at home, often to enhance a husband's social position: a wife who could sing or play was a valuable asset. Other women searched out ways to perform, establish, and support music in their homes, churches, and communities, but always on a nonprofessional basis. When necessary, of course, the conservatory graduate was able to support children, parents, ailing spouses, or other dependents and, indeed, a number of them did so.

Those from the artist-musician class, however, used their education to further their professional career in teaching and performing. The great majority of conservatory graduates turned to teaching: some taught in home studios; others joined men on the faculties of the institutions for higher musical education. Here class was not an issue but gender was. Women taught in the Paris Conservatoire from its inception but were generally kept in the lower ranks and received lower salaries even within the same rank. Louise Farrenc, professor of piano at the Paris Conservatoire (in the women's section) from 1842 to 1872, received her appointment at the same time as Henri Herz (who also taught in the women's section), but Herz's annual salary was 200 francs higher than Farrenc's. Not until 1850, after her *Nonet* was successfully premiered in Paris, did she take the unladylike step of requesting that her salary be brought up to the level of the other professors, several of whom had been appointed well after she was.[35] Despite her achievements as a composer and editor, Farrenc was never appointed a professor of composition; she remained in the piano department. Between 1795 and 1859, there were some 26 women out of a total of about 325 faculty members and administrators on the faculty of the Paris Conservatoire; without exception, they taught voice, keyboard instruments, and such practical subjects as keyboard harmony, accompaniment, and solfège.[36]

Many concert artists joined conservatory faculties when they retired from the concert stage. There were, however, restraints even on such celebrities. The Brussels Conservatoire took pride in the presence of Marie Pleyel on its faculty, but she was only permitted to teach girls. Male

35. Friedland, *Louise Farrenc*, p. 42.

36. This information was taken from the alphabetical list of names of teachers and administrators in Lassabathie, *Histoire du Conservatoire impérial*, pp. 424–46. Among the twenty-six women were several actresses, who taught *déclamation*.

professors in most schools, by contrast, taught students of both sexes.[37] As a rule, whatever their background, women professors received neither the rank nor the salary of their male counterparts.

The women conservatory graduates from the artist-musician class who were performers had problems never faced by men. As a professional, the woman musician was paid for her work and consequently regarded as unfeminine; a male agent or manager was necessary to protect her "femininity." He could bargain for her fees, provide an escort, make tour arrangements, and, often, guarantee the public that the pianist, singer, or composer in question gave her womanly responsibilities first priority— whether it was true or not. An article in the *Illustrated London Weekly* of 19 July 1862, for example, assures its readers that Mrs. Lucy Anderson, teacher of and pianist to Queen Victoria, is "a woman [who] adorns her art by her domestic and social virtues, and enjoys the esteem and regard of every one who knows her." And Berthold Litzmann concludes the preface to his biography of Clara Schumann, first published in 1902: "The biographer has fulfilled his task only if he has succeeded in making the figure of this great artist stand out clearly, and through her inmost being has revealed her personality as a whole, showing her as an example of noble, pure, and true womanhood."[38]

Along with the charge of disloyalty to one's gender or the threat of being "unsexed," an emotional burden was borne by the women who had to leave home and tour in order to maintain careers and earn good fees. Some women traveled with husband, children, and nursemaids. Other married artists parted with husbands and children, sometimes for as long as two or three years at a time, leaving their sons and daughters in boarding schools or with servants or family members.

Margarethe Stockhausen (1803–1877), singer and mother of the great baritone Julius Stockhausen, gave birth to six children between 1826 and 1837, at the height of her career. Her fees provided the greater part of the family livelihood; the father, a harpist and composer, never earned as much as she. Julius, the oldest child, was first placed in a foster home with his wet nurse while his parents worked in England. He and the younger siblings were brought to see their mother from time to time, but until he was sixteen he lived either with grandparents or in a boarding school. Summer months were the only times the family spent

37. Note that for many years the regulations of the Paris Conservatoire required that the mother or guardian of each female pupil be present at the lessons (ibid., pp. 250, 327). This undoubtedly referred only to lessons with male professors. How long this injunction continued in force is not clear.

38. Berthold Litzmann, *Clara Schumann: Ein Künstlerleben*, trans. Grace E. Hadow, 3 vols. (Leipzig, 1902–1908), vol. 1, p. vii. Here Litzmann is quoting Julius Allgeyer, who began the biography but did not live to complete it.

together. It was through the post that the mother, who found each parting exceedingly painful, learned of her children's illnesses and even death.[39]

Pauline Viardot (1821–1910) began her touring life at the age of five when her parents, the Garcias, brought an Italian opera company to North America. As an adult, Viardot left her eldest child at home and toured with her husband-manager, her younger children, and servants, as she went the rounds of Europe.[40] Arabella Goddard (1836–1922), a leading English pianist, embarked on a three-year tour in 1873 that took her to India, Australia, and North America. Her husband, music critic J. W. Davison, and two children remained behind.

Neither concert managers nor even an accompanying husband, however, could protect these women against the prurient curiosity that attended all women artists, even the pious Jenny Lind or "the priestess," Clara Schumann. Such flamboyant artists as Teresa Carreño (1853–1917), pianist, singer, and composer, deemed the equal of Louis Gottschalk and other male contemporaries, could not escape the interest in her sexuality and may even have exploited it, much as some female artists do to this day. Marie Pleyel was described as flirting with the members of the orchestra as well as with the audience.[41] Critics thought nothing of describing women performers in such terms as the "fat" Fraülein Auernhammer.[42] When, in 1809, Johann Friedrich Reichardt heard Caroline Longhi, a harpist and pianist, he lingered on details of her beautiful figure and wrote, almost as an afterthought, "her harp playing itself was quite delicate and pleasing." Reichardt was not the only critic who took delight in "the lovely harpist from Naples." Carl August Varnhagen, the Prussian diplomat and journalist, reported details of Longhi's love life in letters to Rahel Levin, later to be his wife.[43]

39. See Julia Wirth, *Julius Stockhausen: Der Sänger des deutschen Liedes* (Frankfurt, 1927), esp. pp. 15, 17, 19, 21, 22.

40. Louise Héritte-Viardot, the eldest child of Viardot, who had disappointed father and grandmother because she was a girl, was left with her grandmother soon after her birth, while her parents went on tour. At six she was sent to a boarding school, and from then until she was twelve she saw her parents only in the summer months. See her *Memories and Adventures*, trans. E. S. Buchheim (1913; rpt. New York, 1977), pp. 18, 22, 26–27.

41. Madame Lea Mendelssohn, the mother of Fanny and Felix, wrote a description of Pleyel's December 1839 Leipzig performance which was copied into Clara Schumann's unpublished diary. See my *Clara Schumann: The Artist and the Woman* (Ithaca, 1985), pp. 152–53.

42. Eduard Hanslick, *Geschichte des Concertwesens in Wien* (Vienna, 1869), p. 125.

43. Johann Friedrich Reichardt, *Vertraute Briefe geschrieben auf einer Reise nach Wien und den österreichischer Staaten zu ende des Jahres 1808 und zu Anfang 1809*, ed. Gustav Gugitz, 2 vols. (Munich, 1915), vol. 1, pp. 193–95. Gugitz gives excerpts from Varnhagen's gossipy letters.

As theatrical performers, opera singers were especially vulnerable to comments on their sexuality. Consequently, even the violinist and conductor Joseph Joachim, who had many women students, insisted that his fiancée, Amalie Weiss, leave the stage after their marriage and confine her singing to song recitals and oratorio. The twenty-four-year-old mezzo obeyed but wrote to a friend that at her final performance in Beethoven's *Fidelio*, just before her wedding in 1863, she was so agitated and unhappy about giving up operatic performances that Florestan's costume was soaked with her tears.[44] Clara Kathleen Rogers, who married a Boston lawyer in 1878, wrote in her memoirs that "the mere thought of giving up that which from earliest childhood had been the one and only deep interest in my life was like death to me."[45] She compromised by leaving public life but continuing to teach.

Two musicians, Fanny Hensel, née Mendelssohn, and Clara Schumann, née Wieck, can serve as paradigms of the nonprofessional and the professional woman musician of the nineteenth century. Contemporaries and friends, they represented two different traditions and classes.

Fanny Caecilie Hensel (1805–1847), older sister of Felix Mendelssohn, was a member of a bourgeois-aristocratic German-Jewish family that had converted to Christianity. The women in both the maternal and the paternal line were well educated and musically accomplished. Among Fanny Mendelssohn's aunts was Dorothea Veit Schlegel, the eldest child of Moses Mendelssohn, who had been educated by the philosopher himself. Dorothea Schlegel, a writer, was an independent spirit who left her well-to-do husband and the world of Berlin salons to live with and subsequently marry Friedrich Schlegel. Although her work did not appear under her name, it is known that she was the author of at least one novel that was published with her husband's name as "editor."[46] Two other

44. "Angesichts solcher Erfolge [auf dem Bühne] bedarf es kaum der Versicherung, dass sich Fräulein Weiss nur schweren Herzens dem Wunsche ihres Verlobten fügte, der Bühne zu entsagen. Wenige Monate vor ihrem Tode hat mir die Künstlerin selbst noch erzählt, wie sie in der Abschiedsvorstellung als Fidelio vor innerer Erregung kaum imstande gewesen sei, ihre Rolle zu Ende zu führen. Und an Scholz, der zur Zeit der Aufführung nicht in Hannover war, sondern in Rom weilte, schrieb sie unter dem unmittelbaren Eindruck der Begebenheit, sie habe den ganzen Abend über so viel weinen müssen, dass der Rock von Gunz [der den Florestan dargestellt hatte] auf einer Seite ganz nass war." (Andreas Moser, *Joseph Joachim: Ein Lebensbild*, new and expanded ed., 2 vols. [Berlin, 1910], vol. 2, pp. 120–21. Note that an earlier [1898] edition of this biography, written during Joachim's lifetime, does not give this information.)

45. Clara Kathleen Rogers, *The Story of Two Lives: Home, Friends, and Travels* (Norwood, Mass., 1932), p. 4.

46. An English translation of her *Florentin: A Novel* has recently appeared, translated, annotated, and introduced by Edwina Lawler and Ruth Richardson (Lewiston, N.Y., 1988).

gifted great-aunts in the maternal line, Baroness Fanny von Arnstein and Baroness Caecilie von Eskeles (after whom Fanny Caecilie Mendelssohn was named), and Arnstein's daughter, Henriette von Pereira, played significant roles in the Viennese musical world as amateur pianists and prominent patronesses.[47] Also in the maternal line was great-aunt Sara Levy, a Berlin *salonnière*, a student of Wilhelm Friedemann Bach and patroness of Carl Philipp Emanuel Bach. "Tante" Levy's music library of priceless Bach manuscripts and prints was donated to the Singakademie, of which she was an early and active member.[48]

Fanny, like her younger brother, was an heir to the musical traditions and talents of her family. Like her brother, she had a superb musical education as well as the discipline, initiative, and ambition necessary to succeed as a professional musician. Like her brother, she was an unusually skilled pianist of professional caliber and, like her brother, a composer who wrote in all forms: she composed over four hundred works including songs, piano music, string quartets, cantatas, and orchestral and choral works. Unlike her brother, however, she did not become a professional musician—indeed, that even a son of this banker's family should have turned professional was extraordinary; for a daughter it was unthinkable.

Throughout her childhood and adolescence, both parents were as delighted with and took as much pride in Fanny's talent and progress as in her brother's. But this was accompanied by reminders of her position as a woman and her ultimate role in the home. These reminders haunted her throughout her life. Fanny's husband, Wilhelm Hensel, a court painter and son of a rural minister, was a member of the artist-musician class and had no objection to his wife's composing, performing, or publishing. His own sister, Luise, was a well-known poet.[49] He, Fanny's mother, and family friends encouraged her to publish her work, but she was inhibited by the lack of support and outright disapproval she received first from her father and then from the brother to whom she had close artistic ties. Felix, like her father and other educated men of

47. See Reichardt, *Vertraute Briefe*, vol. 1, pp. 104–5, 112–13, 120–23; translated in my dissertation, "A Commentary on and a Translation of Selected Portions of *Vertraute Briefe* . . . ," New York University, 1972, pp. 259–61, 262–63, 266, and 269–73. See also Spiel, *Fanny von Arnstein*.

48. See Eric Werner, "Levy, Sara," *Die Musik in Geschichte und Gegenwart*, ed. Friedrich Blume, 14 vols. (Kassel, 1960), vol. 8, col. 684; Georg Schünemann, "Die Bachpflege der Berliner Singakademie," *Bach-Jahrbuch* 25 (1928): 144; and *Die Singakademie zu Berlin 1791–1941* (Regensburg, 1941), p. 71.

49. For a hitherto unknown picture of Wilhelm and Luise Hensel, see Susan Youens, "Behind the Scenes: *Die schöne Müllerin* Before Schubert," *19th-Century Music* 15 (1991): 3–22.

his class, echoed Rousseau, Basedow and Campe, and Humboldt, disapproving of any attempt on Fanny's part to move out of home music-making.[50]

Fanny Hensel directed her musical energies and talents into the Mendelssohn family Sunday musicales, which were given in her home. In doing so, Madame Hensel was continuing an established Berlin tradition: many of the salons of 1790–1806 were headed by Jewish women to whom she was related. But for the *Sonntagsmusik*, which became brilliant Berlin musical events, Fanny Hensel was far more than a *salonnière*; she served as musical director, pianist, composer, and conductor. Her brother gave her his full support in this endeavor—so long as it remained nonprofessional.[51]

At the age of forty, Fanny Hensel at last decided to abandon the amateur tradition of her maternal relatives and accepted—although with some trepidation—a paid offer from a Berlin publisher. Heartened by reassurance from the successful Sunday musicales, the encouragement of her artist-husband, and the respect and admiration of several young musicians (including Charles Gounod, whom she had met in Rome in 1840),[52] she did not ask but *informed* her brother that she was prepared to publish her work and face the world as a musician.

Fanny Mendelssohn Hensel's efforts to cross the line to professionalism were defeated by death. Her obituary appeared in the *Allgemeine musikalische Zeitung* of 26 May 1847. It was followed one week later by a review of her piano works, ops. 2, 4, 5, and 6, in that journal.

The ultimate professional, Clara Wieck Schumann, was born in Leipzig in 1819 to Marianne and Friedrich Wieck. Both parents were members of the artist-musician class: her father was a piano teacher and a merchant of pianos, music, and related equipment and accessories; her mother, Marianne Tromlitz Wieck, was a professional musician and the daughter and granddaughter of working musicians. In addition to performing in the Leipzig Gewandhaus as a singer and a piano soloist, Marianne Wieck worked in Wieck's business, taught piano, and gave birth to five children in the eight years she was married to Wieck. She left her husband when her children were five, three, and one year old, and a divorce followed within the year. Soon remarried to Adolph Bargiel, also a pianist and teacher,

50. See Felix's letter to Lea Mendelssohn, translated in Marcia J. Citron, "Women and the Lied, 1775–1850," in Jane Bowers and Judith Tick, eds., *Women Making Music: The Western Art Tradition, 1150–1950* (Urbana, 1986), p. 231.

51. See her descriptions of these events in Marcia J. Citron, ed., *The Letters of Fanny Hensel to Felix Mendelssohn* (Stuyvesant, N.Y., 1987), esp. pp. 116, 119, 121, 147.

52. See Eva Weissweiler, ed., *Fanny Mendelssohn: Italienisches Tagebuch*, 2d ed. (Darmstadt, 1982), esp. pp. 21–22, 101, 106.

she supplemented the family income again by teaching, and supported her second family of four children in this way when Bargiel died.

Clara Wieck, her oldest child, worked for over sixty years as a pianist, composer, teacher, and editor. Because she came from a family of teachers and musicians who had to earn a living and because she married a man whose income was always modest, money was an important incentive throughout her life. In her childhood, when she toured under the aegis of her father, it had the highest priority: Wieck personally collected, kept, and invested the fees she earned. Later, during the years of her marriage to Robert Schumann, her income paid for such necessities as rent and school fees for the children. This was known to friends and recorded in the household account books but, because of the tradition of male support of the family, not discussed publicly.

Like all professional performer-composers of her time, she had to withstand not only the criticism of friends and colleagues but also the attacks of reviewers and critics. Moreover, Clara Schumann, as a widow—and even as a girl—acted as her own agent-manager.[53] All arrangements for solo concerts were made by the artist herself: she negotiated the fees, chose the program, organized travel and housing, rented the hall, tested the instruments, hired the supporting artists, scheduled the rehearsals, had the programs and tickets printed, and looked after the advertising and newspaper announcements. All these details required action quite inconsistent with the image of the nineteenth-century German woman. The "priestess," as she was called, was often peremptory, aggressive, commanding, and demanding. She had a strong ego and sense of self, and these "unfeminine"—that is, atypical—characteristics often aroused antagonism. Her correspondence attests to her occasional discomfort with this "unwomanly" role, but she was a professional: she needed the money and expected to be paid for her artistic efforts. A letter to Ferdinand Hiller describes an experience from which she learned much. At her first concert in Düsseldorf, in 1850, she appeared on the same program as her husband, newly appointed director of music in that city, and received only a basket of flowers in payment. She wrote:

> It is simply incomprehensible that the men could think that for the first time here I will play gratis. Moreover, I cannot understand the indelicacy of just demanding this! Do they take us for rich people? Or do they think I will play whenever they like for the salary my husband receives? Dear Herr Hiller, if I had no children and if I were wealthy, I would play as often as they wanted, and would be happy to play gratis, but in my circumstances,

53. On her nineteen English tours, she had managers and/or friends to help with arrangements. On the Continent, however, she continued making her own arrangements even after the 1860s, when concert management was available.

I cannot do this. What shall I do now? I cannot discuss it with them nor can Robert. . . . My playing is a separate matter on which they could not count when they engaged my husband.[54]

The distinction between nonprofessional woman musicians like Fanny Hensel and professionals like Clara Schumann was found throughout Europe. A nineteenth-century phenomenon, it influenced musical life well into the twentieth century. Fanny Hensel was a supremely gifted wealthy woman whose musical ambitions were frustrated by the male members of her bourgeois aristocratic family and whose social position prevented her from achieving her full potential. Conversely, Clara Schumann was a professional pianist and composer who, with family support and generations of musical tradition behind her, was able to reach the artistic heights to which her gifts entitled her. Their experiences demonstrate that we cannot overlook the intersection of gender and class and their impact on music history.

Appendix

Letter from Ernst Rudorff, deputy director, to Joseph Joachim, director of the Berlin Königliche Hochschule für Musik, 18 December 1881. (From *Briefe von und an Joseph Joachim*, ed. Johannes Joachim and Andreas Moser [Berlin, 1913], 3: 230–31. My translation.)

I would like to ask you to consider seriously whether it is right for us to allow women to take part in orchestra classes and performances. They add nothing to the orchestra performances; indeed, I am more and more convinced by the last few rehearsals that the weak and uncertain playing of the young girls not only does no good at all but actually makes the sound indistinct and out of tune. If we were to make an exception of a personality like Frl. Soldat, that would not weight the question in any way. To my mind, the point of view that it will be useful to the girl students is simply not plausible. They can learn rhythm and sight-reading in other ways, and they should not be trained to become orchestra players as such anyway. It is bad enough that

54. "Es ist doch ganz unbegreiflich, wie die Herren denken können, dass ich zum ersten *Male* hier *gratis* in ihren Concerten spielen werde, noch dazu kann ich die Undelicatesse nicht begreifen, so etwas nur zu verlangen! Halten sie uns für reiche Leute? oder denken sie, dass ich für den Gehalt, den mein Mann erhält, auch spielen soll, wenn sie es wünschen! Lieber Herr Hiller, hätte ich keine Kinder und wäre ich reich, dann wollte ich spielen so oft es die Leute wünschten, und würde es mich beglücken, es nie anders als gratis zu thun, aber in meinen Verhältnissen kann ich das nicht. Was soll ich nun thun? Ich kann mit den Herren nicht darüber sprechen, Robert auch nicht . . . .Dass ich spiele, ist ja eine Sache für sich, auf die sie doch nicht rechnen konnten, als sie meinen Mann engagirten!" Reinhold Sietz, ed., *Aus Ferdinand Hillers Briefwechsel (1826–1861)* (Cologne, 1958), p. 85. My translation.

women are meddling in every possible place where they don't belong; they have already taken over in almost every area of music. At the very least, we have to make sure that orchestras will not have men and women playing together in the future. It is possible that the general currents are heading in that direction and in the coming decades we may see the last bit of disciplined behavior and artistic seriousness driven out of public productions of pure instrumental music. In any case, I would not like it to be said that an institution like the Royal Hochschule has taken the lead in entering upon this path toward immorality.

Thus I propose that in the new year, which offers the opportunity for a good beginning, the participation of women in orchestra classes and performances come to an end, once and for all. If I had to add anything to this, I would go one step further and exclude the women from auditing the orchestra classes as well. With only a very few exceptions, they do *nothing* but exchange looks with the men and chatter. Their need for artistic knowledge would be well enough served if we permitted them to attend the final rehearsals before the performances, since they shall not be studying conducting, composing, nor instrumentation.

[Ich] möchte dich bitten, die Frage ernstlich in Erwägung zu ziehen, ob es richtig ist, daß wir Damen in Orchesterstunden und Aufführungen mitwirken lassen. Für die Leistungen des Orchesters selbst kommt Nichts dabei heraus; ja, ich habe auch mich bei den letzten Proben mehr und mehr überzeugt, daß das schwächliche, unsichere Mitspielen der jungen Mädchen nicht nur Nichts nützt, sondern im Gegentheil den Klang verschwommen und unsauber macht. Wenn eine Persönlichkeit wie Frl. Soldat hier eine Ausnahme bilden würde, so fällt das der Frage im Ganzen gegenüber nicht ins Gewicht. Der Gesichtspunkt, den Schülerinnen nützlich sein zu wollen, ist meiner Ansicht nach auch nicht stichhaltig; Rhythmus und Vomblattspielen können sie auf andere Weise lernen, zu Orchesterspielerinnen als solchen sollen sie aber nicht ausbilden. Das Hineinpfuschen der Frauen in alle möglichen Gebiete, in die sie nicht hineingehören, ist schon genug an der Tagesordnung; die Musik haben sie schon fast in allen Theilen in Beschlag genommen; man sollte wenigstens Sorge tragen, daß nicht auch in Zukunft unsere Orchester gar aus Männern und Weibern zusammengesetzt werden. Möglich, daß die allgemeine Strömung dennoch in Jahrzehnten dahin führt und den letzten Rest von Haltung und künstlerischem Ernst auch aus den öffentlichen Vorführungen der reinen Instrumentalmusik vertreibt; jedenfalls möchte ich nicht, daß es heißen könnte, eine Anstalt wie die Königliche Hochschule hätte auf diesem Wege zur Unsitte die Führung übernommen.

Also ich beantrage, daß wir mit dem neuen Jahr, das einen guten Anfang abgiebt, dem Mitspielen der Damen in Orchesterstunden und Aufführungen ein für alle Mal ein Ende bereiten. Wenn ich zu verfügen hätte, so würde ich noch einen Schritt weiter gehen und die Damen auch vom Zuhören in den Orchesterstunden ausschließen. Sie thun mit ganz wenigen

Ausnahmen *Nichts* da oben, als mit den Herren Blicke wechseln und schwatzen, und ihren Bedürfnissen nach künstlerischer Erkenntniß würde vollauf Genüge geschehen, wenn man ihnen zu den letzten Proben vor den Aufführungen Zutritt gewährte, da sie doch weder dirigiren, noch komponiren, noch instrumentiren lernen sollen.

Interpretive Strategies

Miriam Sings Her Song:
The Self and the Other in Anthropological Discourse

Ellen Koskoff

It is Friday evening and Miriam is alone in her apartment waiting for her husband to return from work. As she lights the candles for the Sabbath, she begins to sing a *nigun*, one she has composed herself. She loves to sing and is pleased to be able to offer such a gift to the Sabbath queen who will soon descend. Miriam is observed by a married male neighbor, who retreats into his own apartment next door, observing the law of *kol isha*. Miriam hears her neighbor's door close and continues singing.

Scenes such as this, and countless others noted by anthropologists in the field, constitute the "raw data" from which convincing cultural pictures and analyses will later be derived. The anthropologist, seen essentially as a translator between—or an analyst of—cultures, interweaves the bits and pieces of others' lives into stories and collages, often of immense power and integrity.

Two common perspectives found in the anthropological literature result in what will be called here *descriptive* and *analytic* ethnography. In descriptive ethnography, which is usually limited to portraits of one culture, all of the parts seem to be uniquely and correctly connected, much like a completed, intricate jigsaw puzzle. They are written ostensibly from an insider's perspective, yet the reader understands that this is a fiction; it is the ethnographer who, in selecting and thereby privileging some bits of data over others, has constructed a convincing story. Such ethnographies are essentially distillations, presenting no individual view, yet somehow representative of the whole.

Analytic ethnography, by contrast, often attempts to expose and change systems that oppress or dominate. In this sense it is openly political

I would like to thank Gretchen Wheelock for helping to clarify many of the points expressed in this essay, and to offer special thanks for her editorial eagle eye.

in its purpose. Recent feminist anthropology, for example, often comparative and clearly written from an outsider perspective, points to deeper social structures that have been obscured or mystified (in the Marxist sense) by political or religious ideology.

Although it can be an occupational hazard of anthropology to portray cultures either as neat ethnographic packages or as evidence for a particular political viewpoint, it is clear that the resulting portraits are essentially outsider perspectives. But what of the insider, the person actually living the culture, the so-called Other of ethnographic presentation? This essay explores the differences in presentation that result when cultures and their musical systems are presented from these very different perspectives. The ethnographic data come from many years of observing and participating in the musical practices of a group of Hasidic Jews (Lubavitchers) living in Brooklyn, New York.

I first don the describer's hat (perspective 1): I present, as in a monograph, the Lubavitcher religious and philosophical belief system and the resulting social roles that Lubavitchers adopt to create and maintain a sense of social order and balance. Next, I move to a more openly analytic perspective (perspective 2), as in a feminist political text, examining gender roles within this society, using Jewish laws pertaining to gender differences and musical performance as evidence of the asymmetry of value between Lubavitcher men and women. Third, I offer the insider's viewpoint (perspective 3), as in a diary, based on direct quotations taken from field notes and from conversations with Lubavitchers during which they expressed to me their misgivings about outsider perspectives. Finally, I offer a way to understand these perspectives, by introducing the dynamic of power that exists between the observer self and the observed Other. In doing this, I hope to clarify both the voice that is speaking in these cultural presentations and the end to which it speaks.

Perspective 1: The Describer, Looking In

The Ethnographic Setting

In Hasidism, one of the most important things is the happiness of the heart, and the adherence of the heart to the worshipping of our God. The Hasid can only allow his soul expression through melody. Only melody has the strength to elevate the soul.[1]

Woman's body reflects more of the aspect of G-d's essence than does man's, as Chassidus [sic] explains. For woman has the ability to create within herself new life, a new creature, a "something from nothing," and this parallels, and derives

---

1. *Sefer Ha-Nigunim*, ed. Rabbi Samuel Zalmanoff, trans. Yehuda Bardugo (New York, 1948), p. 19.

from the power of the essence of G-d to create ex nihilo, to create from utter nothing. This is one of the ways in which woman is in a more sensitive spiritual position than man.[2]

Hasidism is an orthodox and mystical Jewish movement, the modern phase of which was begun by the seventeenth-century Polish Rabbi Israel ben Eliezer, the Ba'al Shem Tov (1698–1760).[3] The Lubavitcher court was founded in the late eighteenth century by Rabbi Schneur Zalman of Liadi (1745–1813), a Lithuanian Rabbi who codified his essential philosophy in the *Tanya*, a four-volume collection of writings and commentaries upon Talmudic and mystical texts. At the core of Schneur Zalman's philosophy is the concept of the *benoni*, or the "intermediate," that is, any Jew who stands between two opposing souls, expressed metaphorically as the "animal" and the "divine" soul. The status of *benoni* is within the grasp of anyone who succeeds in living his or her life without intentionally committing an evil act.[4] Lubavitchers today often speak of the polarization of animal and divine souls, of the process of moving upward and inward from the animal to the divine realm, and of the considerable tension between these two equally powerful forces in everyday life.

Rabbi Schneur Zalman's form of Hasidism came to be called HABAD, an acronym based on three Hebrew words: *hochma* (conceptualization), *binah* (cognition), and *da'at* (understanding). After the death of Schneur Zalman, his followers moved the center of HABAD Hasidism to the town of Lubavitch, from which the community has since derived its name. The contemporary Lubavitcher court is led by Rabbi Menachem Mendel Schneerson, known as *Rebbe*, or *Tzaddik* (Holy One), who emigrated to the United States in 1941 and settled in Brooklyn, New York. There are roughly 150,000 Lubavitchers worldwide, the majority of whom live in Crown Heights.

Lubavitchers, unlike other Orthodox Jews, practice a mystical form of Judaism that focuses on the concept of *devekuth*, or adhesion to God ("oneness" or unity with the divine). The process of achieving *devekuth* is described as moving from the animal to the divine soul (or, often, from the "heel of the foot to the top of the head"); when the divine soul is reached, the animal "falls away."[5] The metaphor of heel and head is further expressed through the Lubavitcher notion that as the generations

---

2. Shaina Sara Handelman, "Modesty and the Jewish Woman," in *The Modern Jewish Woman: A Unique Perspective* (Brooklyn, 1981), p. 25.

3. See Ellen Koskoff, *The Concept of Nigun Among Lubavitcher Hasidim in the United States* (Ann Arbor, 1977), for a fuller discussion of the historical and present-day social context of this group.

4. Rabbi Shneur Zalman, *Likutei Amarim (Tanya)*, trans. Nissan Mindel (New York, 1969), pp. 77–83.

5. Zalman, *Likutei Amarim (Tanya)*, pp. 22–30.

pass they move "upward" in spirituality. For example, Moses, Rabbi Schneur Zalman, and other ancestral males are often referred to as existing at the "top of the head," and people living today are in the realm of the "heel of the foot." Finally, the animal, or mundane, soul is conceptualized as disordered, often needing restricting laws or codes, whereas the divine soul is seen as being ordered, or having the capability of ordering. One's spiritual quest for *devekuth*, then, is regarded as a movement away from disorder toward order.

Devekuth is brought about by adhering to the laws of Orthodox Judaism and by living all aspects of one's life with the proper godly intention (*kavannah*). *Kavannah* is prepared for ("awakened") by the expression of two essential emotional states: *simhah* (joy) and *hitlahavut* (enthusiasm). Lubavitchers regard their melodies, or *nigunim* (singular *nigun*), as essential vehicles for expressing *simhah* and *hitlahavut*, as *nigunim* are believed to hold traces of these properties that are "freed" through active performance.

Nigun *and Its Performance*

Nigunim are paraliturgical melodies, often borrowed from, or newly composed to resemble, both Jewish and non-Jewish Eastern European folk melodies. They are performed on a variety of occasions, including the Rebbe's *farbrengens* (Hasidic gatherings where the Rebbe speaks), the Sabbath or other festive meals, or during private moments of prayer and contemplation. Lubavitchers believe that performances of *nigunim* ready them for divine communication enabling them to communicate with God and with their spiritually elevated ancestors. *Nigun* performances, especially during *farbrengens*, are often marked by an intense, at times frenzied singing style that can temporarily render the performers emotionally or physically out of control.

The dichotomy between the animal and divine souls discussed above also appears in the Lubavitcher distinction between texts and melodies in music: text is connected to the mundane or animal soul, music to the spiritual or divine. Thus, many *nigunim* are wordless, sung to vocables, which occupy an intermediate spiritual position between the mundane and the spiritual. Furthermore, *nigun* tunes are frequently borrowed from the music of the host culture, as this music is regarded as especially mundane, needing "freeing" from its mundane setting by Lubavitcher intervention. Borrowed *nigunim*, then, are tunes that are considered to be "raw" but to contain trapped properties of *simhah* and *hitlahavut* and therefore to be worthy of adoption and adaptation by Lubavitchers. In order to be incorporated into the repertoire, however, *nigunim* must be performed in the presence of the Rebbe in a socially sanctioned context such as a *farbrengen*.

Two primary factors affect the performance, composition, and acceptance of *nigunim*: the spiritual lineage of the performer, and the performer's gender. Many Lubavitchers now living in Crown Heights were born into Hasidism, and many come from powerful Hasidic lineages that extend back to Eastern Europe and to the seventeenth century. In this country, in the late 1960s and the 1970s, Hasidism, especially HABAD Hasidism, saw the growth of the Ba'al Teshuvah,[6] or "returnee" movement, which resulted in a heavy influx of new, predominantly American-born, non-Orthodox Jews who wished to return to orthodoxy. Ba'alei Teshuvah often describe themselves as being on a perpetual journey toward spirituality. This journey takes years of study and contemplation and parallels, if on a different plane, the spiritual journey of Lubavitchers who have been Orthodox (or "observant") since birth. Many Ba'alei Teshuvah, however, are regarded as slightly suspect by lifetime Lubavitchers, as their roots are in the mundane world of contemporary U.S. culture. It is usually only with marriage—often to another Ba'al Teshuvah—and the birth of children that they are truly accepted.

The second factor that affects the performance, creation, and acceptance of *nigunim* is gender. In Orthodox Judaism, men and women are prohibited from praying, singing, or otherwise engaging together in social activities that offer a danger of unacceptable sexual behavior. Restrictions upon males prohibit them from hearing women singing, and from talking freely to women who might cause them to become *ervah*, or sexually stimulated in a "prohibited" way.

In Orthodox and Hasidic Judaism, women are believed to be inherently closer to spirituality than men. As is noted in the quotation cited above, their fertility—their ability to create, like God, something from nothing—puts them closer to God, and thus makes them more "naturally" and powerfully holy. This natural superiority is reflected in many ways, one of the most important of which concerns women's exemption from many of the 613 commandments that Orthodox Jews follow.[7] For example, women are exempt from commandments that are linked to time and place (going to the synagogue at a specific time for prayers, and so forth) because their duties in the home are seen as already fulfilling a commandment of greater spiritual value. But a woman's voice, especially in singing, is problematic in that it can lead to promiscuity. The singing voice of a woman has the potential to connect the body to prohibited sexuality, and thus to the mundane world and the animal soul.

6. The masculine plural of Ba'al Teshuvah is Ba'alei Teshuvah; the feminine singular is Ba'alat Teshuvah; the feminine plural, Ba'alot Teshuvah.

7. Orthodox Jews follow all of the commandments as set forth in the first five books of the Bible, not only the ten given by God to Moses. There are 365 negative and 248 positive commandments.

Kol Isha

An entire body of Jewish laws known as *kol isha* (the voice of a woman) addresses the issue of illicit sexual stimulation, with specific reference to musical performance. The question of *kol isha* centers on the interpretation of a small passage in the Bible from the Song of Songs, "Let me see thy countenance, let me hear thy voice, for sweet is thy voice and thy countenance is comely."[8] The first to comment on this passage was the sixth-century Talmudic scholar Samuel, whose interpretation firmly linked women's voices to prohibited sexuality. Commenting on the above passage from the Song of Songs, he wrote, *"Kol b'ishah ervah"* ("The voice of a woman is a sexual incitement").[9] During the tenth century another scholar, Rabbi Joseph, added a refinement: "When men sing and women join in, it is licentiousness; when women sing and men answer, it is like a raging fire in flax."[10]

Later scholars debated other issues, such as whether *kol isha* referred to the speaking as well as to the singing voice, or whether a woman's voice was sexually stimulating all of the time, only when one (male) was reciting the *Shema* (the holiest of Hebrew prayers), only when one was engaged in religious study, or only when one was nude. One commentator, Rabbi Judah He-Hasid (d. 1217), anticipating a feminist argument that would not surface for another seven hundred and fifty years, proposed the notion of *kol ish* (the voice of a man) as constituting the same sexual problems for women as *kol isha* for men.

Perhaps the most important commentary for our purposes, for it is the one that is followed today by most Orthodox and Hasidic Jews, is that of the great philosopher Moses ben Maimon (Maimonides, 1135–1204). He saw the word *ervah* as referring to the woman and to the performance context, not specifically to the woman's voice. He preceded the word *ervah* by the definite article, *ha*. To Maimonides, the original commentary by Samuel read, *"Kol b'ishah ha-ervah,"* or, "The voice of an illicit woman is prohibited."[11] He states in the fifth book of his *Code*, in the section titled "Forbidden Intercourse":

> Whoever indulges in [having intercourse with an illicit woman] lays himself open to the suspicion of forbidden unions. A man is forbidden to make suggestive gestures with his hands or legs or wink at a woman within the forbidden unions, or to jest or act frivolously with her. It is forbidden even

8. Song of Songs 2:14.
9. Rabbi Ben Cherney, "Kol Isha," *Journal of Halacha* (n.d.) from the Talmud, Tractate Berachot 24a, p. 57.
10. Cherney, "Kol Isha," p. 58.
11. In Hebrew writings, long vowels are generally omitted, and occasionally definite articles are not given. Thus, the interpretation of texts is often problematic and over the centuries has provided much grist for the scholarly mill.

to inhale her perfume or gaze at her beauty. Whosoever directs his mind toward these things is liable to the flogging prescribed for disobedience. He who stares even at a woman's little finger with the intention of deriving pleasure from it, is considered as though he had looked at her secret parts. It is forbidden even to listen to the singing of a woman within the forbidden unions, or to look at her hair.[12]

The word *ervah* in Maimonides's interpretation referred only to a woman of the "forbidden unions"—that is, one who was not likely to become a marriage partner, one with whom a man might establish an illicit relationship. Maimonides in effect shifted the emphasis from the inherent sexuality of women and their voices to the context of a potential illicit relationship between a man and a prohibited woman within a nonsanctioned context. Sexual stimulation in itself was not prohibited; rather, it was the potential to create a context of sexual stimulation that was restricted.

Thus, in theory, men may listen to their wives and premenstrual daughters—in the first case because the couple is already married, and in the second because it is unlikely that an illicit relationship will develop between two close relatives, especially when one is a child. In addition, unmarried women (with whom a marital relationship could be possible) and one's wife while she is a *niddah*, a menstruant (because sexual intercourse will soon be possible) are also excluded from this prohibition.

Although *kol isha* prohibits men from hearing women sing, it does not prevent women from singing. Thus, women, especially Ba'alot Teshuvah and young, unmarried women, when not in the presence of males, freely engage in many of the same musical activities as their male counterparts. It is not uncommon, for example, to hear women singing *nigunim* in the home while lighting Sabbath candles. One particular event, the *forshpil*—a party given for a young woman on the Sabbath before her wedding— rivals the musical and spiritual intensity of the predominantly male *farbrengen*.

Thus, Orthodox and Hasidic Jews make a distinction between the natural spirituality and positive sexuality of sanctioned women, and the perhaps unintentional, yet powerful and potentially destructive, sexuality of prohibited women. This destructive sexuality, symbolized by the speaking and singing voice, can create the context for illicit sexual relations that can threaten the very existence of the group and hence must be restricted.

From the Lubavitcher point of view, then, *kol isha* and many other laws of Orthodox Judaism are socially agreed-upon rules for various forms of interaction between men and women that guard against their loss of

12. Moses ben Maimonides, *Code*, Book Five, "The Book of Holiness," 21:2, trans. Louis I. Rabinowitz and Philip Grossman (New Haven, 1965), p. 133.

sexual and physical control. In controlling women's voices, Lubavitchers (both men and women) believe that they are balancing out the shift of power that might result in group disintegration if women were permitted true freedom, for in such a case the animal soul would dominate. Such laws are thus necessary to Lubavitcher life, for they preserve the essential binary contrasts that lie at the heart of Lubavitcher identity and form the underlying structure of Lubavitcher social relations.

Perspective 2: The Analyst, Looking In

Hierarchies of Value in Lubavitcher Life

The cultural celestialization of the sources and nature of male power over women and juniors has an important consequence. Those who are subordinated are locked into the system not by a political and legal superstructure of state power but by their encapsulation within a closed universe of cosmic power. . . . If rules, such as pollution rules that exclude women from religious and political realms, were visibly the creations of men, they could be challenged. But if they are imposed by ancestors, who hold powers of life and death over the living, they are beyond challenge. [13]

If we examine Lubavitcher gender relations in terms of the relative value between men and women a different picture emerges. [14] Let us move beyond the restrictions of *kol isha*, as outlined in the Talmudic writings above, and observe what happens in everyday practice, for in doing so we can expose the hierarchy of value that underlies Lubavitcher gender relations. Although in theory *kol isha* does not restrict men from hearing their wives sing, in practice married women almost never sing in the presence of their husbands, for they might inadvertently be overheard by a close male neighbor, relative, or one of their husband's students. Living in the close quarters characteristic of large urban centers, with the risk of being heard, even inadvertently, women have been effectively silenced. The restriction of *kol isha*, for all practical purposes, affects not only "prohibited" women but virtually *all* adult (menstruating) women.

In contrast, all males are encouraged to sing, especially at *farbrengens* in the validating presence of the Rebbe. Indeed, some of the most highly regarded males are those who act as the Rebbe's musical assistants, suggesting specific songs and initiating the long, intense singing sessions that

13. Roger M. Keesing, *Cultural Anthropology: A Contemporary Perspective,* 2d ed. (New York, 1981), pp. 298–99.
14. For a fuller discussion of gender issues, see my "Gender, Power, and Music," in Judith Lang Zaimont et al., eds., *The Musical Woman: An International Perspective,* vol. 3 (New York, 1991), pp. 769–88.

are so much a part of these gatherings. For Ba'alei Teshuvah singing is especially important. Such a high value is placed on "correct" *nigun* performance that many Ba'alei Teshuvah gain a measure of social and spiritual acceptance through intense and heartfelt singing styles displayed during *farbrengens*.

Women, especially married women, do not usually attend the Rebbe's *farbrengens* or, for that matter, Sabbath or other religious services, as their exemption from commandments of time and place have "freed" them to fulfill commandments in the home that have a higher spiritual value. Women who do come to the main Lubavitcher synagogue in Crown Heights sit in the women's gallery, a balcony high above the area occupied by the men, to ensure strict separation of the sexes. The gallery is enclosed by darkened sheets of plastic, so women's view of, and participation in, the proceedings below is quite limited.

In practice, then, a sharp social division arises for women, but not for men, in regard to musical performance: the division by marital status. Thus, if we ranked the various subgroups within Lubavitcher society, we might end up with a hierarchy of value that places the Rebbe and all males who have been Lubavitchers from birth (as well as all male ancestors) at the top; all adult married lifetime Lubavitcher women slightly beneath them; and unmarried Ba'alot Teshuvah at the bottom. It is no coincidence that unmarried Ba'alot Teshuvah tend to be the most active musically and the most adventurous concerning their musical practices, often singing under their breath during the Rebbe's *farbrengens* or religious services, composing their own tunes, calling their own *farbrengens*, and, at times, listening to current popular music. Thus it appears that the status hierarchy for women is in inverse proportion to their musical activity. Women in the most valued social and religious position, achieved through "correct" origins and marriage, tend to have the least active connection with music.[15]

Using the model of a hierarchy of value to analyze Lubavitcher society can bring us closer to an understanding of the underlying complexity of Lubavitcher social interactions surrounding gender and of their implications for music performance. The Rebbe, as the spiritual and symbolic head of this group, controls its fate through his spiritual lineage, personal holiness, and, most important, his access to the divine realm. That he is also male and elderly tends not only to validate his spirituality

15. This social and musical hierarchy is presented in a more detailed form in Ellen Koskoff, "The Sound of a Woman's Voice: Gender and Music in a New York Hasidic Community," in Ellen Koskoff, ed., *Women and Music in Cross-Cultural Perspective* (Westport, Conn., 1987), pp. 213–23.

but also to reinforce the relatively high value that this group places on gender and age.

Members of the group of least value, unmarried Ba'alot Teshuvah, are believed to be still somewhat connected to the mundane world and are relatively out of control in that they have not yet married and produced children. This belief is borne out in everyday Lubavitcher life, for of all the social groups within Lubavitcher society, it is unmarried Ba'alot Teshuvah who are most encouraged to continue on their spiritual path not only by hard study and close observance of traditional laws, but, more important, by marrying and producing children. Ba'alot Teshuvah, the least valued group, are exploited in a pure Marxist sense, as the group at the top (older, lifetime Lubavitcher males) controls, through the ideology of spirituality, the fruit of their true labor—their children. Ba'alot Teshuvah could be called "collaborative," in that they work within the system and seem not to be oppressed by it.

Returning now to the binary contrasts represented in the Lubavitcher worldview, we see that they seem to line up as follows: the mundane domain consists of, among other things, the animal soul, Ba'alei Teshuvah (especially females), contemporary U.S. culture, non-Lubavitcher music, texted music, and women's voices. The spiritual realm consists of the divine soul, all adult lifetime Lubavitchers, Eastern European Jewish culture, *nigunim,* and male voices. Things perceived as mundane have the potential to go out of control—accumulate too much animal soul—and must therefore be restricted, controlled, or otherwise limited for the protection of the group.

Women, especially Ba'alot Teshuvah, who perform music accumulate a threefold dose of potential out-of-controlness: that associated with music, with their fertility, and with their sexuality. It is the accumulation of too much potential out-of-controlness that creates tension. The tension relates to whether women's musical performance will bring on social integration or destruction; whether or not the power of music will cause women and men to lose control sexually or withdraw their fertility; and whether or not raw sound, in the hands of a woman, will really become music (*nigun*).

From the feminist perspective, then, the laws pertaining to *kol isha* indicate part of a carefully constructed and historically validated ideology that explains, rationalizes, or otherwise obscures the asymmetrical relationship of Lubavitcher men and women as social groups. *Kol isha,* in its effective silencing of women's literal and figurative voices, is at its core a strategy of males to deny women their sexuality, hence their power over group survival. *Kol isha,* like many of the restrictive codes of Orthodox Judaism, is a complex elaboration upon a theme of male dominance within a strongly patriarchal system that, in spite of protestations to the contrary, values the actions and behaviors of men over those of women.[16]

Perspective 3: Miriam, Looking Out

The idea is that a woman's voice is beautiful. It has a lot of qualities that would be enticing to a man. This is a fact known everywhere. It's been looked over a lot because "liberated" woman is pushing away all her ideas about being different. [For us] the facts are taken as they really are. Woman is woman and man is man. Now, one of the considerations is that when a woman sings, it has a very appealing aspect to another man, and it should not.[17]

Over the years, in my work with Lubavitchers, I have often discussed my portraits of their culture with them. Hopeful that I have presented a true picture of their lives, I ask them to comment on my interpretations, to tell me whether or not "I've got it right." The consensus is that I often come close but that I cannot really understand the true nature of Lubavitcher life while I still remain on the outside.

For example, they say that I make too much of the artificial distinction between lifetime Lubavitchers and Ba'alei Teshuvah. Worse, I completely reverse the status hierarchy: lifetime Lubavitchers say that Ba'alei Teshuvah are *more* spiritual, *more* intense, *more* connected to the divine than they. After all, look at all they have given up to become Orthodox! Everyone does *teshuvah* (repentance), they say, but to be called a Ba'al Teshuvah is a tremendous honor. Many lifetimers say they long to have this title. Of course, there are those who look down on the Ba'alei Teshuvah, seeing them as still part of the "secular" world, but they are not in the majority.

Concerning *kol isha*, I am told that I have understood the legalities but have missed the real point by inadequately portraying the positive and vital power of women's sexuality. This is the reason, women say, that the restrictions of *kol isha* are so necessary. *Kol isha* protects them, not only against prohibited men, but also against their own sexual power. Furthermore, I have not adequately described the sense of relief that obeying the laws of *kol isha* (and all other laws and codes) has provided for the community at large in its struggle to maintain balance. I have not successfully captured the real and constant combat between animal and divine souls.

---

16. Indeed, this is the view of many Jewish feminists who have in recent years challenged the historical and legal bases of many of these restrictive laws by becoming Rabbis, cantors, and other synagogue and community leaders.

17. Miriam Rosenblum, personal interview, Pittsburgh, Pennsylvania, August 1975.

Finally, they say, my analysis of their gender roles and statuses is simply wrong. Don't I know how important women are to maintaining Jewish continuity? How central home life is to Jewish culture? How can I suggest that women are a subordinated social group or that individual women are pawns, manipulated by powerful social forces beyond their control—at best, unconscious of their subordinated position; at worst, victims of a dominant male hierarchy that seeks to deny them their powerful sexuality? It is easy, they say, simply to dismiss this description; it is too secular, too much a part of the "outside."

Is it possible that I have been mistaken in my descriptions and analyses? Have I not observed carefully enough? Have I allowed my biases to creep in and to skew what I have seen? Or, worse, are my informants not being truthful with me? Are they, tired of being misinterpreted by researchers and the press, expressing a "party line" to the latest outsider, however well-intentioned she may be?

Out and In Together

Lately, in these self-reflexive days of postmodernism, there has been an attempt in anthropology to integrate inside and outside perspectives better by interweaving the voices of informants and ethnographers into a more convincing picture that represents cultural collaboration rather than presentation. Known as the new or reflexive ethnography, this style has perhaps been best represented in works by James Clifford and George E. Marcus and by Marjorie Shostak, among others.[18] In allowing the Other to speak, the new ethnography attempts to equalize the traditional power relationship between the observer self and the observed Other by reversing, or at least minimizing, the differences between these perspectives. On the surface this goal appears laudable, in that the ethnographer no longer appears to speak for the informant, and the insider perspective is apparently integrated into the analysis. Even the new ethnography, however, is still somewhat encumbered by the voice of the ethnographer, who, in openly attempting to acknowledge and minimize the power differential between self and Other, can actually highlight it.

How, then, can we uncover the separate, often competing voices that inform cultural descriptions? First, we must make clear whose voice is really speaking, and to what purpose. In the spirit of the new ethnog-

18. James Clifford and George E. Marcus, eds., *Writing Culture: The Poetics and Politics of Ethnography* (Berkeley, 1986); Marjorie Shostak, *Nisa: The Life and Words of a !Kung Woman* (Cambridge, Mass., 1981). For a good description and some sample readings in the new ethnography, see Frances E. Mascia-Lees, Patricia Sharpe, and Colleen Ballerino Cohen, "The Postmodernist Turn in Anthropology: Cautions from a Feminist Perspective," *Signs: Journal of Women in Culture and Society* 15 (1989): 7–33.

raphy, I suggest that we examine more closely the dynamic of power, not only within the societies we study, but also as it affects cultural presentation.

The Dynamics of Social Power

Underlying all social relations are cultural notions of power that are continuously enacted in everyday and ritual behaviors. According to Roger Keesing, in an analysis of power relations we need to "look *through* cultural conceptualizations as well as *at* them. . . . We need to see the realities of power: who has it, who uses it, in what ways, to what ends."[19]

In an important article devoted to modeling the dynamics of social power, Richard Adams argues that power is "the ability of a person or social unit to influence the conduct and decision-making of another through the control over energetic forms in the latter's environment."[20] Control over valued resources is maintained through elaborate interactions that articulate explicit or implicit threats of withdrawal. Simple control over resources, though, does not necessarily create a dynamic of power. Rather, power is an outgrowth of the *ranking* of differences and the assignment of value and status to certain differences over others. A central feature of power, according to Adams, is the manipulation of tensions between cultural notions of control and out-of-controlness. Adams cites the tendency in many cultures to associate elements of relative control in their world and to place them in binary opposition to elements that are relatively out of control.

Developing Adams's model, let us distinguish between states of in-control and out-of-control—states of differing degrees of order or balance, based on culture-specific notions of those states—and "controlling," that is, exercising a degree of constraint upon another. Second, let us place this system within a specific context.[21] Power, in a general sense, can be seen as part of a larger, closed system involving culture-specific (or idiosyncratic) notions of states of in-control and out-of-control, belief systems of tremendous complexity that help to define and give validity to these notions, and controlling behaviors of various styles (ranging from influence to coercion) that are brought into play for the purpose of stabilizing the system. The system itself is embedded in a context that defines the specific people or social units and their long-term or immediate interests.

19. Keesing, *Cultural Anthropology*, p. 299.
20. Richard N. Adams, "Power in Human Societies: A Synthesis," in Raymond D. Fogelson and Richard N. Adams, eds., *The Anthropology of Power: Ethnographic Studies from Asia, Oceania, and the New World* (New York, 1977), p. 388.
21. See Keesing, *Cultural Anthropology*, p. 299.

We have not yet introduced specific people (or "social units") into the model. Doing so will isolate and crystallize the relevant dynamic of power. Carefully defining in-control, out-of-control, controlling behaviors or laws, and the context of their interaction by "inserting" specific people, groups, and behaviors into these categories helps to clarify the voice that is speaking, and to what end it speaks.

We can now isolate at least two general kinds of power relationships that exist simultaneously and are embedded in any portrait of a culture: (1) the dynamics that exist between the people or social groups being described or analyzed; and (2) the power dynamic between the ethnographer and the informant, each with his or her own agenda. In this essay we have been concerned primarily with describing and analyzing the first set of power relationships: those within Lubavitcher culture. Let us now focus on the second dynamic, through which the first dynamic is filtered: that between the narrating self and the carefully constructed Other. To illustrate, let us return to the scene with which we began, of Miriam singing her song as she lights Sabbath candles. Using the model I have been developing, I will show how differing power dynamics between the presenter and the presented create the widely different portraits seen above.

In Perspective 1, the so-called descriptive portrait, the ethnographer is primarily interested in portraying a convincing picture of a culture largely foreign or "exotic" to his or her anticipated audience. This observer sees the system as a whole as in balance; individual differences are smoothed over, possibly seen as irrelevant or even problematic. This observer is not making an explicit judgment about either the validity of Miriam's actions or their value.[22] What is highlighted is the balance of life in the big picture. To give authenticity to this portrait, the ethnographer may give the impression that Miriam herself is speaking. However, we know this is a fiction, that it is really the ethnographer who has recorded the event and who has fitted this piece together with others, locking them into a satisfying whole.

Miriam, for her part, wishes to present her culture carefully and truthfully. She knows that the researcher (possibly a professor from a major university) has access to the larger world outside, and if the description is "right," many people will be affected by the beauty and strength of Lubavitcher philosophy. Both she and the researcher need each other: their relationship must be kept in balance, or the chance for her truth to reach the secular world will be lost.

Now we move to Perspective 2. Here the outsider analyst's agenda is to expose the underlying structures that govern Miriam's life and, by

22. However, the very act of having observed and perhaps participated in this scene attests to its implicit value as data.

implication, those of all Lubavitcher women. There is no pretense of an insider's perspective here. Miriam is not even presented as an individual. What are highlighted are the potential instabilities of the system and the controlling factors, in the form of codes of behavior imposed by one social group on another for the purpose of maintaining a status quo of male dominance. Miriam will no doubt be offended by this portrait. She will see it as simply wrong; it will be of no use to her. She may attribute this skewed analysis to the dominance of the animal soul in the researcher and will dismiss this picture of her world.

Finally, in Perspective 3, Miriam's agenda (the word seems odd here) is to light the candles and to greet the Sabbath joyously. She is simply acting, not observing herself act. There is no audience for her actions (except perhaps God). She understands, without really thinking about it, the need for *kol isha*, because she has internalized the Lubavitcher world-view that sees her as more inherently spiritual than a man. *Kol isha* validates her spirituality and sexuality and links her to other women in a positive way. Miriam is empowered by this, secure in the knowledge that she occupies a structurally superior and more powerful position than her male counterpart. However, she is also aware of the threatening potential of her voice and understands that for the moment the animal soul has the potential to dominate. Here the animal and divine souls and the controlling code of *kol isha* are not in balance but are widely fluctuating, their outcome uncertain.

The ethnographers, for their part, might or might not be aware of or sensitive to Miriam's ideas. They may feel that they have the right to present her as they wish, for their main goal is not to please Miriam or to become like her but, rather, to present their own picture for a different audience. Their audience is not God or other Lubavitchers but, most probably, other academics—historians, ethnomusicologists, and feminists—who form part of a larger scholarly and political community.

I do not wish to imply that observers of any stripe are simply a bunch of insensitive louts, constructing fictitious accounts of others' lives to serve a malevolent colonialist or political purpose, much less that they do not care about or that they demean the people with whom they work. Nor do I wish to suggest that cultural informants are always politically motivated, purposefully untruthful, or eager to trick ethnographers—although there are certainly such cases. Rather, I simply wish, in this small academic exercise, to call attention to the many intentional or unintentional biases through which all so-called raw data, whether currently ethnographic or historic, are filtered, and to suggest that we begin to integrate perspectives so that we may better portray the wholeness of cultures, both observed and lived, rather than remain content telling stories that are less about the Other than about ourselves.

Lesbian Fugue: Ethel Smyth's Contrapuntal Arts

Elizabeth Wood

Write a poem on the ruses of cruising, fears in the street, long strolls seeking those who run away, "looking for love where it can't be found and waiting for love where it will not come," how to evade with the happy foreknowledge of being caught, how to reject gracefully and ungraciously, etc. And call it: The Art of the Fugue.[1]

If we think about meaning in music and how it is produced, about music as a socially constructed discourse whose meanings are decipherable once we learn to interpret its rules and codes, we may find composers using music in special ways. In life, and in their narratives about life, composers may resort to music and musical procedures as a source of allusions, metaphors, roles, and techniques. They may also use music as a sound-form of narrative: as a way to tell truths about life, shape subjectivity, and make audible feelings that are essentially private, whose meanings words may only partially reveal.[2] If we read together works of music and autobiographical texts, we in turn may use musical techniques and allusions to explicate texts, listen to life, and hear its secrets.

Or so I speculate from reading the music and texts (memoirs, diaries, and letters) composed by Ethel Smyth (1858–1944). As her biographer, I am interested in the ways Smyth, an acknowledged lesbian, represented her sexuality to a reading public. Although apparently candid in print

Early versions of this essay were read at the Columbia University Institute for Research on Women and Gender, the Graduate Center of the City University of New York Committee for Lesbian and Gay Studies, and the Fourth Annual Conference of Lesbian Gay and Bisexual Studies at Harvard University. I am grateful to the participants at those events for their responses, and to Julie Abraham, Teresa de Lauretis, Lawrence Mass, Miranda Pollard, Ruth A. Solie, Catharine R. Stimpson, and Elizabeth Vantrease for their comments.

1. Ned Rorem, *The Paris and New York Diaries of Ned Rorem, 1951–1961* (San Francisco, 1983), p. 299.

2. Jacques Attali suggests that music is an instrument of understanding that "prompts us to decipher a sound form of knowledge" (*Noise: The Political Economy of Music*, trans. Brian Massumi [Minneapolis, 1985], p. 4).

about "a certain twist" in her sexual composition and lifelong attachments to women, whenever (and repeatedly) she tried to tell the story of the unhappy ending of her first major love affair, her writing becomes oblique and oddly secretive.[3]

Although Smyth was not one to lie or duck such issues, her attempt to camouflage a lesbian theme seems at first sight complicit with social realities that constructed the lesbian as invisible and inaudible. During the 1920s and 1930s in England, where in old age Smyth published her memoirs, it was hazardous, if not impossible, for any writer openly to proclaim her lesbianism, given prevailing discourses on homosexuality as congenital inversion and deviancy and, in an atmosphere of increasing hostility, when lesbian work was censored.[4] One of Smyth's closest friends, Lady Ponsonby, had nicknamed her "the Contrapuntalist" for the multiple, often violently conflicting themes and dramas she met in life and managed in love and work.[5] I decided to follow Lady Ponsonby's example. Reading Smyth's work—both music and writing—together with her life, I found "the Contrapuntalist" using music in ways that simultaneously reveal and conceal lesbian experience; that her narrative invention, which inscribes a musically coded lesbian message, is derived from the craft as well as the metaphor of fugue and fugal counterpoint.

"Human beings are constructed, like fugues," she said, "on one or two chief themes, which recur again and again; and if the 'treatment' varies a little each time, it is as obviously predetermined by the Great Composer as the themes themselves. Perhaps Death may deliver us from these fugal bonds—but Life never does!"[6] Smyth's fugal theme of lesbian desire, with its counterpoint of conflict and concord, was a bond in both senses: a restraining force (a shackle that enslaves), and a uniting tie (the pledge that binds).

Lesbian autobiographical narratives such as Smyth's "are about remembering differently, outside the contours and narrative constraints of conventional models," according to literary critic Biddy Martin. "Events or feelings . . . become signs that must be reread on the basis of different

3. Ethel Smyth to Harry Brewster, 15 March 1892, in Ethel Smyth, *As Time Went On* . . . . (London, 1936), p. 76. I am using *lesbian* in the sense of Adrienne Rich's phrase "lesbian continuum," as a range of erotic and emotional relationships between women; see Rich's "Compulsory Heterosexuality and Lesbian Existence," in her *Blood, Bread, and Poetry: Selected Prose 1979–1985* (New York, 1980), pp. 23–75.

4. See George Chauncey, Jr., "From Sexual Inversion to Homosexuality: Medicine and the Changing Conceptualization of Female Deviancy," in Robert Boyers and George Steiner, eds., *Homosexuality: Sacrilege, Vision, Politics,* special issue of *Salmagundi,* no. 58–59 (1982–1983): 114–46.

5. Ethel Smyth, *Impressions That Remained* (1919; rpt. New York, 1946), p. 474, and *As Time Went On* . . . ., pp. 84, 184.

6. Ethel Smyth, *What Happened Next* (London, 1940), p. 161.

interpretive strategies."[7] I believe Smyth constructed her autobiographical literary narratives in ways that replicate the horizontal and vertical lines of musical counterpoint, as "a string of musical items [read as] executions of gestures codified by musical convention."[8] My interpretive strategy, then, is to reread according to contrapuntal principles her work that both "constitutes and . . . transforms the codes, . . . [and] the individuals using the codes, performing the work."[9]

Two distinct lines—one represented by Smyth's musical scores, the other by her letters written at the same time—comprise the horizontal element in counterpoint. In my contrapuntal reading, her correspondence suggests (melodic) voices and (thematic) threads that, read together with the scores, constitute a chronological sketch of a personal and professional identity in the process of construction. Smyth's memoirs represent the vertical element in counterpoint. They function in ways similar to the incidental occurrence of intervals in musical counterpoint, suggesting a controlling (and harmonizing) voice that retrospectively reconstitutes and reinterprets identity and comprehends the strands of experience.

When we consider that fugue is supreme among baroque and academic genres for its prestige and technical authority, we can see Smyth's fugal code and narrative invention as an audacious and rebellious subversion of musical convention. My reading proposes, moreover, that it was fugue's historical association with the mounted hunt and, metaphorically, with sexual seduction that suggested to Smyth referential as well as form-defining ways in which to reconstruct her erotic relationships with women and to shape lesbian experience.

To outline, first, fugue's generic pattern and musical protocol: fugal counterpoint constructs two or more voices on horizontal narrative lines. As these voices sound together or coincide, vertical chords or harmonies are produced. Sections in which the main subject or theme of the fugue appears (first in one voice, then in another) are called expositions. Sections that do not include a statement of the main subject are episodes, based mostly upon short motifs derived from the subject or its continuation or countersubject. For the sake of variety and intensity, such episodic motifs are put through different sequences at different pitches. These motifs may be freer than the expository subject and lighter in

7. Biddy Martin, "Lesbian Identity and Autobiographical Difference(s)," in Bella Brodzki and Celeste Schenck, eds., *Life/Lines: Theorizing Women's Autobiography* (Ithaca, 1988), p. 85.

8. Carolyn Abbate, "What the Sorcerer Said," *19th-Century Music* 12 (1989): 225.

9. Teresa de Lauretis, *Alice Doesn't: Feminism, Semiotics, Cinema* (Bloomington, 1984), p. 167. De Lauretis also discusses the relation of experience to subjectivity as a process by which subjectivity is constituted, through which the self is placed in social reality (pp. 159 ff.).

weight and texture; they may involve modulations to a minor or relative key and may interrupt or intervene during the course of a later exposition. Filling the spaces between appearances of the main subject is a narrative counterpoint unified by use of recurrent motifs derived from that theme itself or, more often, from its continuation, which forms an answering counterpoint. Fugal procedure in music employs various complex devices to manipulate the subject and its countersubject—such as augmentation, diminution, inversion, or stretto—but whatever the preceding explorations, the main theme returns in a final coda which reaffirms its original characteristics and tonality.

In its original meaning of flight, *fuga* articulated and served certain social functions and values that had specifically to do with the mounted hunt. Fourteenth-century contrapuntal art music with naturalistic hunting sounds or scenes includes the French *chace*, Spanish *caça*, and Italian *caccia*, words used synonymously with *fugue* to denote passages or entire pieces written in canon with the notion of one voice chasing another before capture, and imitation and exchange among the voices.[10] Participants in the hunt, like voices in fugal counterpoint, enact a colorful display of power and agility in a heroic mode in which chance and change play variations on themes of pursuit and flight. Brass instruments of the hunt (the natural horn, forest horn, and military bugle) have been signaling and ceremonial instruments since ancient times, when their distinctive fanfares and call-and-answer motifs were features of courtly and military ceremony, warfare, and sporting competition.

The mode and movement of the hunt as pursuit, flight, conquest, and capitulation, and its musical representation in fugal counterpoint, have obvious associations with sexual seduction. For example, Maynard Solomon bases his revelation that Franz Schubert was gay on decoded evidence of pederastic cruising in bawdy letters among Schubert and his circle of friends that allude to the memoirs of Benvenuto Cellini, a literary source of homosexual code-words in hunting and fowling images of the pursuit and capture of young game pheasants, peacocks, peahens, and "pretty things."[11]

Ethel Smyth, herself a skilled hunter, horse rider, and player of the hunting horn, was also literate in hunting's musical and sexual meanings. What I call her strategy of narrative "subterfuge" enabled her first to flee lesbian conflict and consequently to claim the lesbian bond. Her coded use

10. Some French compositions that imitated hunting-horn calls were titled "La Chasse." See *The New Harvard Dictionary of Music*, ed. Don Michael Randel (Cambridge, Mass., 1986), pp. 120, 130, 145, 153, 328. My accounts of fugal form and procedure are standard and can be found, among other places, in the same *Dictionary*, pp. 327–39.

11. Maynard Solomon, "Franz Schubert and the Peacocks of Benvenuto Cellini," *19th-Century Music* 12 (1989): 193–206.

of fugal counterpoint—in patterns of simultaneous revelation and con-
cealment—technically resembles Bach's brilliantly deceptive work, *The Art
of Fugue*, which stands outside traditional fugal concepts in that, although
several themes appear at the outset, the main theme enters only later to
combine with them. Eventually, because of its more complete melodic
characteristics, this theme dominates over all the others. As it usurps their
function, they sound subsidiary by comparison.[12] Smyth's fugal disguise
and delay on the theme of lesbianism was perhaps only in part a strategy
to prevent public disclosure or further censure. Long after this particular
relationship had ended, she seemed unwilling to permit its destructive
effects either to silence her or to usurp and dominate ways she subsequently chose to live and to represent lesbian identity.

Smyth intended to "set life to music as I myself have seen and overheard it" as a series of dramatic acts and scenes.[13] In her memoirs, amid
the anecdotal recitative of daily life and extended aria-portraits of her
friends and lovers, Smyth depicts life as contrapuntal struggle among
conflicting themes: of "my music, . . . the absorbing passion for sport
and games, . . . the impossibility of bearing moral pain, . . . the pull of life
and the constant longing for calm, the fascination of difficulties and
barriers, the need of human contact and affection, the love of one's own
ways."[14] Unlike life, which she represents as a confused, restless, and
often desperate journey, a piece of music is a "rounded-off episode, its
proportions settled to start with."[15] If music shaped life and gave it
meaning, in composing life she might find musical ways to resolve and
reconcile its conflicts.[16]

Smyth's fugal treatment of lesbian conflict in the central narratives
about her first love affair embodies forms and procedures of continuation
and repetition—or both combined, since these are not contradictory—
with certain phrases occurring again and again, sometimes the same,
sometimes changed, across a writing span of twenty years. The story of
a relationship that began in 1878 and ended in 1885 appears first in
chapters 18 to 26 in the first volume of *Impressions That Remained* (1919);
dominates the entire second volume; recurs in the first chapter of her
seventh book, *As Time Went On* . . . . (1936); and returns once more, four

12. Roger Bullivant, *Fugue* (London, 1971), p. 160.
13. Ethel Smyth, "A New Departure in Comic Opera," in *A Final Burning of Boats, Etc.*
(London, 1928), p. 202.
14. *Impressions That Remained*, p. 339.
15. *As Time Went On* . . . ., pp. 138–39.
16. "Autobiography occupies a zone between self-discovery and self-invention . . . [and]
is often a medium for reconciling conflicting aspects of the self," says Maynard Solomon,
in "Charles Ives: Some Questions of Veracity," *Journal of the American Musicological Society*
40 (1987): 445.

years before Smyth died, in the prologue of her last, *What Happened Next* (1940).

The structure of each narrative is similar. Clusters of chapters, presented chronologically, are interrupted by "Letter Sections" of excerpts Smyth edited from her extensive correspondence with the leading characters in her story. These letters function in several ways. First, as private texts representing the real time of events portrayed, they fuel the public narrative by serving as autobiographical documentation and illustration of its themes.[17] Second, their placement in the narrative structure disrupts the interplay of time past with the present time of writing and reading, enabling Smyth simultaneously to act as writer, reader, and editor. Third, letters written by others to Smyth vary the narrative voice, perspective, and texture: a musical strategy represented in fugal procedures as episodic modulations to different keys among different and fragmented voices.

Smyth's synopsis before each chapter outlines in brief its main themes. My example comes from the first chapter of *As Time Went On. . . .* , headed: "Life in Leipzig. The Herzogenbergs. The story of myself and the Brewsters. Lisl Herzogenberg breaks with me and I with Harry Brewster." I interpret her treatment of these themes as a construction of alternating expositions and episodes in which elements of the main subject, her lesbian bond with Lisl, reappear throughout. My summary of the story and its division into a fugal scheme is not Smyth's narrative but my interpretive reconstruction of its several versions. It does not try to capture the uniquely funny, spunky, and candid tone of Smyth's voice. In spite of her seemingly effortless and artless style, Smyth told this particular story in so many versions and at such convoluted length that it is difficult to know precisely what is going on. Mine is but a sketch of a plot whose complications rival any nineteenth-century tragicomic opera.

Exposition 1: When she was a student of composition in Leipzig in 1878 at the age of twenty, Ethel Smyth had fallen in love with Elisabeth (Lisl) von Herzogenberg, at thirty-one a beautiful, musically gifted aristocrat, the friend of Johannes Brahms and Clara Schumann, and wife of Heinrich, a notable music pedant who had begun to give Smyth private lessons in harmony and counterpoint. For the following seven years, Smyth was a third partner, the child, in Lisl's childless marriage. "MotherLisl," as she had Smyth call her, reciprocated her love passionately and possessively.

17. Letters may "exemplify a particular women's text, one that is neither wholly private nor wholly public," and form "an autobiography of the self with others," says Catharine R. Stimpson, "The Female Sociograph: The Theater of Virginia Woolf's Letters," in her *Where the Meanings Are: Feminism and Cultural Spaces* (New York, 1988), p. 130.

Episode 1: On holidays at home in England or in Lisl's absence, Ethel initiated other love affairs that caused Lisl anxiety and jealousy. One that momentarily threatened Lisl's preeminence was Ethel's love for Rhoda Garrett, member of a well-known family of English feminist activists, but the brief affair was ended late in 1882 by Rhoda's death from tuberculosis.

Exposition 2: In that year Ethel made the first of several visits to Florence without Lisl and against Heinrich's advice. There she became entangled in the lives of two married couples who were mutual friends: the German sculptor Adolf Hildebrand and his wife Irene; and the part-American, part-French writer Harry Brewster and his wife Julia. Lisl, who was Julia's younger sister, knew the quartet well and warned Ethel of their bohemian, sexually sophisticated ways. The Brewsters favored a form of open marriage based on friendship, freedom, and trust. Should one weary of the other or be attracted to another, they had agreed amicably to dissolve the marital bond.

During this time in Florence, Ethel embarked on *secondary episodes* that involved both couples. At first, she thought she might be falling in love with Adolf—in part, she said, from a desire to be loved and cared for, but in part knowingly protected by his ineligibility as a married man and her own instinct for independence. Ethel confessed these feelings to Irene Hildebrand and tried in her letters to Lisl to reassure her that all was well between them. In fact, Ethel was more disturbingly attracted to Julia Brewster and regularly wrote to Lisl in Leipzig details of her amorous campaign to breach Julia's cool reserve. These letters caused Lisl considerable anguish.

Episode 2: Just as Ethel had decided she was winning Julia's affection, Julia's husband Harry told his wife that he had fallen in love with Ethel and had determined to make her his mistress. On their first meeting Ethel had disliked Harry intensely, but she had come to enjoy intellectual combat and companionship with him. His declaration of love flattered and confused her and caused much havoc among the Herzogenberg, Hildebrand, and Brewster marriages. In panic, Ethel raced back and forth between Florence, Leipzig, and her Surrey home, unsure what to do and what she wanted.

Exposition 3: Lisl's desire to fight for Ethel and their relationship was steadily eroded by conflicting loyalty to her sister Julia and their stern, formidable mother, who had arrived in Florence. Julia's fine ideals about marriage crumbled, and she became manipulative and devious toward Ethel and Lisl. Harry pursued Ethel to Leipzig and tried to persuade her to an affair. Gossip abounded, spread by an irate Irene Hildebrand and Lisl's mother and brother. The prospect of public shame and scandal so overwhelmed Lisl that in 1885 she broke off with Ethel and insisted on permanent silence between them. They never saw each other again.

Coda: In the aftermath of events in 1885, Harry left Julia for a time and went to live alone in Paris, where he wrote his first book of metaphysics called, appropriately, *Theories of Anarchy and Law.* Angry, confused, suffering a nervous breakdown in exile in England, and afraid for her musical future in Europe, Ethel formed concurrent passionate attachments with the mothers and daughters of the Benson and Trevelyan families. Shortly before Lisl died of heart disease in 1892, Ethel again and unexpectedly met Harry Brewster in London at her orchestral concert debut. A deep and lasting friendship flourished with Harry's collaboration in the librettos of her first three operas. When he unwisely proposed marriage after Julia died in 1895, Ethel furiously refused him but did agree to meet him in Paris to have sex, an oddly moving experience that she said she had no wish to repeat. Harry had to settle for a chaste long-distance friendship that endured until his death in 1908. In Ethel's subsequent memoirs, begun during the First World War, Harry is represented as a prominent but strangely insubstantial figure in comparison with numerous personal portraits of her women lovers and friends.

What follows is my three-part commentary on the texts of this particular story: Smyth's retrospective memoirs; contemporary letters in the narrative; and music composed during its course.

The Memoirs: More than thirty years beyond the ending of Smyth's relationship with Lisl, when she had entered her sixties and grown deaf, and all the other characters of the drama were dead, she repeatedly tried to tell the "inner history of that fantastic triangular duel, that mad essay in three-part counterpoint."[18] But even as she reshaped it to permit new details gradually to emerge, what is said and left unsaid remains on casual reading problematic. Her camouflage of lesbian cause and explanation serves to replicate the actions of those who forced Lisl to reject Smyth: Lisl's family, and friends including the Hildebrands who, representing Smyth as an outsider, a dangerous interloper to their class, kin, and social position, had expelled her from their midst. Smyth's subterfuge—a more conventional, if scandalous, heterosexual plot in which Lisl is eclipsed by Harry Brewster—effectively denies the lesbian by inscribing in her place the presence of a different sexual subject that renders Smyth's self-representation more paradoxical and unconvincing.

18. *As Time Went On . . . .,* p. 10.

For Ethel Smyth wanted readers to believe that she, too, found the ending of her affair with Lisl "unusual, puzzling, indeed almost inexplicable as psychological study."[19] The muzzling as well as deafening effect of the silence Lisl imposed was as if, Smyth said, "when I first heard a Beethoven quartet, and felt endless possibilities for further comprehension, someone said: 'You may never hear a note of music again.'"[20] Although Smyth refused to permit her voice or music to be silenced, her retellings have a repetitive, almost obsessive sound, as if silence still dazed and dominated her as receding time cast memory as myth. Once upon a time, she would begin again, "there lived in Leipzig a very remarkable couple . . . an inseparable trio."[21]

Only once did Smyth hint that the "mad essay" hid a homosexual theme. In her 1919 version of the story, she confessed that "dissolution . . . has always interested me even more than origins" since her childhood preoccupation with the destruction of Saul's love for David—a "form of death in life" which the loss of Lisl resembled.[22] The ending of her first great passion so shattered her, its circumstance so distorted her identity, that she never forgot it. Applying to the experience of "death in life" the principle of repetition, a structural aspect of music that also means rehearsal and that has the effect of intensifying time past by moving it into a present time of writing and reading, she might relive the love, repossess the beloved, and rewrite the loss. Repetition, more an artifice of discourse than a property of the story it represents, enabled Smyth to articulate feelings that had been disguised and fugitive but to keep invisible both her lesbian relationship with Lisl and its subsequent cover-up by others. To expose the cover-up would risk exposure of its source. One of the paradoxical effects of Smyth's use of repetition, its disarming candor, is a chattering echo that distracts readers from learning the source of the truth.[23] While obsessive repetition may also be an effective strategy for managing anxiety, its devices of imitation or mimicry, variation, and sequential treatment create a structure for thematic continuation, a way to reclaim identity.[24] Repetition immersed Smyth in

19. *Impressions That Remained*, p. 366, and "a tragic inexplicable mystery," p. 488.

20. Ethel Smyth to Harry Brewster, 1885, in Christopher St. John, *Ethel Smyth: A Biography* (London, 1959), p. 46 n. 3.

21. *As Time Went On . . . .*, pp. 6–7; another version in Ethel Smyth, "I Knew a Man: Brahms," speech broadcast on the BBC National Program, London, 27 December 1935; typescript p. 5, Recorded Item 11666-7.

22. *Impressions That Remained*, p. 365.

23. On reading the Echo myth, see Tania Modleski, "Feminism and the Power of Interpretation: Some Critical Readings," in Teresa de Lauretis, ed., *Feminist Studies/Critical Studies* (Bloomington, 1986), pp. 126–27.

24. Mary Jacobus discusses repetitive anxiety in Charlotte Perkins Gilman's "The Yellow Wallpaper" in *Reading Woman: Essays in Feminist Criticism* (New York, 1986), p. 246.

order to deliver her. Only then might she forgive Lisl and Lisl's family and friends for rejecting her.

Although the memoirs disguise the homoerotic nature of their relationship, allusions to Lisl's hands and hair, "a lovingness that had the sweetness of ripe, perfect fruit," and "an almost bewilderingly rich, tender form to affection" encode both a familiar nineteenth-century romantic rhetoric and an effect of cultural repression: the absence of a structure in which to describe forbidden desire.[25] An absence of cultural structures, writes Julie Abraham, is as much an effect of oppression and social taboo as is a "fear of punishment that forces silence." Lesbian artists, Abraham continues, found indirect ways of "saying things that could not have been imagined without the forms they created, and through creating the forms they spoke."[26] In the discourse of her music profession, Smyth found alternative ways to conceptualize, understand, and represent a lesbian erotic, ways that displace the discourse of a heterosexist, homophobic system represented by Lisl's family and a society that had exiled and silenced her.

Smyth likened herself to an instrument with two strings that embodied two lovers and vibrated to their touch, a triple play on love, for her favorite ensemble formation was a love triangle.[27] A trio strategy configured her intense need to be loved, to belong to a musical group, and to replace her own inadequate and unreliable parents. Smyth took the part of a prodigal child to an adored older woman who eagerly adopted her as the longed-for daughter. "MotherLisl" acted as sexual subject and agent of erotic desire, while her maternal protection nurtured Smyth's art and freed her to pursue untraditional female paths. The passive husband acted as teacher. An underlying tension to the trio—Smyth's sexual attraction to the woman and her need to have the attraction both disguised and contained by a cooperative husband—only added creative intensity to the musical bond on which the trio openly was founded. For it was music that made attraction and participation legitimate, just as it was through music that Smyth could fully and freely express passion. A

25. *Impressions That Remained*, pp. 232, 487. See Carroll Smith-Rosenberg, "The Female World of Love and Ritual: Relations Between Women in Nineteenth-Century America," *Signs: Journal of Women in Culture and Society* 1 (1975): 1–29. Teresa de Lauretis suggests that to disguise erotic and sexual experience, or to inscribe the lesbian erotic in code, was to suppress representation of its specificity: lesbian writers "dislodge the erotic" in order to escape, deny, and transcend gender ("Sexual Indifference and Lesbian Representation," *Theatre Journal* 40 [1988]: 162–64).

26. Julie Abraham, "History as Explanation: Writing About Lesbian Writing, or 'Are Girls Necessary'?" in Lennard J. Davis and M. Bella Mirabella, eds., *Left Politics and the Literary Profession* (New York, 1990), p. 264.

27. *As Time Went On . . . .*, p. 139.

man might teach her contrapuntal technique. Only a woman could inspire it.

From early youth, Smyth was attracted to maternal power, to women's "peculiar understanding, mothering quality."[28] Older, married, mostly upper-class women, who represented a more complete and powerful version of her ideal self, granted her a privileged position as resident "child-bride" within heterosexual marriage, which she regarded as "the most perfect relation of all" but from which, "given my life and outlook," she was sexually excluded.[29] Smyth's trio formations, however, subvert the normative heterosexual triangle, a male-female-male erotic paradigm of male domination and patriarchal control in which women are "between men."[30] Rather do they represent the musical structure of a trio sonata in which the contrapuntal lines for the two upper parts (each representing a female voice) have a similar range and design, while the bass or lower part (representing a male voice) provides their support or ground. Not surprisingly, given her female-female erotic bias, Smyth was totally unprepared for a man (especially a husband, whom she counted ineligible on account of his marital responsibility and supportive role in the triangle) to break rank and interrupt her lesbian counterpoint with expressions of male desire. She failed to recognize that Harry Brewster, by virtue of his open marital agreement with Julia, considered himself eligible. Phallic desire, penetrating the trio, destroyed it. Hereafter, Smyth's love triangles comprised women only.

As if human relationships were constructed on contrapuntal principles, Smyth represented her lesbian affairs as a series of consecutive cycles, each lasting continuously for at least seven years. A new cycle invariably began, she said, with the cry, "My God, what a woman!"[31] After themes of desire had run their ecstatic and turbulent course and the relationship established harmony in lifelong friendship, another triumphant shout announced a new subject of desire and the start of a new exposition.

Letters in the Narrative: Smyth made public in her memoirs excerpts from an extensive correspondence with Lisl in which, she claimed, "all the

28. *Impressions That Remained*, p. 259. Jessica Benjamin discusses a psychoanalytic "triangulation" theory that defends the father and phallus against maternal power in the formation of a young girl's gender identity ("A Desire of One's Own: Psychoanalytic Feminism and Intersubjective Space," in *Feminist Studies/Critical Studies*, pp. 85–89, p. 100 n. 17).

29. *Impressions That Remained*, p. 258.

30. This is the form of Eve Kosofsky Sedgwick's "erotic triangle" of male homosocial desire, in *Between Men: English Literature and Male Homosocial Desire* (New York, 1985), p. 26; an alternative lesbian configuration, a female-male-female triangle in which "men are 'between women,'" is suggested in Terry Castle, "Sylvia Townsend Warner and the Counterplot of Lesbian Fiction," *Textual Practice* 4 (1990): 213–35.

31. *As Time Went On . . . .*, p. 38.

secrets of my heart stand revealed."[32] Here the reader finds a private layer of lesbian experience, although by no means all its secrets, since their complete correspondence has never been published. In their letters the two women played role inversions and variations upon them, mostly fantasized by Lisl for Ethel's enactment, on "a fantastic progress through an eternal transformation scene."[33] In the guise of mother and child, Ethel played "Little Euphorion," child of Goethe's Faust and Helen of Troy and personification of the union of romantic with classical poetry. In a wry comment after the break, Smyth acknowledged the impermanence of euphoria in that Goethe had also intended the child to represent Lord Byron, who "came to grief through wilfulness and daring."[34]

On holiday in England, where Smyth dallied in pursuit of Rhoda Garrett and indulged a passion for foxhunting to the neglect of Heinrich's "horrid" counterpoint exercises, she received letters from Lisl that likened their relationship to *The Magic Flute* and cast Ethel as Tamino, the susceptible outsider and foreigner seeking knowledge but wanting wisdom, herself as an ardent, loyal Pamina, apprehensive of the impending tests of their endurance.[35] But on Ethel's departure for Italy, shortly before Rhoda's death, Lisl's distressed epistolary imagination cast Ethel as "poor little Tannhäuser," a hero seduced and corrupted by Venus, whose true beloved, faithful Elisabeth, was destined to stay at home to pray for their eventual reunion while her lover went on fruitless pilgrimage to Rome in search of moral purification.[36] (The Herzogenbergs both detested opera, particularly Wagner's, but made an exception of Beethoven's *Fidelio*, in which Lisl identified with Leonora, the good wife and rescuer.)

As their affair began to unravel, Smyth's letters to MotherLisl further infantilized herself as innocent victim, target of unseen betrayals, a motherless waif. Lisl, however, reminded her of a previous self-representation as a "great rough egoistic young colt" with violent energy and "ridiculous fancies."[37] Since Lisl scorned Ethel's hunting and sporting activities, her letters voiced a scorching countersubject that inverted rough horse into ruthless rider. "You are a Juggernaut, a blind horsewoman blinded by self-love, galloping roughshod over all," she blazed. "I say your guilt lies

32. *Impressions That Remained*, p. 258.

33. *Impressions That Remained*, p. 487.

34. Elisabeth von Herzogenberg to Ethel Smyth, 27 May 1878, referring to Goethe's *Faustus*, Part 2, Act 3 (*Impressions That Remained*, p. 220 and n. 15).

35. Lisl erroneously reversed these characterizations: Elisabeth von Herzogenberg to Ethel Smyth, 9 June 1878, *Impressions That Remained*, p. 223.

36. Elisabeth von Herzogenberg to Ethel Smyth, 10 April 1880, in *Impressions That Remained*, p. 283.

37. *Impressions That Remained*, p. 353.

in that tendency to make elbow-room for yourself . . . to develop your own being at any cost, to revel in your power over others, to let your personality work its own will, to deny that it could or should be subject to restriction, to be careless of the harm it may do others." As parting shot, Lisl said she had no doubt Ethel would soon find consolation elsewhere, "given your gift for getting the most out of life."[38]

Smyth does seem at times to have been careless of Lisl's feelings, particularly her jealousy of her sister Julia and longing for affection from her mother. Lisl felt she had given Ethel the mother-love she herself lacked, and it had appalled her to imagine, as she read Ethel's letters from Florence, that Julia, who was "so richly endowed" with two children, could also take *her* "child" if she chose.[39] Ethel had not undermined Lisl's marriage. If anything, she had been its consolation and compensation: for Lisl's failure to conceive both musically and maternally; for Heinrich's failure as a composer and, perhaps, as a lover.

That Lisl reciprocated Ethel's passion is clear from an unpublished, unfinished, unsigned letter that broke her two-year vow of silence for a single last time. It ended: "I was never and am not unfaithful to you and our mutual past. What separates us now is stronger than you and I [and here the words 'and our passion' are heavily scored out]. . . . Don't try to make me say more I can not."[40] Reading this provoked in Smyth a frenzy of rage and bitterness. If reading forced recognition that the break was final, rage refused to accept it. After Lisl died and Heinrich returned to Smyth all of her letters, she angrily placed them away unread, locked in one of her soldier-father's disused military despatch boxes, a symbolic burial of secret messages of lesbian desire locked out by warrior patriarchal power.[41]

In her excerpts from private letters Smyth significantly, perhaps guiltily, edited out her erotic attraction to Julia Brewster. Her correspondence with Harry Brewster appears only from 1890, that is, after they had remet in London. Ironically, it is in the letters to Harry selected for publication in her memoirs that we find Smyth first identifying her attraction to women as homosexual desire and discussing the long-delayed fugal bond.

38. Quoted from Smyth's paraphrase of Lisl's letter, in *Impressions That Remained*, p. 371; see also Lisl's letter in English translation given to Mrs. Minnie Benson, ca. 1892, copied in St. John Small Notebook, University of Michigan Library, Ann Arbor.

39. Elisabeth von Herzogenberg to Ethel Smyth, 10 October 1883, in *Impressions That Remained*, p. 358; and 11 January 1884, MS in McMaster University Library, Hamilton, Ontario. When Smyth excerpted this letter for her memoirs, she cut out evidence of her attraction to Julia Brewster (*Impressions That Remained*, pp. 359–60).

40. Elisabeth von Herzogenberg to Ethel Smyth, 19 December 1887; MS in McMaster University Library, Hamilton, Ontario. Smyth's edited version is in *Impressions That Remained*, p. 393.

41. *Impressions That Remained*, p. 182.

Harry was all she had salvaged from the end of her affair with Lisl. As reading survivor, as memory, Harry became witness to her process of retrieval and renewal; his encouragement and understanding legitimized both the lesbian love and the loss. It was lesbian legitimacy that Smyth celebrated in Harry, not a hat-trick illusion of heterosexuality that his love for her has conjured among Smyth's biographers.[42] Of all the original voices in the fugue, only Harry had never rejected her. On the contrary, his modern views on sex and marriage accommodated and found healthy her homosexuality. Possibly it was this that had attracted him to her in the first place.

The Music: Autobiographical and representational features in Smyth's music created concurrently with her relationship with Lisl seem especially interesting if we think of musical genres "in terms less of transcendental shapes than of often-complementary discourses."[43]

Between 1878 and 1882, her apprentice years in Leipzig, Smyth worked under Herzogenberg's tutelage to acquire fluency in the contrapuntal setting of Lutheran chorale tunes in the style of Bach.[44] Lisl asked to be included in these lessons and diligently completed more exercises than Smyth reluctantly began. Heinrich's somewhat sterile habit was to write a daily dozen canons and fugues arranged as keyboard duets to play with his wife. Smyth preferred the intimate forms of song and sonata to perform alone at the piano or sing with Lisl in a reciprocal sharing of work, space, and voice. Among her earliest songs modeled on Schubert's lieder are settings of hunting, riding, and chase texts whose unmistakable rhythms, calls, and fanfares reappear in her later operas and instrumental works. In her romantic songs, Smyth's mezzo soprano voice represented in performance an ardent page or young suitor yearning for a woman's love.[45]

42. Louise Collis, for example, represents Smyth both as a "slightly hysterical" bisexual virgin and as "a chaste woman and also emotionally immature," in *Impetuous Heart: A Biography of Ethel Smyth* (London, 1984), pp. 15, 73.

43. Celeste Schenck, "All of a Piece: Women's Poetry and Autobiography," in *Life/Lines*, p. 286.

44. Heinrich von Herzogenberg was one of the founders of the Bach Verein in Leipzig. Smyth's exercises on chorales in Bach's *St. Matthew Passion* are among her earliest music, dated June–July 1879, in the collection of her music manuscripts in the British Library. A chronological *List of Works* compiled by Jory Bennett from autograph and published sources, incorporating Smyth's revisions, extracts, and arrangements, and with timings and details of scoring derived from a personal inventory Smyth made shortly before her death, concludes *The Memoirs of Ethel Smyth*, abridged and introduced by Ronald Crichton (London, 1987), pp. 373–81. My forthcoming book contains full citations of manuscript sources and locations. Smyth's works to which the following notes refer are in British Library Additional Manuscripts 45949–46938 unless otherwise noted.

45. *Lieder und Balladen*, op. 3 (Leipzig, 1886), and *Lieder*, op. 4 (Leipzig, 1886): for example, op. 3 no. 2, the ballad "Der verirrte Jäger" (Eichendorff) with halloahs, bugle

Her training included arranging from manuscript in two- and four-hand piano score Brahms's latest symphony or concerto that he sent the Herzogenbergs in advance of publication, and making fair copies of Brahms's new piano pieces. Smyth's original work from that time includes three piano sonatas, each with a literary program that dramatizes personal experience.[46] In England in 1878, she wrote her first set of *Variations on an Original Theme of an Exceedingly Dismal Nature* for piano in D♭ Major, during her first separation from Lisl, whose letters then portray Ethel as beautiful Helen's darling, daring Little Euphorion.[47] Maynard Solomon has characterized variation as the most "open" of musical procedures: a discursive form "in flight from all messages and ideologies" that mirrors life's unpredictability and offers the greatest freedom to fantasy.[48] One of Smyth's variations is dedicated to her filly, Phyllis, who had thrown her on a riding expedition, a harmless accident illustrated on the score in the composer's pencil sketch of herself coming a cropper, arms and legs flailing from a watery ditch.

On her return to Leipzig that summer, she composed another piano study dedicated to Lisl and "To Youth!!" Smyth's friend Edvard Grieg begged her to tell him its program, but it has remained a secret.[49] Two further works composed in 1880, which correspond in time to Lisl's Tamino/Pamina fantasy, are notable for wildly exuberant themes and dance rhythms.[50]

In 1882, when "Tannhäuser" left Leipzig to try working on her own in Florence, Lisl joked in an edgy aside to Brahms that Ethel "imagines she can finish all her fugues on the dominant there unrebuked."[51] Smyth rebelled against Heinrich's canonical example shortly after she met the

---

horn, and hunting call in $\frac{6}{8}$ rhythm; op. 4 no. 4, "Nachtreiter" (Karl Groth), an emphatic, dashing riding song in E Major; op. 3 no. 5, "Schön Rohtraut" (Möricke), love song of an ardent page.

46. In 1877, Sonata No. 1 in C Major (dedicated to *la Madre*); Sonata No. 2 in C♯ Minor, the "Geistinger"; Sonata No. 3 in D Major (two movements, unfinished). She also wrote variations, canons, dances, inventions, and suites for piano at this time.

47. Completed July 1878; of eight variations, the fourth ("filly") is in A Major with $\frac{6}{8}$ rhythm.

48. Maynard Solomon, *Beethoven* (New York, 1977), p. 303.

49. *Aus der Jugendzeit!!* piano study in E Minor. Edvard Grieg to Ethel Smyth, Copenhagen, 17 April 1879; *Impressions That Remained,* p. 301.

50. Sonata in C Minor for cello and piano; and Trio in D Minor for violin, cello, and piano (MSS Durham University). Smyth described as "a mere piece of student's work" a String Quartet in D Minor composed and performed in Leipzig in June 1880, whose manuscript is presumed lost (*Impressions That Remained,* p. 254). She had also begun a String Quartet in A Minor in March 1878, of which one movement survives.

51. Elisabeth von Herzogenberg to Johannes Brahms, 18 May 1882, in *Johannes Brahms: The Herzogenberg Correspondence,* ed. Max Kalbeck, trans. Hannah Bryant (1909; rpt. New York, 1987), p. 161.

Hildebrands and Brewsters and discovered that Adolf was a talented amateur violinist and violist, Harry a rusty but competent cellist. With their assistance, she experimented with her first series of string quartets, some merely sketches or single movements, two complete.[52]

On learning of Rhoda Garrett's death that November, Smyth composed a quintet for two violins, viola, and two cellos.[53] Its central adagio movement, dedicated to the memory of Rhoda, gives the main theme to viola, instrumental kin to Smyth's mezzo voice, inviting speculation that the accompanying counterpoint on paired upper and lower strings may have been intended to represent Irene and Julia, Adolf and Harry. Smyth missed the public premiere of this quintet in Leipzig in 1884, but Lisl was there. She told Ethel she had listened with mingled pride and shame, as if Smyth "were undressing before the horrid Leipzig public." Lisl was relieved that nobody present knew the source of the feelings the adagio aroused, whose name was inscribed upon the score.[54]

During the "second episode" in Florence in 1884, at about the time Harry Brewster confessed his love, Smyth again set to music sacred texts of German Lutheran chorales, some in three-part counterpoint for unaccompanied women's voices, others in four parts for both male and female soloists or mixed chorus.[55] The texts she chose travel emotionally from mourning and grief that welcomes "sweet Death," across a slow passage of time toward acceptance and tranquility, to an exultant sense of beauty at the dawn of a new day. Two, those for women's voices only, seem especially personal. One beseeches "my lover" to "think, think"; the other asks, "Why can I scarcely see you?"

52. String Quartets in E♭, E♭ (one movement), E Minor (203 bars only), C (167 bars), "Hildebrand" String Quartet in C (58 bars), and String Quartet in C Minor (four movements and a discarded set of variations; MS Durham University).

53. String Quintet in E, op. 1 (Leipzig 1884), manuscript lost. She also began a String Quintet in B Minor, two movements only (Prelude and Fugue); both quintets are scored for two violins, viola, and two cellos on the model of Schubert's String Quintet in C Major, D. 956 (1828).

54. First performed at the Leipzig Gewandhaus, 26 January 1884; Elisabeth von Herzogenberg to Ethel Smyth, 27 January 1884, in *Impressions That Remained*, p. 360.

55. Five Sacred Part-Songs Based on Chorale Tunes, for soprano, alto, tenor, and bass. Smyth also arranged Four Short Chorale Preludes for Strings and Solo Instruments (originally titled Short and Solemn Interludes for Sectional Orchestra), and Short Chorale Preludes for organ, both of which were revised and published in 1913, the latter dedicated to her organ teacher, Sir Walter Parratt (MSS in Royal College of Music). In 1882, she wrote two partsongs for women's voices and a portion of an elegy, *Sur les Lagunes*, for voice and piano on a text by Théophile Gautier (41 bars). Of the eight chorale texts set by Smyth, *O Traurigkeit, O Herzeleid*, which appears in all three settings, may have held special significance: in March 1878, soon after she and Ethel had met, Lisl had played from memory Brahms's setting for organ of a chorale and fugue on this tune (*Johannes Brahms*, ed. Kalbeck, p. 52).

The mixed-voice chorales, with their serenely controlled contrapuntal texture in the style of Bach, suggest that Smyth had retreated to Heinrich's musical example and aesthetic in search of consolation and a stability of faith displaced by Rhoda's death and the ensuing tensions in her relationship with Lisl. Her involvement with Hildebrand and Brewster may be mirrored in her inclusion of male voices. Fifty years later, Smyth inserted one of these chorales, a hymn of praise, into her last composition, a symphony for soprano and bass soloists, mixed chorus, and orchestra whose text she compiled from Brewster's book *The Prison*, a dialogue between a prisoner facing death and his immortal soul. She dedicated this work to his memory with a motto from his text, "I am striving to release that which is divine within us, and to merge it in the universally divine."[56] Although Smyth dedicated none of her music to Heinrich and only one short study to Lisl, Rhoda has a string quintet, Adolf Hildebrand a string quartet, named for them, while for Harry there are songs, operas, the choral symphony, and the chorale composed in the summer of 1884.

As her relationship with Lisl neared disintegration, on one of Smyth's brief escapes to England she met the Oxford professor of music the Reverend Sir Frederick Gore Ouseley who, like Herzogenberg, was learned in academic fugue.[57] After dinner together, Ouseley seated himself at the piano and invited Smyth to scribble down a short melodic theme. He proceeded to extemporize upon it in freely inventive ways that Smyth found inspiring. What she heard was her theme first plain and unadorned, then answered, echoed, imitated, inverted, transposed, varied with new melodies and challenged by new themes: the whole a seamless and inventive counterpoint that finally returned her theme in its original simplicity but seemingly transformed. Ouseley's extemporized performance was nearer in spirit than Herzogenberg's strictly academic rule to the original meaning of fugal flight.

Smyth herself was in flight. In exile at home, she believed herself trapped between desire for reconciliation with Lisl and an instinct for self-renunciation that Julia had rightly detected and manipulated. She was fleeing her own wild, unmediated impulses. She was also pursued: by

56. *The Prison* (London, 1930), Symphony for Soprano and Bass soli, chorus and orchestra, libretto compiled by Ethel Smyth from the book by Harry Brewster (MS Faber Music). The chorale tune is *Schwing dich auf zu deinem Gott*, no. 4 in Smyth's arrangement of Four Short Chorale Preludes for Strings and Solo Instruments (see note 55). The motto is Andrew Lang's translation of the last words of Plotinus.

57. Ouseley (1825–1889), Oxford professor from 1855 to his death in 1889, and in 1874 first president of the Musical Association, has to his credit the improvement of British instructional standards of composition and church music on Bach models. See *Impressions That Remained*, p. 349; and Bernarr Rainbow, "Music in Education," in Nicholas Temperley, ed., *The Romantic Age 1800–1914*, vol. 5 of *The Athlone History of Music in Britain* (London, 1981), pp. 30–31.

Harry's love and its emotional reverberations; by the mocking Hilde-brands; by Lisl's jealous rivalry with Julia and Julia's devious withdrawals; by the chaos that Europe had become. If she could compose feeling into form, into the fluent, coherent, and consoling measures of the fugue, she might disguise and evade a terrible anxiety and rage; she might transform desire to gain control and conquer conflict. At this devastating time of flight from her beloved's rejection of her and common gossip about their affair, and simultaneously prey to her lover's brother-in-law, whose pur-suit threatened publicly to expose them all, she composed at her keyboard a series of self-contained three-, four-, and five-part fugues that literally invent themes of flight and chase.[58]

Given Smyth's active participation in hunting since early adolescence, she very likely drew creative purpose as well from fugue's historical association with the mounted hunt in time of war. Her home was within earshot of her father's artillery depot at Aldershot, where she had learned as a child to play the bugle and to memorize its military and hunting calls. She was clearly familiar with hunting's sexual meanings. In the late 1890s, for her second opera, *Der Wald*, she arranged and transcribed literal hunt calls that function as sequential signs of the huntress-heroine's discovery, pursuit, catch, and kill of her male quarry and female rival, to alert a knowing audience to precise moments of seduction and capitulation in the drama.[59]

Furthermore, Smyth's correspondence and memoirs abound in vig-orous images, analogies, and metaphors of the hunt that she related specifically to eros and creative energy. "I feel I am in for a good run," she declared of her passion for Lady Mary Ponsonby in 1893, repre-senting desire in a lusty Arabian horse legend: "Ride me like an enemy, feed me like a friend."[60] Reckless physical energy, sexual appetite, and craving for pleasure and love were driving forces in Smyth's creativity. She considered prowess in sport and sex healthy and natural for women, although both were traditionally identified with masculinity and manly self-esteem and presented many women in the Victorian era, identified as she was in youth and adolescence as tomboys, with questions about their

58. Fugue a 5 in B♭ Minor for two-staff organ, with another version in B Minor for three-staff; sketches for two three-part fugues; and one four-part fugue in D Minor. Probably also at this time Smyth completed an organ study (a canon on the chorale *Wie selig seid Ihr Frommen*), a Prelude and Fugue in C Major for piano, and a fugal exposition in B♭; incomplete MS, Fawcett Library, City of London Polytechnic.

59. *Der Wald*, music-drama in one act with Prologue and Epilogue, after an idea by Harry Brewster; libretto in German and English by Harry Brewster and Ethel Smyth (Mainz, 1902). She began the opera in 1899 and completed it on 31 October 1902; it was first performed in Berlin, 9 April 1903.

60. Ethel Smyth to Harry Brewster, and quoted by Harry Brewster in reply, Rome, 8 March 1893, in *As Time Went On . . . .*, pp. 235, 99.

femininity and sexual proclivities.[61] Proud of her strength in daring athletic performances, in hunting she relished encounters with physical danger; in mountain-climbing, the conquest of natural obstacles that tested her courage, agility, and powers of endurance.

If the art of fugue as flight and the hunt as chase suggested Amazonian meanings to Ethel Smyth that she put to personal action in music and words, she also drew upon fugue's material history. When Lisl imposed silence upon her, Smyth appropriated the power and authority of fugue as invested in Lisl's husband (and Smyth's teacher), and used it as a resource of allusion and influence for her own subversive purpose: to disaffiliate herself from patriarchal heterosexual marital norms and rules in order to regain control of a sexual conflict that named her outcast and threatened to destroy both her lesbian identity and her musical career.

Although Smyth never again composed an academic fugue, she continued to incorporate fugal procedures in choral passages in her operas and among her choral and orchestral works, notably in her *Mass in D Major*, a powerful, substantial work that some describe as her "masterpiece" on the model of Beethoven's *Missa Solemnis*, and that premiered in January 1893, one year after Lisl died.[62]

At the conclusion of the Credo, "*Et vitam venturi saeculi*: I look for the resurrection of the dead and the life of the world to come," a baroque trumpet announces the theme of a mighty fugue scored for massed chorus and full orchestra. Perhaps this passage suggested to Smyth reconciliation with Lisl in another life, or that death had finally "delivered [them] from fugal bonds." The score is dedicated to a new beloved, but several of Smyth's old Leipzig friends who remained loyal in the aftermath of scandal believed that this magisterial and triumphant work consummated Smyth's love for Lisl; that without the suffering incurred by loss she might never have been able to write it.[63]

61. See Patricia Del Rey, "Apologetics and Androgyny: The Past and the Future," *Frontiers: A Journal of Women Studies* 3 (1978): 8–10. Hunting in mid- and late-Victorian England simulated aristocratic society but "allowed a limited amount of class mixing in the field. . . . Hunting and riding were the only outlet for physical activity allowed . . . girls and women" that also relaxed strict rules of chaperonage. See Leonore Davidoff, *The Best Circles: Society Etiquette and the Season* (London, 1986), pp. 28–29, 50.

62. *Mass in D Major*, composed 1892 (London, 1893, 1925; reprinted New York, 1980, ed. Jane Bernstein). First performed London, 18 January 1893. Manuscript believed lost. MS sketches: Lady Boult; incomplete MS vocal score, Royal Academy of Music; Ethel Smyth corrections to percussion parts in BL Add. MS 46863. Donald Francis Tovey, among its first admirers, compared it with Beethoven's *Missa Solemnis* in D Major, op. 123 (1823) in "Vocal Music," vol. 5 of *Essays in Musical Analysis* (London, 1937), pp. 235–42. Lisl died 7 January 1892.

63. The *Mass* is dedicated to Pauline Trevelyan. Hermann Levi, on first seeing the score in February 1892, thought it "the strongest and most original work that had come out of England since Purcell's time" and evidence of a dramatic gift. He advised Smyth to write

Coda: In 1922, Smyth visited the Leipzig museum to view for the first time the marble bust of Lisl that Adolf Hildebrand had sculpted the year their relationship ended. She told a friend, "It was like being with her again . . . Oh! the hair—how can he have caught the texture and colour of that soft gold hair! . . . It makes me so happy . . . All the enthusiasm, faith, purity and poetry of this youthful friendship has been renewed. No one ever loved me quite as she did, and no love responded more to the deepest needs of my heart, and of hers. That was the secret."[64]

---

an opera (Ernest Newman, Introduction to *Impressions That Remained*, p. xii). "But for the Lisl tragedy, she could never have written it," Smyth quotes Levi as having written to Mary Fiedler (*As Time Went On* . . . ., pp. 222, 47).

64. Ethel Smyth to Lady Betty Balfour, August 1922, quoted by St. John, *Ethel Smyth*, pp. 205–6.

Reading as an Opera Queen

Mitchell Morris

Your first question is very likely to be "What is an opera queen?" To provide a rough definition: an *opera queen* is any member of that particular segment of the American gay community that defines itself by the extremity and particularity of its obsession with opera.[1] So much for bare description. Connotations of the term become visible only in the appropriate surroundings. If you have attended a performance in an American opera house, you have seen them without recognizing them: those (gay) men at intermission disputing the details of the diva's personality, the production, the performance, and the music itself with a passion that startles when compared to the well-heeled middle-aged couples grumbling about this year's seats. For an opera queen, an evening at the opera is never simply a chance to meet new and interesting people, nor to doze in an expensive setting, nor to display the outward and visible signs of his class—it is also (and primarily) another session of a continuous half-hidden seminar, debating society, and social club conducted between the acts of each production. Opera queens are arguably the largest, most knowledgeable, and most devoted single section of the opera-going public.

I am not merely describing a gay man who is interested in opera, however, nor even a gay man who has an all-consuming passion for it. In the gay community, a whole battery of specific tastes and attitudes are

---

1. In gay slang, the noun *queen* is a faintly derogatory epithet for any gay man. The word used to modify *queen* indicates his particular interests: "drag queen" (very loosely speaking, a gay transvestite), "leather queen" (a man who is more or less involved in the gay sado-masochistic subculture), "disco queen," among countless others. The construction is meant to trivialize the indicated obsession, and it may be used to refer to any gay man who is perceived as a fanatic. But the flippant description may be taken up seriously and worn self-consciously: opera queens are apt to wear the phrase the way a diva wears a tiara.

attributed to the stereotypical opera queen. Although we ought to recognize this as an in-house simplification and, like all such "ideal types," only partly corresponding to reality, still the truth contained in the stereotype tends to suggest a coherent aesthetic stance which is at least partially opposed to that of the majority of the audience (especially those who are musicologists or critics), gay or straight.[2] Furthermore, this aesthetic stance extends beyond the boundaries of the opera and its surrounding commentary: the music and its performances become a ruling metaphor for life, and a serious opera queen is apt to make many of his day-to-day decisions in the spirit of *imitatio operae*.

The sensibilities attributed to opera queens preserve a great number of features characteristic of nineteenth-century opera audiences. Such a sensibility is generally regarded in our society as marginal—it is understood and respected mostly by those who share it, derided or passed over in embarrassed silence by those who do not. Members of the musical academy, in their public role as legislators and enforcers of cultural attitudes toward music, seem especially wary of the torrid late-romantic sentiments now most forcefully expressed in the gay community; yet this vision of the genre can lead to readings as emotionally compelling as any readings ventured in musicological literature.

In this essay I want to describe the stance of a stereotypical opera queen and take it as seriously (and at the same time as playfully) as do the queens themselves, as a way to challenge and perhaps even to displace the dominant critical understandings of the musicological academy. Let me add that this essay is only an opening gesture; the discursive node occupied by opera queens is historically complex, and the space of one essay can at most begin to trace the discourse and suggest further inquiries.

Your second question might be "Who are you to describe this phenomenon?" I take a lesson from feminism and invoke the authority of personal experience. I am not myself an opera queen, but as a gay man who frequents opera houses, knows self-described opera queens, and has read the discussions of opera queens that have appeared in the gay community, I count as a "competent informant."[3] Knowledge is not

2. This might correspond to Stanley Fish's notion of an "interpretive community," whose consensus establishes a set of concepts and procedures for dealing with works of art. The existence and coherence of such a community seem confirmed by the ease with which gay writers extrapolate their stereotypical opera queens from the people they know, as well as by the lack of any apparent protest within the community when these stereotypes have been presented. See Stanley Fish, *Is There a Text in This Class? The Authority of Interpretive Communities* (Cambridge, Mass., 1980).

3. A word about the literature: the literary magazine *Christopher Street*, for instance, devoted most of one issue (no. 69, October 1982) to opera queens and opera. (The issue also included a Maria Callas coloring book.) *The Advocate*, a national gay newspaper, used to run a regular column on opera, and it continues to run features, though more sporad-

necessarily acceptance, of course; I am in fact uncomfortable with some aspects of the characteristic discourse of opera queens. But a position on the margins of this admittedly—and perhaps advantageously—marginal aesthetic provides a certain amount of analytical space. As Susan Sontag once noted about a related phenomenon, "No one who wholeheartedly shares in a given sensibility can analyze it; he can only, whatever his intention, exhibit it. To name a sensibility, to draw its contours and to recount its history, requires a deep sympathy modified by revulsion."[4] Although "sympathy modified by revulsion" is too extreme a formulation to describe my reaction to the sensibility, I do find a certain value in my ambivalence. The greatest fault of the traditional opera queen's perspective is its tendency to deny even the possibility of social and political action, thus in effect acquiescing in the status quo.[5] As long as the opera house provides a space—a closet, we might say—in which the spirit may soar free, everyday injustices seem to matter much less. This separation between opera house and "real world" effectively neutralizes most of the potential social impact of the oblique interpretations that "queer" the opera; the best remedy for this split is the reminder that all aesthetic choices inevitably imply ideological choices.

I want to discuss opera queens in their relation to three things: the aspects of opera most important to them; the rhetoric used to discuss those aspects; and the use and abuse of opera in gay life. After sketching out some of the positions these topics suggest, I will provide a brief example of how an opera queen might read part of the canon by giving a paraphrase of *Parsifal* from a hypothetical opera queen's point of view.[6]

An opera queen's attention is focused rather differently from the ways we tend to focus attention in musicology; what is actually present matters

ically. Most gay newspapers in cities with opera houses review opera productions carefully. And several books of gay cultural criticism have included chapters or articles examining the relationship of gay men to high culture, and particularly to the opera. See, for instance, Michael Bronski, "Opera: Mad Queens and Other Divas," in *Culture Clash: The Making of Gay Sensibility* (Boston, 1984), pp. 134–43.

4. Susan Sontag, "Notes on 'Camp,'" in her *Against Interpretation and Other Essays* (New York, 1961), p. 276. Later in the essay I will discuss the ways in which the sensibility of the opera queen contains elements of Camp.

5. As a gay music critic once noted, "One need only recall the audience at performances of *Die Frau ohne Schatten* (where it looked as if the entire membership of the Mineshaft had arrived en masse) to wonder why such a devoted congregation has failed to harness its strength in numbers toward anything more than casual cruising at intermission." (George Heymont, "Opera Companies and Opera Queens," *Christopher Street*, no. 69 [October 1982]: 51.)

6. This essay is principally an ethnography. A recent article by Wayne Kostenbaum, "Callas and Her Fans" (*Yale Review* 79 [1989]: 1–20) came to my attention too late to be discussed here, but it traces some of the same issues from a different perspective.

most. In practical terms this means that the music and the drama do not seem to exist for their own sakes, but, rather, for the possibilities they create for performance. And the performance in general is less important than the individual singers. One observer of gay opera audiences notes:

> Gay opera lovers can be divided into two groups: the opera queens and those who merely like the music and would probably be just as turned on by a good string quartet. The latter group shows a suspicious tendency to frequent lieder recitals given by singers who never made it on the big stage. . . . They appear satisfied with a single decent performance of a favorite opera and cannot recall who sang it two years ago. Some far-gone cases become critics.[7]

Central to the "true" opera queen's aesthetic is the cult of the singer—specifically, the female singer. All else pales beside the figure of the prima donna, who is from the opera queen's point of view the dominant figure in every opera of any importance.

The worship of great singers is a tradition of long standing in all opera audiences, of course, but from general audiences the male singers have received just as much adulation as (if not more than) the women.[8] In the circles of the opera queens, however, tenor and bass never seem to have inspired the same frenzy as the soprano. In one self-proclaimed opera queen's words:

> Gay as well as straight male artists were admired and were occasionally objects of fantasy. But primary allegiances and identifications were always with the ladies. There is no male opera singer who has commanded the legions of gay male fans that framed the careers of Zinka Milanov, Renata Tebaldi, Joan Sutherland, and Maria Callas; just as there is no male counterpart in gay male fandom to Mae West, Joan Crawford, and Judy Garland.[9]

According to convention, an opera queen admires one prima donna in particular, and he will defend every one of her performances, legally recorded or pirated, against all challengers. The divine Whoever is at the peak of his hierarchy of singers, and all other divas are ranked after her. If the opera queen perceives a rival for his diva's position, he will use all

7. Ivan Martinson, "How to Be an Opera Queen," *Christopher Street*, no. 69 (October 1982): 18.

8. Witness the number of people who will rush to buy opera tickets in order to hear, say, Placido Domingo. The opera queens are much more likely to converge on a performance by Jessye Norman or Teresa Stratas.

9. Lawrence Mass, "Confessions of an Opera Queen," *Christopher Street*, no. 69 (October 1982): 26.

his knowledge and rhetoric to subdue the usurper and her adherents.[10] The more illustrious the diva, the larger and more vehement her claque becomes. In the case of an extraordinary singer like Maria Callas, the claque of opera queens may by its interest help to spawn a small industry.[11]

The prima donna's musicianship and acting ability are crucial to her winning a claque, but in the minds of her devotees these become merely aspects of her personality, ingredients of her mystique. As in Camp taste,

> character is understood as a state of continual incandescence—a person being one, very intense thing. This attitude toward character is a key element of the theatricalization of experience embodied in the Camp sensibility. And it helps account for the fact that opera and ballet are experienced as such rich treasures of Camp, for neither of these forms can easily do justice to the complexity of human nature. Wherever there is development of character, Camp is reduced.[12]

Opera by its nature tends to aim at grand gestures and passions as elements of a dramatic essentialism, and this colors the public view of the prima donna both on and off the stage. The publicity industry also works by creating essences, and so the primary means of gaining information about the beloved diva inevitably guides the devotee into painting her in a few broad strokes. In Albert Innaurato's short story "Solidarity" the relationship between a gay fan (nicknamed Rose Hips) and Montserrat Caballé is strongly colored by the diva's public persona:

> Although we all loved operatic sopranos, especially fat ones, Rose Hips was the maddest Caballé Queen I have ever met. He attained heaven alive by becoming part of the team treating her during one of her innumerable health crises some years before. Since he was the only one of her doctors who loved opera, and spoke Spanish, she had discovered his home phone number, called him, gotten his answering machine, and sung all of "Vissi

10. We thus have a Camp version of chivalry. See Martinson, "How to Be," p. 20. It might be worth considering the role of the diva in creating a *homosocial* bond between gay men, just as women typically serve to establish such a bond between straight men. See Eve Kosofsky Sedgwick, *Between Men: English Literature and Male Homosocial Desire* (New York, 1985).

11. This claim may seem extravagant, but considering the scope and intensity of the passions "La Divina" still arouses in the circles of opera queens, I cannot help suspecting that they must be the primary purchasers of her recordings and memorabilia.

12. Sontag, "Notes," p. 286. Other gay theorists and critics have noted Sontag's extremely reductive view of Camp; the varied languages and practices that constitute Camp become for her a deliberately apolitical stance, incapable of any genuinely subversive critiques of majority culture. It is true that Sontag's reified notion of Camp fails when brought to bear on most aspects of gay and lesbian culture in the twentieth century. There seems to be a better fit between the attitudes she describes and the ones expressed by opera queens at intermission. See note 5.

d'arte" as a way of saying thank you. Rose Hips walked on air for years afterward.[13]

At a very advanced point, the "real presence" of someone like Maria Callas on the stage or disk becomes more significant than her dramatic and musical power, since these latter are the results of her personal power.

The central position given the figure of the prima donna does not mean that an opera queen sees *only* her and not her role, however. Opera queens read the dramas they see on stage with great care, if only because of the vicarious identifications and deliberate "over-interpretations" gay people must use to make a "straight" plot generate analogies between their day-to-day experiences and the operatic situations:

> At the opera we hear our most extreme feelings take over individuals and work themselves out to just the melodramatic catharsis we can but fantasize in real life, and liberate us, somewhat, from the miasma of reality. Next *Don Giovanni* you go to, identify yourself with Donna Elvira and picture a recent flame as the callous Don. You'll enjoy it so much more when he gets his.[14]

To adjust an opera in this way you must perform an elaborate chain of cross-gender identifications. An example of this kind of identification is provided in Terrence McNally's *The Lisbon Traviata*. One of his characters describes a past romantic situation:

> MENDY: And here I was on the other side of the door feeling like a combination of the Marschallin—all gentle resignation, *"ja, ja, ja,"* age deferring to beauty and all that shit—and the second act of *Tosca*—stab the son of a bitch in the heart. (Mendy seizes a knife from a fruit bowl and raises it dramatically.)
>
> STEPHEN: Careful, Mendy.
>
> MENDY: *Questo é il baccio di Tosca!* (He "stabs" Stephen, who reacts melodramatically.)
>
> STEPHEN: *Aiuto . . . aiuto . . . muoio. . . .*
>
> MENDY: *E ucciso da una donna . . .* Killed by a woman! *Guardami! . . . Son Tosca, o Scarpia!*
>
> STEPHEN: *Soccorso!*
>
> MENDY: *Tu suffoco il sangue? . . . Muori! muori!! muori!!! Ah e morto! . . . Or gli perdono!* (Stephen starts to get up.) Just a minute! I'm not finished. *E avanti a lui tremava tutta Roma.*[15]

13. Albert Innaurato, "Solidarity," in *Men on Men 2: Best New Gay Fiction*, ed. George Stambolian (New York, 1988), pp. 110–11.

14. Martinson, "How to Be," p. 24.

15. Terrence McNally, *The Lisbon Traviata*, in *Three Plays by Terrence McNally* (New York, 1990), pp. 19–20. When I saw a recent performance of this play in San Francisco, the passage quoted began in serious nostalgia, but as the characters became more and more caught up in the impromptu performance of *Tosca*, they became more and more manic,

The subject position of the heroine—never the hero—is the locus of investment here. Note that the incidents mentioned in the quotation, and especially the scene from *Tosca* played out to its end, are epiphanic moments within their operas. The ability to invent and sustain intense personal revelation is typical of the characters that the great divas play. These are invoked to justify emotional states in everyday life, and, conversely, personal experience is brought to bear on their interpretation.

The preferred works are those in which great female singers can make the maximum impact—in practical terms, the *bel canto* repertory. Such operas as *Norma*, *Lucia*, and *Maria Stuarda* are the ranking pieces, because they display divas to their best vocal and dramatic advantage. Wagner and Strauss, as well as Puccini, are generally successful, too, though with a more butch set of opera queens; they attract those who admire power perhaps more than agility.

If an opera queen's interests appear too personal for most musicological tastes, the language in which he discusses those interests is even more idiosyncratic. We might situate this language somewhere between histrionics and hysteria as a self-consciously artificial mode, alternately hyperbolic and attenuated, veering—sometimes within the same sentence—between deliberately prissy diction and vulgarity. More alive to stagy rhetorical effects than most other idiolects of American English, the opera queens' discourse revels in ambiguity; what seems like an insult may be a compliment, and more than likely it is both. What matters is that neither blame nor praise is meant entirely seriously, for this kind of Camp speech is usually defiantly antinomian—it inverts all basic categories and subverts any claims to privilege, including its own.[16]

Examples of this way of speaking appear in journalism and in literature. The gay music critic George Heymont wrote an opera column for a San Francisco gay newspaper under the name Tessi Tura. Tessi's prose style "aims for the immediacy of the intermission queen exclaiming 'Oh my dear, Leontyne just *peed* on that note!' and [s]he is not above describing Leonie Rysanek as 'screaming her tits off.'"[17]

---

without, however, losing a serious undertone. I can't help wondering if we were meant to understand Mendy's use of the opera as a way of redeeming his past sorrows.

16. Camp as a style seems to have reached its fullest and most subtle development in the 1950s, perhaps in response to tension between the homo-baiting antics of official U.S. political culture, the greater visibility of homosexuality in countercultural movements, and the homosexual community's own attempts to build a civil rights movement on the African-American model. See Sontag, "Notes," for a description of what must have been Camp style in the 1950s.

17. Carl Maves, "Opera Queens: A New Breed Way Out West," *The Advocate*, no. 432 (29 October 1985): 51, 110. Although the last part of the quotation may seem like simple

Let us turn back to literature, to examine the first act of *The Lisbon Traviata*. The scene is a long conversation between two opera queens who are Callas fans; the play in fact takes its name from a famous performance of *La Traviata* that took place in Lisbon on 27 March 1958. Stephen and Mendy idolize Maria Callas and, in the course of their conversation, abuse other sopranos. For instance, the two are trying to remember who sang the role of Clotilde in various performances of *Norma*:

MENDY: I bet she [Callas] remembered who sang Clotilde with her in London on November 8, 1952.

STEPHEN: The whole world remembers who sang Clotilde with her in London in 1952: Big Joan Sutherland herself, The Beast From Down Under.

MENDY: Maria said Sutherland didn't have the legato to sing a good Clotilde.

STEPHEN: The rhythm to sing it is what Maria said.

MENDY: I read "legato."

STEPHEN: Well, you read wrong. Besides, Sutherland has legato. Even I would grant her that. But she always sings behind the beat. That's why Maria said she didn't have the rhythm to sing even a decent Clotilde. God knows what Maria thought of her Norma.

MENDY: You're too butch to know so much about opera.

STEPHEN: I'm not butch. Risë Stevens is butch. Are you still looking for that *Medea*?[18]

This may at first seem simply like degrading women for the sake of male bonding, but it isn't. Nicknaming Dame Joan Sutherland "The Beast From Down Under" is primarily a way for Stephen to elevate Callas further. At the same time, the epithet allows a kind of backhanded identification with the object of his scorn. The critics Michael Moon and Eve Kosofsky Sedgwick have recently explored an emotional attachment between gay men and fat women they refer to as "divinity"—a mixture of "abjection and defiance" which results in a peculiar kind of grandeur.[19] The passage quoted from Innaurato's "Solidarity" suggests the kind of relationship Moon and Sedgwick are describing, but it is made explicit only near the end of the story, when Rose Hips and Caballé go skiing: "He said seeing

---

misogyny, the complex irony of the discourse makes any such direct analysis quite tricky. See below.

18. McNally, *The Lisbon Traviata*, pp. 17–18.

19. The term is used in tribute to Divine, an actor who played many drag roles in the films of John Waters. His name is in turn a cliché of Camp language, where "divine" is one of a number of standard extravagances for anything a speaker likes. And "Divinity" probably refers as much to the calorie-laden confection of that name as it does to the exalted status of the star. Michael Moon and Eve Kosofsky Sedgwick, "Divinity: A Dossier," paper read at Stanford University Conference on Gender at the Crossroads, 9–10 March 1990.

her toboggan slowly down the beginner's hill, her hippopotomic bulk swathed in tons of multicolored furs, singing Castilian folk songs, was as close to the beatific vision as he expects to get."[20]

Moon and Sedgwick explicitly tie their concept of "divinity" to opera, primarily by noting the girth of the stereotypical diva. In doing so they imply a number of resonances. The world of opera is filled to bursting with examples of behavior that would connote "divinity": Tosca singing "Vissi d'arte," Brünnhilde desperately justifying herself to Wotan, Lucia at the height of her insanity. And the mixture of abjection and defiance is carried over to an opera queen's use of cruel epithets and gossipy stories about embarrassing incidents, which place the diva in the "divine" position of a *monstre sacré*.[21] As strange as it may seem, then, such epithets indicate a certain acceptance and, indeed, a certain identification within the world of opera queens.

Stephen's comment about Risë Stevens adds yet another twist to the connotations I have been tracing out here. Calling the diva "butch" implicates her further in the world of opera queens by suggesting that she is a lesbian, closely related to her audience by homosexuality as well as art. As one of our opera queens remembers:

> The more operatic I became, the more it seemed to me that anybody who had anything to do with opera was at least "potentially gay." In the world of opera we would entertain and rival one another with long, tittery stories about the secret lives of famous artists. The more famous, respected, and loved the artist, it sometimes seemed, the greater was the challenge to expose *her* as notorious, flamboyant, outrageous, or at the very least, gay.[22]

The same impulse is at work when McNally has Mendy claim that Marilyn Horne was actually a truck driver. The diesel fumes still cling to her concert dresses—an aspect of "divinity."

Gay cultural analysts as well as thoughtful opera queens have at times speculated on why opera exerts such a powerful fascination for many gay men, and why a role like that of the opera queen would be so prevalent. The relationship created by the impulse toward "divinity," as I have outlined it above, is one answer. If the members of an oppressed minority find on stage adequate and cathartic representations of an emotional state central to their affective lives as shaped by the repressive social order surrounding them, it is no wonder that they invest so heavily in the art form. Gay men (and lesbian women) who attend the opera find that it

20. Innaurato, "Solidarity," p. 118.
21. It is appropriate that the phrase was used most memorably by the "divine" Sarah Bernhardt herself. This points to the historically complex web of resonances surrounding the discourse of opera queens.
22. Mass, "Confessions," p. 26.

provides a situation where most of their rigidly controlled desires and attitudes may have free rein without social censure:

> Gays, even the most liberated, have each lived part of their lives in a vise, a tension between what society urged and what their own needs demanded. In each of us . . . was born a tendency, perhaps, to hold back on certain types of self-expression, at least in general company. Few of us, I put it to you, entirely outgrow that. Hence much gay creativity, bubbling up, inspired, by the long repression, and hence our thrill at opera's explosions of bare feeling, the sublime musical metaphor for passion.[23]

This account supports Philip Brett's suggestion that part of the function of music and musicality in our culture is to frame and control (homo)sexual impulses.[24] Opera includes at least four such mechanisms of enforcement: the notion that art and reality intersect only in the most trivial ways—opera as absolute music; the various stage paraphernalia, which by their mediation prevent the proliferation of illegitimate meanings; the overwhelming tendency of (nineteenth-century) opera to provide social closure by the death of the heroine as a parallel to the tonal closure of the music;[25] and the association of opera with the less publicly sexual upper classes. Within the boundaries created by these mechanisms, interpretation and identification can take place without disrupting the standard (heterosexual male) cultural productions of meaning.

Before trying to dismantle opera's mechanisms of enforcement, I want to give some sense of the various ways interpretation and identification might work for opera queens. Sedgwick has proposed that "our culture's crystallization of gay identities over the past hundred years has persistently been structured by two conceptual impasses or incoherencies, one concerning *gender* definition and the other concerning *sexual* definition."[26] She articulates this conceptual terrain as a four-part structure, with all elements available for various discursive purposes.

According to Sedgwick, a "topos of inversion" defines gay identities by the extent to which they partake of characteristics of the opposite gender, such that people defined as gay are conceived of as in some sense androgynous. Simultaneously, gay identities can be construed by the op-

23. Martinson, "How to Be," p. 25.

24. Philip Brett, "Musicality, Essentialism, and the Closet," paper read at the annual meeting of the American Musicological Society, Oakland, 1990, and at the Conference on Music and Gender, London, 1991 (unpublished manuscript, pp. 11–12).

25. See Catherine Clément, *Opera, or the Undoing of Women*, trans. Betsy Wing (Minneapolis, 1988).

26. Eve Kosofsky Sedgwick, "Across Gender, Across Sexuality: Willa Cather and Others," *South Atlantic Quarterly* 88 (1989): 57.

posing "topos of gender separatism," which treats a gay man as a "man's man," a lesbian as a "woman-identified woman." There is a choice, then, between considering homosexuality as a state on the margins of a specific gender or as a state at the center of that gender. These opposed integrative and separatist positions on gender definition recur in the discourse of sexual definition, in the positions Sedgwick calls "universalizing" or "minoritizing." Is homosexuality a fixed, "inborn" predisposition toward the members of one's own sex, or is it a manifestation of a basic human bisexuality? These latter terms operate at present in the debate between "social constructionist" and "essentialist" positions on gay identity; social constructionists understand sexual desire as labile and radically historical, whereas essentialists find homosexuality to be a transcultural, transhistorical state.

Within Sedgwick's paradigm, an opera queen's identifications would operate by "topoi of inversion." The diva and her roles are both central. The language used to constitute these strong female presences makes the features of inversion even more apparent. As was noted earlier, the variety of Camp speech used to discuss topics of importance to opera queens constantly plays upon various conventions of discourse; boundaries of tone are self-consciously transgressed, and established values are ironically and ambiguously reversed. The overall effect is one of extravagance—it might be termed a verbal drag show.

Let me return to my earlier pairing of *histrionic* and *hysterical*. Both of these highly feminized terms connote a kind of artificiality, the linguistic equivalent of a mask. The actor is a professional liar; Freud's female patients are always "hiding something." But in a sense they are opposed; an actor's disguise is deliberately assumed, but Freud's hysterical women conceal the sources of their troubles unconsciously. Pushing harder, we may say that an actor's secret is constructed, whereas an hysteric's secret is essential. To situate an opera queen between histrionics and hysteria, then, suggests the difficulty of locating him within his network of discursive practices.[27]

At the same time that patterns of identification work by "topoi of inversion," they depend implicitly on a stance toward character that seems to be linked to an essentialism of personality. This notion is related to Susan Sontag's declaration that Camp understands character as a single, intense state. Favored moments within operas are moments of great

27. See the crucial article by Eve Kosofsky Sedgwick, "Epistemology of the Closet (I)," *Raritan* 7 (1988): 39–69. Sedgwick suggests that a whole host of such pairings are densely imbricated with the opposition homo/heterosexual, which ends up as a central locus of epistemological struggle throughout the past century. The issues Sedgwick presents here and in her article on Willa Cather are developed at dazzling length in her recent book, *Epistemology of the Closet* (Berkeley, 1990).

theatrical revelation—to put it more bluntly, when a character "comes out." But the process of coming out in this case tends to depend on some sort of self-definition, which becomes in effect an essentializing maneuver. An implied separatist position on sexual definition is hooked to an integrative position on gender definition. A fixed sexual object-choice is linked to a fluid sense of gender.

Or is it? The incoherencies Sedgwick notes extend to the coming-out process, where sexual object-choice may suddenly shift gears in either direction. As a result, the act of revelation is immediately liable to interpretation by any of the definitions listed above. Even more important, it often happens that all four definitions operate simultaneously, at different levels of discourse. It seems that the attempt to interpret someone else's coming out (of whatever kind) is fraught with undecidables.

This kind of epistemological crossing is apparent in Figure 1. Concern with opera intersects with drag (both figuratively, in verbal identification with the diva, and literally, since the boys dress for the party as divas). But the humor of the cartoon, obviously, is contained in the host's shock at the enthusiastic cooperation of his parents. We are treated to the spectacle of Sonny's father as a prima donna, from his costume all the way to his hand-waving gesture. What kind of an action is this? For a reader in the gay community, the cartoon explicitly depends on the common gay situation of discovering the homosexuality of someone previously unsuspected. But, although this sumptuary reversal deliberately evokes an unexpected liminality of gender meant to suggest homosexuality, there is no way to decide whether Sonny's father is therefore revealed to have been already always gay, or whether he is shown manifesting a mobility of sexual tastes. Either way, his identity *as it is constituted by others* is thrown into doubt by his assumption of the role of the diva.

Role-playing and sincerity; public and private; male and female. Opera is a crucial locus for these issues, and opera queens participate in their elaborate transactions, whether they use one set of polarities to undermine another or whether they hover willfully between definitions. Having suggested the complexities involved in assuming the stance of an opera queen, I nevertheless will provide a rough summary of its general outlines with an eye toward disarticulating the sexist and homophobic interpretive paradigm that prevails in musicology at present.

An opera queen's aesthetic stance is profoundly personal; it values the *effect* of the strong performance, the diva's character, and the beauty of the music on the individual listener rather than any intersubjective analysis of vocal, dramatic, or compositional craft. Although reasonably ver-

Figure 1. From Brad Parker, *Oh Boy! Sex Comics by Brad Parker* (San Francisco, 1988), unpaginated.

ifiable musical terms such as *intonation, diction, legato,* and *phrasing* are employed, they are invoked fairly casually, to support an already established conviction, rather than to build up a deductive argument. Rhetoric and not logic is the chosen mode of arguing for or against the merits of a particular opera, production, or singer, because personal taste overrules everything else.[28] "What kind of an impact do I feel?"—on this question any opera queen's argument will stand or fall.

A survey of the opera queen's canon suggests that the intensity of discrete moments matters more than large-scale dramatic coherence; unrelated operatic repertories are scanned for operas that permit nodes of gorgeous musical violence. The *bel canto* repertory, for instance, is cherished for theatrical confrontations such as Lucia's mad scene and the clash between Mary Stuart and Elizabeth Tudor. And much of Wagner's vaunted "art of transition" consists of giant build-ups to climaxes of great intensity but relatively brief duration. A reading that followed this sensibility would not try to explain what musical and dramatic elements in the opera might connect all these moments, but would instead concentrate on elucidating the unique qualities of the moments and the nature of their intensity.

The language opera queens use to describe their loves and loathings suggests that they perceive music primarily as a means of articulating the erotic and that they respond to it strongly on this level. This perception and response may be at least partially a result of their general preoccupation with eroticism—when one's sexuality is contested, that sexuality will occupy one's thoughts rather often—but it is just as much a result of the gay tendency to assume multiple meanings in every cultural product, whether casual conversation, advertisement, or high art. This is a gesture of self-defense that probably carries over into all gay interpretation of culture. In any case, it leads to an interpretive stance that emphasizes sexual politics of one sort or another.

The opera queen's aesthetic position is thus intensely subjective, temporally discontinuous, and eroticized—I might say "Dionysian." Although much of the opera-going public might react with similar emotion, they do not seem to give themselves as totally to this sensibility as do gay men in general and opera queens in particular. The primary gay operatic aesthetic is opposed to the more logically rigorous, abstract, "Apollonian" stance found in the public discourse of musicology. But it

---

28. It is easy to see how an opera queen's trust in personal taste alone could be the result of coming to terms with a sexual desire explicitly prohibited by his society. Once he has accepted that the sexual taste society prohibits is nevertheless correct for him, he will be inclined to accept his intuitive preferences in nonsexual realms as well.

would not do to dismiss the opera queen's position as hopelessly individual, hence useless for scholarly endeavors. It is the aesthetic stance of a large and sophisticated community of listeners, interesting as an oppositional gesture to traditional scholarly readings as well as on its own terms.

As I mentioned above, such an oppositional aesthetic might provide a challenge to traditional academic readings of the operatic canon as well as of individual operas. This opposition performs two functions. First, it uncovers the (hetero)sexist assumptions that direct much of our customary interpretation of opera and, by extension, of all music. Second, it might humanize the impact of our field. Traditional (positivist) musicology has never felt much responsibility for meeting the educated music-loving public on terms that that public understands, and the consequence has been not only the lack of interest of that public in musicology but also the apathy of other scholars in the academy. Only resistance within the field to this detachment can ever cause musicology to broaden its appeal beyond the circles of the scholarly elect. I would like to think that the readings of opera queens could help expand the appeal and effectiveness of musical scholarship.

This said, it is worth experimenting with various ways of "queening" the canon.[29] I will examine *Parsifal*, mostly because, though it seems at first glance to be an unlikely candidate for productive reading as by an opera queen, it turns out to allow several useful observations. A look at the elements an opera queen is likely to notice prompts the observation that Wagner structures the drama by means of a vast disparity in sexual (hence, moral) power. For an opera queen, who interprets by assuming "feminine" subject positions, the sexual imbalance is so apparent that the opera misfires.

We start by ranking the characters in terms of their affective and dramatic importance. The most interesting character in the opera is Kundry, to all intents and purposes the only woman. And she is a passionate woman, although it is part of her nature that she wants to be rid of passion. Her suffering is likely to evoke a pang of sympathy from every opera queen who has at one time or another wished that he were straight. There is a tie for the position of second most interesting character between Amfortas and Klingsor. Although Amfortas gets more stage-time and suffers more theatrically, his histrionics become rather tiresome rather quickly. Klingsor at least gets to gnash his teeth and chuckle evilly; if he had a better—that is, stagier—death, he would definitely be first

29. I explore other aspects of this topic in "On Gaily Reading Music," *repercussions* 1, no. 1 (Spring 1992): 48–64.

runner-up. Gurnemanz is probably next, mostly because he is on the stage practically *all* the time and because he has some nice music. Parsifal, unfortunately, is a callow bore of interest only to chicken queens. Titurel is little more than a bit part. The flower maidens are transparently a straight man's fantasy of inert flesh waiting for whoever happens to come along, and as such they are uninteresting. And finally we have that chorus line of *Graalsritter*.

Act I is somewhat appealing, because we get to meet most of the characters. The opera queen's ear will be attracted to whatever Kundry is singing, of course (even though it isn't very much); consequently, her chromaticism is the most striking feature of the act. In comparison, all of the sublime restraint of the diatonicism that surrounds her is noble, inspiring (in fact, quite beautiful), but in the last analysis rather featureless. What we might in other circumstances consider "the real story" is actually a background for Kundry's reactions to Parsifal.

Act II fares considerably better from the very beginning, which Klingsor kicks off in his best villainous style. We feel for Kundry, since she just can't help herself when he is around to urge her on. There is a relaxation of the tension when the cloying flower-maidens rush onto the stage (but the *bel canto* queens will like this part best). Then we reach the supreme moment: Parsifal encounters Kundry in all her glory in her natural hothouse environment. Note that she gets the closest thing to an aria in the entire opera when she relates Herzeleide's death. Since she keeps on singing about sex and death in those slithery lines, we might be reminded of Isolde; this time, though, we must reluctantly cheer our heroine on to failure, because we know that she does not *want* to win. Masochist that she is, she would rather bathe Parsifal than bed him. Even though she wants to lose, she tries to snare him, and only his naiveté keeps him from her clutches. It may be difficult to see what she finds attractive about him, of course—the bars are jammed full of Parsifals. But we have all had our follies, and they were not unlike this one. At any rate, Parsifal rejects her, and the drama is over.

Act III, the mopping up, is one long drama of straight male transcendence. Parsifal assumes Amfortas's kingly and priestly duties step by step and is rather pompous and smug about it, while everybody else sings hymns. An opera queen can't help but be a little frustrated by Kundry's silence; Parsifal is reaching for heights and she acts like his stepladder. This does seem to be what Wagner showed her as desiring, but after all of her sultry moves in Act II this blank self-denial seems a pity. By the middle of this act, an opera queen will have to force himself to pay attention to tenors and basses if he is not to drift off into total boredom.

This kind of summary—a misfire, as I termed it earlier—is a long way from the traditionally reverent readings of Wagner's Grail legend; it seems far as well from those revisionist readings that would turn *Parsifal* into a proto-Nazi tract. Both these other readings make some sense, and it is likely that in the past they would have been more convincing to a majority of the audience; but in our present intellectual climate, what might appear more prominent—to more members of the audience than just the opera queens—is just how Wagner's lofty male drama is grounded upon a bruised female presence.

Serious and playful. The preceding summary is flippant and willfully trivializing, conscious of the gap between the opera and its description, but it is meant all the more seriously for that reason. The opera queen who speaks is a performer no less than his divas: both exist in the gaps between themselves and their roles. The awareness of this gap, which leads to a very "gay irony," is of course not exclusive to gay sensibilities, but it is so frequent that it perhaps becomes exemplary here. This gay irony employs the instabilities of gender and sexuality to question authority, whether it is the speaker's own or that of those the speaker speaks against; at the same time it acknowledges its own status as an artifact of its speaker's personality. And listening to this irony may lead us to a way of writing about music that leaves a space for—to paraphrase Roland Barthes, himself at times nearly an opera queen—the grain of our own voices.

Schwarze Gredel and the Engendered Minor Mode in Mozart's Operas

Gretchen A. Wheelock

In noting music's influence on listeners, Jean-Jacques Rousseau expressed a view widely held throughout the eighteenth century: "Each key, each mode, has its own expression which must be understood, and this is one of the means by which the skillful composer becomes master, in some manner, of the affections of his audience."[1] Recent demonstrations of historical tunings and temperaments of the period lend support to Rousseau's first claim,[2] and Rita Steblin's study of eighteenth- and early nineteenth-century descriptions of key characteristics provides ample evidence that composers and theorists associated individual keys with

This essay is an expanded version of a paper I presented at the International Mozart Congress 1991, in Salzburg, to be published in the Proceedings of that meeting. Additional presentations were made at the national meetings of the American Society for Eighteenth-Century Studies, Pittsburgh, 1991, and of the American Musicological Society, Chicago, 1991. For helpful comments I am grateful to Wye J. Allanbrook, Ellen Koskoff, Ruth Solie, Jürgen Thym, and James Webster.

1. Jean-Jacques Rousseau, *Dictionnaire de musique* (Paris, 1768), p. 516.

2. Whatever the particular adjective a listener might choose in describing the character of a key, temperament was surely an important factor in distinguishing one key from another. A range of unequally tempered tunings was in use throughout the century, and advocates of equal temperament far fewer than is often assumed. Live demonstrations by Mark Lindley of tempered tunings used in the mid to late eighteenth century offer persuasive evidence of the distinctive qualities of scales and the alterations of those qualities in transposition; see his entry on "Temperaments," *The New Grove Dictionary of Music and Musicians*, ed. Stanley Sadie (London, 1980), vol. 18, pp. 660–74. For a recent compendium of documents bearing on eighteenth- and nineteenth-century tempered tunings, see Owen Jorgensen, *Tuning: The Perfection of Eighteenth-Century Temperament, the Lost Art of Nineteenth-Century Temperament, and the Science of Equal Temperament* (East Lansing, Mich., 1991).

specific affective qualities.[3] Since the particulars of such descriptions varied (sometimes wildly) with the theoretical orientations and personal preferences of their respective compilers, it is not possible to discover here a precise semiotic of affect—a "key-code" of the emotions—that is transportable from one composer to another. A turn to the minor *mode*, however, would be easily recognized. And here there was considerable agreement among eighteenth-century writers that minor keys signaled regions of gloom—of melancholy, weeping, languishing laments—a domain associated in turn with the tender ministrations of women.

As both Leonard Ratner and Susan McClary have observed, theorists and composers of the period construed the minor mode itself as "feminine," as weak and unstable.[4] Indeed, the very foundation of the minor mode was judged shaky: in agreement with the theoretical pronouncements of Rameau's *Traité de l'harmonie* (1722), Rousseau judged the minor triad as lacking fundamental resonance with the *corps sonore* of Nature, and therefore to be "discovered only by analogy and inversion" from the naturally healthy major triad.[5] It is not surprising, then, that the "less natural" minor mode was construed as the weaker sex to the major's strength, and as "therefore suitable," as Johann Kirnberger put it, for "the expression of sad, doubtful sentiments, for hesitation and indecision."[6]

Functionally, though, the minor mode acted as a more robust agent of instability. Sketching a model of the triads useful for modulation within a major key, Joseph Riepel captured both aspects of the "feminine" mode in his *Grundregeln zur Tonordnung insgemein* (1755). Assigning class status as well as sex to the various keys subordinate to the master tonic, Riepel proposed a hierarchy of key relations in which the primary, major harmonies were male, and the secondary, minor ones female.[7] In this con-

---

3. Rita Steblin, *A History of Key Characteristics in the Eighteenth and Early Nineteenth Centuries* (Ann Arbor, 1983). Steblin's impressive study documents the pervasiveness of key associations during the eighteenth century and provides a number of explanatory models for their origins, including unequally tempered tunings, circle-of-fifths modulation schemes, flat- and sharp-key relationships to C Major, and tone quality of instrumentation. I have relied in this study on the extensive appendices to her book.

4. See Leonard G. Ratner, *Classic Music: Expression, Form, and Style* (New York, 1980), p. 50; and Susan McClary, *Feminine Endings: Music, Gender, and Sexuality* (Minneapolis, 1991), pp. 11–12.

5. Rousseau, *Dictionnaire*, s.v. "Mode" (p. 287).

6. *Die Kunst des reinen Satzes in der Musik*, vol. 2 (Berlin, 1771), part 1, p. 70. For Andreas Werckmeister, whose theories of harmony derived from modal practices, the "natural" mode, with its major third over the fundamental note, provided a more perfect proportion than the "less natural" and "imperfect" minor third (*Musicae mathematicae Hodigus curiosus* [2d ed. Frankfurt, 1687], pp. 124–25); cited in Joel Lester, "The Recognition of Major and Minor Keys in German Theory: 1680–1730," *Journal of Music Theory* 22 (1978): 68.

7. *Anfangsgründe zur musikalischen Setzkunst*. Volume 2: *Grundregeln zur Tonordnung insgemein* (Frankfurt, 1755), pp. 65–68. I have arranged the triads in my diagram to reflect

I
Meyer
[master/landowner]

IV
Taglöhner
[day laborer]

V
Oberknecht
[chief manservant]

ii
Unterläufferin
[errand girl]

vi
Obermagd
[chief maid]

iii
Untermagd
[lower maid]

i
schwarze Gredel

figuration of the tonal estate, the parallel minor tonic is dangerously androgynous (see above). The power of *schwarze Gredel* is not far to find: unnaturally feminine/masculine, she shares the Master's tonic, and her chromatic mutability is capable of destabilizing his natural domain.[8]

---

the implicit hierarchy of mode in Riepel's treatise. For a discussion of Riepel's theoretical writings, see Nola Reed, "The Theories of Joseph Riepel as Expressed in His *Anfangsgründe zur musikalischen Setzkunst* (1752–1768)," Ph.D. diss., Eastman School of Music of the University of Rochester, 1983. Reed (p. 115) notes that Riepel allowed occasional use of the parallel minors of IV and V but restricted the parallel majors of ii, iii, and vi to local functions as applied dominants (*Änderungsabsätze*). The introductory chorus ("Che lieto giorno") of Mozart's *La finta giardiniera* (1775) offers a parallel, to some extent, of Riepel's gendered estate. Stepping out of the framing D Major tonic, each of the characters expresses his or her private unhappiness: Ramiro, the castrato role, in B Minor, Sandrina and Serpetta in E Minor, the Podesta in G Major, and Nardo in A Major. I do not suggest, however, that Mozart knew Riepel's *Grundregeln*.

8. I have been unable to confirm Ratner's explanation of Riepel's "schwarze Gredel" as being "a nickname for a Swedish queen whose swarthy complexion made her look like a man" (*Classic Music*, p. 50). The only Swedish Queen Margaret reigned in the late thirteenth and early fourteenth centuries. Whether or not her complexion was "swarthy," she was a powerful ruler who consolidated Norway, Denmark, and Sweden into a single Nordic empire to suppress expansionist moves on the part of north German states. (I am grateful to Alfred Mann for bringing this information to my attention.)

Grimm's *Deutsches Wörterbuch* (s.v. "Grete"—also Gredl, Grîte, Greet, etc.) lists various references to this short form for Margarethe that might have informed Riepel's use of the

If such a scheme seems little more than an idiosyncratic effort to schematize the emerging functional relations of keys in tonal harmony, "feminizing" the minor mode was not short-lived. Surveying the views of eighteenth-century theorists, Ratner finds an explanation for the dominance of the major mode in its natural advantages at cadential points—the minor mode must "borrow" the leading tone, chromatically altering its (already less than natural) diatonic form, in order to confirm closure. Ratner's characterization of the two modes is a suggestive gloss on the terms of his historical predecessors: "In later baroque music, the pull of the cadence begins to reach back into the phrase; eventually its thrust starts with the opening chords; hence the more fragile minor mode gave way to the peremptory major."[9]

Extending the dichotomy of masculine and feminine to the minor mode itself, Roland Tenschert characterizes the use of G Minor in Mozart's operas in polarized affective domains. He asserts that for Mozart this key "represented in manly activism more the expression of passion, of the daemonic, of defiance or rebellion against an adverse fate, and in womanly passivity the soulful condition of despondency, grief, painful resignation, and despair. Often, however, both of these sides are found bound together in a remarkably iridescent unity."[10] Given this model of gendered expression, it is striking that in his account of the opera arias in G Minor Tenschert does not mention that all but one of the nine he discusses are sung by female characters. Tenschert is not alone in failing to note the predominance of female voices in Mozart's minor-mode arias—indeed, none of the studies I have located that address Mozart's choice of keys has mentioned this fact.[11] He also joins (albeit with a twist)

name. As early as the sixteenth century, Grete was a pejorative nickname for an effeminate, womanly man. More often used in reference to women, "Grete" had generally unsavory connotations as a wanton, immoral peasant girl or female farmhand; sometimes also a sullen, bad-tempered wife. To be "gretig" was to have inordinate desire, perhaps explaining a proverb current in the mid-eighteenth century: "Don't get too close to Grete or you'll grow slowly grey." Grete was also a popular name for the Turkish black caraway plant, and in north German folklore a "schwarze Greet" was an empty, worm-eaten nut.

9. Ratner, *Classic Music*, p. 56. My interest in eighteenth-century notions of a "feminine" mode was sparked by the sources quoted in Ratner's book and his observations about them.

10. "Die G-moll-Tonart bei Mozart," *Mozart-Jahrbuch 1951* (Salzburg, 1953): 122.

11. Werner Lüthy, *Mozart und die Tonartencharakteristik* (Strassburg, 1931), the single monograph on the subject, was summarized by F. O. Souper in *The Monthly Musical Record* 63 (1933): 202–3 and prompted responses in this same journal from A. H. King: "Mozart's Tonality," 66 (1936): 153–54 and "The Consistency of Mozart's Use of Keys," 67 (1937): 104–7. Like Lüthy, Alfred Einstein treats both vocal and instrumental music in his discussion of keys (*Mozart: His Character, His Work*, trans. Arthur Mendel and Nathan Broder [New York, 1945], pp. 157–63). See the following for characterizations of the minor mode specific to Mozart's operas: William Mann, *The Operas of Mozart* (New York, 1977), pp.

a long history of assigning manly and womanly attributes to mode and key.

I want to examine aspects of that history in seemingly disparate constructions of the minor mode—as weak and passive in affect, but also as powerful and subversive in function—by eighteenth-century writers. I will look first at perceived connections between the minor mode and female affections in contemporary descriptions of key characteristics. In turning to the minor-key arias in Mozart's operas, I will consider the implications of a feminized sphere of expression in somewhat more embodied terms. With primary focus on a limited number of arias by a single composer, I do not mean to propose the minor mode as a litmus test for gender stereotyping in late-eighteenth-century opera. More complex and interesting, in my view, is the ambivalence that the minor mode introduces, in destabilizing masculine/feminine dichotomies as well as the tonal order that contains them.

Recent feminist analysis of opera has insisted on the power of patriarchal narratives to silence women's voices, or to control them within a hierarchic system that demands submission to tonal closure.[12] Viewed in eighteenth-century terms, however, Mozart's dramatic works suggest the power of women's voices to undermine and transform conventional categories of gendered expression. Of particular interest is his use of the minor mode to invoke powerful associations with the supernatural, the furies of Nature, human passions out of control, delirium and fainting, and death. These are hardly fragile emotions of "hesitation and indecision." Rather, the minor mode was a vehicle for often menacing forces, the expression of which threatened to exceed the bounds of the "natural." I will suggest that ambivalences in late-eighteenth-century concepts of woman's nature and views of female physiology and temperament provide a broader context for study of the mutable mode.

If we take seriously the claims of eighteenth-century theorists and composers—Mozart's father among them[13]—the various keys had intrinsic

---

20–24; Edward J. Dent, *Mozart's Operas: A Critical Study* (2d ed. London, 1947), p. 54; Martin Chusid, "The Significance of D Minor in Mozart's Dramatic Music," *Mozart Jahrbuch 1965/66* (1967): 87–93; and Daniel Heartz, "Tonality and Motif in *Idomeneo*," *Musical Times* 115 (1974): 382–86.

12. The former position, with primary focus on the stories of opera libretti, is taken in Catherine Clément, *Opera, or the Undoing of Women*, trans. Betsy Wing (Minneapolis, 1988); the latter claim is more comprehensively treated in musical terms by Susan McClary, both in her foreword to Clément's book and in her own *Feminine Endings*. See also below, n. 31.

13. The particular qualities of keys are noted by Leopold Mozart of his *Versuch einer gründlichen Violinschule* of 1756 (English translation by Editha Knocker as *A Treatise on the Fundamental Principles of Violin Playing* [2d ed. Oxford, 1985], p. 64 n. 1): "Even if all the modern keys seem to be made only from the scale of C Major and A Minor; yea, in reality

and recognizable differences. In line with traditional characterizations of the major mode as hard (*dur*) in contrast to the minor's soft (*moll*), theorists sought to describe the specific character of each major and minor key. The mutability of the minor mode, acknowledged as particularly useful in modulation, also made it something of a moving target for those who attempted these characterizations—the minor had, after all, a variety of forms and changing chromatic shapes. One such author, whose account was published in Carl Friedrich Cramer's *Magazin der Musik* (1787), assigns specific qualities to the character of each major key but excuses himself from a similar list for the minor keys: "Difficult as it is to fathom the inner quality of a major key, it is more difficult by far to discover the nature of a key that consists of a mixture of various different things. Moreover, it seems that the character of the minor key is not so precisely circumscribed, so unchangeable, as that of the major."[14] Other writers were less reluctant to circumscribe the elusive minor keys, and tended to assign them generic labels as somber and weak; their major and sharp key counterparts were more often characterized as joyful and strong.[15]

---

are only built up by adding ♭ and ♯: how comes it then that a piece which, for instance, is transposed from F to G, never sounds so pleasant, and *has quite a different effect on the emotions of the listeners*? And whence comes it also that practised musicians, on hearing a composition, can instantly specify the key note if it be not indeed different in character?" (My emphasis.)

Even if recorded by the often unreliable Schindler, the alleged comment by Beethoven suggests the staying power of key associations in the nineteenth century: "When I make Pizarro sing in harsh keys (even in G-sharp major) when he makes his heinous accusations of Florestan to the jailer, I do it to convey the nature of this individual." Cited in Steblin, *History of Key Characteristics*, p. 146, from Anton Felix Schindler, *Beethoven as I Knew Him: A Biography*, ed. Donald W. MacArdle, trans. Constance S. Jolly (Chapel Hill, 1966), p. 369.

14. G. G. R . . . r, "Etwas von Tönen und Tonarten," *Magazin der Musik*, ed. Carl Friedrich Cramer, vol. 2 (Hamburg, 1786), p. 1190; quoted in Steblin, *History of Key Characteristics*, pp. 120 (translation) and 360–61 (original): "Schwer ist es, ins Innere einer Durtonart einzudringen,—noch weit schwerer aber, die Beschaffenheit einer Tonart entwickeln, die aus der Mischung verschiedener Andrer besteht. Ueberdem scheint auch der Character der Molltonart nicht so genau begränzt, so unveränderlich zu seyn, als der der Durtonarten, mehr wenigstens als der Character dieser mit der Natur und dem Vortrag der musikalischen Stücke selbst zusammenzufließen." (I have modified Steblin's translation of this passage somewhat in my text.)

Felicity Nussbaum notes a comparable unease among English writers of the mid eighteenth century in distinguishing precise qualities of "character" in women (see her "Heteroclites: The Gender of Character in the Scandalous Memoirs," in Felicity Nussbaum and Laura Brown, eds., *The New Eighteenth Century: Theory, Politics, English Literature* [New York, 1987], pp. 144–67). A close relative to "G. G. R."'s estimate of the minor mode is Pope's claim that in comparison with men, women were "inconsistent," "incomprehensible," but also "more uniform and confin'd" (*Epistles to Several Persons*, 3: 2: 46–74; cited in Nussbaum, "Heteroclites," p. 147).

15. As one who promoted the idea that each key had its own affective qualities, Johann Mattheson protested that "those who are of the opinion that the entire secret [of a key's affect] resides in the minor or major third and would prove that all minor keys, speaking

Table 1 compares the minor keys most commonly used by Mozart with their parallel majors in a representative sampling of descriptions by theorists, composers, and teachers from Johann Mattheson to Francesco Galeazzi.[16] Despite some obvious discrepancies, certain consistencies can be noted in descriptions of minor keys in general, and in characterizations of specific minor keys in comparison with their parallel majors. The first is a tendency early on to group minor keys, when they are mentioned at all, as "sweet and tender," suited to "plaints and sad songs"—the sadness deepening with additional flats in the key. With later writers, more intense versions of sadness reach beyond simple passivity to downright immobility: from calm and tender melancholy to languishing laments over unhappy love, to misery, weeping, deep depression, and funereal gloom.

A concomitant tendency (making an early appearance in Mattheson) is toward greater polarization of affect between parallel minor and major keys; in several cases gender is invoked either directly or by association (Schubart's D Major "triumph, war-cries" versus the "melancholy womanliness" of D Minor, for example, and Knecht's "pompous, noisy" versus "gently sorrowing"). Overall, descriptions of minor keys suggest interior, privately expressed feelings within a relatively restricted affective field, in comparison to the more overtly sociable and public functions attributed to major keys. The more numerous and distinctive "personalities" represented by major keys may well reflect less frequent use of minor keys, as was certainly the case among Mozart's contemporaries. In any event, the broad spectrum of affections attributed to these major keys excludes the sadness that afflicts their parallel minor counterparts.

No doubt the origins—or confirming evidence, at least—of many such lists were the pieces known to their respective compilers. What is striking, then, about the minor keys described here by later writers is the relative scarcity of adjectives we commonly apply to minor-mode works of the late 1760s and early 1770s—works in the so-called *Sturm und Drang* style. Galeazzi's "tragic, ominous" for C Minor and "frenzy" for G Minor surely qualify, and Schubart's "uneasiness" for G Minor might do, but, by and large, pieces in the minor mode—as represented *here*—must have moved

---

generically, are necessarily sad, and on the contrary, that all major keys commonly foster a lusty character—it is not so much that they are wrong, but they have not yet gone far enough." (*Das neu-eröffnete Orchestre* [1713], p. 232; quoted in Lester, "Recognition," p. 101 n. 66.)

16. A number of factors governed my choice of these sources: relatively complete lists for the major and minor keys compared here; chronological and geographical range; and variety of orientations in assigning characteristics (tuning systems, circle of fifths, etc.). These characterizations are representative of others listed in Steblin's Appendix A (pp. 222–308).

TABLE 1 Contemporary Descriptions of Major and Minor Keys

	Mattheson (1713)	Rameau (1722)	Rousseau (1768)	Schubart (ca. 1784)	Knecht (1792–1798)	Galeazzi (1791–1796)
A Minor	Calm, plaintive			Pious womanliness	Sorrowful	Lugubrious, gloomy
A Major	Playful, jesting	Mirth, rejoicing	Gaiety or brilliance	Innocent love, hope	Cheerful, bright	Laughing, playful
D Minor	Calm, devout, contentment	Sweet, tender	Touching, tender	Melancholy womanliness	Gently sorrowing	Extremely melancholy and gloomy
D Major	Noisy, joyful, war-like	Mirth, rejoicing, grand	Gaiety or brilliance	Triumph, war-cries	Pompous, noisy	Tumultuous celebration
G Minor	Grace, tenderness	Sweet, tender	Touching, tender	Discontent, uneasiness	Moving	Frenzy, despair
G Major	Serious, brilliant	Gay and tender		Rustic, calm, idyllic	Pleasant, rustic	Innocent, simple
C Minor	Sad, lovely, sweet, induces sleep	Tender, plaints	Brings tenderness to the soul	Lament of unhappy love, languishing	Extremely lamenting	Tragic, ominous, lugubrious
C Major	Rejoicing, impudent	Mirth, rejoicing		Pure, innocence	Cheerful, pure	Grandiose, military
F Minor	Mild, calm, despair	Mournful plaints	Sadness, lugubrious	Misery, deep depression	Extreme grief	Grief, weeping
F Major	Generosity, *à bonne grace*	Tempests, furies	Majesty, gravity	Complaisance, calm	Gentle, calm	Majestic

SOURCE: Rita Steblin, *A History of Key Characteristics in the Eighteenth and Early Nineteenth Centuries* (Ann Arbor, 1983), Appendix A. The original treatises are: Johann Mattheson, *Das neu-eröffnete Orchestre* (Hamburg, 1713); Jean-Philippe Rameau, *Traité de l'harmonie réduite à ses principes naturels* (Paris, 1722); Jean-Jacques Rousseau, *Dictionnaire de musique* (Paris, 1768), s.v. "Ton"; Christian Friedrich Daniel Schubart, *Ideen zu einer Aesthetik der Tonkunst* (written ca. 1784; published Vienna, 1806); Justin Heinrich Knecht, *Gemeinnützliches Elementarwerk der Harmonie und des Generalbasses*, 4 vols. (Augsburg, 1792–1798); Francesco Galeazzi, *Elementi teorico-pratici di musica*, 2 vols. (Rome, 1791–1796).

listeners at a rather slow pace within relatively narrow bounds! The persistent association of minor keys with tender sadness and gentle melancholy does not, I think, need Schubart's cues of "womanliness" to point up a perceived connection between the minor mode and the expressive domain of women.

In the gendered construction of mode that I am suggesting, it might be suspected that the mutable, potentially disturbing powers of *schwarze Gredel* are effectively suppressed by underreporting.[17] For evidence that the minor mode was confined neither to laments nor to women we can turn to opera. In that most public of genres, the relation of mode and affect to gender had clearly visible and audible referents.

Mozart's contemporary, Anton Salieri, wrote of composing an opera that his first attention after several readings of the libretto was to the keys of his arias: "Following the practice of my teacher [Florian Gassman], I decided first on the key appropriate to the character of each lyric number."[18] Salieri's first compositional concern for an appropriate fit of key and affect indicates the importance he attached to arias' role as "characterizing" both the dramatic situation and the characters themselves. In drawing attention to this remark, Daniel Heartz notes that Salieri's priorities were very likely shared by many Viennese composers, including Mozart.[19] From this it should not be inferred that a single composer will consistently use a particular key to characterize a given sentiment, character, or dramatic situation; various factors might influence key choice, such as instrumentation and larger tonal structures, as well as the range and tessitura of the singer. But as a vehicle of charac-

17. An interesting ambivalence in attitudes toward the minor mode with respect to women as performers of instrumental music is reflected in the notion that pieces in minor keys were "too difficult" for the fingers of young ladies at the keyboard. See Peter Schleuning, *Das 18. Jahrhundert: Der Bürger erhebt sich* (Hamburg, 1984), pp. 220–21 and 381.

18. Cited in Daniel Heartz, "Constructing *Le nozze di Figaro*," *Journal of the Royal Musical Association* 112 (1987): 83.

19. Heartz, "Constructing," p. 83. As attention has increasingly been focused on the relationships of keys in large-scale tonal structures, discussions of key characteristics in analyses of Mozart's operas have become rather unfashionable. Even Heartz, who emphasizes the significance of Salieri's remark, examines Mozart's key choices as driven primarily by the tonal structures of extended finales, these in turn reaching back to determine earlier choices. Yet if the listener is to be expected to understand the intricate and long-range symmetries alleged as means of unifying the beginnings and endings of acts (and of operas), some presumption of key recognition seems unavoidable. Granted, the audibility of such relationships will not rest on key recognition alone, nor are key relationships in themselves guarantors of unity. In arguing for a more directly experienced *coherence* in Mozart's operas, James Webster demonstrates the complex web of musical and textual associations that accompany key as an agent of meaning (see, most recently, "Cone's 'Personae' and the Analysis of Opera," *College Music Symposium* 29 [1989]: 44–65).

terization in arias, the minor mode might be expected to carry associations of its theoretically constructed gender.

On first inspection, Mozart's opera arias seem to confirm an association of the minor mode with women and with grieving (see table 2). Sparing in his use of minor tonic keys, he assigned the great majority to female characters: of twenty-four minor-mode arias, seventeen are sung by women, two by castrati, and five by male voices.[20] Except for a single aria in A Minor, all are in flat keys, most of them in G or C Minor. It is beyond the scope and intent of this essay to discuss the unique features of each of these arias. The more general concern here is to determine who sings minor-mode arias and under what circumstances—in short, what affective work "minor-modeness" does in the context of an opera, and what relation this might have to more broadly constructed associations of the minor mode.

Taking texts, dramatic situations, and congruences of stylistic features into account, for purposes of initial comparison I have assigned decidedly reductive characterizations to these arias. A rough typology of affect might be represented by the general categories of grief, fear, and rage; arias of mixed emotions arising from conflicting loyalties might tend toward one or another of these. (Colas's magic spell and Osmin's folk song seem to stand apart; I will return to these.) Representing a varied lot, arias of male characters are found in each category, though often as "qualified" affections, as we shall see. A far more consistent association of mode and gender attaches to the affection of grief—the category that accounts for the largest number of minor-key arias, and for those most often sung by women.

The question, though, is one not simply of male versus female characters but also of the comic and serious genres in which we meet them. For the context of genre that frames the affect of an aria may also multiply its connotations—for example, in comic opera, when irony and parody deflate the potency of rage. Since parody relies on recognition of a prototype, the minor mode can be used to signal mixed messages about both character and situation. Thus for Barbarina, the simple servant girl in *Le nozze di Figaro*, unself-conscious mimicry is an appropriate frame for her naive and anxious lament over the loss of a pin. But even if the minor mode might be considered a conventional vehicle to convey the mock-tragic, F Minor sounds a rather dark anxiety here. (This particular pin is, after all, a crucial item in the unfolding plot of the opera.) Barbarina's

---

20. Chusid ("Significance of D Minor," p. 88) gives the total number of vocal numbers in the operas as more than 400, and of minor-mode numbers as 34. He includes in these figures duets, ensembles, and choruses. In my count I have included Electra's C Minor aria, "D'Oreste, d'Ajace," in *Idomeneo*, even though in final revisions Mozart cut this number. See below, n. 27.

anxiety may be brief and simply expressed, but the minor mode conveys an atmosphere of unease that extends beyond her interrupted song to frame the events of the opera's final act.[21]

We might pay attention, too, to the way conventions of serious and comic opera delineate emotion in broadly ideological terms. The heroines of *opera seria* represented in minor-mode arias (Aspasia, Giunia, Ilia) sing of their griefs and fears in the elevated style appropriate to their status and situation, often with an *agitato* intensity. Falling melodic lines and erratic phrasing, halting diction, chromatically inflected *appoggiature*, dissonant melodic intervals, and leaps into diminished or augmented harmonies: all are common musical markers of these agitations. Granted, many such elements may be found in a major-mode aria of high passion, but the minor mode provides an added affective charge, together with an expanded chromatic vocabulary, that elevates the laments of women in comic operas as well. As might be expected, their texts make explicit reference to physical symptoms: tears, sighs, trembling, pounding heart, loss of breath, faltering voice, even fainting. Whereas such evidence of weakness could undermine the credibility of heroes (and villains), it was eminently suited to heroines expressing their fears for and love of men.

Whether in comic or *seria* operas, the arias of grieving heroines instantiate their fidelity, the constancy of their love. At the same time, however, contemporary views of the minor mode as weak, changeable, and indecisive create a somewhat unsettling paradox in these arias: in its chromatic mutability, its wide-ranging access to remote harmonic regions, the minor mode is unpredictable, unstable, *in*constant. In view of gendered constructions of the minor mode, the role of the lamenter becomes a puzzling double bind. If women are invested with the responsibility for expressing their loving fears and sorrows in the minor mode—regarded as changeable, inconsistent—a more widespread uneasiness about the constancy of women's affections might be suspected.

I will come back to consider the implications of this ambivalence, but I want to pursue the theme of inconstancy, looking briefly at minor-mode arias for male characters and then at those for female characters whose passions escape the "natural" expressive domain inscribed for women. In

21. Wye Jamison Allanbrook points to the reduced orchestration and "nursery-rhyme simplicity of the phrase structure" as features appropriate to Barbarina's naiveté and to the mock-tragic effect in her Cavatina of grand gestures mimicked from *opera seria*, such as the augmented sixth chord into which she leaps at "Ah, chi sa dove sarà?" Allanbrook's *Rhythmic Gesture in Mozart: Le nozze di Figaro and Don Giovanni* (Chicago, 1983) is a sensitive and revelatory study of the many dimensions of affect conveyed in eighteenth-century topoi of dance gestures and meters. In her discussion of Barbarina's lament (pp. 158–59), she notes its larger function in connecting the "note of unrest" at the close of Act III with the anxious mood of the pastoral in Act IV.

TABLE 2   Minor-Mode Arias

A Minor			
Sandrina	Fear, exhaustion, weeping, fainting	"Ah dal pianto, dal singhioso" (Allegro agitato)	La finta giardiniera 22
D Minor			
Electra	Rage, Furies, jealousy, revenge	"Tutte nel cor vi sento" (Allegro assai)	Idomeneo 4
Queen of the Night	Rage, Hell's vengeance, death	"Der Hölle Rache kocht in meinem Herzen" (Allegro assai)	Die Zauberflöte 14
G Minor			
Aspasia	Grief, fear for lover's peril	"Nel sen mi palpita dolente" (Allegro agitato)	Mitridate 4
Giunia	Grief, addresses dead father's spirit	"O del Padre ombra diletta" (Molto adagio)	Lucio Silla 6 (framed by E♭ Major chorus)
Arminda	Rage, jealousy, conflict of scorn and love	"Vorrei punirti indegno" (Allegro agitato)	La finta giardiniera 13
Zaide	Rage, defiance in face of death	"Tiger! Wetze nur die Klauen" (Allegro assai)	Zaide [incomplete] 13
Ilia	Grief, guilty love, divided loyalties	"Padre, germani, addio!" (Andante con moto)	Idomeneo 1
Osmin*	"Exotic" folk song on women's infidelity	"Wer ein Liebchen hat gefunden" (Andante)	Die Entführung aus dem Serail 2
Constanze	Grief, separation from lover as fate	"Traurigkeit ward mir zum Loos" (Andante con moto)	Die Entführung aus dem Serail 10
Mme Herz	"Grief" (parody in the pastoral mode)	"Da schlägt des Abschiedsstunde" (Larghetto)	Der Schauspieldirektor 1 (concludes in G Major)

Character	Aria	Affect	Opera
Pamina	"Ach ich fühl's, es ist verschwunden" (Andante)	Grief, weeping, despair, longing for death	Die Zauberflöte 17
Queen of the Night	"Zum Leiden bin ich auserkoren" (Andante)	Grief, maternal sorrow for lost daughter	Die Zauberflöte 4 (concluding Allegro: B♭ Major)
C Minor			
Giacinta	"Che scompiglio" (Allegro)	Fear, confusion, trembling, fainting	La finta semplice 24
Colas*	"Diggi, daggi" (Andante maestoso)	Magic spell (pastoral-exotic)	Bastien und Bastienne 10
Sifares* (castrato)	"Se il rigor d'ingrate sorte" (Allegro agitato)	Conflicting loyalties, resolve to die	Mitridate 20
Giunia	"Frà i pensier" (Andante – allegro)	Grief, fainting, hallucination of death	Lucio Silla 22
Sandrina	"Crudeli, fermate, oh Dio!" (Allegro agitato)	Fear, abandonment in wild forest, pleas for pity	La finta giardiniera 21
Ramiro* (castrato)	"Va pure ad altri in braccio" (Allegro agitato)	Rage, jealousy, rejection by lover	La finta giardiniera 26
Agenor*	"Sol può dir, come si trova" (Allegro)	Conflicting loyalties, anger, torture of love	Il re pastore 12
Electra	"D'Oreste, d'Ajace" (Allegro assai)	Rage, madness, death, tortures of Furies	Idomeneo [29]
Ferrando*	"Tradito, schernito" (Allegro)	Rage, wounded pride as betrayed lover	Così fan tutte 27 (concludes in C Major)
F Minor			
Barbarina	"L'ho perduta! Me meschina!" (Andante)	Grief, anxiety, lament-mimesis (pastoral)	Le nozze di Figaro 23
Alfonso*	"Vorrei dir, e cor non ho" (Allegro agitato)	"Grief," false voice of feigned sorrow	Così fan tutte 5

*Male character

these arias, the question of masculine versus feminine expression becomes considerably more ambiguous and suggests the need for an alternative perspective on the mutability of affect and mode.

The only minor-mode aria of grief for a male character is at the same time
a charade. It is also dramatically pivotal, for the feigned grief of Don
Alfonso in *Così fan tutte* sets his plot of deception in motion. Not only must
Alfonso's "Vorrei dir" be sufficiently persuasive to convince the young
girls of their lovers' imminent departure for war, it must also convince the
listener that these two are taken in by simulated grief. In choosing F
Minor Mozart perhaps sets Alfonso apart from genuinely grieving
women (heard typically in G Minor); in any case, the older man displays
all the physical symptoms of their weakness (weeping, trembling lips, loss
of breath and voice), along with the halting speech in which they express
their fears. In other words, Alfonso persuades in the vocal disguise of a
grieving and fearful woman.[22] The minor mode is essential here, both to
the success of Alfonso's affective disguise and to the irony of his duplicity:
the young women recognize and respond to the conventional signs of
sorrow in his song, while the audience comes to know that Don Alfonso
can express pity only in a borrowed voice. But if the jaded philosopher
proposes an object lesson in the inconstancy of women's affections, he also
reveals in this aria his own disturbingly mutable character.

Ferrando's jealous rage in his C Minor aria "Tradito, schernito" is a
fitting turnabout on the subject of constancy. He is railing against Dorabella's infidelity when he has himself conspired in the graver injustice of
setting her up! Although his anger is genuinely felt (perhaps most keenly
as wounded pride: "Alfonso, how you will laugh at my stupidity"), the
irony of his complicity in Alfonso's plan undercuts the effect of his rage.
The opening gestures of his aria strike conventional poses of outrage in
the *opera seria* mode, but here and in the preceding accompanied recitative the minor mode rings false—indeed, the aria turns quickly to the
relative E♭ Major, and it finishes in C Major. One gets the distinct impression that Ferrando is as changeable as Dorabella and that his emotion
is as self-centered as hers.

In its hyperbole, Ramiro's jealous rage in *La finta giardiniera* is not
unlike that of Ferrando. But his grand style and castrato voice are more
audible markers of an *opera seria* transplant. With more than enough bait
for an accompanied recitative ("heartless woman, malignant monster of
cruelty," and "I am breathless with fury . . . hate, indignation, anger,
rage, and spite") Ramiro delivers himself of his outrage in a *secco* pre-

22. The arias of Sandrina and that of Aspasia, for example, have many of the gestures
mimicked here.

liminary to his C Minor aria. Wavering between scorn and "wretched" love, he seems to parrot the affections, and clearly poses no threat to his intended, Arminda.

Ambivalence of a rather different sort attends the rage of Osmin in *Die Entführung aus dem Serail.* Here the theme of women's inconstancy—a subject that preoccupies the men in this opera—is explicitly sounded within the frame of a lied in G Minor. Following upon the opening exclamations of hope and love in Belmonte's C Major aria, Osmin's strophic song offers a dark and sensuous contrast, with a growing sense of menace as the foreigner's questions increasingly irritate the Turkish overseer. For Osmin's is the exotic folk-wisdom of Islam, a culture that for Europeans had a decidedly erotic cast.[23] Modal coloration is prominent in the sensual chromaticism that alters the accompaniment in each strophe of the song. From an opening stanza that advises sweetness and kisses as the rewards due a faithful sweetheart, the song takes a sinister turn in the second: "But to make sure she remains true to you, lock the darling up carefully; for loose women snatch at every butterfly and have far too great a fancy for sampling foreign wine." The third stanza aims more direct insults at the stranger, and in the angry duet that follows without break Osmin's Otherness (and his fulminating rage) continues to sound in reversions to the minor mode.

With a monopoly on the minor mode throughout the opera, Osmin's deep bass voice is far from sweet and tender, grieving and fearful! In representing an exotic and erotic power, he may be a stand-in for *schwarze Gredel* (though he has not been degendered, as some would have it).[24] The mutability of his character, however, is most forcefully expressed in the short fuse of his temper, his propensity for out-of-control rage when crossed. In a letter to his father Mozart himself made reference to this quality in a context that makes specific mention of the minor mode. As this is the only evidence, so far as I know, that we have of Mozart's reasons for using a specific minor key, the often-quoted passage deserves attention here.

In composing the F Major aria "Solche hergelauf'ne Laffen" for Osmin, Mozart added an unexpected coda after intervening dialogue:

> As Osmin's rage gradually increases, there comes . . . the allegro assai, which is in a totally different measure and in a different key; this is bound

23. On this point see the discussion of "Oriental Opera" in Thomas Bauman, *W. A. Mozart, Die Entführung aus dem Serail* (Cambridge, 1987), pp. 27–35. In an excellent analysis of Osmin's lied and duet (pp. 69–71), Bauman points to several examples of the ambivalence of major and minor in this and other numbers of the opera.

24. The notion that Osmin is a eunuch persists among those who want to imagine an entertaining irony in his *basso profundo* voice. For correction on this point see Bauman, *W. A. Mozart,* p. 66.

to be very effective. For just as a man in such a towering rage oversteps all the bounds of order, moderation and propriety and completely forgets himself, so must the music too forget itself. But as passions, whether violent or not, must never be expressed in such a way as to excite disgust, and as music, even in the most terrible situations, must never offend the ear, but must please the hearer, or in other words must never cease to be *music*, I have gone from F (the key in which the aria is written), not into a remote key, but into a related one, not, however, into its nearest relative D minor, but into the more remote A minor.[25]

It goes without saying, apparently, that the uncontrolled, "towering rage" of Osmin should be expressed in a minor key. What Mozart seeks to justify to his father is his choice of the "more distant" A Minor rather than the relative, D. The parallel, F Minor, is not a candidate here, one reason being the accompaniment Mozart specifies, earlier in this letter, for the coda: "Osmin's anger is made comic by having Turkish instruments introduced." Identifying Osmin's out-of-control passion with music that "forgets itself," Mozart locates the bounds of this seeming irrationality within a rational system of tonal order. He also defuses that fury with reminders of Osmin's own exotic music—here captured in the fashionable *stilo alla turca*. Thus controlled, Osmin's rage is doubly impotent in being "colonized" by a European version of exoticism. Ultimately, of course, Osmin's power is contained by that of his master, the enlightened Pasha, and by the context of comic opera.

What, then, of a female *schwarze Gredel*? Although men do have some purchase on anger in the minor mode, truly convincing expressions of rage fall to Zaide, Electra, and the Queen of the Night, all three of whom display powerful and menacing voices in the expression of "unnatural" passion.[26] The defiant rage of Zaide, heroine of the unfinished opera that bears her name, is directed toward her captor in a G Minor aria with a shockingly gory text: "Sharpen your claws, tiger . . . suck the innocents'

25. Letter to Leopold, 26 September 1781, in *Letters of Mozart and His Family*, trans. Emily Anderson (2d ed. London, 1966), pp. 768–69. Many have commented on the various aesthetic and dramatic ramifications of this passage. Two of the most recent are Peter Kivy, *Osmin's Rage: Philosophical Reflections on Opera, Drama, and Text* (Princeton, 1988), pp. 59–61, and Bauman, *W. A. Mozart*, pp. 66–68.

26. Although the arias of Electra and the Queen of the Night are most similar in scoring, all three have many features in common. Comparison of their *allegro assai* entrances reveals explosive short phrases accompanied by agitated syncopation, and upward-striding figures that emphasize the tonic triad; repetitions of nervous neighbor-tone figures alternate with striding descents and prodigious leaps. The instability of melodic and harmonic forms of the mode in the vocal line is particularly audible here in "ungrateful" augmented seconds, ascending and descending. As additional proof of her supernatural powers, the Queen of the Night displays an almost superhuman virtuosity and vocal range.

warm blood, tear the heart from the entrails." (A *larghetto* middle section in E♭ Major softens into the grieving chromaticism of other G Minor arias, turning back to the tonic at the words "only death will end our bitter distress," before the opening section resumes.) If Zaide's passions are aroused by earthly love, those of Electra and the Queen of the Night are allied with supernatural forces. And both seek vengeance in D Minor, the only examples of this key among the minor-mode arias.

It is Electra's aria that best exemplifies the potential of the minor mode to undermine tonal order. The legacy of Electra's past might be enough to call her sanity into question, but in Mozart's setting her derangement is heard as an immediate disruptive force on several levels. First, the tonic of her entrance is approached indirectly, in an open-ended continuity that is seen in many of the minor-mode arias, as is the lack of closure at its end. The second key area is also unstable, vacillating between F Major and Minor. Most telling, perhaps, is the formal instability at the recapitulation, in which the D Minor tonic return is displaced by an extended recall of opening material in C Minor. Like Osmin's, Electra's music "forgets itself," but here is a character who embodies the Furies themselves as well as the manifest disruptions of Nature in the storm around and within her. Many have noted that the C Minor of Electra's irregular recapitulation anticipates the key of the chorus of shipwrecked sailors in the scene that follows, without a break, from her aria. What might also be noted is that, on a larger scale, the mode of her aria sounds the dark side of the opera's D Major tonic. The other D Minor numbers belong to the chorus, in its frightened responses to the supernatural powers of Neptune. Elsewhere D Major is heard as the official, kingly key of order and celebrations. Electra's madness haunts the end of the opera as well, as she makes a (permanent) exit in D Minor, although without benefit of an aria.[27]

The differences between Mozart's treatment of Osmin's and of Electra's rage are obvious on the level of comic versus serious characterization, but the use of the minor mode to represent uncontrolled fury in both cases is significant when examined from the standpoint of *schwarze Gredel*'s potential for undermining the hierarchic order of a governing tonic. For the mutable properties of the minor mode promote both instability and power, by providing access to chromatically altered harmonies remote

27. Mozart provided a final aria in C Minor ("D'Oreste, d'Ajace") for Electra, but he excised it—and much else—in revisions to shorten the final act. As revised, Electra leaves the scene after Neptune's announcement with an accompanied recitative in "her" key. (In a parallel to the contrasting responses to the news of Idomeneo's death in Act I, her C Minor aria was to follow this recitative.) With many similarities to her first outburst, "D'Oreste, d'Ajace" is a fitting reminder of Electra's origin and of the Furies and madness that plague her as she embraces the "horned serpents" of Hades.

from the controlling major tonic. Had Riepel sketched a jurisdiction for the natural form of a minor tonic, the tables would be turned on gendered triads: i, III, iv, v, VI, VII. In the expanded estate of its harmonic and melodic forms, the minor mode could accommodate a full range of secondary dominants, including IV and V, for easy modulation. Indeed, Mozart's modulations in the flat direction reach minor regions never heard as tonic keys in their own right—B♭ Minor and E♭ Minor, even A♭ Minor—where the darkest of human fears and traumas can be expressed: the attempted rape of Zerlina in *Don Giovanni*, as well as the shocked memory and recounting by Donna Anna of her own assault; the terrors of the crowd in *Idomeneo*; the dialogue between Tamino and the Priest in Act I of *Die Zauberflöte*, to name but a few examples.[28]

This mutability is suggestive, I believe, when we look at Mozart's use of the minor mode from another perspective. For, although we find some patterns in his use of specific minor keys to "represent" particular affective states (and statuses) of his characters, these arias as a group suggest a more far-reaching topos of the minor mode in its association with altered states of consciousness, with forces beyond rational control. The quality of unreason can be as comic as the nonsense syllables of Colas's magic spell in *Bastien und Bastienne* or as terrifying as Giunia's hallucinations of death in *Lucio Silla*. But in the broadest sense the minor mode accompanies emotional, and even physical, passage into darkness.

We see this in many domains throughout Mozart's operas, and often on several levels at once. Barbarina's anxiety in F Minor, for example, evokes the atmosphere of the dark garden in Act IV of *Le nozze di Figaro*—an effect that is heard in other night scenes out-of-doors in Mozart's operas.[29] In some cases a minor key takes on a symbolic meaning that dominates an entire opera. D Minor, for example, becomes a ruling darkness of the supernatural in both *Idomeneo* and *Don Giovanni*, played out in raging storms of the natural world in the earlier opera and in the "whirlwinds and flames" of Hell in the latter; in both operas the governing key of D Major is powerfully undermined by its *schwarze* counterpart. In *Die Zauberflöte* C Minor comes to represent the dark superstitions of the "witching hour" in which the magic flute was carved, and the kingdom

28. In a close analysis of this last, James Webster aptly describes Tamino's move, from B♭ Minor's "musical dark night of the soul" through a chain of fifth-related minor keys to E Minor, as a "struggling up toward clarity"—ultimate enlightenment being the E♭ Major tonic of the opera. See his "To Understand Verdi and Wagner We Must Understand Mozart," *19th-Century Music* 11 (1987): 188.

29. Other examples include the courtyard and cemetery scenes in *Don Giovanni*; the midnight rescue in *Die Entführung*, signaled by Pedrillo's strangely minor-major Romanze; the dark kingdom entered by Tamino in the opening scene of *Die Zauberflöte* (and to which the Queen exits in the finale of Act II); and the rocky landscape that surrounds the abandoned Sandrina in *La finta giardiniera*.

of darkness to which the Queen and her army return, "gestürzet in ewige Nacht." The appointed task of conquering fears of darkness and death (and of unreason) is sounded in the C Minor chorale of the armored men in black, to which both Tamino and Pamina answer in affirming the C Major power of love and music. (Similarly, in *Idomeneo* the voice of Neptune sounds the triumph of love in a movement from C Minor to C Major.)

Darkness and loss of reason are allied in passage to and from unconscious states. The raging passions of Osmin and Electra have their counterparts in the external storms and internal delirium of Sandrina and Belfiore, the lunatic lovers in *La finta giardiniera*. And the theme of madness in Giunia's premonitions of death returns in the distracted despair of Pamina. Loss of consciousness in fainting spells is itself a kind of dementia, through which the character passes to a newly awakened self—as in Donna Anna's reaction to her father's death, Sandrina's fainting exhaustion, and Tamino's swoon of fear. Even mock suicides by comic characters are heard in minor keys: G Minor is common to the feigned attempts of Bastien and Papageno (which lead to reconciliation with their lovers), and to those of Ferrando and Guglielmo (which lead to the undoing of theirs). The actual death of a character on stage, which shocks even Don Giovanni, prompts a move from the duel's D Minor to the darker shades of F Minor.

Many of the examples cited above, all involving movement to minor keys on the "flat" side of C Major, are embedded in extended and continuous musical numbers such as finales and *introduzioni*. As Mozart mastered these large-scale dramatic and tonal structures in his mature operas, he increasingly used minor keys as vehicles of characterization in continuously developing action and reaction. The dynamic psychology of affect becomes similarly fluid in arias and ensembles whose progressive forms are tailored to reflect the emotions of more complex characters. But for male and female, comic and serious characters alike, episodes in the minor mode expose the darker side of human passions, memories, and actions. In reaching to universal fears of irrationality and death, the elusive and mutable mode effected inclusive passage.

In view of the minor mode's audible powers to destabilize tonal order and to evoke disordered states of human consciousness, it is tempting to dismiss contemporary associations of minor keys with grieving and passive gloom as simply limited. None of our writers mentions the supernatural, for example, as D Minor's affective force; for Rameau, F Major was the key of storms and tempests, and closer contemporaries of Mozart thought of D Minor as "melancholy womanliness" (Schubart) and "gently sorrowing" (Knecht). The implications of a "feminized" mode suggest a deeper ambivalence about woman's nature, however, one aspect of which can be traced in eighteenth-century theories of consciousness and of the physiology of female temperament.

In an age that celebrated the powers of reason, the preoccupation of philosophers and scientists with the physiology of consciousness and rationality had its counterpart in studies of the pathology of irrationality by men of medicine. In his study of the sociology of madness in the eighteenth century, Michel Foucault locates the origin of changing explanations of irrationality in shifting paradigms of the relation between inner consciousness and the external world. In the late-eighteenth-century "science" of sensitivity, the unconscious is necessarily contained in the conscious, its control requiring a kind of fine-tuning of the nerves: "In the psychology of madness, the old idea of truth as 'the conformity of thought to things' is transposed in the metaphor of a resonance, a kind of musical fidelity of the fibers to the sensations which make them vibrate."[30] (Foucault's own metaphor of musical "in-tuneness" is itself suggestive of eighteenth-century theories of human temperament and notions of a minor triad's imperfect resonance with nature.) Viewed as naturally soft and delicate, the nervous "fibres" of women were susceptible to excessive sensibility and to vibrations "out of true," whether in gentle melancholy or convulsive *crise*. Melancholic disorders, classified by medicine as among the "hysterical affections," came to be seen as female maladies.[31] On this view, it is not surprising that musical expressions of

30. Michel Foucault, *Madness and Civilization: A History of Insanity in the Age of Reason*, rev. ed., trans. Richard Howard (New York, 1973), p. 127.

31. Foucault, *Madness and Civilization*, pp. 140–54. See also William B. Ober, M.D., "Eighteenth-Century Spleen," in Christopher Fox, ed., *Psychology and Literature in the Eighteenth Century* (New York, 1987), pp. 225–58. For a study of the ramifications of this association in the nineteenth century, see Elaine Showalter, *The Female Malady: Women, Madness, and English Culture, 1830–1980* (New York, 1985). McClary traces female madness in Monteverdi's *Orfeo*, Donizetti's *Lucia di Lammermoor*, and Strauss's *Salome* as the representation of sexual excess ("Excess and Frame: The Musical Representation of Madwomen" [*Feminine Endings*, pp. 80–111]).

Recent research in the history and sociology of medicine has begun to fill in the details of eighteenth-century medical and popular views of woman's physiology and pathology—heretofore less well documented than nineteenth-century views. In addition to studies by associates at the Wellcome Institute of the History of Medicine, the following sampling reflects the range of this literature: Barbara Duden, *The Woman Beneath the Skin: A Doctor's Patients in Eighteenth-Century Germany*, trans Thomas Dunlap (Cambridge, Mass., 1991); Barbara M. Stafford, *Body Criticism: Imaging the Unseen in Enlightenment Art and Medicine* (Cambridge, Mass., 1991); Londa Schiebinger, *The Mind Has No Sex? Women in the Origins of Modern Science* (Cambridge, Mass., 1989); Thomas Laqueur, *Making Sex: Body and Gender from the Greeks to Freud* (Cambridge, Mass., 1990); G. S. Rousseau, ed., *The Languages of Psyche: Mind and Body in Enlightenment Thought* (Berkeley, 1990); Peter Wagner, "The Discourse on Sex—or Sex as Discourse: Eighteenth-Century Medical and Paramedical Erotica," in G. S. Rousseau and Roy Porter, eds., *Sexual Underworlds of the Enlightenment*

grief and fear—especially in public representations of such emotions on the stage—were associated with women. Nor is it curious that contemporary descriptions of the minor mode circumscribe its expressive space as one appropriate for tender laments and even gloom—or simply find it too elusive to describe at all.

But if in the "feeling mode of knowing" there lurked instability of conscious control, that inner world also held the possibility of revelation. In tracing the etymology of the "inward-tending" word *conscious*, Jean Hagstrum notes the paradoxes that persist in eighteenth-century meanings as: "guilty or innocent, referring either to a shared secret that chooses the dark over the light or to an inner awareness that drives outward from the recesses of the heart."[32] If in states of altered, heightened consciousness, women were susceptible to "mistunings" of the nerves, they were also empowered to mediate in the inner world of passion, fear, desire. There are resounding voices of this power in Mozart's operas, most especially in characters through whose agency the minor mode becomes a force both of darkness and of revelation: Aspasia, Giunia, Sandrina, Electra, Ilia, Osmin, Barbarina, Donna Anna, the Commendatore, the Queen of the Night, Tamino, and Pamina. Although disruptive and disordered passions were contained by the rational order that eighteenth-century opera's dramatic and tonal conventions required for resolution and closure, the disturbing presence of *schwarze Gredel* could elude such closure in powerful voices released to the resonance of memory. In Mozart's operas, these voices are overwhelmingly female.

(Chapel Hill, 1988), pp. 46–68; Roy Porter, *A Social History of Madness: The World Through the Eyes of the Insane* (New York, 1987); and L. J. Rather, *Mind and Body in Eighteenth-Century Medicine: A Study Based on Jerome Gaub's De regimine mentis* (Berkeley, 1965). These are but a few of the studies that point directions for tracking, in primary sources of the period, the metaphors by which men of music and science constructed a feminine mode and temperament. The observations offered in this essay are a preliminary to that larger project.

32. Jean H. Hagstrum, "Towards a Profile of the Word *Conscious* in Eighteenth-Century Literature," in Fox, ed., *Psychology and Literature*, pp. 25–26.

Critical Readings

Opera; or, the Envoicing of Women

Carolyn Abbate

A diva's voice, the politics of interpretation and performance, Gluck's *Orfeo*, a crystal ball, the Veil and the Delusion, certain B♭s in Strauss's *Salome*, and a castrato: a tantalizing litany, but seemingly unconnected themes. These separate motifs are entangled nonetheless, brought secretly together in Patrick Conrad's *Mascara* (1978), a film in which opera haunts a strange scene of unmasking. This cinematic scene draws two older works, Gluck's *Orfeo* and Strauss's *Salome*, into a counterpoint in which each part illuminates the others. For instance, *Mascara* asks us to wonder whether Salome is revealed (when the final veil falls) as a man— not literally a biological man, but bearing nonetheless some frightening sign of maleness, symbolizing visually her usurpation of powers conventionally assigned to men. The film makes other, similarly explosive suggestions about opera and about critical questions of female voice and male authority, questions that dance behind its vision of Salome's unseeable secret.

How? *Mascara* is a murder mystery set in a nightclub called Mister Butterfly, in which male transvestites costumed as female opera characters lip-synch their favorite roles. The club's name has a double edge. As a play on Puccini's title, it evokes in one stroke both opera (*Madame Butterfly*) and a conversion of female to male (as Madame becomes Mister). But "butterfly" is also slang for a male transvestite and thus suggests a sexual crossover in the opposite direction, men becoming women in the masquerade implied by the film's title.[1] Real women don't go to Mister

---

1. The same transposition of Madame to Monsieur Butterfly, again evoking both opera and male transvestism, recurs in David Henry Hwang's play *M. Butterfly* (1988), based in part on a true incident. The "butterfly" is a male Peking opera singer who specializes in female

Butterfly. But police inspector Bert Sanders, the club's owner, has convinced Pepper (whose round breasts, repeatedly exposed, assure us that she's a girl) to dress as Eurydice and perform a passage from Act III of *Orfeo*—the recitative in which Eurydice begs for Orfeo's glance, and dies when her lover turns to look upon her. Pepper, in love with Bert, is more than willing to comply, but this impersonation leads to a more primal scene. Backstage with Bert after the performance, Pepper takes off her Eurydice costume, as we hear (far away) music for the next number on the Mister Butterfly stage: the final moments from *Salome*. While *Salome* sounds in the background, the camera's eye freezes in horror as Pepper turns, naked, to face that eye and expose her secret: her male genitalia. Unmasked as male, Pepper nonetheless repeats Eurydice's plaint, begging Bert (whose back has been turned to her) to "look at me," to *see* her true maleness. As the camera begins to cut quickly between the lip-synching Salome impersonator and the tragedy backstage, Bert does at last *see*. He confronts the truth, and when the taped Herod screams out the final line of Strauss's opera, "man töte dieses Weib!" ["let this female be killed!"], Bert, in a terrible rage, strangles Pepper. Like Eurydice, she dies when her lover gazes upon her.

In this one cinematic sequence we have been presented with a rich mélange of motifs, knotting the scene to a background of gender, voice, performance, and authority. On one level Bert is a closeted homosexual whose rage at his "discovery" of Pepper's maleness points up his guilt over his own sexuality. Bert will repeat the symbolic murder when he convinces another transvestite to enact Eurydice, killing "her" as he had Pepper—as "she" undresses. Attracted to the Eurydices as long as he can pretend they are women, he is maddened when he must admit that the object of his passion is forbidden.[2] This parable concerning the dangers of the closet, however, seems less central than the motif of the masked-costumed female, her desires, and the delusions she engenders. On these subjects nonoperatic texts feed the film as well. *Mascara* composes out Nietzsche's vision of Woman as a being without visible essence, an unseeable core, concealed by a sheen of adornment (cosmetics, ribbons, false hair, jewelry, and more intangible ornaments such as physical

---

roles; his lover, the French official Gallimard, claims to have been deluded for decades into believing he was truly female.

2. Alice A. Kuzniar discusses a similar drama of disguising-unveiling in *Blue Velvet* and points out that the classic Freudian interpretation of the fetish object (for Bert, the Eurydice costume) is that it "protects its user from acknowledging his homosexuality"; it covers and replaces the phallus as the object viewed, so "promising" that when it is removed the person will be revealed as female. The Eurydice costume is thus a failed fetish object, since in the end it reveals exactly what it had promised to disguise. See "'Ears Looking at You: E. T. A. Hoffmann's *The Sandman* and David Lynch's *Blue Velvet*," *South Atlantic Review* (1989): 7–21.

beauty). As Nietzsche intimates, you undrape her at your peril; perhaps (the film adds) what you may discover is the monstrosity of her secret maleness. Beyond this, the film evokes Joan Riviere's "Womanliness as a Masquerade" and her complementary notion that femaleness means no more than a self-conscious display of conventionally defined femininity.[3] Male transvestites' onstage acts take the masquerade to real-life, low-life extremes. The title *Mascara* is thus (like "Mister Butterfly") an evocative double-entendre, referring both literally to eye makeup (paraphrasing Nietzsche, to the face-paint that signifies Woman) and to "the female masquerader" (*la Mascara*).

Mascara nonetheless goes beyond the masquerade of its title. It associates two operatic passages—the recitative from *Orfeo* and the final scene in *Salome*—to uncover a common librettistic motif, for Eurydice's demands that Orfeo "look upon her" are indeed echoed in Salome's plaint to Jochanaan's dismembered head, "open your eyes, lift up your eyelids, Jochanaan! Why don't you look at me? Are you afraid of me, Jochanaan, that you won't look at me?" (324–25).[4] Thus *Mascara* alludes to a theme explored in both operas: the female longing to attract male glances; the female role as object of male observation. In all three works, the consequences of being looked upon are fatal: Pepper is choked, Eurydice collapses, and Salome is crushed. Salome's death (we should recall) is especially elaborate. Herod's final orders ("Extinguish the torches. Cover the moon, cover the stars" [354]) darken the scene to *erase* the figure he once so greedily observed. But the moon, reemerging from its cloud, betrays him, and Salome, revealed by moonlight, must be not only killed but eliminated from sight. The stage directions dictate that she be "begraben"—that is, both buried and hidden—beneath Herod's soldiers' shields.

When it replays Eurydice's and Salome's deaths in its own primal scene, *Mascara* is, in a queer way, "lip-synching" the two background texts. There is nonetheless one obvious difference. Reassigning the female's (putative) desire to be gazed upon to someone whose real maleness is disguised by a costume, *Mascara* confuses the conventional female-object male-subject dichotomy invoked by the two operatic plots even as it draws upon them. The film makes the freely anti-essentialist suggestion that positions of gender are masks, to be assumed or laid aside. Most important of all, in the intersection of the three works we can sense a subversive

---

3. See Friedrich Nietzsche, *The Gay Science*, trans. Walter Kaufmann (New York, 1974), p. 317; Joan Riviere, "Womanliness as a Masquerade" (1929), reprinted in Victor Burgin, James Donald, and Cora Kaplan, eds., *Formations of Fantasy* (London, 1986), pp. 35–44.

4. References to the text and music are throughout given by rehearsal numbers in the 1905 Fürstner orchestral score, reprinted by Dover (New York, 1981). All translations of the German text are my own.

suggestion about power in opera. *Mascara* shows, of course, how the desired (female) object may be undraped to reveal maleness, making opera the background (*Salome*) and the context (*Orfeo*) for this striptease. Precisely by invoking opera at this moment, however, the film also whispers how an excessive and at times maddening genre in itself eternally replays similar inversions of the conventional status quo between the sexes. For opera (as we shall see) enacts the dangerous obverse to *Mascara*'s primal scene (female object unveiled as male)—by unveiling an authorial voice *as a woman's*.

Mascara takes up this idea, allegorizing this dangerous obverse in a quite concrete way: in the Mister Butterfly transvestites, with their lip-synching of female singers. To understand the allegorical force of the singing transvestites, we need to think for a moment about the phenomenology of their performances. In lip-synching drag acts, the text being performed is not the operatic passage in question (an excerpt from *Orfeo*, authored by Gluck), which has receded to a more distant remove. Rather, the text is the female singer's voice, Eurydice-sound, authored by, say, Benita Valente, and caught forever on tape. This taped voice is the permanent material basis for generating a performance (Pepper's lip-synching and miming), just as a score of *Orfeo*—paper and ink and binding—constitutes a permanent material basis for any live performance of the opera. On the Mister Butterfly stage, female voices make the sound-text that sets biologically male puppets spinning in an interpretive dance. In this sound-text the women's singing voices themselves have an explicitly *authorial* force, and these strange lip-synching scenes represent women as the *makers* of the musical sonority in opera. This representation is affirmed within individual operas (especially Richard Strauss's) by specific musical gestures and is inherent in *all* opera by virtue of its phenomenology (live performance, unavoidably involving women singers).

The transvestites' high-camp horror show, complete with vampy bad acting, thus serves a more than ornamental function, and there are grounds for the drag singers' mockery of the feminine. This mockery can be understood as a compensatory move to assuage the disturbing reality of what is represented in transvestite lip-synching: a vision of the female voice usurping the traditionally male role of originating creative voice. Female authority is thus parodied and deflated in a revenge-comedy, which (like all parody) also reinforces the power it tries to unman.

Mascara, in short, raises this startling question: whether opera, far from being a revenge-tragedy that Catherine Clément calls "the undoing of women," is a genre that so displaces the authorial musical voice onto female characters and female singers that it largely reverses a conventional opposition of male (speaking) subject and female (observed) object.[5] The film offers us two operas, *Orfeo* and *Salome*, ostensibly as plots parallel to its own tale of a murdered, gazed-upon "woman." Yet this metonymy suggests others: how opera, the masquerade of gender, and aural delusion come together in an intricate web. In what follows I touch upon the female voice in opera and how traditional assumptions of a male composing voice may be challenged by perceptions of multiple voices, a dispersal of authority suggested all but irresistibly by opera. Moving then from theory to practice, I will argue that the music of *Mascara*'s background opera, *Salome*, draws on motifs of acoustic delusion (a phenomenon that is, incidentally, at the heart of both transvestism and lip-synching) to suggest this liberating confusion of subject that speaks and looks and object silent and observed.

Female Authorial Voices

The scandalous inversion suggested by *Mascara* devolves upon a central issue: can we identify what might be called a musical *écriture féminine* as a female authorial voice that speaks through a musical work written by a male composer?[6] One cannot now, of course, lightly invoke the "female authorial voice" without recalling the doubt that has accrued to its account; that doubt rests, in part, on ironies inherent in two pedigreed strategies for dealing with feminine creative voices.[7] Put bluntly: a liberal humanist might unearth works by female writers or composers and scrutinize them with the care routinely accorded to canonic works; a poststructuralist might suggest disentangling authority and meaning from the historical author and allowing all artworks to be heard in alternative ways. But—as many critics have pointed out—the liberation promised by the poststructuralist program may itself be rather dubious. For instance, two classic essays, Barthes's "The Death of the Author" and Foucault's "What Is an Author?" have seemed to offer means of redressing our invariable association of *author* and *he*, since both suggest that the historical author (whoever he was) is not equivalent to the poetic voices whom we now perceive as animating the work. Many women have paused to scrutinize what Barthes and Foucault seem to offer to their sex: a jewel-casket filled

5. Catherine Clément, *L'Opéra, ou la défaite des femmes* (Paris, 1979); trans. Betsy Wing as *Opera, or the Undoing of Women* (Minneapolis, 1988).

6. I attempted to describe such a female authorial voice "inside" the music in "Elektra's Voice," in Derrick Puffett, ed., *Richard Strauss: Elektra* (Cambridge, 1989), pp. 107–27.

7. See, for instance, Peggy Kamuf, "Writing like a Woman," in Sally McConnell-Ginet, Ruth Borker, and Nelly Furman, eds., *Women and Language in Literature and Society* (New York, 1980), pp. 284–99; and Luce Irigaray, "Any Theory of the 'Subject' Has Always Been Appropriated by the Masculine," in *Speculum of the Other Woman*, trans. Gillian C. Gill (Ithaca, 1985), pp. 133–46.

with liberating interpretive moves. Peggy Kamuf agrees that the writer's gender identity is irrelevant, and "reading like a woman" might well mean laughing off the idea of the authorial sign; "if, on the other hand, by 'feminist' one understands a way of reading texts that points to the masks of truth with which phallocentrism hides its fictions, then one place to begin such a reading is by looking behind the mask of the proper name, the sign that secures our patriarchal heritage." As the formulation implies, any reading detached from certain conventions becomes a "feminine" reading. Thus rhapsodies to "feminine" interpretive indeterminacy are a common topos in poststructuralist writings.[8]

I Will Give You A Crystal,
into Which No Female May Gaze

Yet, as Margaret Homans has pointed out, this has given rise to the rather odd situation that "if reading like a woman . . . means to adopt a position of destabilizing marginality from which culture and literature can be seen to deconstruct themselves, then anyone can be 'a woman.'"[9]

This vision of a subject who can at will see, read, or hear like a woman (or, presumably, like a man) promises an attractive anti-essentialism, an escape from cultural determinism. Yet while imagining a subject whose mental gender can float freely about *seems* an enfranchising mechanism, Homans would claim that it is secretly weighted against women. It appears to invite male and female writers to graze together in grace in some poststructuralist meadow, from which gender politics have been banished, but it has actually pushed women into a passive position. For when a positive critical concept—"indeterminacy"—is tagged as something "feminine," what has happened is that Woman is converted into the Muse, an objectified female figure to be gazed upon and learned from by men, who then go on to do what they have always done: lay down the (critical) law.[10] Thus no matter how creamy the writing of someone like Barthes, and no matter how enticing the poststructuralist bond between freer interpretation and "feminine" openness, the "death of the author" may represent a denial of cultural and historical contexts that might be seen as critical for women.[11]

8. Kamuf, "Writing like a Woman," p. 286. Margaret Homans includes Derrida's recurring association of destabilizing readings with images of "woman" and "the feminine" in this pattern ("Feminist Criticism and Theory: The Ghost of Creusa," *Yale Journal of Criticism* 1 [1987]: 153–82).

9. Homans, "Feminist Criticism," p. 168.

10. See Homans, "Feminist Criticism," p. 158.

11. See, for instance, Nancy K. Miller, "Changing the Subject: Authorship, Writing, and the Reader," in Teresa de Lauretis, ed., *Feminist Studies/Critical Studies* (Bloomington, 1986),

Poststructuralist female critics, in short, seem to occupy a rather elaborately ironic position. They adopt strategies inspired in men by "the feminine iconicized"—but they are not women reading like women; they are deluded transvestites who have put on the theory-costume of men, disclosing their secret desire to "see like a man." The dilemma of the woman who writes seems, in short, to be that she can adopt either the (androcentric) strategies of traditional humanism or the (androcentric) strategies of poststructuralism, but in either case she must guard against being remade by her theory-costume into something risible or false. In terms of the jewel-box model, poststructuralist theory might be seen as crystal balls or magic turquoises. These items are marketed as objects that liberate you to "see freely (like a woman)" but you gaze into them because, in secret, they promise that you will see "like a man." And they become ornaments on a woman weighed down by precious stones, a beautiful and glittering woman, on permanent display.

The Castrato

Rereading such poststructuralist classics as Barthes's "Death of the Author," one might nonetheless ask whether his ideas are as abstracting, hence masculinizing and tainted, as some would have it. Kaja Silverman's interpretation of Barthes's author politics is more generous. While aware of the ambiguities in Barthes's proposal (and in "iconicizing the feminine"), Silverman untwists Barthes's celebration of the grounded and the feminine as a rejection of abstraction. Although she notes that by "fragmenting the authorial body . . . Barthes attempts to hold it outside the perspectival frame of classic representation . . . [and] also attempts to sustain it outside gender," she goes on to suggest that he is on the whole not performing a typically male abstraction but, rather, accepting the images of sexual difference that are inevitably cast up by his intensely physical imagery.[12] Thus "The Grain of the Voice" or *The Pleasure of the Text* indeed reconstrue the Author quite explicitly as a collection of sensual sonorous events, in passages whose recurrent acoustic metaphors are striking: "the grain of the throat, the patina of consonants, the volup-

---

pp. 102–20, esp. p. 106. Miller rejects Barthes's destabilization of the author on the grounds that female writers and readers simply do not have (and have not had) the same relation to literature that men do, arguing that Foucault's reduction of the author to "transcendental anonymity" ("What Is an Author?" in Donald F. Bouchard, ed., *Language, Counter-Memory, Practice: Selected Essays and Interviews* [Ithaca, 1977], p. 120) implies that it does not matter who writes or reads, a stance that dismisses as irrelevant the whole cultural question of how *women* write or read.

12. Kaja Silverman, "The Female Authorial Voice," in her *The Acoustic Mirror: The Female Voice in Psychoanalysis and Cinema* (Bloomington, 1988), p. 191.

tuousness of vowels, a whole carnal stereophony; the articulation of the body, of the tongue, not that of meaning, of language."[13] Rather than killing the author, Barthes proposes the rebirth of an author "inside" the artwork, one that reveals herself in the "grain" of the voice(s) that speak what we read (hear); he eliminates a specifically male position (the Author), supplanting it with this overtly female and musical force (the Voice).

Barthes's alignment of male with discursive language, female with music, should sound familiar: it is dogma in certain schools of psychoanalytical and feminist writing.[14] The way that his switch is pulled, however, is significant. Female voice replaces male author with one critical cutting stroke, as Barthes symbolizes the author's "death" in La Zambinella (a character from Balzac's *Sarrasine*): the castrato as male-who-has-become-female. A male author is replaced, not by an androgynous voice but by a female who has been explicitly artificially constructed and, more than this, by one who is a singer.[15] Just as castration creates the castrato's all-conquering female and soprano voice, so a newly freed way of interpreting artworks enables us to hear the (female) voice that speaks from within them.

13. Roland Barthes, *The Pleasure of the Text*, trans. Richard Miller (New York, 1975), pp. 66–67.

14. One classic instance: Irigaray ("Any Theory of the 'Subject'") famously argues that gender distinctions are the foundation of all binary oppositions and thus that language itself (since the signified-signifier division is predicated on a binary distinction that can be associated with male-female) is based on "male desire" that defines female sexuality as a lack. Irigaray's *écriture féminine* would be as close as possible to presymbolic speech and as far as possible from representation, would attempt to slip away from the subject-object distinction that must inevitably be figured as male-female. Put this way, *écriture féminine* begins to sound a lot like "music" as traditional Western clichés would have it, since music, at least in the conventional formalist view, establishes no signifier-signified system and is wholly nonrepresentational. The alignment of music with "the female cry," "the feminine," and "presymbolic speech" is pervasive in much French feminist theory (as, for example, in Kristeva's notion of the *chora* as enveloping but nonlinguistic sound)—so much so that many writers simply take it for granted that what is spoken by the prelinguistic, female, or maternal voice is "music." (See, for instance, Michel Chion, *La Voix au cinéma* [Paris, 1982], pp. 52–57, or Claude Bailblé, "Programmation de l'écoute (1)," *Cahiers du Cinéma* 292 [1978]: 53–54; and the critique in Silverman, *The Acoustic Mirror*, pp. 72–100.) Such assumptions resonate powerfully with conventional nineteenth-century musical metaphysics, which could bluffly identify music as "she," language as "he" (as, for instance, in Wagner's *Oper und Drama*, Parts II and III).

15. For Silverman, "The Death of the Author"—as well as Barthes's later writings in general—fantasizes a "narrative event through which Barthes dramatizes the demise of the traditional (male) author, and the production of a feminine singing voice. . . . Male castration becomes the agency not merely whereby the masculine subject is forced to confront his own lack, and is remade in the image of woman, but whereby the female author constructs herself as a speaking subject, and emerges as a figure 'inside' the text." (*The Acoustic Mirror*, p. 224.)

But one could, with Silverman, take Barthes's evocation of the castrato as a rather dubious, even dangerous, gesture:

> [The crisis of authorship] is also motivated by the fact that the voice has taken up residence elsewhere, that it has migrated from a masculine to a feminine position. The castration which Zambinella undergoes not only "unmans" him, making it impossible for him to speak any longer from a masculine position, but it produces a *female* singing voice. Significantly, singing is one of the privileged tropes through which Barthes describes "vocal writing" or the author within the body of the text. The Barthesian fantasy would thus seem to turn not only upon the death of the paternal author, but upon the production of a female authorial voice, as well. It would also seem to insist upon male castration or divestiture as one of the conditions of such a production—to insist that insofar as the female voice speaks authorially, it does so at the expense of a system of projection and disavowal.[16]

Silverman is brought up short by the "unmanned" castrato—aren't we all? A terrible monster, she/he suggests violence, pain, emasculation, and the bloody removal of the one certain physical sign that differentiates male from female. Thus finally drawing back from Barthes's pretty idea of the singing voice inside the text, Silverman argues that as Barthes sets them up, female authorial voices are in the end audible solely through the agency of a horrifying subtraction. He merely rewrites an old song: the feminine is imagined once more in terms of what is missing. Can a female voice within a work, in other words, ever be defined except by a negative, as that which can be heard to sing only after a real Author is methodically eliminated from what we read (hear)?

When a castrato enters the conversation (as in the passage cited above), we sense immediately a certain queasiness. Grim verbal formulations begin to proliferate—as if linguistic knees were being subconsciously pressed together. Indeed, so strong is our culturally conditioned revulsion at the castrato that we cannot imagine her/him as a positive symbol for the hidden female voice. But is castration, after all, so bad?[17] Can we

16. Ibid., p. 193.

17. Our revulsion at castration—which we tend to imagine as complete and bloody removal of all genitalia—is largely formed by Freud's fantasies about castration and his scandalization of the image, themselves a summary to the highest power of nineteenth-century attitudes; this revulsion means that we find operatic castrati (as Balzac does in *Sarrasine*) inevitably pitiable and monstrous. Thus we also tend to be baffled by the wit, energy, and humanity that are communicated by their memoirs (as by their happy love-affairs and lasting sexual relationships)—a bafflement that suggests that the cultural and metaphorical space in which they existed is one our histories have yet to touch. For a summary of nineteenth-century views of the castrated see Sander L. Gilman, "Strauss and the Pervert," in Arthur Groos and Roger Parker, eds., *Reading Opera* (Princeton, 1988), esp. pp. 314–24; excerpts from memoirs of Italian castrati in the eighteenth and nineteenth

think of the castrato without pain, see the singer as a female *constructed* but not necessarily monstrous? And recognize that this feminine voice, though Barthes makes it vivid through the metaphor of castration, can nonetheless be imagined without automatic terror caused by the thought of what is gone? I would suggest that Barthes's castrato in "The Death of the Author" is (in part) a *joke*, a tongue-in-cheek moment, one which our deep revulsion at castration prevents us from understanding as laughter. Just as the castrato (like the transsexual) is a figure who confuses real with constructed woman, so Barthes, by using the castrato, is mocking the positivist distinction between the real meaning and a real author's intentions, and all those ungrounded readings that might identify a female authorial voice in works authored by men. At this, gentler readers might well wince.

Authority in Performances

Yet, where does music itself stand? Debates about author politics need to be entirely rethought when we move from the written textual genres that inspired them to live performed arts, whose phenomenologies are another matter. *Performed genre* can be defined as any classic verbal or musical text that exists in live executions by performers; operatic performances are in fact exaggeratedly pure in their liveness, since no technology (amplification) is supposed ever to interfere. The central point about such genres is that the work does not exist except as it is given phenomenal reality—by performers. We might even say (in deliberately exaggerated terms) that the *performer* in some sense usurps the authorial voice.

The power politics of this Jacobin uprising have always been recognized on the street—expressed anecdotally, by performers, playwrights, librettists, and composers. We speak of performers "creating" a role or "making" music; playwrights and composers often document their sense of powerlessness vis-à-vis the performers who make their works, for performers are vital, yet their strange role as a second author is threatening. Composers will assuage this sense of passivity in rage—we need only recall Wagner's tirades against the singers who interpreted his music. Biographers usually excuse this as justifiable anger in a man who saw his

---

centuries are given in Angus Heriot, *The Castrati in Opera* (London, 1956). Nineteenth-century fantasies about the violence and thoroughness of the operation that produced castrati are not borne out by the medical treatises of the seventeenth and eighteenth centuries; Charles Ancillon, in the *Traité des eunuques* (Paris, 1707), reported that the operation involved a minor nick, severing blood vessels and seminal ducts from the testicles, which were not themselves removed (though they might later shrink). Thus, at least initially, boys who were castrated were visually indistinguishable from other boys.

intentions thwarted by, say, Madame Tedesco (the mezzo-soprano who created Vénus in the Paris *Tannhäuser*). Yet temperamental as the Madame Tedescos may actually be, does not some part of all authorial rage at performers spring from resentment at a second voice who completes the work in her (or his) own interpretation? The Jacobin performer is not, however, perceived as the sole source of music; the case is more complicated. Thus if we ask whose are the originating voices in opera (who, that is, do we assume is singing?) we do not only mean "Which singers are singing at the performance?" We also mean "How do we conceive the origins of the sonorities—verbal and musical—that we are hearing?"

A traditional musicological answer to that question reverts to the historical Composer, suggesting that, in the metaphor of a voice singing *Fidelio*, this voice is always Ludwig van Beethoven's or (more abstractly) that of the Composer—*he* who created the piece, and he whose intentions should now police its interpretation.[18] Any critic committed to the positivist notion of the Author Beethoven and his reconstructable opinions concerning his work would see little point in inquiring further. This enterprise demands extensive renovation, not because it runs counter to pedigreed poststructuralist author politics (with their inherent ironies), but, rather, because music is not a novel or a poem, and the unique phenomenal realities of musical performance demand their own tribute.

Musical performance enacts a bizarre drama, in which the performers—as noisy sources of resonance—shout out that *they* are creating the work literally before our ears (and eyes). We know this is not true: Wagner wrote *Tristan*. But at the same time we are deluded by the transgressive acoustics of authority that operate during performance. No single (and, in opera, all-knowing) composer's voice sings what we hear. Rather, the music seemingly has other sources; it strongly encourages listeners to split the sonorous fabric into multiple originating speakers, whose bodies exist behind what is heard. The locus of creation is not, in short, simply shifted from the composer to the performer; rather, the fact of live performance encourages its relocation to other places. The phenomenological peculiarities of music's production urge us to imagine originating singers, voices not simply that of a single historical composer, hence potentially indeterminate or variable in gender.[19]

18. This, for example, is how the metaphor of voice is used in Edward T. Cone's *The Composer's Voice* (Berkeley, 1974).

19. Richard Taruskin ("The Pastness of the Present and the Presence of the Past," in Nicholas Kenyon, ed., *Authenticity and Early Music: A Symposium* [Oxford, 1988], p. 189) argues that, to earlier centuries, the fact that either the composer or the performers are "speaking" a musical work would seem obvious. He argues that "to ask 'who is speaking' . . . is to propound an irrelevancy, for it presupposes the existence of a . . . ghost in the machine." It is a divine irrelevancy, as he indicates. I would argue that with their capacity

Author politics in music are thus in great measure also performer politics, for when confronted with human sources of sonority in live performance we create for ourselves a polyphony, in which the noise-making of the human individuals before us—as a little drama of usurpation that powerfully disperses the "composer's voice"—encourages us to assume the other singers, inside the music. Thus while one might well prefer to be skeptical (as are many literary critics) about poststructuralist interpretive strategies that murder authors and dismiss the notion of intention, one must also recognize that the mechanisms for dispersing authority are radically different in different genres, that the effect of dispersion is strongest in all the genres that are played live, given life in the visible and audible efforts of performers. For opera especially, the Barthesian (female) "singing voice," the hidden castrato who is producing the music from within, is not just a striking metaphor born of interpretive high spirits. The image summarizes the phenomenological realities of opera, the way that opera composers celebrate and enhance its inherently polyphonic nature, and the particular hermeneutic strategies that opera will encourage. Given this encouragement, one might well (as it were) look for the castrato. We can start looking with *Salome*.

Another Monster (Salome as a Man)

A castrato is hiding in the *Salome* score, and analyzing the character Salome is one means of coming to recognize the eerie moment at which she/he begins to speak. This castrato could suggest many things: more open interpretive strategies, the relationship between (male) author and (female) performer, the female authorial voice. But hearing the castrato involves thinking first about one of opera's most notorious women, who famously embodies dangerous oscillations between male and female, author and performer.

Salome has always been deemed a horror. For Sander Gilman, Salome is monstrous because "she serves as an audience's focus for a set of representations of difference," differences that include hysteria, seductiveness, Jewishness, and perverted sexuality. In reviews of the Salome image in painting, literature, drama, and music, both Elliot Gilbert and Lawrence Kramer reinforce this reading; for Gilbert the story plays out "an embattled patriarchal culture . . . under attack by a corrosive, disobedient, unbridled female sexuality"; for Kramer, Salome is a "focal point for the representation of . . . instabilities produced by the *fin-de-*

---

somehow to speak what they have not (literally) created, the performers, by decentering authority, lend music its tremendous uncanny resonance. It would be dreadful to think that music is a machine *without* a ghost.

siècle gender system." Françoise Meltzer sees Salome as a grotesque, an unnatural melding of "virgin and devouress."[20]

Salome's monstrousness is associated with transgression, with her taste for decapitated Jochanaan's salty lips. She, like Carmen, can be interpreted as a monster who is punished by plot because she inverts nineteenth-century culture's stereotyped gender roles (she wants sex and says so) and thus claims a powerful male privilege.[21] In Wilde's play, Salome's desire for Jochanaan and Herod's for her are made verbally equivalent; Salome expresses her disgust at Herod's gaze, "Why does the Tetrarch constantly look at me like that, with his mole's eyes under twitching lids?" (22), and Jochanaan asks concerning Salome, "Who is this woman who is looking at me? . . . why does she look at me like that, with her golden eyes under gliding lids?" (81–82).

Even more scandalously, she insists on her status as an artist (she speaks a self-consciously poetic language) and thus is not so much a "feminiz[ed] . . . artist" as something more distressing: a female author.[22] The libretto leaves little doubt as to Salome's male side, and Gilman's, Gilbert's, and Kramer's readings of Wilde's *Salome* and Strauss's opera all touch upon it at some length. But Salome, significantly, masculinizes *herself*. Listening for the sounds of Jochanaan's execution, she aligns herself with heroic male resistance by comparing Jochanaan's passive (female) acceptance of violence with her own hypothetical valor: "If someone were coming to kill me, I would cry out, I would defend myself, I would not suffer it!" (305).[23] She cannot *be* a man, but she can postulate herself a man in a series of speculative moves; impossible in reality, the statements are made by means of grammatical magic, in the subjunctive mood.

Herod the Essentialist (or, Salome as a Woman)

An ambiguous tribute to Salome's claims of masculinity is put into Herod's mouth. Shocked by her request for Jochanaan's head, he offers other rewards for her dancing. His series of treasures—which begins rather conventionally with emeralds and pearls—culminates in two sym-

20. Gilman, "Strauss and the Pervert," p. 317; Elliot L. Gilbert, "'Tumult of Images': Wilde, Beardsley, and 'Salome,'" *Victorian Studies* 26 (1983): 150; Lawrence Kramer, "Culture and Musical Hermeneutics: The Salome Complex," *Cambridge Opera Journal* 2 (1990): 271; Françoise Meltzer, *Salome and the Dance of Writing: Portraits of Mimesis in Literature* (Chicago, 1987), p. 18.

21. Carmen has been reinterpreted in much these terms by Clément in *Opera, or the Undoing of Women*, pp. 47–53, and by Nelly Furman in "The Languages of Love in *Carmen*," in Groos and Parker, eds., *Reading Opera*, pp. 168–83.

22. Kramer, "Culture and Musical Hermeneutics," p. 279.

23. It would be interesting, given her claim, to stage the final seconds of the opera accordingly: to have Salome resist her execution.

bols of male hierophantic glory: "I will give you the robe of the High Priest; I will give you the veil of the Temple" (297).

Perhaps realizing he cannot tempt her with feminine trinkets, Herod mentions instead *transvestite costume* (a priest's mantle, a veil) that could convey male force. The offer of Power Dress is nonetheless preceded by two significant alternatives, coming at the end of the catalogue of jewels: "I'll give you all of them, all of them, and more. I have a crystal, into which no female is permitted to gaze. In a mother-of-pearl casket I have three miraculous turquoises; whoever wears them on his forehead can see things that aren't real. These are priceless treasures" (291–94). Herod, who will give Salome the crystal "into which no female is permitted to gaze," offers her a place as *the one who is staring*—the place prohibited to women. Yet his next line, associating the crystal with the three turquoises, indicates that the offer remains empty. A woman who usurps the male position of observer and speaker will "see things that aren't real"—what she sees when stationed "as a man" is delusion, and she can no more "see as a man" than she can "be a man." Herod's bribes thus resonate with Salome's subsequent series of subjunctives. All argue for the unreality of her self-identification with maleness. All suggest metaphysical trans-vestisms, couched in terms of magic visions, delusions, and the grammar of the impossible, summarized symbolically in the High Priest's mantle and the veil of the Temple, as draperies that could, paradoxically, unveil Salome's inner and unreal (nonphysical) maleness—what might be called her masculinity in the subjunctive.

There Are Other Herods, Too

One uncanny aspect of *Salome*'s reception is that Herod's essentialism (women must act as women: they should not gaze and cannot compose) has been reenacted in judgments both of the play and of the opera, as the Herodian tactic (elaborating or *complimenting* Salome's claims to male force but *concluding* they are empty) is repeated by *Salome*'s critics. Gilbert, for instance, notes that "androgyny recapitulat[es] misogyny," and the plot must crush Salome in the end.[24] Kramer causes the *music* of *Salome* to affirm the plot's paternal shutdown by understanding it as omniscient authorial commentary. Music, he argues, functions to objectify Salome as a target of male gazes, acting as a sonic representation of the male observer's eye and ear. Salome's final monologue is "the contribution of Strauss's music to the masculine projects of scopic triumph and aesthetic vindication." Music helps put Salome back in her place. Strauss "pun-ishes" her in music, and this slap on the hand is endorsed: "Salome

---

24. Gilbert, "'Tumult of Images,'" p. 156.

assumes—tries to assume, fantasizes about assuming—the logocentric authority of the voice on behalf of the female subject . . . it must, of course, come to nothing [!], but that judgement is not imposed by the music, or not by the music alone."[25]

What are we to make of a vision of music as Herod's accomplice? It is hard not to suspect that the male author is luxuriating a bit in Salome's alleged defeat, relieved that it all comes "to nothing."[26] What is most telling, however, is the assumption that *Salome*'s music (which is given the final interpretive word) originates in a male voice who nudges the audience with his musical elbow, since the assignment of an omniscient commenting function to operatic music is put to work in defeating Salome. How? Interpreting operatic music as an elaboration of plot is, after all, a conventional opera-analytical habit. What has not been remarked, however, is that it involves an *automatic* sexing of operatic music as the voice of a male observer, and an accompanying transformation of libretto drama and characters into a female body, gazed upon and elaborated upon by that music. Thus when Kramer speaks of "internal complications" to *Salome*'s patriarchal happy end (he points out that Salome is associated with rather chromatic music which refuses to be "incorporated in tonal order," much like Strauss's own style in 1905—has she got a bit of "logocentric authority" after all?), the brief nod to a Salomeic authorial voice seems a bad-faith gesture, undermined a priori by the terms of the interpretation itself.[27] And a basic strategy of opera analysis—that music underscores the moral of the libretto—can now be seen as highly charged, both sensual and gendered (all-knowing male voice, caressing female body with his comments). Because traditional, this analytical assumption has seemed both neutral and natural.

It is not.

---

25. Kramer, "Culture and Musical Hermeneutics," pp. 285, 282, 293.

26. Investigating how male writers interpret "phallic women" is an instructive pursuit ("must come to nothing" seems to be the universal refrain), but one that would demand an entire separate essay. Sarah Kofman sees a significant univocality in male interpretations of such women, as in Freud's interpretation of Judith in "The Taboo of Virginity." Freud, according to Kofman, must defeat Judith by arguing that she is deformed and incomplete, thus in effect mutilating *her* to confirm the whole and pleasing "truth" of his analytic theory. See *Quatre Romans analytiques* (Paris, 1973), pp. 84–100. As Mary Jacobus points out in discussing the Judith problem, criticism that discovers ringing endorsements of alleged psychoanalytic laws or social prejudices seems suspicious at best. Less patriarchal readings might show how those laws are called into question, so much so that male hegemony cannot be understood as having been restored at the final curtain. Triumphal critical finales concerning the alleged vindication of male order in the end sit rather uneasily on the vapors of disturbingly ambiguous artworks, and especially on something as polyphonic as the opera *Salome*. See her *Reading Woman: Essays in Feminist Criticism* (New York, 1986), pp. 115–19.

27. Kramer, "Culture and Musical Hermeneutics," pp. 286, 293.

But falling into Herodian essentialism need not be inevitable in interpreting the music of opera, least of all in interpreting the music of *Salome*. I would propose instead that any notion of operatic music as an objectifying "male voice" is precisely what Strauss, in *Salome*, struggles to invert. The *Salome* music resonates with small and strange details of Salome's characterization, to subvert Salome's defeat-in-plot ("must . . . come to nothing") and speak against the revenge-tragedy that ends in her death.

Music Is Not on Your Side, Herod

To trace this dismantling of masculine law we must go back to those inversions clustered around Salome. They do indeed suggest why her monstrousness becomes identified with claims to male privileges (and her revenge when denied them). But they also reflect more abstract oppositions, played out elsewhere in the libretto and in the music. The inversions form a suggestive imageric web—veils that unveil maleness, a sensory delusion that places one's consciousness in a position it doesn't occupy. These two motifs, the Veil and the Delusion, symbolize as well an escape from the interpretive habit that has operatic music gazing in manly fashion and booming with revelations concerning what has been seen. They confuse the boundaries, the terms that define male and female, from within.

The Veil (Why We Must Hide the Dance)

The two motifs are allied to the two notorious practical problems in staging *Salome*. One, of course, is the Dance of the Seven Veils: few sopranos negotiate it with success, and many directors prefer to erase the singer and replace her temporarily by a dancer. The other is that Jochanaan, a powerful presence, spends most of the evening out of sight in a cistern, so everyone must react to an invisible man.

The impossibility of staging the Dance is not limited to Strauss's opera or Wilde's play. As Meltzer has pointed out, Salome's Dance has essentially remained "veiled," left undescribed, because it is indescribable. In biblical versions, though all the circumstances leading up to and following the Dance are recounted, the Dance itself is not, and elaborate multiple framing devices distance us from the tale, as if the narrators are afraid of it. The story thus is "remarkably lacking the sensual and the visible." Later literary retellings, though unlike the biblical sources in lavishing attention on the Dance's details, retreat in other ways from this unseeable mystery:

Huysmans's description (in *A rebours*) describes, not the Dance, but Moreau's painting, creating (despite the sensuality of vocabulary) a representation of a representation. Meltzer interprets this recurrent unrepresentability as a metaphor for the "dance of writing": perfect mimesis staged as an impossible dream. Any live representation of the Salome plot (including the Rita Hayworth–Charles Laughton movie version) must on some level make the Dance real, yet its failure is eternally guaranteed (no staging can be the Dance in all its mythic force); the Dance will always escape.[28]

This pattern of unrepresentability links the Dance to Salome herself, in the sense that she becomes, like the Dance, something that is hidden and unseeable. Jochanaan, castigating Salome in Scene 3, mandates this fate: "Cover your face with a veil" (88). And Herod's soldiers' shields are the tangible equivalent of all the literary equivocations and narrative frames, all the shields of figuration that veil the Dance from us in its literary forms. If seeing Salome, like seeing the Dance, is ultimately fatal, we can appreciate that the Page urges Narraboth *not* to look at Salome, that Herod must hide her from view.

Yet in all this we can reformulate the meaning of Salome's unseeability—which has, famously, been seen as the suppression of a dreaded image (the scar left by castration)—by arguing that this monstrosity is self-willed. Indeed, Kramer notes that Salome actively fends off male gazes; in Flaubert's version of the Dance, she "turns the gaze back against itself by making it impossible for the male spectator to structure the visual field . . . subjuga[ting] the eye that subjugates her."[29] Salome's revenge, in other words, is to make herself monstrous because she thus escapes being an object: she becomes Medusa, on whom no male eye can ever safely fall.[30] In this, unlike her operatic cousin Eurydice (or her cinematic relative Pepper), she is unseeable because being seen is deadly, not to her, but, rather, to the *observer*. The Veil motif is thus two-sided: as the soldiers' shields, the veils in the dance, it serves to hide a Salome who is perilous, but as Herod's offers of symbolic male dress, the High Priest's mantle or the veil of the Temple, it is not a disguise but the *sign* of a fearful inner essence, a veil that denudes.

28. Meltzer, *Salome*, pp. 38, 42–44.

29. Kramer, "Culture and Musical Hermeneutics," p. 274.

30. The Medusa-theme is clear enough: Perseus's shield—the mirror in which he is able indirectly to see Medusa (and hence defeat her in battle)—is both multiplied and made nonreflective in the shields that cover and crush Salome. On Wilde's invocation of the Medusa image and Freud's famous reading of Medusa as male fear of female castration— displaced onto those ultra-phallic snakes—see Gilbert, "'Tumult of Images,'" pp. 158–59, and Kramer, "Culture and Musical Hermeneutics," p. 277.

Splitting the Visible from the Audible

Jochanaan underscores another subterranean motif (common to *Salome*
and *Mascara*), one that enables the radical dispersion and unmanning of
authorial voice in the *Salome* music—a motif of acoustic delusion.

Jochanaan is a directorial problem because he is (mostly) invisible but
must be audible. He represents a split between the visual and the acoustic,
in which meaning is conveyed mainly through sound, not through sight,
in what Alice Kuzniar, speaking of lip-synching, has called "the disjunction of sound from image, hearing from seeing, voice from body."[31] The
libretto reiterates this disjunction in various forms. The first scene (the
Mauerschau, in which the characters describe audible off-stage doings)
compels the theater audience to experience sightless hearing, spectator-
ship denied, which anticipates the more significant invisibility of Jochanaan. There are other invisible (but audible) players: several times, characters hear "the sound of wings rushing through the palace"—the sound
of the *unseen* Angel of Death. The music of the opera (as we shall see)
hides invisible but audible bodies, bodies not present in the plot.

Salome's encounter with Jochanaan is, finally, a drama of acoustic
displacement. Motivated by her desire to see the Jochanaan who is otherwise merely heard, the scene serves instead to reaffirm the schism
between visible and audible. Salome is entranced by the timbre and
resonance of Jochanaan's voice. When she sees him, however, she finds
him revolting (his eyes are places where dragons hide, oceans glittering
with insane moonlight). She imagined a body of surpassing beauty, but
what she envisaged as ivory, as clusters of fragrant grapes, turns out to
be leprous skin and matted tangles.[32] Only one body part corresponds to
the aesthetic intimations of his voice: his mouth, a scarlet band, a pome-
granate, red roses. In her final and mixed metaphor for Jochanaan's
mouth, Salome struggles to sustain the impossible congruence of visual
and aural by associating the color of his mouth with *sound itself*: "Even the
red fanfares of the trumpets . . . are not as red as your mouth" (117). In
his mouth alone she discovers this confluence of seen (body) and unseen
(voice). Her desire to see Jochanaan thus transcends sexual appetite, as

31. "'Ears Looking at You,'" p. 7. Kuzniar shows how assumptions that the visual is a
more secure witness than the acoustic may be inverted by texts that juxtapose the two forms
of information. For another discussion of the separation of sound from body, see Mary Ann
Doane, "The Voice in the Cinema: The Articulation of Body and Space," *Yale French Studies*
60 (1980): 33–50. Doane describes how unnaturally separated voices and bodies are devised
to suggest transcendent meaning (as with the "voice of God incarnated in the Word").

32. It seems astonishing that almost all interpretations of *Salome*, while inevitably de-
voting much attention (and a fair amount of crypto-pornographic prose) to Salome's
"worship" of Jochanaan's bodily and phallic glories, seem literally not to hear her dismissal
of those glories upon closer examination.

a utopian quest that would eliminate the blindness inherent in separating sound from sight and would discover meaning behind the sign in confirming that the rich "music" of Jochanaan's voice signifies an equally fair corporeal reality.[33]

But when the visible is split from the audible, which sense—seeing or hearing—is reliable, which deluding? At first *Salome* seems to privilege the acoustic, contradicting what theorists of film propose as an overwhelming cultural tendency to trust the visible—ocular proof—above the audible.[34] In *Salome*, as in all opera, sound can read the narrative's palm. Put another way, the music assumes a temporary identity as that male-gendered voice, that all-seeing observer. There are musical equivalents to the libretto's "sound of the Death Angel's wings" (a *sound* that alludes to the future). All the famous proleptic leitmotivic asides, such as the orchestral foreshadowing of Salome's "ich will den Kopf des Jochanaan" (153–54), represent prophetic sound. The motif hints at what Salome has in mind and at what will happen to Jochanaan. Though Strauss employs traditional leitmotifs—and this may well work to suggest that the acoustic can convey deep secrets—the theme is nevertheless treated far more equivocally over the course of the opera. Sound takes another form: as Delusion, how Salome hears Jochanaan's voice, how we hear her perception of his death.

The Music of Jochanaan's Voice

Jochanaan's voice, the soldiers say, is something that has no discursive meaning: "We never understand what he's saying" (35). What is this sound that signifies nothing? Salome answers directly: his voice is *music*,

33. Jochanaan is the opposite; he struggles not to know, repeatedly denies wishing to hear or see, refuses to look. This might seem "blind" Christian faith confronting curious pagan (or even Jewish) skepticism. Gilman argues that the opera's initial reception reveals how the character herself came to be aligned with contemporary perceptions—both negative and positive—of Jewishness ("Strauss and the Pervert," pp. 314–27). Yet Salome's desire is linked to the actions of Christ himself, who when he comes will (as Jochanaan says) have the power to "make the eyes of the blind see the daylight, to open the ears of the deaf"—that is, to expunge, from an imperfect world, the despair in meaning that comes of hearing without seeing, seeing without hearing. Gilbert ("'Tumult of Images,'" p. 156) points out that Wilde's Jochanaan is dealt with rather ironically as a "seer" who refuses to look, "because he withdraws from a direct confrontation with the real world, the better to perceive and manifest the ideal," and that Herod's final orders "hide the moon, hide the stars," resonate (almost comically?) with Jochanaan's blind-prophetic style.

34. Christian Metz, for instance, points out that the very term *voice-off*—meaning a character who speaks when he or she is not at that moment framed by the screen—indicates the priority of the visual: the voice is not (cannot be) acoustically "not there," but our habits of reading for sight encourage us to understand it as somehow "gone." ("Le Perçu et le nommé," in his *Essais sémiotiques* [Paris, 1977], pp. 153–59.)

"Speak, Jochanaan; your voice is like music sounding in my ear" (85–86). Possessing beauty that is sheerly sonorous, this voice-sonority speaks in no comprehensible language.

The voice-sonority without sense possesses, like music itself, an immense sensuality and ("the red fanfares of the trumpets . . . are not as red as your mouth") assumes visual embodiment as Jochanaan's mouth. This mysterious and sensual music is, however, also aurally embodied, first and foremost as sheer voice, the overpowering dark baritone multiplied within the resonant chambers of the cistern (which should ideally act as a giant speaking-tube).

Jochanaan's *voice* takes a second and more significant aural form as a motif, the seven-note theme heard first during the interlude between Scenes 2 and 3, as he emerges from underground (cellos, 61–62). The motif recurs several times (it is sung by Jochanaan and resurfaces as well in the orchestra) and reflects this strange "voice-music" conceit by refusing to act as a leitmotif.[35] Put another way: the motif has no fixed association with any verbal formula, no semiotic significance; it is never used to convey decipherable plot information. Precisely because it lacks a concrete equivalent ("Idea of Decapitation," "Jochanaan") the motif remains (like Jochanaan's voice) purely "mysterious music" that can never be understood. Strauss remakes the pure and sensual sound of Jochanaan's dark baritone as "pure music" within the orchestra and, in this, postulates voice in a distinctly Barthesian sense, a motif as "carnal stereophony" rather than as "the articulation . . . of meaning, of language."

The motif acts throughout to *delude* our senses as it does in its most musically potent recurrence, in Salome's final monologue (338–39), at a significant moment: "Nothing in the world was as white as your body. Nothing in the world was as black as your hair. In the whole world, nothing was as red as your mouth. Your voice was an incense-vessel; and when I looked at you, I heard mysterious music." Here, Salome's quest to rejoin image and sound as meaning reaches its end in that strange final sentence. The invisible voice is corporealized as a palpable, seeable vessel, and the silent, gazed-upon body is erased and made sonorous as the mysterious music. At the same time we hear this etherealized body and this corporealized voice, in flutes, oboes, and English horn (ex. 1). This moment presents what seems at first a musical affirmation of Salome's hopeful gesture. One *envisages* Jochanaan as sound, and simultaneously hears his voice-music: a visionary melding of visual and acoustic?

The high-cadential shutdown is nonetheless hardly absolute. An acoustic delusion (the separation of body from voice), denied in poetry by Salome's metaphorical mixing of Jochanaan's voice and body, is set to

35. The motif is sometimes labeled "Jochanaan." This seems inadequate.

EXAMPLE 1 Jochanaan's Voice-music

(continued)

EXAMPLE 1 *(continued)*

music at highest volume when the orchestra offers Jochanaan's "mysterious" unsung voice. For if Jochanaan's *voice* is this *music*, the motif
becomes a "voice" that issues from some *other* Jochanaan-body, one not
only invisible but metaphysical. This second Jochanaan inhabits the web
of instrumental sound; his mouth is the shadow in the mouths of the
brass. Thus the seven-note motif bespeaks ultimately, not merely the
"music" of "voice," but, in a most powerful way, the schism between visible body and incorporeal voice that haunts the libretto.

Delusions

Jochanaan's voice-music issues from a body hidden in the musical score.
A second voice speaks out only during the gaudiest of delusion-scenes,

the scene of Jochanaan's murder, a scene unseen, only heard: it all happens in the cistern.

As Salome listens, we see a grotesque visual juxtaposition of big mouth and little ear, the mouth of the cistern from which noise emerges and Salome's cupped ear as she bends over it. She misinterprets the noises that issue from that mouth and is played false by sound:

> There's not a sound. I don't hear anything. Why doesn't he cry out, this man? Oh! If someone were coming to kill me, I would cry out, I would defend myself, I wouldn't suffer it. Strike, Namaan, strike, I tell you. . . . No. I don't hear anything. There's a terrible silence! Ah! Something's fallen on the ground. I heard something fall. That was the executioner's sword. He's afraid, this slave. He let the sword fall! He doesn't trust himself to kill! He's a eunuch, this slave. Send soldiers! [to the Page] Come here, you were the friend of Narraboth, no? Good, to you I say, there aren't enough dead yet. Go to the soldiers and order them to go down, and bring me what I demand, what the Tetrarch promised me, what belongs to me! Over here, you soldiers, go down into the cistern and bring me that man's head! Tetrarch, Tetrarch, order the soldiers to bring me the head of Jochanaan! [An immense, black arm—the executioner's arm—rises up out of the cistern, holding Jochanaan's head on a silver tray. Salome seizes it.] (305–13)

The "something falling" is Jochanaan's severed head, which makes its appearance seconds later. Salome's misreading of that sound ("that was the executioner's sword") becomes the spark that ignites others; the executioner, with his "immense, black arm," is clearly not afraid to kill. Jochanaan is dead, while she thinks him still living. The monologue gives us a deadly little melodrama of misinterpretation as born of mishearing, initiated by the silence that Salome tellingly identifies as a state of not being able to hear. What most disturbs her, though, is that the silence comes because Jochanaan himself says nothing; in other words, that his voice refuses to utter sounds that will convey the desired meaning.

This scene is critical to understanding how Strauss *rejects* the notion of operatic music as an objectifying gaze, and how he makes an unusual and more radical move: he coaxes the listening ear into occupying a female position, by *erasing* any sense of a male authorial voice and replacing it with a deluding chorus of disembodied singers. In filling out the silence, Strauss might (rather banally) have offered us either the "real" sound that Salome mishears (Jochanaanian groans, some orchestral onomatopoeia of the dull thud of a falling head) or music that could be read as a leitmotivic betrayal of Salome's thoughts at this moment. Music's male-gendered role in opera—to speak as the observer-commentator who gives a secret clue to the action onstage—would thereby have been confirmed.

What happens instead is quite different. Strauss multiplies the aural delusions that wind through Salome's world. He refuses to compose the unseen reality of what's happening in the cistern or in the hearts of the characters. In this, he in effect relinquishes male authority, frees the music from complicity in Herod's essentialism.

The B♭s

A single phenomenon, the repeated high B♭s of the basses (from 7 measures after 304), is the liberating stroke (ex. 2). In these few instants we hear the most bizarre noise invented by a composer whose instrumental *Effektmalerei* is notorious. The silence surrounding Salome becomes the low E♭ tremolo and unpitched bass-drum roll. But something is added to the silence, as one solo bassist, instead of pressing her or his fingers down on the string, pinches the string between thumb and index finger and (as the directions indicate) "bows with a very short, sharp stroke, so that a tone is produced that resembles the suppressed groaning of a woman." Thus even as Salome sings "there's not a sound," we hear this strangled pitch, repeated and building (305–6) to a chorus of pinched-off B♭ explosions.

What (on earth) is this sound? The answer is: nothing (on earth). This is an instrumental noise that comes into the world at this moment, a newborn acoustic grotesquery. It is an *unknowable* sound. The lowest of low instruments, the string bass, plays far above its normal register—something strange is singing in soprano range. No true soprano (a violin, a viola) produces the note. As an unknowable sound, the B♭s cannot be fixed by any interpretation, thus cannot *be* an instrumental symbol for some event in the Salome drama (noise from the cistern; a comment on Salome's mood). Who is the "woman" who is "groaning" (according to the instructions to the solo bassist)? Where is her body, from which this noise issues? The otherworldly sound, along with those suggestive directions to the bassist, open up a sonic and interpretive underworld.

The Ear of the Listener Is a Woman's Ear

The sound as sheer timbre is presented as unguessable, an impossible sound whose true instrumental origin (bassist pinching rather than pressing a string) cannot be identified. If the sound is the voice of an unidentified woman, she speaks unseen and resides nowhere in the Salome plot, but rather within the music. As both, the sound is an ultimate acoustic delusion: sound issuing from a body is not there, sound without decipherable origin. When we are forced to hear such a sound, the

EXAMPLE 2 The B♭s

(*continued*)

EXAMPLE 2 (*continued*)

EXAMPLE 2   *(continued)*

Delusion motif is pressed upon us, the listening spectators of this performance, in a purely musical and utterly uncanny form.

In other words, our ears are forced to become female. For when one's subjectivity attempts to occupy a place that culture forbids to it, one will see and hear "things that aren't real." Sensory delusion (so Herod the essentialist) is the condition of a woman who thinks like a man, who gazes into a crystal into which only men may gaze. Claiming a place as an active subject who sees and speaks, she can only hallucinate, and what a woman will see in that crystal is as deluding as these B♭s that could not have originated in the real world, that cannot be fixed by any interpretation. Hearing those B♭s, we are remade by the sound into the Woman who slides into the male subject-position, the Woman mentally cross-dressed. Our subjectivity is (in a broad sense) brought into absolute identification with Salome, at precisely that moment when she, through grammatical magic, in the subjunctive, imagines herself as woman become man. *Wenn einer mich zu töten käme, Ich würde schreien, ich würde mich wehren.*[36]

36. Kramer ("Culture and Musical Hermeneutics," p. 286) also quotes the passage with the B♭s at length, but, once more, interprets the repeated B♭s as an authorial-musical whisper to the male-gendered audience, as a representation of Salome's secret sexual or parturitional groaning. Again, music is interpreted as a trace of an omniscient (male)

Within the B♭s there is also a paradox. If they are Delusion (a sonorous quintessence of Herod's prescription), then are they not a musical notification that women merely have *delusions* of authorial power ("must . . . come to nothing")? But if they are Delusion (thus remaking the observer's eye, the listener's ear, as a woman's), then do they not stir up dizzy anti-essentialist flights between genders? The subject position might be female; the object position might be male; the composing voice might be the voice of a woman. Salome might have made this music. Or, more radically still, the very idea of such divisions (subject/object, male/female) might be the *delusion*. In the deliberately unknowable B♭s Strauss relinquishes a traditional operatic-compositional power, refusing to use music to reveal secrets (what is happening in the cistern). The usual authorial voice is replaced by a disorienting sound that urges us to rethink *Salome*'s musical web. With other uncanny voices hidden within the orchestra—like Jochanaan's "mysterious (voice-)music"—the B♭s enhance a fundamental sense that the music is not sung by the historical author or by some goggling, commenting, omniscient, and monologic narrator who acts as his local representative. The authorial voice of music, dispersed by Strauss's odd acoustic tricks, is no longer exclusively male.

The Castrato (Again)

A female authorial voice inside the music, Salome's self-identification as an active subject—these, too, are suggested by the B♭s, but in an indirect way.

For the B♭s, as unknowable sound, must continually be rethought. They are a soprano noise made by a bass instrument; (more vaguely) a female sound made by a male. They are a bizarre high sound that suggests how the maleness of its originator is questionable. In these ways they are a sound that after 1905 was indeed no longer one of this world: the sound of the castrato voice, unknown to us except as the ancient voice of Moreschi, the Last of the Castrati. There's a castrato who speaks from within the music of *Salome*, singing at rehearsal number 304, and her/his voice is resonant indeed. That castrato, Barthes's governing symbol for the "female authorial voice," is another singer inside *Salome*. And she/he sings, among other things, *for* Salome's claims to a composing self.

Gazing and Hearing (Beginning of the Conclusion)

What happens when we see Salome? Or, more generally, when we watch a female performer?

---

commentator's covert knowledge (that Salome really feels desire or pain). That this interpretation is assigned to the most powerfully unmanning moment in the score seems odd indeed.

The question has carried a heavy charge since Laura Mulvey's "Visual Pleasure and Narrative Cinema," in which she argues that classical film (in its apparatus, in a taste for certain plots) is inevitably complicit with a male "scopophilic ideology," defining the spectator as he, the thing observed as she; "in a world ordered by sexual imbalance, pleasure in looking has been split between active/male and passive/female."[37] Reactions to Mulvey's sweeping idea have been passionate and have raised the obvious questions: What about films that feature men as pretty matter for visual consumption (*Pumping Iron*, westerns)? How does a female spectator interpret and understand the woman on display, and the plot that exhibits her? Can classical films force the spectator position to be male, even when the observer is a woman?[38] Does authorship change the game—how does Mulvey's theory sit with films directed by women?[39] Finally, are there no films that can inspire shifting senses of the hypothetical observer's gender identity whatever her (his) actual sex, setting off what Barbara Klinger calls a "complex play of identifications across the apparent borders of fixed sexual identity"?[40] This is one thing that happens by means of the B♭s in *Salome* (as I whimsically suggested). They will reconstrue anyone who hears them as an elaborately gender-confused listener, a woman who has assumed male dress.

Mulvey's essay echoes suggestively with a book that seems destined for equal notoriety in musicological territory, Catherine Clément's *Opera, or the Undoing of Women*. There is the same concentration on a spectacle that objectifies women (indeed, aestheticizes their powerlessness), the same attention to plot as a means of enforcing male power and sexual status quo. Both women offer ideas whose critical punch is in part a consequence of stubborn insistence upon the universality of the pattern. For Clément, opera plots kill off women: end of story. No doubt Clément's book (like Mulvey's essay) will continue to generate rebuttals or extensions of her central thesis. As Paul Robinson has said, however, it seems pointless to reproach Clément for choosing not to deal with comic opera (in which nobody dies) or to demand affirmative action (men die too! they die just as often!) for she is concerned not just *that* women die but exactly *how* those deaths happen, how they are treated within plots that, reflecting the

---

37. Laura Mulvey, "Visual Pleasure and Narrative Cinema," reprinted in Philip Rosen, ed., *Narrative, Apparatus, Ideology: A Film Theory Reader* (New York, 1986), p. 198.

38. Mulvey herself took up this question in "Duel in the Sun: Afterthoughts on 'Visual Pleasure and Narrative Cinema,'" *Framework* 15–17 (1981): 12–15. The "female spectator" is also discussed in Mary Ann Doane, "Film and the Masquerade: Theorising the Female Spectator," *Screen* 23 (1982): 74–87.

39. Silverman is concerned to address this issue in *The Acoustic Mirror*.

40. See her "In Retrospect: Film Studies Today," *Yale Journal of Criticism* 2 (1988): 135; see also pp. 131–36 for a summary of fallout from Mulvey's essay.

social conditions of their time, treat women quite differently from men.[41]

Robinson has a more telling objection: Clément chooses to neglect the locus of women's operatic triumph, even though it is exemplified in the very works she discusses, in the overwhelming sound of female operatic voices and the musical gestures that enfold those voices into a whole. This is a realm beyond narrative plot, in which women exist as sonority and sheer physical volume, asserting themselves outside spectacle and escaping murderous fates. *Mutatis mutandis*, the same could be said of Mulvey (as of many film theorists): taken with film's great visual suasions, "framing" plot, they all but overlook sound.[42] My initial question—what happens when we watch a female performer?—refers to this ocular prejudice. But opera's meaning is not conveyed in primarily visual terms (one obvious sign: opera has long been consumed wholly blind, in the form of recordings, but who would sit and listen to the entire soundtrack of a movie?).

For opera the question is: What happens when we watch and *hear* a female performer? We are observing her, yet we are also doing something for which there's no word: the aural version of staring. And looking and listening are not simply equivalent activities in different sensory realms. Seeing a female figure may well more or less automatically invoke our culture's opposition of male (active subject) and female (passive object), as Mulvey describes it. But listening to the female singing voice is a more complicated phenomenon. Visually, the character singing is the passive object of our gaze. But, aurally, she is resonant; her musical speech drowns out everything in range, and we sit as passive objects, battered by that voice. As a voice she slips into the "male/active/subject" position in other ways as well, since a singer, more than any other musical performer, enters into that Jacobin uprising inherent in the phenomenology of live performance and stands before us having wrested the composing voice away from the librettist and composer who wrote the score.

In the house (as it were), opera buffs have always recognized opera's aural subversiveness, though presumably without putting it through such elaborate theoretical hoops. We go to hear "Behrens's *Walküre*" or "the Freni–Domingo *Don Carlos*"; we listen to recordings of "the Melchior

41. Paul Robinson, "It's Not Over Till the Soprano Dies," *New York Times Book Review* (1 January 1989): 3.

42. This is, of course, a relative inequality: provocative work on cinematic sound and voice has been done by (among others) Chion, Doane, Silverman, and Robert Altmann; still, as Silverman points out, reading classic cinema "has focused primarily upon the image track" (*The Acoustic Mirror*, p. viii). What seems uncanny about this writing (to someone concerned with opera) is how many traditional operatic-analytical assumptions about the "omniscience" of musical discourse in opera are asserted in a different form, relating to a very different genre, in discussion of sheerly acoustic features in film.

Tristan." As for the tyranny of the visual: despite directorial claims that today's audiences demand attractive singers, opera remains the one spectacle in which conventional physical beauty counts for next to nothing. Imperfect and disappointing bodies are literally overlooked for the sake of a voice, unseen through the roar of the singing. In a world where one sex has been condemned "on sight" to being understood as "lacking" something, this is a rallying thought.[43]

Salome addresses these issues in ways I have tried to describe, as Salome oscillates between subject/object and male/female identities and as the musical fabric sets out alternative voices that suggest—like operatic performance itself—a re-sexing of authorial speech. Yet the *Salome* plot ends with Salome eliminated from the scene, and while Clément may exaggerate the incidence of librettistic gynocide, this does make us wonder why this opera plot undoes this particular woman. Clément assumes that such plots reflect our culture's state of sexual inequalities and that they perform cultural work by intimating, over and over, that women occupy certain places and those alone, that women's defeat is a pleasurable sight for men.

Revenge

But perhaps opera librettists and composers favor plots that murder women (and men, too) as a form of revenge, to assuage the anxiety born of the Jacobin uprising of performance. Composers' dependence on *women* is unique to opera. Beethoven piano sonatas can be played by men, and men are capable of playing the trombone or conducting an orchestra, but no boy soprano could ever sing operatic female roles. Women are thus critical in authoring the operatic work as an audible reality; they cannot be prohibited from the work's production unless (as Britten did) the composer limits himself to an all-male cast. And once they start singing, these women—cozily envisaged as pleasurable objects—will begin creating sound instead.

Mascara, a true revenge-tragedy, plays out these tensions in physically explicit terms. When Pepper is unveiled as male, when Bert kills her in response, the author has killed a performer because she turned out to be another author—a woman turns out to be secretly male. This disastrous on-camera unveiling, we can now see, resonates obliquely with *Salome* (the music off-camera), suggesting at last why the Dance of the Seven Veils has

43. Mary Jacobus, reviewing the terms by which femininity is seen as a "lack," notes that Freud's theorizing on castration assumes an entirely visual perception of the world, and that as soon as perception is formed through the other senses, women might well be understood as "lacking" less than men. See her *Reading Woman*, pp. 21, 29–30, and esp. 110–36, 243–44.

remained unrepresentable: because what is revealed by the last veil is a Salome endowed with the bodily sign of her frightening and real capacity to create (the sign that it has not all "come to nothing"). At the metamorphic moment when *Mascara* undrapes its Eurydices, it reveals a physiological maleness that is a symbol for the "male" force of the female performer. Those Eurydices must be destroyed—significantly, by having their throats, the source of their singing, literally crushed.

The Masquerade

In opera, singers, as well as characters, are refigured subtly in the listener-spectator's mind as creating what they sing. Given the traditional assignments of power and creative force in our culture, this envoicing seems especially subversive when character and singer are female. Are we not, however, speaking of a masquerade, an illusion of force ended by the iron tongue of midnight, when the performance is over?

Consider *Mascara*'s transvestite lip-synchings, where the text is a sound recording, the master figure who made it a female opera singer. Here the Svengali lurking behind the performer is in fact a woman, and the reversal allegorizes opera's "envoicing of women." But the allegory is staged in the context of yet another masquerade and delusion, since lip-synching (like the acoustic delusions explored in *Salome*) is engineered by dividing body and voice. Indeed, even without their lip-synchings the transvestites in *Mascara* create an acoustic rift, for the one thing a transvestite cannot disguise is his or her *voice*, whose pitch and timbre will contradict his or her visual identity. Similarly, fieldwork among the surgically altered has shown that the hardest job for male transsexuals is not learning to walk like a woman, but attempting to speak in falsetto (Adam's apples can be shaved, but vocal cords that thickened in puberty can never thin back to soprano range).[44] Radical as the statement may seem, it appears that voice-type (and not physical appearance) is the common mark of gender and hence of position in the culture—subject or object, observer or observed.

An essentialist (like Herod, and like many critics who have written about *Salome*) would take this as symptomatic, arguing that transvestism represents a failed fantasy of self-disguise and that wearing the High Priest's robe or looking into the crystal cannot unmake your fate. The timbre of your voice will always put you in your place. A similar essentialism marks certain feminist criticism (like Mulvey's) that postulates gender as determining the way the world must be seen and heard. Any

44. See Anne Bolin, *In Search of Eve: Transsexual Rites of Passage* (South Hadley, Mass., 1988), pp. 38, 97, 134–35.

woman who "reads like a man" (Salome) is castigated as a transvestite, and the notion that men could "read like a woman" is dismissed as ludicrous. Essentialism undoubtedly has its attractions, especially since it has served women as one defense against what must remain an unappetizing figure: the male critic who takes up "feminist" interpretation, with chanted refrains ("scopophilia," "hegemony," "phallocentric," *e tutti quanti*) as a politically correct or, more reprehensibly, professionally profitable move. (To female writers might be offered the following anti-essentialist advice: be intelligent about the crystal and the three turquoises. Remember the High Priest's mantle is for show. Get the head of Jochanaan. And avoid the soldiers with the shields.)

Feeling (rather like Salome) that essentialism has worked against me in the past and will probably do so again, I would on the whole prefer to strike out for a less grounded and grounding territory, in which Trilby can be heard to drown out Svengali.[45] That Salome's envoicement is conveyed through symbolic acoustic delusions does not expose that envoicement as *illusion*; it suggests, rather, that acoustic delusion reflects a masquerade in several directions. To give this last (whimsical) turn to the allegorical screw: lip-synching tells how the music being heard comes from someone Other (Salome?) than the person assumed to have created it (Strauss).

Thus the music of *Salome*, as well as *Mascara*'s allegory, conveys the other side to the essentialist story—that subject-position and object-position are masks that can be assumed, not easily, not without peril. Strauss allows acoustic delusion to dissolve boundaries, as the disembodied voices that speak through the score (which have no fixed gender) and the sound-image of the castrato cast up by the B♭s force us to envisage, not androgyny, but a Tiresias-like oscillation between male and female, through which the female voice emerges.

Mascara's primal scene involves a Eurydice and a Salome. But there is a significant character who hasn't been mentioned, who skitters at the edges of all I have said: Orfeo. The film opens with a night at the opera, as Bert watches a (real) performance of Gluck's *Orfeo* (the confrontation of Orfeo and Eurydice preceding her death). Eurydice is sung by a beautiful, rich-voiced woman who resembles Benita Valente; Orfeo by a countertenor. When Pepper comes to lip-synch the same scene at Mister

45. Indeed, although we generally regard such classic pairs as exemplifying the male artistry behind the female voice, they can be seen instead as subtly disrupting the conventional arrangement. Nina Auerbach notes that Du Maurier's Trilby is too large, too strong, for the narrative that tries to contain her; in every realm except that of sheer plot (in the sonic realm, through her voice, and in the visual, through Du Maurier's illustrations of his own tale) she is the dominant speaking force. See her *Woman and the Demon: The Life of a Victorian Myth* (Cambridge, Mass., 1982), pp. 17–19.

Butterfly, however, she does a solo act; she converses with an Orfeo-voice on the tape, but nobody mimes the part. Orfeo is—visually—completely absent.

How suggestive that Orfeo has become so fugitive a body! Gluck's Orfeo (in the Italian original) was a castrato, and the castrato body has fled (like Orfeo in *Mascara*) out of history. The parts now mainly belong to women. Over historical time, the master-figure for the Opera Composer has mutated from male (Monteverdi's baritone) to a voice that oscillates between signifying male and female (the castrato of Gluck's Italian version), becoming today a male image often taken over by a female body and a female voice. Hence, the *Realpolitik* of operatic performance reconstrues the Performer of the Composer as a woman, and in the prologue to *Ariadne auf Naxos* the Composer is sung by a woman, not just because the high voice is meant to signal youth, but as Strauss's homage to this re-sexing of our archetypal Opera Composer. The line that begins with Monteverdi's *Orfeo* and continues through Strauss's Composer might indeed be seen as a secret narrative, a history that traces symbolically opera's capacity to disrupt male authority. This historical transformation enacts diachronically the strange Jacobin uprising inherent in operatic performance itself; its story tells of women who take over musical sound. For if libretto plots struggle against this narrative by portraying operatic women as objects, by killing them when they are at their most dangerous, the history of voice-types for Orfeo gives us at least one plot that is different: how opera, with *music* that subverts the borders we fix between the sexes, speaks for the envoicing of women.

Britten's Dream

Philip Brett

For Sue-Ellen Case

"How can a minor third be gay?" This response from a prominent lesbian feminist, on hearing that I was engaged in gay musicology, encapsulates what is thought to be the main question. But we need not subscribe to its implied finality. Granted that music as many of us have studied it—my interlocutor was once herself a music major—has been presented most rationally to us both as a symbolic system with no connotations and as a series of works of transhistorical significance. As gay scholars we ought constantly to interrogate this training and its implications. One strategy would be to assert (and exert) the right to propose meanings that are grounded in an inside awareness of the cultural conditions under which homosexual composers in this century and before have functioned. Another is to insist on going beyond the text: what people perform or hear, what meaning they invest in it, and within what framework they place it will be a valid interest for gay inquiry (as Mitchell Morris demonstrates so ably in this volume); it will also put into question the fixation on the composer and his intentions which have dominated historical musicology for so long.

Another tactic is to question the unspoken assumptions behind the original question—that the minor third will have no part in a composite sign that includes words, that if it does the game is too easy, the results unfairly won. The superiority of "absolute" music is not merely an unhistorical notion but also an oppressive one: it must be contested all the time by being placed in its cultural and historical context. When we do overcome all the obstacles (including our own internalized reluctance to

This essay is a revised and much expanded version of one first written for the Los Angeles Music Center Opera production of Britten's *A Midsummer Night's Dream* in Spring 1988.

do so) we are liable to be the target of the latest and dirtiest word in academic polemics, *essentialism*. If so, let us be aware of the power relations involved: a graduate student throwing this word around may be plucky rather than homophobic; there is no reason to give an established male scholar the benefit of the doubt. It may be that the presentation of knowledge gleaned from a minority position ultimately enhances the authority of the dominant discourse: oppositional interpretations may "reinscribe" what they would erase. But before succumbing to this argument we should ask in whose interests it would be not to produce such knowledge. For what ought to be evident is that fear of certain kinds of meaning and knowledge are deeply ingrained in the musical community, and especially in its musicological component. It is hard to imagine, for example, that the spontaneous eruption of approval, at the 1991 Chicago meeting of the American Musicological Society, greeting an attack on Maynard Solomon's delineation of Schubert's homosexual circumstances sprang from genuine devotion to the detachment of scholarly method. At stake is the status of a major mainstream European master (rather than, say, a deviant Russian one), and the energy that has gone into suppressing the notion that he might have been sexually as well as emotionally involved with others of his own sex is but one indicator of the fear and repression on which the notion of musicality and musical scholarship in the West is built.[1]

Producing knowledge about homosexual artists of the past is not without its dangers, of course. One is a tendency to essentialize homosexuality as a condition of creativity, a tendency which at its most grotesque reflects the elitism of certain kinds of privileged male homosexual subcultures.[2] For those of us who would abandon what Alan Sinfield, in a recent article on Noel Coward, calls the "discretion model" for an explicit gay identity, there is the almost opposite danger in decoding the work of closeted homosexual artists—not only of suggesting that all gay creativity must be covert but of simply uncovering a gruesome record of oppression and humiliation.[3]

In this regard, the composer Benjamin Britten poses a problem comparable to, but different from, that of Coward, his contemporary. Both

1. I began to explore this question in "Musicality: Innate Gift or Social Contract?" a paper first delivered at the annual meeting of the American Musicological Society, Oakland, 1991.

2. A. L. Rowse's *Homosexuals in History: A Study of Ambivalence in Society, Literature and the Arts* (London, 1977) is an example of this approach, which at its best might be called a search for role-models, at its worst snobbery.

3. Alan Sinfield, "Private Lives/Public Theater: Noel Coward and the Politics of Homosexual Representation," *Representations* 36 (1991): 43–63; I also paraphrase here from his *Literature, Politics, and Culture in Postwar Britain* (Berkeley, 1989), p. 301.

were leisure-class individuals whose discreet homosexuality helped to maintain the power of that troublesome mechanism the "open secret," which in D. A. Miller's formulation functions "not to conceal knowledge, so much as to conceal the knowledge of the knowledge"; it reinforces the dominant culture by confining homosexuality to the private sphere while making it obscurely present in public discourse as an unthinkable alternative.[4] Both wrote in forms that demanded a negotiation with the dominant discourse in theater or music: until 1968, plays on the public stage in England had to be licensed by a state official (the Lord Chamberlain), and until 1958 all mention of homosexuality was specifically forbidden; modern opera was almost a contradiction in terms, at least in England, until Britten almost single-handedly created a space for it. Whatever subversive or oppositional encodings their works incorporate, therefore, had to be contained, available only to a portion of their audiences. The very difference between their responses to these conditions—the one adopting a camp sensibility, the other rigorously rejecting it—undermines any fixed or stereotypical notion of a British homosexual subculture that might be used to dismiss them. It also supports Sinfield's conclusion that it is important to study such figures: "This is some of the history that we have; it is foolish to imagine that we can be free of it, and dangerous to leave its interpretation to others."[5] After all, the conditions they worked under may all too easily return, making the knowledge of how they dealt with them doubly valuable. And, yes, the power of Britten's music and its connection to the various stages of my own search for a means of self-determination are critically present in the following attempt to understand the broad outlines of his operatic development.

When Benjamin Britten turned to Shakespeare for a libretto, he was a veteran composer of forty-six with six major operas and four other musico-dramatic works to his credit. The occasion for the opera was the remodeling of the tiny Jubilee Hall at Aldeburgh. Britten decided as late as August 1959 that a full-length stage work was needed to celebrate its reopening at the 1960 Festival: "There was no time to get a libretto written," he wrote, "so we took one that was ready to hand."[6] The statement can be taken with a grain of salt, for no composer's closet can have been littered with a greater number of unused libretti than Britten's. Nor had an apparent necessity ever prevented him from doing exactly what he pleased, at least in terms of artistic decisions. The drastically truncated version of *A Midsummer Night's Dream* that Britten concocted with the help

4. D. A. Miller, *The Novel and the Police* (Berkeley, 1988), p. 206.

5. "Private Lives/Public Theater," p. 59.

6. "A New Britten Opera," *The Observer*, 5 June 1960; quoted in Eric Walter White, *Benjamin Britten: His Life and Operas*, 2d ed. (London, 1983), p. 90.

of Peter Pears that fall finds a logical place in the composer's operatic output, representing a climactic end to a special line of development within it.

His three operas of the 1940s had all been concerned with a public world in which one individual is abused or victimized. They are fundamentally social, not psychological, dramas, and are all at one level or another parables of oppression. In *Peter Grimes* (1945) a society bound together by its common battle against the sea ostracizes one of its own members because he doesn't fit in. Tragedy results, however, only when the victim, internalizing society's condemnation at the climax in Act II, Scene 1 ("So be it, and God have mercy upon me!"), succumbs to the shame and self-hatred that eventually lead to his suicide, which is utterly unremarked by those who have pushed him to it. Shame is also the downfall of the heroine in *The Rape of Lucretia* (1946): she allows her imagination to create her own guilt out of Tarquinius's crime and, like Grimes, commits suicide as a result. *Albert Herring* (1947) mirrors *Grimes* more closely but reinterprets the predicament of the individual against the crowd through comedy: the young Albert turns the tables on his oppressors.[7]

In an unguarded moment the normally reticent Britten related the story of *Grimes* to his and Pears's predicament as pacifists and conscientious objectors returning to England during the war.[8] At a deeper level, however, the intensity of *Grimes*, and perhaps the composer's pacifism itself, had its roots in his personal experience as a homosexual—an experience which became central to his art but which he himself could never discuss or even mention in public.[9] Coming as he did from a cultured middle-class family, the security he undoubtedly felt was accompanied by those other middle-class characteristics, a compulsion to work and a puritan ethic from which he never really wanted to break free. His homosexual nature found expression in the lifelong relationship with Pears, which society could accept because its basis was ostensibly professional. But it also resulted in an equally lifelong sense of unworthiness and alienation.[10] The tension between these elements was apparently greater

7. Britten's own recording and the productions with which he was associated emphasized the comic, even patronizing, elements in the opera rather than its serious side. For the arguments concerning this latent side, see my "Character and Caricature in *Albert Herring*," *Musical Times* 127 (1986): 545–47.

8. To Murray Schafer, in *British Composers in Interview* (London, 1963), pp. 116–17.

9. Robin Holloway made the connection in an interesting passage on *Owen Wingrave*: "The private, almost fetishistic quality of this word [peace] in Britten's output explains itself—warrants its full warmth—only if it is understood as the pass- or code-word for his sexuality." ("The Church Parables [II]: Limits and Renewals," in Christopher Palmer, ed., *The Britten Companion* [Cambridge, 1984], p. 224.)

10. The biographies give the tell-tale signs—indications of black moods and utter depression, an avoidance of direct conflict, a lack of confidence and even a sense of failure

for Britten than it was for the many other twentieth-century composers who shared his homosexual orientation. It was a tension that could not be worked out in the usual ways, because of the puritanical streak that served him so well in other respects—we know that he was horrified by manifestations of gay subculture, and even by the word *gay* itself.[11] Prevented from any open discourse by the self-imposed silence on the matter of sexuality which he shared with most prominent homosexual men of his generation—a situation which has still not changed much in the world of classical music—covert treatment of the issues of sexuality in his music may have offered itself as a personally effective remedy. The result was an engagement in his work, first with the social issues of his experience of homosexuality, later with the metaphysical ones, that trod various fine lines between disclosure and secrecy, allegory and realism, public and private—the binarisms that in our culture mark what Eve Kosofsky Sedgwick has aptly labeled the "epistemology of the closet."[12]

Britten seems to have grasped certain truths intuitively: he recognized that oppression is not simply an economic matter along Marxist lines but a multidimensional phenomenon in which the oppressed in one situation is the oppressor in another; and he saw that its toll on the individual comes most devastatingly not by means of unjust acts (which tend to ennoble the sufferer) but through the ordinary individual's unthinking internalization of society's values and judgment. What makes *Grimes* so modern an opera is the very unheroic nature of its title figure. What makes it so brilliant from a political standpoint is that it forces the audience to identify with a figure they have been socially conditioned to spurn: the frightening alternative is to identify with the Borough (which, of course, several music critics have been willing to do). As an allegory that springs from his own experience, then, *Grimes* suggests that at some conscious level Britten realized that "the homosexual condition" is in essence a social construction brought about by labeling and its consequences. The works of the 1940s are in this sense prophetic, for such

---

in the midst of tremendous success—which most gay readers will immediately recognize. The testimony of Ronald Duncan, who harbored a good deal of resentment as a rejected librettist, cannot be taken uncritically. There is surely some truth, however, in this description of Britten: "He remained a reluctant homosexual, a man in flight from himself, who often punished others for the sin he felt he'd committed himself. He was a man on a rack." (*Working with Britten: A Personal Memoir* [Welcombe, Devon, 1981], pp. 27–28.)

11. See, for instance, Christopher Headington, *Britten* (The Composer as Contemporary Series) (London, 1981), pp. 34–35, and Pears's statement, "The word 'gay' was not in his vocabulary . . . 'the gay life,' he resented that," in the ITV film, "A Time There Was," dir. Tony Palmer, quoted in my *Benjamin Britten: Peter Grimes* (Cambridge Opera Handbooks) (Cambridge, 1983), p. 191.

12. *Epistemology of the Closet* (Berkeley, 1990).

ideas were not current until the minority movements articulated them in the sixties and beyond.[13]

Did anyone hear any echoes of all this in the music? The determination with which contemporary music critics avoided any mention of allegory in their response to *Peter Grimes* suggests a collective subconscious effort to repel meanings that might lead down a dangerous path (such an effort is paralleled at the end of Britten's life by the opposite tendency, to *invoke* allegory to get them out of a similarly tight spot with *Death in Venice*). Into this arena Edmund Wilson's intervention comes like a breath of fresh air; he attended *Grimes* and saw in it a message about the universally deleterious effect of war on the victors as well as the vanquished; his views on the brutalization of English society did nothing for his popularity at the time.[14] But there was at least one person who created a homosexual meaning for himself out of *Grimes*. The writer Colin MacInnes confided to his private notebook in the late 1940s:

> The theme and tragedy of P. Grimes is homosexuality and, as such, the treatment is quite moving, if a bit watery.
> Grimes is the homosexual hero. The melancholy of the opera is the melancholy of homosexuality.[15]

MacInnes's odyssey—from someone who at the time of this note had had sex with men without regarding himself as homosexual to someone who at the end of his life wrote a column entitled "Captain Jockstrap's Diary" for *Gay News*—was quite different from that of Britten.[16] Nevertheless, he pinned down here an element that is always present in Britten's portrayal of the "homosexual condition," and he also hinted at its sentimental underpinnings.

Developments in Britten's own life and in British society made the continuing exploration of the oppression/liberation theme an unlikely way forward—the children's opera *The Little Sweep* (1949) was its last manifestation. The repressive atmosphere of the thirties, like so much else in British life, was swept away in the aftermath of World War II. Yet, paradoxically, Britain under a socialist government seems to have been less stimulating for left-wing idealism than those earlier days. Alan Sin-

13. Particularly important texts for the gay movement in this regard were Mary McIntosh, "The Homosexual Role," *Social Problems* 6 (1968), rpt. in Kenneth Plummer, ed., *The Making of the Modern Homosexual* (London, 1981), pp. 30–44; and Dennis Altman, *Homosexual: Oppression and Liberation* (New York, 1971).

14. Wilson, *Europe Without Baedeker* (New York, 1947), rpt. as "An Account of *Peter Grimes*" in my *Benjamin Britten: Peter Grimes*, pp. 159–62.

15. Quoted in Tony Gould, *Inside Outsider: The Life and Times of Colin MacInnes* (London, 1983), p. 82.

16. See ibid., esp. pp. 89–100, 227–28. Especially attracted to men of color, MacInnes crossed the boundaries of race, which Britten appears to have kept intact.

field has shown how artists and writers responded negatively to the threat the welfare state presented to the notion of individuality they prized so highly as a condition of art.[17] In Britten's case, his change of priorities may perhaps be further attributed to his detaching himself from W. H. Auden, who had been a dominant (and dominating) influence in several spheres of his life. Furthermore, his increasing acceptance by all levels of society began to alleviate his paranoia, at least on the surface—already by 1947 the disgruntled Communist librettist of *Grimes*, Montagu Slater, was complaining that Britten had become a "court musician."[18]

The first opera of the fifties occupies a special place in Britten's output, for it is one he himself preferred. The librettist was the novelist E. M. Forster, who had endeavored to suggest elements of homosexual experience in his fiction but had given up writing novels altogether while maintaining a position of great spiritual and intellectual authority among the left-wing gay artists of the thirties—Christopher Isherwood called him their unheroic hero. Forster and Britten lighted on Melville's *Billy Budd* with such enthusiasm that the co-librettist, Eric Crozier, could not even get them to consider the implication of their choice, that this would be the first all-male opera.[19] The subject was still at one level that of injustice and oppression, but Billy's forgiving act of sacrifice for the inadequate Vere underpins the work with a universal quasi-Christian symbolism that did not (as in the less happy *Lucretia*) need to be spelled out. First and foremost, though, Britten's *Billy Budd* (1951) is a work of ambiguity, in which an apparent surface "libretto" truth is questioned at a deeper musical level: a remarkable example occurs in the Epilogue, where the aging Vere's rapturous confidence in his salvation is undermined by the throbbing pulse of the militaristic music of the earlier sea chase. The almost embarrassingly epiphanic arrival of an otherwise unclouded B♭ chord in this epilogue, moreover, could be heard as almost literally anticipating Sedgwick's vision of Vere "retiring from his agonistic public performance, only, once alone at last, to hug himself in delight under the covers, getting off on the immutable visual glory of the boy who 'ascending, took the full rose of the dawn'": the excitement of those drum beats after all, the music obliquely suggests, is not entirely removed from the thrill of orgasm.[20] If at some level Forster hints at a potential Ricky-

17. *Literature, Politics, and Culture*, pp. 43–58.

18. As reported by Bridget Kitley, Slater's daughter, to whom Britten taught piano. See Donald Mitchell, "Montagu Slater (1902–1956): Who Was He?" in my *Benjamin Britten: Peter Grimes* p. 30.

19. See P. N. Furbank, *E. M. Forster: A Life* (London, 1977–1978), vol. 2, pp. 283–86.

20. *Epistemology of the Closet*, p. 118. This is the only crucial feature of the score that Arnold Whittall misses in a fine recent article, "'Twisted Relations': Method and Meaning in Britten's *Billy Budd*," *Cambridge Opera Journal* 2 (1990): 145–71.

Stephen or even Maurice-Alec alliance between the upper-class Vere and
the Handsome Sailor, Britten seems to be admitting in this final moment
that the captain is every bit as destructive as his less ambiguously homosexual (and evil) master-at-arms, John Claggart.[21]

While composing *Gloriana* (1953), his ambivalent act of homage to the
new British Queen, in his mind Britten was already working toward
another chamber opera, commissioned for the 1954 Venice Biennale. It
is with *The Turn of the Screw*, an operatic version of Henry James's famous
ghost story, that the composer entered the phase of development that was
also to find powerful expression in *A Midsummer Night's Dream*. In *Billy
Budd* he had already relegated his earlier concerns with oppression to
second place in hinting at the metaphysical issues that lie beyond the
dynamics of power within social relationships. A further way to explore
relationships themselves, especially the irregular kind Britten was interested in and those dynamics in which they become entangled, was to
cultivate dream, fantasy, and the exotic.

There was another reason why, if Britten were to approach, through
opera, matters of deepest concern to him, he would have to find stories
that were in no sense "real." On his return to England from the United
States in 1942, Britten was bidden farewell by his friend Auden in a letter
that anatomized some of the composer's main problems as the poet
viewed them. In opposing bourgeois complacency to bohemian lack of
discipline, Auden was expressing the dichotomy (his own, as well as
Britten's) that the composer was to explore so movingly in *Death in Venice*,
his last opera. In characterizing Britten's bourgeois side, however, Auden
drew attention to his attachment to "thin-as-a-board juveniles," and it is
no secret now that Britten's homosexuality involved a fondness for, and
an idealization of, young boys.[22] It is of course misleading simply to throw
the late-nineteenth-century word *homosexual*, with its implications of pathology and "medicalization," into the ring with an older and more
universal phenomenon of Western paternalistic society that has typically
involved the teaching of younger men by older ones, sometimes with an
erotic element (as in the case of that prototypical teacher, Socrates) and
sometimes not. For modern society, however, pederasty is a dangerous

21. Ricky and Stephen are half-brothers who end up living together in Forster's novel
The Longest Journey; Maurice is the chief character in the posthumously published *Maurice*
and Alec Scudder, the other gamekeeper of English fiction, is his lover.

22. The letter is reprinted in Donald Mitchell, *Britten and Auden in the Thirties: The Year
1936* (Seattle, 1981), pp. 161–62. Donald Mitchell has stated that "*Death in Venice* embodies
unequivocally the powerful sexual drive that was Britten's towards the young (and sometimes very young) male": *Benjamin Britten: Death in Venice* (Cambridge Opera Handbooks)
(Cambridge, 1987), p. 21.

area—the side of paternalism which when it manifests itself physically becomes "sexual abuse."

Just as Britten, who had never suffered real persecution for his homosexuality, came to terms—in the terrifying manhunts of *Peter Grimes*—with the paranoid fears common to most homosexuals, so in *The Turn of the Screw* the composer, who seems never to have forced himself on his young friends, explored (or exorcised) through the agency of Henry James the possibility of a dominant man-boy relationship implicitly sexualized. Bringing the ghosts alive and giving them words meant that the Quint-Miles connection had an effect very different from the suggestive, ambiguous horror of the story (which depends for much of its effect on the reader's own vulnerability). Britten's Quint sings songs of allure and delight to which Miles fully responds. The ambiguity in the opera does not depend on whether or not the ghosts exist but springs from a musical question as to how different in kind are the relationships, and which is worse for the poor boy: that with the predatory ghost, or that with the smothering governess.

A deeper ambiguity surrounds the very nature of Quint's "threat" to Miles. The seductive theme in which he utters Miles's name in, for instance, Scene 8 of both acts, and which is formalized in the Ceremony of Innocence episode (Act II, Scene 1), is first vocalized by the Governess in Scene 1 and is again heard on her lips in Scene 5, after the disclosure by Mrs. Gross of the fact of Quint's death. "See what I see, know what I know, that they may see and know nothing," cries the Governess, singing this theme to the bewildered housekeeper. Are we to understand musically that Quint's relations with Miles are projections of her fears and desires? If it hints at that, the Ceremony of Innocence theme also suggests the crisis of secrecy, sight and knowledge constructed around the "love that dares not speak its name." And listeners' reactions confirm it. Disquieted by the implications of this theme, analysts underplay the fact that it occurs first in the score under the heading "THEME" and is as much part of *the* theme as the twelve-note motive that claims their attention.[23] In abstract serialism—however different from the Schoenbergian model—lies safety. The slippage here betrays the importance of the issue.[24]

---

23. Peter Evans, with his usual perspicacity, notes its derivation from the inversion of the first five notes of that chromatic series: *The Music of Benjamin Britten* (London, 1979), p. 214.

24. Patricia Howard goes so far in not seeing/hearing as to claim that the theme "first occurs in Act I scene 1 at a significant point in the governess's musings," quoting the passage seven measures after figure 3 ("O why, why did I come?") to support her observation; *Benjamin Britten: The Turn of the Screw* (Cambridge Opera Handbooks) (Cambridge, 1985), p. 82.

It may seem a far cry from James to Shakespeare, but the progression from intense tragedy to more healing comedy had after all been traversed before, from *Grimes* to *Herring*. Britten, who was adept at covering his tracks, once said that *A Midsummer Night's Dream* appealed to him as the work of a very young man and as a story that involved three different and separate groups—the Lovers, the Rustics (as he called the mechanicals), and the Fairies—who nevertheless interact.[25] It seems more likely that after exploring the ambiguity of relationships in a realistic setting in *Billy Budd*, and the fantasy of the unthinkable in the context of James's ghost story, the composer should have found in Shakespeare's subtle and adventurous play an ideal vehicle for pursuing his interests in the possibilities of relationships.

Until after World War II it was common to refer to plays like *A Midsummer Night's Dream* as Shakespeare's romantic or idyllic comedies. Productions emphasized the magical qualities of the play, its fairy enchantment and illusion, and its romance. (Indeed, the first production of Britten's opera as designed by John Piper and Carl Toms, especially in its enlarged form at Covent Garden, had a share in that tradition.)[26] Around the time the opera was written, however, C. L. Barber was arguing that Shakespeare's comedies were saturnalian rather than romantic and that they depended for their effect not on nineteenth-century notions of "character" but on ritual as embodied in holiday archetypes. In *A Midsummer Night's Dream* the lovers, like celebrants on the eve of May Day, run off to the wood at night and gain release from everyday restraint under the influence of Oberon. Both they and we gain clarification as a result. In accordance with this scheme, Shakespeare's play begins in town, in Theseus's palace, to which it returns, and into which Oberon and Tytania enter, bringing the blessing of fertility to the bridal couples much as country gods brought their tribute when Elizabeth I was entertained.[27]

As the curtain rises on Britten's opera we cannot fail to notice a crucial difference from the play. Even without the scenery we know that we are already, in more senses than one, in the woods. It is almost impossible to resist the association with breathing and sleep, or at the least with the wood as a primeval force, that is so powerfully suggested by the eerie

25. *The Observer*, 5 June 1960, quoted in Eric Walter White, *Benjamin Britten: His Life and Operas*, p. 90.

26. See Plates 82–89 of David Herbert, ed., *The Operas of Benjamin Britten* (London, 1979), pp. 275–78.

27. "May Games and Metamorphoses on a Midsummer Night," in *Shakespeare's Festive Comedy: A Study of Dramatic Form and Its Relation to Social Custom* (Princeton, 1959), pp. 119–62. See also Louis Adrian Montrose, "'Shaping Fantasies': Figurations of Gender and Power in Elizabethan Culture," *Representations*, no. 2 (1983): 61–94. I have adopted Britten's spelling, Tytania, derived from the quarto, rather than the more usual Titania. In Britten's performances the first syllable was pronounced as a long "i" (as in "tie") not a short one.

sound of the *portamenti* strings. We open at once into a world of dreams—clearly of the post-Jungian variety—the "real" world of the opera. In Britten's scheme it is the court of Duke Theseus that seems unreal and limiting, the final entry of the fairies marking a return to "normal." In other words, Britten has simply dispensed with the social context of Athens and with the background of reality as an initiating device. He has moved here the furthest distance from the realistic borough of *Peter Grimes* into a completely private world, a world of possibilities rather than of limitations. The folk-festival or May-games aspect of Shakespeare's play, then, has been matched by a contemporary notion of misrule, the world of the libido.[28]

The very nature and conditions of opera, of course, appear to go against its expression of anything so radical. Opera is after all an anachronistic performance art, set in a museum context and patronized by a convention-loving public almost as exclusive as the aristocracy for which it was first created. But opera and masquerade have historical links, and today it is perhaps the carnivalesque, libido-enhancing as well as convention-bound characteristics of opera that give it a special place in gay culture.[29] Britten, moreover, had already shown ingenuity in injecting modern concerns into conventional formulas (most notably in *Peter Grimes*). In *A Midsummer Night's Dream*, operatic convention itself becomes part of the subject of the opera.

This concern is most immediately noticeable in the broad comedy of the mechanicals' play. Pyramus and Thisby's exploration of the crudest

28. Ruth Solie has suggested to me the possible connection of this opposition between court and woods to that between "the two fundamental types of sociality: the Norm and the Festival" as proposed by Jacques Attali in his analysis of Breughel's painting *Carnival's Quarrel with Lent* (*Noise: The Political Economy of Music*, trans. Brian Massumi [Minneapolis, 1985], pp. 21–24). It may be useful to consider to what degree Britten's explorations of a transgressive order here and elsewhere have to do with his patent efforts to change the "political economy" of music-making in post–World War II Britain—by starting the English Opera Group, founding the Aldeburgh Festival, and exploring alternative performance-spaces and methods (in such works as *Noyës Fludde*, *Saint Nicolas*, and the Church Parables) and by his leading role in the immense effort to encourage music in schools (which the Thatcher government reportedly did its best to dismantle). My notion here, however, was derived from C. L. Barber and enriched by ideas of the carnivalesque associated with Mikhail Bakhtin and articulated in the English context by Terry Castle in her fine book *Masquerade and Civilization: The Carnivalesque in Eighteenth-Century English Culture and Fiction* (Stanford, 1986).

29. Terry Castle indicates the historical association of masquerade and opera in London—the first public masquerades, like Handel's first productions, took place at the Haymarket—and points to the survival in "the conservative institution of the opera" of masquerade in such works as Verdi's *Un ballo in maschera* long after it had been exhausted as a topos in literature (*Masquerade and Civilization*, pp. 339–40). Representing flamboyant feelings beyond those allowed in "real" circumstances, opera offers solace and promise of fulfillment to gay men (no strangers to repressed emotions); hence its potent role in the social control of homosexuality. See Mitchell Morris, "Reading as an Opera Queen," in this volume.

side of nineteenth-century opera exposes them to ridicule from the audience within the opera while giving a sense of superiority to the audience without. There is a feeling of wicked fun about the whole scene, from its more obvious effects to those little moments of malice such as the Schoenbergian *sprechstimme* in which (as Peter Evans noted) Snout wails out his song as Wall.[30] The episode clearly appealed to Britten's schoolboy sense of humor, but it also constitutes his closest approach to camp, especially in the transvestite role of Thisby memorably performed by Peter Pears in the original production. Yet Britten's delight in parody here is tied up with a tendency of the work as a whole to parody convention in a more subtle way. As in other operas, the chorus opens *A Midsummer Night's Dream*, but it is a chorus of unbroken boys' voices, singing in unison—as different from the romantic notion of fairies (and opera choruses) as could be imagined. Shortly after comes the expected entry of the *prima donna* and the male lead, who in this case is far from the ardent tenor of the romantic era and as close as one can get nowadays to the *primo uomo* of eighteenth-century *opera seria*, the castrato. Along with the historical reference, however, goes the association of unmanliness, and thus of gender liminality, that haunts the modern image of the homosexual. Squeaking in a falsetto voice, the emasculated, misogynistic, boy-desiring Oberon is almost literally a figure of the closet.[31]

The casting of Oberon as a countertenor (the part was written for Alfred Deller) sent Britten back for models to his beloved Purcell. In Oberon's first set piece, "I Know a Bank" (Act I, at figure 47), we can hear echoes of the fantastically elaborate style of Purcell's "Sweeter than Roses," which Britten had once arranged for Pears. The formality of the slow march that announces the fairy king and queen and accompanies several of their moments together also harks back to the seventeenth century. We notice that the fairy denizens of the wood, whether in Oberon's florid aria, Tytania's ecstatic "Come Now, a Roundel" (Act I, at figure 94) or the attendants' bouncy "You Spotted Snakes" (Act I, at figure 97), are much more likely to sing in rounded set pieces than are the Rustics or Lovers who invade their territory. Theirs is a world of formality, of decorum, of

30. *The Music of Benjamin Britten*, pp. 253–54.
31. See Castle, *Masquerade and Civilization*, pp. 35–36, for "squeaking" in the masquerade and its possible parody of the castrato. In an extended and fascinating demonstration of the connection (in singing manuals and other documents) between the falsetto voice and unnaturalness and degeneracy, Wayne Koestenbaum shows how "the discourse of degenerate voice (one of several models of the unnaturally produced self) enfolds and foretells the modern discourse of the homosexual"; see "The Queen's Throat: (Homo)sexuality and the Art of Singing," in *Inside/Out: Lesbian Theories, Gay Theories*, ed. Diana Fuss (New York, 1991), pp. 217–223.

a certain innocent perfection, and ultimately, of course, of nostalgia as well.

Britten's treatment of the role of Puck also suggests a difference from—as well as a reference to—a historical convention. The role of hero's friend or servant in opera is traditionally assigned to the baritone (as in such diverse works as *Don Giovanni, Don Carlos, Tristan und Isolde,* and even *Peter Grimes*); yet Britten's Puck is a boy tumbler who speaks (in an adolescent parody of baritone in the original production) rather than sings. We may remember that the rift between Oberon and Tytania is caused by Oberon's desire for "a little changeling boy / To be my hench-man." But Oberon already has a henchman in Puck, a freer spirit than Miles, and one who snaps to his master's attention with even greater alacrity than Miles to Quint's. Theirs is the central relationship of the wood: it is certainly the one that holds the power in this labyrinth.

The appearance of a quartet of lovers who are constant in all but their affections (as Cecily puts it in *The Importance of Being Earnest*) prompts a modern audience to think almost automatically of *Così fan tutte.* Britten, however, is truer to his poet in suggesting through them the blind, irrational, compulsive—and painful—state of love. These four figures tend to avoid the voluptuous strings of thirds that characterize Mozart's score: they sing lines that are eternally syllabic, in even notes. This is a sure sign in Britten's musical language, as in the case of Grimes's Ellen Orford, that although they are conventionally "good," there is something wrong with them, or limited about them. It is only after very close hearing that we begin to notice the typically Brittenesque subtleties of characterization that distinguish them. Moreover, it is not until their awakening in Act III that their "unending melody" is exchanged for something like a set piece. This is the litany-like chorus that Britten builds out of a speech of Shakespeare's Helena, which she initiates at figure 19a: "And I have found Demetrius like a jewel, / Mine own, and not mine own." On the one hand this suggests that their experience in the ordered/disordered king-dom of the Dream has taught them something, and on the other it seems to consign them to a lifetime of little more promising than double-dating: what many modern critics and directors see as Shakespeare's gloomy prognosis for marriage in patriarchal society finds a modern echo in Britten's own pessimism about it.[32]

One relationship in the play/opera is purposely grotesque. Interest-ingly enough, Britten puts it literally at the center of the opera, halfway through the second act, and lavishes on it some of his most luscious

---

32. See Stephen Orgel, "Nobody's Perfect: Or, Why Did the English Stage Take Boys for Women?" *South Atlantic Quarterly* 88 (1989): 10–13, 26–28.

music. As Bottom, singing an out-of-tune song, wakes the sleeping Tyta-nia, she bursts into a rapturous lyricism that suggests a truth beyond irony. "Certainly on the evidence of her *music* Tytania's love for Bottom misconceived seems deeper than whatever it is she feels for Oberon," as Wilfrid Mellers puts it.[33] Her final statement before they fall asleep together, couched over the four chords that encompass the experience of the wood as well as the notes of the complete chromatic scale (ex. 1a), sounds, in its range, its rhythm and phrasing, and the way its fall com-plements the orchestra's rising pitch, to embody perhaps the most com-plete and definitive statement in a drama whose indeterminacy is one of its chief characteristics.[34]

Tytania's forswearing of her love for Bottom in Act III, contending with and contingent on the moment of musical truth in Example 1a, seems to me to suggest that the opera, like the play, places emphasis on the in-determinacy of meaning and on the disruption of patriarchal power, not its restitution. Women in Britten's operas tend to run to extremes—they are either victims or predators.[35] Tytania is a curious amalgam; she takes over Bottom and at the same time is utterly dominated by Oberon and Puck, whose cruel triumph (as Patricia Howard suggests) causes her even-tually to forfeit not only her Indian boy but also the very stuff of her independent authority, her vocal brilliance—a fate worse than death for a diva.[36] In Act III she sings comparatively restrained phrases in duets or ensembles initiated and controlled by Oberon: both her waking mo-ment (eight bars after figure 9) and her final entry with Oberon (figure 98) are governed by the falling third, G♯, F♯, E, the motive that acts as an *ostinato* to their quarrel in Act I and becomes more clearly identified with Oberon's patriarchal power as the opera proceeds.

If we are led to wonder about the misogyny implied by the composer's treatment of Tytania in Act III, we are also reminded of the power and beauty of her extramarital encounter during Bottom's awakening. At the climactic moment of this scene, when the weaver names the ballad in which he intends to celebrate his experience, he recapitulates Tytania's crucial phrase (ex. 1b). Britten provides only enough differences of detail to accommodate the new words and situation (the forceful dynamic marking *fppp* suggests the waking jolt with which a truly remarkable

33. "The Truth of the *Dream*," in Palmer, ed., *The Britten Companion*, p. 188.

34. See, for the play, William W. E. Slights, "The Changeling in *A Dream*," *Studies in English Literature 1500–1900* 28 (1988): 259–72.

35. See Ellen McDonald, "Women in Benjamin Britten's Operas," *Opera Quarterly* 4 (1986): 83–101. McDonald is surely right to point out that the much-vaunted sympathy of Britten's music for the oppressed did not extend to women.

36. Patricia Howard, *The Operas of Benjamin Britten* (London, 1969), p. 169. On the authority of the diva's voice, see Carolyn Abbate's essay in the present volume.

EXAMPLE 1

a. Act II, seven bars after figure 56

(*continued*)

dream is recalled). Tytania's language of passion, we now realize, was in some way shared by Bottom, who even usurps Oberon's falsetto voice in recalling it. This moment, comic in the richest sense of the word, and open to a number of interpretations in performance, brings with it the realization that the Tytania-Bottom relationship is the only one that crosses the rigid class boundaries of the play's three estates, the only one in which possession and power are not fundamental issues, the only one in which each partner is a victim, the only one in which pure sensuous enjoyment is uncomplicated by societal rights and duties. It is the high point of the carnivalesque side of the opera, and Bottom's waking reverie gently nudges us to savor its transgressive quality.

EXAMPLE 1   *(continued)*

b. Act III, eight bars after figure 32

Another episode of ambiguous meaning occurs at the end of Act II, as Puck arranges the lovers into correct pairs. In the play he speaks in short lines and country proverbs:

> Jack shall have Jill
> Nought shall go ill,
> The man shall have his mare again
> And all shall be well.

Britten gives this speech to the boy-fairies, who sing it to a shapely melody in thirds over rapturous repetitions in the orchestra of the four "motto chords" of the act (ex. 2). The irony of Shakespeare is thus replaced by a statement of faith, if not quite of resolution—the final note of the melody is not vouchsafed in the ending ritornello (ex. 3). Sung by

EXAMPLE 2   Act II, figure 103

EXAMPLE 3   Act II, conclusion

"thin-as-a-board-juveniles," it is hard to interpret it as anything but the vision of innocence and purity that Britten seems to have tried to recapture all his life.

In Auden's terms, of course, this trait was a symptom of the composer's "denial and evasion of the demands of disorder."[37] Certainly when the evening's magic has worn off the critical listener will wonder about this passage. But part of the attraction of Britten's art is the knife-edge it walks between the genuine and the sentimental, between honesty about life's difficulties and a longing for resolution and comfort. It was not until *Owen Wingrave* (1970) and *Death in Venice* (1973) that he went on, after the ritual purification of the Church Parables (1964–1968), to deal directly as well as profoundly with the two major issues of his life, pacifism and homosexual love. *The Turn of the Screw* and *A Midsummer Night's Dream* represent a stage at which he searched for the clarity that eluded him, projected his doubts about the "innocence" he could never recapture, and mulled over the nature of human relationships in a private world created out of the stuff of ghosts and dreams—the private world of the male homosexual and his closet. "He was," as Pears once said when explaining Britten's dislike of "the gay life," "more interested in the beauty, and therefore the danger, that existed in any relationship between human beings—man and woman, man and man; the sex didn't really matter."[38] That sex really did matter is shown, paradoxically, by the de-sexualizing of the creatures of the wood in *A Midsummer Night's Dream*.

Danger is the word that leaps out of Pears's statement, and it is one that bears thinking about. The closet is maintained by the threat, the "danger," of discovery and its reprisals, real or imagined. Even among

37. Letter to Britten; see note 22 above.
38. "A Time There Was"; see note 11 above.

openly gay people today the feeling lingers: there is after all enough potential menace from any number of our institutions (law, religion, the military, medicine, psychotherapy, business, and so forth) to strike terror into the most sanguine person. The closet is a dynamic, not static, shaping presence, and homosexuals with long experience of it can hardly be expected to imagine human relations without its corrosive effect.

But a specific historical situation ought to be in our minds when we consider Britten's music of the period from *Billy Budd* (1951) to *A Midsummer Night's Dream* (1960). In May 1951 the homosexual British diplomats Guy Burgess and Donald Maclean defected to the Soviet Union. The British authorities, urged on by the Central Intelligence Agency of the United States, where the McCarthy era was in full swing, increased surveillance. Use of police as agents provocateurs resulted in a dramatic increase in arrests (five-fold the number from 1938). And it was not simply the "man in the street" who was affected. In 1952 the mathematical genius and computer pioneer Alan Turing was sentenced to submit to estrogen therapy; he committed suicide two years later. A year afterward began the much more notorious and highly publicized series of prosecutions of Lord Montagu of Beaulieu and his friends. One effect of the public hysteria generated by the popular press and the blatant dishonesty of the police was the move toward reform: the Wolfenden Report on prostitution and homosexuality (1957) led (after another ten years) to the "consenting-adults" law.[39]

Britten and Pears may not have been directly affected by any of this—puritans both, they were unlikely to have been picking up men in public places. But someone as sensitive to injustice as Britten cannot have remained indifferent. The climate both encouraged the kind of bravado that seems (in the circumstances) to mark Angus Wilson's *Hemlock and After* (1952) or Britten's *The Turn of the Screw* and at the same time prompted a certain instinct for self-preservation and reticence. It may be true, as Peter Conrad avers, that in his version of *A Midsummer Night's Dream* Britten leads his characters back from the "atonal dubiety" of nature to the shelter of courtly ceremony, that he "flinches from psychological exposure" and "hadn't the fortitude to remain in the wood," but such judgments (which seem not even to pause before projecting the

---

39. Standard accounts are H. Montgomery Hyde, *The Other Love: An Historical and Contemporary Survey of Homosexuality in Britain* (London, 1970), and Peter Wildeblood, *Against the Law* (London, 1955). Chapter 5 of Sinfield's *Literature, Politics, and Culture in Postwar Britain* includes analyses of literature of the time. For Turing (and a wonderfully thoughtful appraisal of the decade) see chapter 8 of Andrew Hodges, *Alan Turing: The Enigma* (London, 1983).

composer directly into his work) reflect a later age in which "danger" is presumed to have been exorcised.[40]

If danger stalks the score of A Midsummer Night's Dream, what musical form does it take? For an answer to that question we must go back to The Turn of the Screw, and specifically to the music in which Quint awakens desire in Miles. The celesta flourish that announces Quint's presence, the remarkable variation 7 with its panoply of sounds—harp tremolandos, celesta arpeggios, gong strokes, and horn—and the cantilena in which Quint calls to Miles: all these belong to a preoccupation of Britten's with the music of Asia that goes back at least to his association in the States with Colin McPhee and its effect on Peter Grimes.[41] Orientalism in music is as heavily loaded as it is in other aspects of Western culture. Britten's usage here surely answers to Edward Said's classic description of it as producing "one of [Europe's] deepest and most recurring images of the Other" and yet being in essence "a sort of surrogate and even underground self" for the West.[42] Even more pertinently for the present case (in the words of Leo Treitler, in relation to the interpretation of chant), "the Other is, in effect, a projection of the Self, or rather of an unacknowledged aspect of the Self that is suppressed as unacceptable to that identity that is the speaker for the Self."[43] Quint is the quintessence of that Other in Britten's presentation. And his music spills over into the Dream: "If it is an accident that E flat is the key both of the immortals in A Midsummer Night's Dream and of Quint's evil in The Turn of the Screw, it is the kind of accident that happens only to genius," as Wilfrid Mellers noted.[44] If Quint/Oberon is decidedly Britten's Erlkönig, in the Dream it is even more noticeably the process itself of erotic binding and power embodied in the juice of the flower that is invested with the "Oriental" sound of the celesta, accompanied in its most sinister appearance—the bewitching of Tytania at the end of Act I (at figure 102)—by harp, tremolo strings, glockenspiel, and the like.

There was clearly no way forward from here. Britten's visit to Asia in 1955–1956 planted a seed of understanding in his mind about the actual

40. Peter Conrad, "The Top Line and the Sub-Text," Times Literary Supplement (10 July 1981): 781–82.

41. The Sunday Morning Interlude in Act II, which bears an obvious resemblance to the Coronation Scene from Boris Godunov, also derives from Balinese music transcribed by McPhee for piano duet and recorded by him and Britten; see David Matthews, "Act II Scene 1: An Examination of the Music," in my Benjamin Britten: Peter Grimes, pp. 122–24. See also Donald Mitchell, "What Do We Know About Britten Now?" in Palmer, ed., The Britten Companion, esp. pp. 39–45.

42. Edward Said, Orientalism (New York, 1978), pp. 1, 3.

43. Leo Treitler, "The Politics of Reception: Tailoring the Present as Fulfilment of a Desired Past," Journal of the Royal Musical Association 116 (1991): 290.

44. "The Truth of the Dream," p. 191.

music of Bali and Japan, which he then heard in context. In a letter to Imogen Holst about the Balinese gamelan he praised the music as *"fantastically* rich—melodically, rhythmically, texture (such *orchestration!*) and above all *formally,*" and said, "At last I'm beginning to catch on to the technique."[45] There occurred at this time no less than a crisis in his career (one that many commentators seem to see as the beginning of his decline). The first large work after the *Dream* was the *War Requiem,* completed in December 1961. Hans Werner Henze conveys something of its importance when he says that it is "a work whose urgency had banished all stylization," that it represents "the other side of Ben's music: a world in which the lyrical is denied, and whose contours have been elaborated in a hard and indeed temperate and unornamented manner."[46] Even greater severity is characteristic of *Curlew River,* not completed until 1964. This Church Parable engages with the music of Asia on terms that are not at all patronizing, because they put so much of Western musical history at risk in an attempt at a genuine relationship that acknowledges and celebrates difference: Britten's grounding of his work musically in Western chant and dramatically in the English mystery play provides the basis for a clear-headed reinterpretation of and homage to Eastern conventions. Such a strategy seemed almost to acknowledge the appropriation and projection that had been involved in the earlier works, especially those of the 1950s. *Curlew River* and its successors *The Burning Fiery Furnace* (1966) and *The Prodigal Son* (1968) were the narrow strait that had to be navigated successfully before Britten could turn back to opera in a more recognizable mold.

One element shared by *Owen Wingrave* and *Death in Venice* is a personal "coming out" drama, constructed in the one case around the young hero's rejection of family values in favor of personal integrity and in the other around the aging writer's abandoning himself to a vision of beauty embodied in the adolescent male whose attraction he has never allowed himself to recognize, let alone enjoy. Pacifism and pederasty are distinct issues, and no doubt they occupied separate areas of Britten's conscious thoughts. Yet they are linked here musically in an Orientalism more utopic than threatening—both peace and the beauty of boys are evoked by the gamelan—and dramatically in the vivid images of "the closet" and "coming out," which condense so many of our Western oppositions into one powerful figure.[47] But both operas downplay the public/private issues of Britten's *Grimes* period in favor of a search for inner peace on the part of the protagonists. Owen's battle with the slightly caricatured living

45. Quoted in Headington, *Britten,* p. 114.

46. Hans Werner Henze, *Music and Politics: Collected Writings 1953–81,* trans. Peter Labanyi (London, 1982), pp. 254–55.

47. Sedgwick, *Epistemology of the Closet,* pp. 72–73.

representatives of the Wingrave family and their allies is far less than what he goes through as the result of the terrible hurt done to the boy with whom he identifies in the ancestral legend. When Aschenbach sings "I love you" at the stirring climax of Act I in his key of E Major, there is no avoiding the sense of personal declaration, the importance of which rests entirely in the private sphere—both for the character Aschenbach and, by implication, for the composer Britten. Such a declaration, it may be thought, would even so have its public effect in robbing the open secret around Britten of its remaining power for his audience. But the way that critical debate grabbed at the straw of allegory offered by the libretto of *Death in Venice* (invoking a round of binarisms such as discipline/licentiousness, classic/romantic, and Apollonian/Dionysian) affords a classic instance of the workings of the open secret and, consequently, of the double bind under which the discerning of sexuality in musical drama operates: "In a mechanism reminiscent of Freudian disavowal, we know perfectly well that the secret is known, but nonetheless we must persist, however ineptly, in guarding it."[48]

48. Miller, *The Novel and the Police*, p. 206.

Of Women, Music, and Power:
A Model from Seicento Florence

Suzanne G. Cusick

It is almost a truism of recent writing on early opera that musico-theatrical stage works dating from before the advent of public theaters were occasional pieces, inextricably linked to the political interests and necessities of the courts where they were produced.[1] Commissioned for performance at events—notably, royal marriages—that conflated the identity of the ruling family with that of the state, the earliest operas unfolded in contexts where, for the ruling family as well as for its invited guests, the personal was self-consciously political. This fact suggests that the operas, like the events of which they formed a part, might be read as political documents in which, as in court life, images of the personal and the political converge.

Indeed, the masterplot shared by such paradigmatic court operas as the Peri/Rinuccini *L'Euridice* (Florence, 1600), the Monteverdi/Striggio *L'Orfeo* (Mantua, 1607), and the Monteverdi/Rinuccini *L'Arianna* (Mantua, 1608) invites a political reading. Each work depicts an ideal world—a paradise—lost, and the restoration of that paradise through one character's recourse to the rhetorical power of speech-song. In such song the truth of the petitioner's experience is expressed in a musically powerful

A substantial part of the research for this essay was completed with the help of a Grant-in-Aid from the American Council of Learned Societies during Summer 1989. A shorter version was presented at the Fourth Biennial Conference on Baroque Music, Royal Holloway and Bedford New College, England, in July 1990. I am grateful for the helpful comments Jane Bowers, Andrew dell'Antonio, Margaret McFadden, Ruth Solie, and Elizabeth Wood made on early drafts of this work.

1. For recent summaries of this view, see Lorenzo Bianconi and Thomas Walker, "Production, Consumption and Political Function of Seventeenth-Century Italian Opera," *Early Music History* 4 (1984): 209–96; and Bianconi, *Music in the Seventeenth Century*, trans. David Bryant (Cambridge, 1987), chapters 19 and 20.

appeal, through the senses, to the imagination. This powerful expression of feeling or powerful pleading seems to persuade the gods to pity and to some sort of restoration of the lapsed order. Thus, these works affirm as merciful and benevolent the "natural" rulers of the world—the gods and their correlatives on earth, the works' royal patrons—while granting agency to those of the ruled who are adept at persuasion and self-expression. Put another way, monarchs—through their stand-ins, the gods—are portrayed as legitimate authorities with the power to control change in the lives of their subjects and to alleviate their pain; courtiers, citizens, and artists—through their stand-ins, the musically powerful persuaders—are portrayed as deriving some control over change in their own lives from their skill at manipulating what others will feel and know of their experience. Individual agency comes from making the monarchs perceive a situation in a certain way.[2]

Because of the balance struck between affirmation of monarchical authority and affirmation of limited individual agency, these works serve as political allegories that show, at important state occasions, how the tensions between the values of Renaissance humanist oligarchies and those of the seicento's ever stronger monarchies might be resolved through the interaction of monarchical benevolence and courtiers' skilled control over appearances.[3]

One of the last Florentine court operas, Francesca Caccini's *La liberazione di Ruggiero dall'isola d'Alcina* (1625),[4] plays within this masterplot

2. From a ruler's point of view, the masterplot of secular operas might have seemed to emphasize the proper relationship of the gods to their human subjects—for it is always some imbalance in that relationship that causes the initial loss of someone's paradise. Restoration of order always involves explicit restoration of the god-human hierarchy; as often as not, the petitioning subject's pleas are answered by provision of a substitute paradise rather than by restoration of the original one. For instance, in *L'Arianna* the famously lamenting heroine's tears are rewarded, not by Teseo's return, but by the provision of an alternative—and presumably better—husband, the god Bacchus.

3. On the playing out of these tensions in late Renaissance Florence, see Samuel Berner, "Florentine Society in the Late Sixteenth and Early Seventeenth Centuries," *Studies in the Renaissance* 18 (1971): 203–46. According to Furio Diaz, these tensions were inflamed anew by the ruling style of Florence's co-regents from 1621 to 1628, Granduchess Christine of Lorraine and Archduchess Maria Maddalena of Austria (*Il Granducato di Toscana: I Medici* [Turin, 1976], pp. 365–66). For allegorical critiques of the courtly monarchical system in Florence from Francesca Caccini's artistic circle, see Claudio Varese, "Ideologia letteratura e teatro nella *Fiera* di Michelangelo Buonarotti il Giovane," in his *Biblioteca di storia toscana moderna e contemporanea. Studi e documenti 26: II. Firenze e la Toscana dei Medici nell'Europa del'500* (Florence, 1983): 585–610.

4. Five printed copies of the published score (Florence: Cecconcelli, 1625) survive, at the British Library, London, the Bibliothèque nationale, Paris, the Biblioteca casanatense, Rome, the library of the Conservatorio Santa Cecilia, Roma, and the Biblioteca nazionale marciana, Venice. The Paris copy was the basis of a modern edition by Doris Silbert in 1945,

to explore the relationship of gender to power, and particularly, given the cultural proscriptions against women's speech, of the troubled relationship of women to the restorative power of rhetoric.[5]

Commissioned for Carnival 1625 by one of Florence's two women regents, Archduchess Maria Maddalena of Austria,[6] *La liberazione* (like its predecessors) seems to have been intended to affirm the authority and ruling style of its patron at a moment when her personal and political interests were to converge. For the work was one of several entertainments with which the archduchess intended to celebrate the betrothal of her favorite daughter Margherita to her visiting nephew, Crown Prince Ladislao Sigismondo of Poland, whose recent victory over the Turks at Wallachia had made him the most admired general in Christendom. This marriage, in turn, was to have been the reflection at a dynastic level of a major shift in Florentine foreign policy engineered by the archduchess: the creation of a Catholic League linking Tuscany, the Papal States, Spain,

---

published as volume 7 of the Smith College Music Archives (Northampton, Mass., 1945). Examples in this essay are my transcriptions from the Paris copy.

5. Caccini's opera is not the only one in which gender is an important issue: indeed, perhaps because many of these works were commissioned for weddings, almost all can be read as allegories of male control over females. Restoration of order coincides with affirmation of that control. Interestingly, the opera most closely resembling *La liberazione* is *L'Arianna*, where the power of female persuasive speech is also an issue. On Monteverdi's treatment of the issue, see notes 16 and 26 below.

On the prohibitions against women's speech in early modern Europe and the particular burdens these prohibitions represented for women poets, see Ann Rosalind Jones, *The Currency of Eros: Women's Love Lyric in Europe, 1540–1620* (Bloomington, 1990), chapter 1, esp. pp. 20–22. An earlier essay by the same author quotes English traveler Robert Coryat on the rhetorical powers of Venetian courtesans: "Also, thou wilt find the Venetian Courtezan . . . a good rhetorician, and a most elegant discourser, so that if she cannot move thee with all these aforesaid delights, she will assay thy constancy with a Rhetoricall tongue." As Coryat's remark suggests, female rhetorical prowess was often equated with sexual license. See Ann Rosalind Jones, "City Women and Their Audiences: Louise Labé and Veronica Franco," in Margaret W. Ferguson, Maureen Quilligan, and Nancy J. Vickers, eds., *Rewriting the Renaissance: The Discourses of Sexual Difference in Early Modern Europe* (Chicago, 1986), p. 304.

6. Maria Maddalena of Austria (1587–1630), widow of Cosimo II and mother of Ferdinand II, shared the regency with her mother-in-law Christine of Lorraine (1565– 1636) from 1621 to 1628. Their joint rule is generally conceded to mark the beginning of a precipitous decline in Florentine public fortunes, a decline blamed on the regents' constant squabbling, political innocence, and shared devotion to Catholic orthodoxy at the expense of Tuscan self-interest. For a general history of the period see Riguccio Galuzzi, *Istoria del Granducato di Toscana sotto il governo della Casa Medici* (Capolago, 1842), vol. 5, and Diaz, *Il Granducato di Toscana*, chapter 3. A recent, unflattering biography of Maria Maddalena is Estella Galasso Calderara's *La granduchessa Maria Maddalena d'Austria: Un'amazzone tedesca nella Firenze medicea del '600* (Genoa, 1985).

Austro-Hungary, and Poland against Lutheran heresy and French territorial ambitions on the Italian peninsula.[7]

Considering the importance to her own career as regent the archduchess assigned to this occasion, it is not surprising that all the surviving works of the 1625 season are to a greater or lesser extent gynocentric: each explores the way a woman's power might create a benevolent outcome to the plot.[8] By far the most gynocentric of these, and the most original in its exploration of the possibilities of female power within the seicento masterplot, is Caccini's *La liberazione*—the one entertainment composed by a woman, and the one paid for from the archduchess's private fund.[9]

7. This view of the occasion for which *La liberazione* was commissioned is based on diplomatic dispatches by Cesare Molza, ambassador from Modena, for December 1624 through February 1625, as preserved in the Archivio di Stato, Modena (henceforth I-MOs), Cancelleria Ducale, Ambasciatore Firenze, busta 53, fasc. 18. Molza's story is substantiated by a briefer series of dispatches from the Lucchese ambassador, Vincentio Buonvisi, preserved in the Archivio di Stato di Lucca, Anziani al tempo della libertà 641, lettere di Firenze 1 gennaio 1622 a 12 ottobre 1630. Florentine diplomatic records reveal vigorous efforts to obtain Pope Urban VIII's participation in the League in late 1624 and early 1625, combined with secret negotiations for a dispensation allowing someone to break a previous commitment and pledge marriage anew. The latter may have been an effort to break Princess Margherita's presumed betrothal to Odoardo Farnese. Archivio di Stato, Florence (henceforth I-Fas), Mediceo Principato 3518, contains the surviving instructions to Florence's ambassador to Rome, Francesco Niccolini. I-Fas, Mediceo Principato 3340, are Niccolini's reports to Secretary of State Curtio Picchena.

Neither the formation of the Catholic League nor the marriage negotiations had been resolved by the time of Ladislao's visit. A further cloud over the event was cast by the sudden death of Maria Maddalena's brother, Archduke Carl, news of which reached Florence two weeks before production of *La liberazione*. Indeed, neither initiative was ever realized: Princess Margherita de' Medici married Odoardo Farnese, duke of Parma, in October 1628. On the fortunes of the League, see Galuzzi, *Istoria del Granducato di Toscana*, vol. 5, pp. 240–45, and Diaz, *Il Granducato di Toscana*, pp. 363–70.

8. The two other entertainments whose texts survive were a revival of *La rappresentatione di Sant'Orsola*, with music by Marco da Gagliano to a poem of Andrea Salvadori, performed in October 1624 for the visit of Archduke Carl of Austria, but apparently written much earlier, for it was rehearsed but never performed before the April 1621 wedding of Claudia de'Medici and Federico d'Urbino (see Angelo Solerti, *Musica, ballo e drammatica alla corte medicea dal 1600 al 1637* [Florence, 1905], pp. 156 and 159); and *La precedenza delle dame*, with music by Jacopo Peri to a poem by Salvadori. For the standard description of all three events, see Solerti, *Musica, ballo e drammatica*, pp. 174–84.

9. Molza's dispatch of 24 December 1624 describes the Medici family's quarrels over the preparations for Carnival 1625, with Maria Maddalena and Cardinal Carlo de'Medici seeming to have usurped all prerogatives from Granduchess Christine and her favored son, Don Lorenzo (I-MOs, Cancelleria Ducale, Ambasciatore Firenze, Busta 53, fasc. 18, f. 249–50). It is clear from Florentine court payment records that only the production costs of *Sant'Orsola* were charged against the official accounts of the Granducato. A note to Granduchess Christine from her personal *maestro di casa*, Vincentio Vespucci, specifies this work, and not others, in a list of the "excessive" costs (9,000 florins) incurred by the court

La liberazione di Ruggiero, then, invites reading as a musico-theatrical essay on women's ways of wielding power within a monarchy-affirming masterplot which, because it conflates the personal and the political, is necessarily patriarchal as well.[10] Such a reading promises us a nearly unique opportunity to learn how the power dynamics of the early seicento, including those of patriarchy, could be imagined by women—by the work's composer, and by its patron.

A Tale of Two Sorceresses

The opera's *invenzione*, by court functionary and poet Ferdinando Saracinelli, derives from an episode in Lodovico Ariosto's epic romance *Orlando furioso*, cantos 6 to 10, in which the young knight Ruggiero is rescued by the sorceress Melissa (sent by his eventual bride, Bradamante) from the love-spell of the sorceress Alcina. Saracinelli's libretto transforms this story into an exploration of the intersections of gender, knowledge, sexuality, and power as they are manifest in each woman's effort to persuade Ruggiero to experience the world as she sees it and to act accordingly to restore a lapsed paradise.

For, just as there are two powerful females in this opera contending for power over one man, there are two parallel lapsed paradises, one within the work's frame and one outside it, in the literary background known to the audience. As Saracinelli recreates the tale, Ruggiero has already broken faith with Bradamante, his betrothed, by coming to Alcina's island. Melissa's mission there, as she announces it in the work's first scene, is to restore Bradamante's paradise by restoring her lover, the man

---

during the Polish visit (I-Fas, Depositeria Generale Antica 1014). *La precedenza delle dame*, staged at Cardinal Carlo's *casino*, was presumably paid for out of his private funds. *La liberazione*, staged at Maria Maddalena's personal retreat, Poggio Imperiale, was presumably paid for out of her private funds. No detailed accounts survive for either household.

The archduchess's intense interest in *La liberazione*'s preparation is attested by Tinghi's noting of her attendance at twenty-seven rehearsals of the work, beginning in December 1624 (I-Fas, Miscellanea Medici 11, f. 96v–103v), by her personal intercessions to the courts of Mantua and Modena for specially trained horses that could dance *La liberazione*'s concluding horseback ballet (I-Fas, Mediceo Principato 6084, letter of 4 January 1624/5; and Mediceo Principato 6085, letter of 2 January 1625), and by her eager conversations about the work with her guests after the performance, reported in Molza's dispatch of 4 February 1625.

10. Before the 1620s regency in Florence, the patrons of all these works—and therefore the figures whose power was being affirmed—were men, part of whose authority to wield power in the world derived from their gender. In our time, we are accustomed to considering the conflation of personal and political as a feminist gesture: in fact, the well-known slogan simply unmasked a connection long obscured by the nineteenth-century ideology of separate spheres.

with whom she is destined to found the Este dynasty. Melissa's success in liberating Ruggiero, however, causes him to break faith with Alcina, to whom he has given a promise of eternal love in the opera's second scene. Alcina then tries to restore her own lapsed paradise by confronting Ruggiero with what she perceives to be his cruelty and treachery. Yet she explicitly names Melissa, not Ruggiero, as her true antagonist.[11] Thus, Alcina prompts the audience to read the plot as turning on a power struggle between two women whose conflict is displaced onto each one's struggle for power over the same man.

Members of a 1625 courtly audience would have brought to *La libera-zione* assumptions about court opera masterplots and about the allegorical meanings of the Ruggiero/Alcina episode that would have further focused their perception of the work. Read through the court opera masterplot, *La liberazione*'s plot is peculiar for having no apparent god-figure to whom appeals for restoration of a lapsed paradise might be made. Instead, as the opera unfolds, both sorceresses appeal to a man who is at best their social equal. The displacement of their power struggle onto competition over this man thus confers on Ruggiero one attribute of the gods in the masterplot, for it is on his perceptions and actions that restoration of one woman's paradise will depend. This reading of Ruggiero as godlike vis-à-vis two women with supernatural powers combines with the absence of other god-figures to reflect a central assumption of patriarchy: that all men are in relation to all women as the gods are in relation to men.[12]

The opera audience, then, is prompted by Alcina to follow the woman-to-woman struggle behind the plot and is further inclined by its knowledge of the masterplot to expect that the outcome of this struggle will depend on how each woman's vision of a desirable world can be made to fit into Ruggiero's presumably patriarchal worldview, the view that confers godlike attributes on all men.

---

11. Alcina's first response to news of Ruggiero's "liberation" is the exclamation, "Ahi, Melissa, Melissa, sol da te riconosc'ogni mio male" ("Ah, Melissa, Melissa, my every woe I recognize as from you"). Her resolve to plead with Ruggiero to return is explicitly described as a response to Melissa's invasion of her realm. And at her final exit Alcina acknowledges Melissa's magic to have been superior.

12. This metaphor for the proper relationship of women to men, widespread in Renaissance prescriptive literature about family life, ultimately derives from I Corinthians 11:3, "But I want you to understand that the head of every man is Christ, the head of a woman is her husband, and the head of Christ is God." For discussions of Renaissance elaborations of this model, see Constance Jordan, *Renaissance Feminism: Literary Texts and Political Models* (Ithaca, 1990), chapter 1, "The Terms of the Debate"; and Daniela Frigo, "Dal caos all'ordine: sulla questione del 'prender moglie' nella trattatistica del sedicesimo secolo," in Marina Zancan, ed., *Nel cerchio della luna: figure di donna in alcuni testi del XVI secolo* (Venice, 1983), pp. 57–93.

Reading through the conventions of late-Renaissance Arioso criticism, the opera audience would naturally construe the episode on which
the opera focuses as an allegory of appropriate and inappropriate power,
symbolically linked to appropriate and inappropriate sexuality and to the
conflicting claims of reason and the senses as means to knowledge. For
the allegory usually seen in this episode in the late Renaissance construes
Alcina as representing illegitimate power: she dominates Ruggiero and
other men by deceiving their senses and promising them both the pleasures of unrestrained sexuality and freedom from their obligations to
(male) society.[13] Ruggiero's "liberation" derives from his acquisition of
reason (in the form of a ring Bradamante sends with Melissa, of which
no mention is made in the opera), which enables him to control his desire
for sensual pleasure, to subordinate its fulfillment to his military and
dynastic obligations. Thus, the episode is usually taken to affirm Ruggiero's successful passage into manhood, a passage paralleling what we
might call a successful oedipal resolution: reason, social responsibility, and
reproductively focused sexuality align with Melissa against the dependence on deceptive senses, self-centeredness, and unproductive sexuality
promised by Alcina.[14]

The woman-to-woman power struggle Alcina points to, whose outcome
(the opera masterplot suggests) will depend on how well each woman's
vision can be fitted into Ruggiero's preconceptions of the world, thus can
be read through the framework of Ariostean allegorical interpretation as
a struggle between two principles. Building on their audience's expectations from previous theatrical and literary experience, Saracinelli and

13. Simone Fornari's influential *Delle espositione sopra l'Orlando furioso, parte seconda* (Florence, 1550) interpreted Alcina as a demonstration of "la violentia et forza che sopra gli
amanti usa cotal femina . . . per Alcina si puo intendere l'ambitione, e la cupidità di do-
minare popoli e terre" ("the violence and force that such women use over lovers . . . through
Alcina we can understand the ambition and the desire to dominate peoples and lands")
(p. 43). It seems likely that the librettist Saracinelli knew Fornari's reading of the Alcina/
Ruggiero episode, for the operatic depiction of Alcina's rhetorical strategy—the evocation
of sensual memory followed by a threat of force—exactly parallels Fornari's reading of the
Ariosto sorceress's twin military expeditions against Ruggiero, by land and by sea.

14. Late-twentieth-century thought is most likely to construe acquisition of these values
as resulting from successful separation from the mother; indeed, Alcina can be interpreted
as representing all the values associated with the mother in Freudian thought. Late Renaissance ideas of human development, however, constructed the passage to adulthood very
differently. Adulthood was reached when a person had learned to use the rational powers
of the *anima* to guide and restrain the tendencies of the body: adulthood was thus marked
by the dominance of reason over desire. See Mario Equicola, *Libro di natura dell'amore*
(Venice, 1525); my description of his notion of human development is drawn from the 1587
edition, ff. 60r–66r. As Equicola does not refer to women in this section except as possible
occasions of voluptuous desire, it is not clear that his model of human development applied
to women. Possibly women were not thought to achieve this sort of adulthood.

Caccini create a complex allegorical model that explicitly links these principles with two opposed ideals of the power balance appropriate to human relationships. Their opera resolves the resulting conflict in a way that challenges the traditional opera masterplot (because successful power—both the godlike and the persuasive kind—is exposed as based on deception, not on reason); challenges the patriarchal masterplot (because Alcina, who resists it, retains the dangerous power of the persuasive exile, and because Melissa comes to replace Ruggiero as the godlike figure in the plot); and challenges the allegorical affirmation of a male adulthood as the only model for responsible behavior. This triple challenge is accomplished by using both plot moves and musical choices to change the principles aligned with Alcina and Melissa as each tries to forge a relationship with Ruggiero that is susceptible to persuasion based on a shared worldview.

Relationship and Reality, Deceit and Dominance

The second scene of the opera, set on Alcina's island, is the first in which we see any relationship modeled. Thus, within the frame of the work we are made to perceive the relationship between Alcina and Ruggiero as normative.[15] Although on the surface a love scene, it is equally a scene of struggle between the lovers over the definition of reality and the definition of an ideal relationship. Ruggiero's opening speech, a conventional exclamation of passionate love inspired by Alcina's beauty, is immediately challenged by Alcina herself. She denies the reality of his claim that her beauty inspires him, and she urges him literally to see her as she sees herself, by using her own mirror as an instrument to avoid the deception of his senses:[16]

> Non ha questo sembiante
> Parte, che pure a sospirar t'alletti.

15. This scene is not found in *Orlando furioso* but is instead superficially based on the so-called mirror scene between Armida and Rinaldo in Torquato Tasso's *La Gerusalemme liberata*, canto 16. On the relationship of Tasso's literary legacy to *La liberazione*, see Roderigo Zayas, "Ferrara, Firenze e una donna," *Schifanoia* 5 (1989): 23–33. Zayas does not, however, compare the two texts systematically to identify Saracinelli's borrowings and consider their meanings. On the mirror scene as an allegory of the oedipal struggle, see Maggie Günsberg, "The Mirror Episode in Canto XVI of the *Gerusalemme liberata*," *The Italianist* 3 (1983): 30–46.

16. In late-Renaissance iconography mirrors were generally construed as instruments of self-knowledge, their use leading to enlightenment and knowledge of the truth. A less common interpretation of mirrors, deriving from Christian rather than classical sources, associated their use with narcissism, vanity, and lust—especially when the mirror was used by a woman. Alcina's proffering of a mirror to Ruggiero hovers uncomfortably in the tension between these two possible meanings. Subsequent developments in the opera suggest that Caccini and Saracinelli intend the mirror in the first sense. Such a reading is made more likely by the long-standing Medici patronage of Galileo Galilei, who used ocular

Parli lo specchio mio, la dove impressa
D'ogni bellezza priva
Ho per costume di mirar me stessa.

This appearance has nothing in it to spark your sighs. Let my mirror speak, in the image in which, deprived of every beauty, I have the habit of looking at myself.

Ruggiero rejects her view, claiming his vision as superior. She defers to his claim, granting him the right to assign to her appearance whatever meaning he chooses for so long as he is a faithful lover:

pur che la fè, la pace
Eternamente nel tuo core si viva,
Sarò qual più ti piace,
O Stella, ò Sole, ò l'amorosa Diva.

As long as faith and peace live eternally in your heart, I shall be what most pleases you, star, or sun, or loving goddess.

Alcina accepts Ruggiero's answering promise of eternal love in a line that reveals the startling premise of her effort at a relationship with him:

Dunque di pari foco eternamente
Arda'l nostro desio.

Therefore with equal fire our desire burns eternally.

---

instruments (telescopes, microscopes, and mirrors) to demonstrate to the senses the truth of the so-called new science's claims against those of Aristotelian cosmology. Furthermore, Caccini was the composer for three stage works by Michelangelo Buonarotti il Giovane (*La Tancia, Il Passatempo,* and *La Fiera*) that include scenes affirming as truth the unusual vision gained from the use of mirrors and telescopes.

Alcina's recourse to a physical mirror in this scene may also be taken as a reference to an extremely common trope in late-Renaissance marriage ideology: that a good wife is as a mirror to her husband. It is for such mirroring—of his passion—that Ruggiero's first speech explicitly asks. By her response Alcina both refuses to participate in the trope by which her identity is to be subsumed in his and proposes an alternative view according to which neither partner would be seen as a projection or reflection of the other. In this response Alcina differs sharply from her operatic ancestor Arianna, who in a similar scene (Scene 2, lines 198–255 of Solerti's edition) also refuses to mirror the feelings of her lover, arguing (lines 222–28) that her mixed feelings about leaving home and family are reasonable. Arianna does not, however, challenge the assumption that her feelings are inextricably connected to Teseo's. Thus, she is trapped within the marriage discourse, as Alcina seeks not to be.

On the iconography of mirrors, especially as used in female self-portraiture, see Mary D. Garrard, *Artemisia Gentileschi: The Image of the Female Hero in Italian Baroque Art* (Princeton, 1989), pp. 361–67. The best short introduction to the mirror trope in Renaissance marriage discourse is Jones, *Currency,* pp. 26–28. Rinuccini's libretto for *L'Arianna* is in Angelo Solerti, *Gli albori del melodramma* (Milan, 1904; rpt. Hildesheim, 1969), vol. 2, pp. 143–87.

Alcina, we thus learn, expects to base their relationship on a shared reality, one untrammeled by preconceptions or sensory deception; and she expects to base it on an equality of passion and a parity in the complementary ceding of personal power to one another.[17]

In both these expectations the Saracinelli/Caccini Alcina differs from the Alcina of allegorical interpretation, who dominates Ruggiero because of her magical ability to deceive his senses. Their Alcina's assumption of equality instead challenges both the traditional view that she dominates men by unnatural means and the patriarchal view that women are the natural subordinates of men. Saracinelli thus transforms the allegorical standard-bearer of sensuality and domination into the standard-bearer of accurate knowledge based on sensory data and of an egalitarian model of human relationships.

Caccini's music for this scene contributes much to its depiction of the power dynamic in this late-Renaissance love relationship. Early in the scene she characterizes Ruggiero as, above all, confused by passion, for she writes him a line whose chromaticism derives from the conflict between two implied finals, G and A (ex. 1).[18] For Alcina, by contrast, she writes serenely controlled, tonal lines (ex. 2)—lines whose tonal goal of F is substantially different from either of Ruggiero's tonal worlds. In thus deftly constructing their difference as partly tonal, Caccini creates the expectation of some musical exchange of territory (each moving to the other's final, or both moving to a third, intermediate area, such as C) to parallel the lovers' verbal exchange of power.

17. Alcina's proposed ideal, of a relationship based on equality, is strikingly similar to the model of political power proposed by the feminist interlocutor of Cristoforo Bronzini's *Della dignità e nobiltà delle donne, giornate prima, seconda, e terza* (Florence, 1622): "Equality, in the household as in ancient republics, was always the keystone and the base on which rested public and private happiness, because [equality] fostered peace, discouraged sedition, gave birth to love and concord, conserved unity and the relations of all the members of the body politic and of the family" (A3v–4; translation in Jordan, *Renaissance Feminism*, p. 268). For more on Bronzini's tract, dedicated to Maria Maddalena yet so threatening to the status quo as to have been placed on the index of prohibited books in 1622, see ibid., pp. 266–69.

Caccini knew Cristoforo Bronzini through their shared status as employees of the court; both were in the households that accompanied Carlo de'Medici to Rome for his elevation to cardinal in 1616 and for the conclave that elected Urban VIII in 1623. The cardinal's 1616 Roman household is listed in I-Fas, Carte Strozziane, serie I.XIII, inserto 36. Descriptions of Caccini's and Bronzini's Roman sojourns in 1623–1624 can be found in the Biblioteca laurenziana, Florence, Archivio Buonarotti, 48, nos. 1037–40, and I-Fas, Mediceo Principato 3645, 3883, 6074, and 6097.

18. Jane Bowers has pointed out to me in a personal communication that the particular harmonic contrast here is a common sound symbol for sweetness in early-seventeenth-century music; indeed, it is so used elsewhere in Caccini's opera. In each case, however, the sweetness of love is portrayed as somehow unnatural and problematic for the speaker.

EXAMPLE 1   "Quanto per dolce," *La liberazione*, Scene 2

EXAMPLE 2   "Ah non ti prender," *La liberazione*, Scene 2

Yet no such exchange of territory takes place when the lovers exchange promises. Rather, Caccini's Alcina modulates to one of Ruggiero's implied finals, G, where he remains with the same adamancy that had characterized his rejection of her mirrored image. Thus, Caccini's music shows Alcina as alone in accommodating herself to her lover's world (ex. 3). Ruggiero, by contrast, is shown as refusing to accept Alcina's vision of an egalitarian relationship, just as he had refused to see her vision of her self. Here, however, his words accept Alcina's vision even as his music rejects it. Caccini's music suggests that Ruggiero's words are false and that his role in their relationship is one of unyielding dominance over what will be acknowledged as real. The composer thus undercuts the audience's presupposition that it is Alcina who represents deceit. Instead, she

EXAMPLE 3   "Vinca Signor," *La liberazione*, Scene 2

skillfully shifts both deceit and dominance from their traditional association with the female to association with the male.

The association of deceit with maleness, and with an unequal power relationship, is reinforced by the next critical scene, in which Melissa appears to Ruggiero in the guise of his white-bearded tutor, the sorcerer Atlante. Melissa's decision to approach Ruggiero as if she were a man, announced in her first-scene speech, allows her appearance and the social meaning assigned to it to match the usual gendering of the allegorical principle for which she stands. Furthermore, it is an infinitely practical choice, for it ensures that she and Ruggiero need not struggle, as Alcina and he did, over reality itself. To respond to her arguments he need not first acknowledge the legitimacy of a worldview other than his own.[19]

19. Late-Renaissance notions of friendship and communication supposed that true understanding was achieved only by those whose life experiences and social class were very similar. See, for example, Equicola's discussion of true friendship, ff. 69v–81r, and Stefano Guazzo, *La civil conversatione, libro terzo* (Venice, 1574), pp. 439–40, on the relative ease of communication between masters and servants who have similar backgrounds.

Although Ruggiero's a priori sharing of Atlante's worldview ought to make his/her effort at persuasion easier, Atlante/Melissa does not persuade but upbraids. From a position of presumed superiority, he/she delivers a strictly androcentric argument about Ruggiero's duty to his military colleagues. This argument, divorced in the opera from any mention of Bradamante's betrayed trust or Ruggiero's dynastic obligations to his descendants, is sufficient to "liberate" Ruggiero. He signals his liberation by expressing shame and deference—in effect, by ceding power to the older man, accepting his domination. Ruggiero, whose relationship to Alcina Caccini has exposed as based on deceit and dominance, recognizes and responds to the assumption of dominance implied in Atlante's speech. He is so comfortable with the ideas that power is dominance through a hierarchical system and that truth comes from white-bearded authorities that he accepts Atlante's arguments without question; ironically, it is here, rather than in his scene with Alcina, that Ruggiero's senses are being deceived.

Ruggiero's acceptance of his interlocutor's superiority transfers effortlessly from the appearance of Atlante to the reality of Melissa, on whom, within the opera's frame, he continues to depend.[20] Melissa, having acquired power over Ruggiero by pretending maleness, becomes the figure through whom a chorus of enchanted plants will gain their liberation, the figure whose power controls the balance of the opera's action and its ultimate restoration of apparent social order. Thus Melissa, by the temporary expedient of seeming to be a man, acquires godlike attributes, becoming the benevolent and powerful figure to whom appeals will be effectively made.

Melissa's relationship to Ruggiero—a relationship of dominance based on an expedient impersonation of patriarchy—is easily read as a model of how a woman such as Maria Maddalena might effectively rule in a monarchical and patriarchal world. She must base her rhetoric and her actions on androcentric premises, and she must engage in cross-gendered behavior at some level, even if that behavior necessarily involves deception.[21] A ruler's need to control how she is perceived—to control the

20. Here Saracinelli's characterization of Ruggiero departs from Ariosto's. The Ariosto hero, once liberated, immediately effected his own escape from Alcina's island. See canto 7, ottave 80 to the end, and canto 8, 1–10, 17–21.

21. The notion that a woman ruler necessarily engaged in behaviors otherwise appropriate only for men is defended by Torquato Tasso's *Discorso della virtù femminile e donnesca* (Venice, 1582). Like his title, Tasso's tract distinguishes between the virtues proper to ordinary women (silence, thrift, modesty) and those proper to women "born of heroic blood." A "heroic woman" is not only allowed but required to act out masculine virtues when she takes on the political role of a man. According to Tasso, failure to do so—clinging to the traditional feminine virtues—constitutes a sin against the virtues proper to her special status.

cultural meaning assigned to her—takes precedence over any desirable allegorical alignment with legitimate power, social and sexual responsibility, and reason-based truth.[22] Thus, Melissa's triumph in the opera both affirms a way Maria Maddalena might successfully rule and points to the paradox in the gender system that forces her to the unsavory choice of deceit.[23] This pointing to the paradox of gender somewhat mutes a politically disturbing element in the opera's construction of Melissa, the alignment of deceit with patriarchal, godlike power. Such an alignment threatens the legitimacy of monarchy itself.[24]

22. Although Melissa's character seems clearly intended to affirm Maria Maddalena's legitimacy within the patriarchal frame of the Medici monarchy, there are unsettling elements to her construction that subvert the presumed intention of *La liberazione*. It would seem that the exigencies of patriarchy require a successful woman ruler to act like a man, that is, to uphold the principles of rationality and social order by behaving contrary to reason. If she acts like a woman, she may fail to exercise her will and may thus cause a collapse of the principles with which she sought to align herself. Furthermore, if she acts like a woman her interlocutors may assume that femininity necessarily brings with it the deceptiveness normally associated with Alcina-figures. Forced to seem what she is not—to deceive—in order to avoid seeming deceitful, a woman ruler is trapped by the contradictions inherent in the overlap between the gender system and the requirements of monarchy.

23. A number of parallels can be drawn between Melissa's character and Maria Maddalena's actual ruling style. The Fornari tradition of Ariosto interpretation reads Melissa as a maternal figure, bringing grace to Ruggiero out of her disinterested concern for him (*Delle espositione*, p. 117). Maddalena cast herself as the disinterested caretaker in her emphatically public prayers for her late husband and for the well-being of all Florence, in her interventions in the dowries and marriages of her *gentildonne*, and in her echoing of her Austrian mother's own practice, as regent of Styria, of inviting the city's poor women to a meal served by the royal children on Holy Thursday. Like the Melissa of Caccini's opera, Maddalena also styled herself an enforcer of sexual restraint, banning makeup among her *gentildonne* as unduly alluring and leading the court's successful effort to imprison and disinherit the former courtesan Livia Vernazza, longtime mistress and last-minute widow of Giovanni de'Medici. Furthermore, Maddalena was perennially criticized by the Florentine bureaucracy for arrogance and inappropriate royalism in her personal habits. Melissa's "liberation" of Ruggiero, which seems to result in her replacing him as the opera's god-figure, may have seemed to symbolize Maddalena's usurpation of the bureaucracy's traditional power.

Finally, Maddalena's gender identity was suspect throughout her association with Florence. As a prospective bride of Cosimo II she was subjected to several physical examinations over a two-year period, because her energetic and "hot" demeanor suggested to Florentine doctors that she was too masculine to reproduce. Later, after having borne Cosimo eight children in nine years, her vigor and excellence as a horsewoman and hunter kept the old murmurings about her hot, dry, masculine humors alive in court gossip.

For more information on the archduchess see Galasso Calderara, *La granduchessa Maria Maddalena*, and Cristoforo Bronzini's biographical essay in *Della dignità e nobiltà delle donne*, pp. 56–74.

24. Tension over the deceit and violence associated with seicento monarchy is expressed in early Italian *romanzi* as well, often in ways that conflate gender or sexual eccentricities with deception and the abuse of power. See Donata Ortolani, *Potere e violenza nel romanzo italiano del seicento* (Catania, 1978).

EXAMPLE 4 "Atlante a te se'n viene," *La liberazione*, Scene 4

Atlante comes to you to ask what folly forces you to dishonor yourself in

these fields... All Libya and all Europe goes to war.

If Melissa's triumph and emergence as the godlike figure in the opera depend on her embrace of expedient deception, the music of her speech as Atlante remains consistent with the allegorical principles for which she is supposed to stand. Unlike the music she assigned to either Ruggiero or Alcina, Caccini's music for Melissa/Atlante is diatonic, firmly tonal, and meticulous in its derivation of all pitch and rhythmic inflections from those of its text. No melodic or harmonic pattern recurs in a way that might draw attention to musical design. The only evident effort at expressiveness is a matching of spatial imagery in the text with sudden, temporary shifts of harmony (ex. 4). Melissa's music is, in effect, excellent word-dominated monody, literal without being expressive, rational rather than either emotional or sensual in its appeal. Like the character who utters it, this speech-song is a model of domination—the word is, here, truly *padrona* of the music which serves it. In that domination of sound by sense, the speech is, too, an excellent model of the culturally desirable domination of sensual pleasure and of emotions toward which Ruggiero is meant to move during the plot. And in that domination of sound by sense, of course, Melissa's music represents the domination of all that is conventionally feminine by the power of masculine reason: her song as Atlante is as firmly cross-gendered as are her appearance and her words. Thus desexed, Melissa's is female speech that is culturally safe.

The success of Melissa's gender-deceptive appeal to Ruggiero promises to lead Ruggiero safely into an adulthood of adherence to rules, responsibility toward other men (his fellow soldiers), and sexual activity channeled toward the production of dynastic power. It promises thereby to restore Bradamante's lost paradise, thus fulfilling Melissa's self-proclaimed mission on the island. But, as we have seen, restoration of Bradamante's paradise requires the destruction of Alcina's.

A Song of Sexual Difference

True to the conventions of the opera masterplot, Alcina's response to the news that her paradise may be lost is an effort to achieve its restoration by passionately projecting her experience into the imagination of Ruggiero, a character she thinks has the power of restoration. She addresses him not as a god-figure, however, but as an equal who has wronged her. She assumes a right to have her grievance heard—a logical consequence of her earlier assumption that their relationship was based on equal, complementary cedings of power. Since he has broken their compact by seeking to leave the island, she too breaks it, reclaiming her right to define for him who she is and how she feels:

> Rimira'l pianto mio, senti le strida
> Senti le mie giustissime querele.
> Ferma, ferma crudele, e questi lumi
> Che pur ora chiamavi e Stelle e Soli
> Mira qual son per te convers'in fiumi.
> Specchiati in questo viso . . .
> Vedrai la tua mancanza, e la mia fede.

Look at my weeping, hear my cries; hear my well-justified arguments. Stop, stop, cruel one, and see that these eyes, which you called stars and suns, are now turned by you into rivers. Look at this face . . . you will see your absence, and my trust.

Caccini's music for this scene of confrontation with Ruggiero, the longest in the opera, emphasizes Alcina's reclaiming of her identity and her insistence that Ruggiero recognize it—her insistence, that is, that he perceive what she perceives. The entire scene is built from the development of motives taken from Alcina's opening speech in the mirror scene discussed above, the speech in which Caccini had constructed her as tonally and melodically different from Ruggiero. Example 5 shows some of the means by which the motive (ex. 5a) that originally announced Alcina's identity is developed in the first two sections of this scene: serving first as a headmotive for her speech "Ferma, ferma crudele" (ex. 5b), it is progressively associated with commands that Ruggiero look at her (ex. 5c), with her sinking into despair (ex. 5d), and finally with her effort to evoke his memory of their shared sensual pleasure (ex. 5e).

Inevitably, Ruggiero and the audience hear the scene as musically working out the implications of Alcina's character, the implications of her difference. Furthermore, because the scene's motivic organization is so easily followed by the ear, its musical organization is foregrounded over its verbal argument. This gradual shift in the listener's attention from words to music parallels Alcina's rhetorical passage from her exordial demand for a fair hearing ("Ferma, ferma crudele") through a *narratio* of broken trust ("Deh, se non hai pietà") to a grief-stricken *peroratio* ("O ferità di Tigre"). As the culmination of this scene's increasing emphasis on musical over poetic form, "O ferità di Tigre" is cast in ritornello form, with the successive stages of Alcina's renunciation framed by the phrases shown as Example 6a and 6b. Both phrases, variously sung by Alcina and her *damigelle*, present striking chromatic variants of Alcina's identity motive; surrounding her renunciation of love's toys ("gli atti cortesi, e l'immortal faretra"/"courteous acts, and the eternal quiver") as vile things, they force the listener to hear the world from within the frame of Alcina's identity.

Completing the scene's insistent realization of the implications of Alcina's character are its chromaticism and its extraordinary tonal range, both of which pose a threat to musical order. Unlike either Melissa or Ruggiero, Alcina is made by her composer to pass through nearly the entire tonal world in this scene, centering her appeal to Ruggiero's sensuality on B only to frame her final renunciation of love with phrases that cadence in the dark and alien world of B♭ Minor. Thus, Alcina's music flaunts her great affective range, her mastery over the formal and tonal means of musical pleasure,[25] and her innate resistance to the conventions that limit Melissa and Ruggiero to a close word/music relationship and to acoustically clear tonal centers. Caccini's music lets us hear, in Alcina's power over the nonrational pleasures of musical discourse, how such a

---

25. Susan McClary has argued persuasively that musical mastery—especially tonal mastery—was used in Monteverdi's dramatic music to represent what she calls "the rhetoric of seduction," a rhetoric available only to the sexually experienced, because it is intended to arouse and manipulate desire. See her "Constructions of Gender in Monteverdi's Dramatic Music," *Cambridge Opera Journal* 1 (1989): 202–23. It should be noted that although Alcina's part displays several kinds of musical mastery, it does not indulge in the virtuosic *passaggi* so often associated with women singers of the time, an indulgence which might have signified a merely sensual control over the voice.

EXAMPLE 5   Variants of Alcina's identity motive, *La liberazione*

a. Scene 2, identity motive

b. Scene 6, "Ferma, ferma crudele," mm. 1–4

Stop, stop cruel one. Where do you go, so pitiless?

c. Scene 6, "Ferma, ferma crudele," mm. 24–30

See my eyes turned into rivers for you, Seek your reflection in this

face, where joy and laughter once held the throne. You will see your absence,

and my fidelity caught between pain and sorrow

EXAMPLE 5 *(continued)*

d. Scene 6, "Deh, se non hai pietà," mm. 1–4

Deh, se non hai pie-tà del mio lan-gui - re muo-va-ti il

Alas, if you have no pity for my suffering, be moved by

tuo fal-li - re sai pur qual mac-chia in-e-stin-gui - bil si - a

your own error, for you know well what an indelible stain it is.

e. Scene 6, "Deh, se non hai pietà," mm. 23–32

al- men dhe, ti sov-ven - ga quai dol - ci ab-brac-cia-

(reversed bass motion)

At least, oh, remember those sweet embraces [which] in the peace of love you enjoyed

men - ti Nel-la pa - ce d'a-mor me - co go - de - ste, E si

with me, And let such sweet memory keep you from leaving.

dol- ce me-mo - ria il piè ri-ten - ga.

(reversed bass motion)

EXAMPLE 6   Damigella and Alcina, *La liberazione*, Scene 6

a.

O fe-ri-tà di Ti - gre,   o cor di pie - tra.

O wound of a tiger, o heart of stone.

b.

An- cor ___ pie-tà tu nie - ghi e ne - ghi pa - ce.

Still you deny pity, and deny peace.

sorceress of pleasure might seduce; she lets us hear the sexually charged danger of a woman's orphic speech.

Her audience may expect Caccini's Alcina to attempt persuasion and dominance of Ruggiero by deception, but it is not deception they hear. Like Ruggiero, they are instead confronted with a sensually appealing— and true—sound-image of Alcina's character. Caccini's music reveals that it is precisely the truth of Alcina's identity, her power over her listeners' experience of pleasure, that cannot be tolerated within the masterplot's frame. By insisting that Ruggiero know Alcina by hearing her in the full development of all that signals her musical difference from him, Caccini implicitly requires that he acknowledge Alcina's femaleness as a differ- ence beyond the control of the projections of his lovesick imagination and beyond the control of the reason that governs his world.[26]

26. In light of other similarities between the two works, it is interesting to consider how Monteverdi constructs the analogous scene in his *L'Arianna*, the famous lament. As Gary Tomlinson has pointed out, some of Monteverdi's most skillful and consistent uses of sequence and motivic variation in that lament serve to connect verbal references to Arianna's lost lover, Teseo. Thus, Arianna's song—in its beauty as much a construction of female speech-as-sexuality as is Alcina's song—gains much of its coherence not from her own identity but from her lover's. Arianna is musically constructed as after all a worthy wife,

What Caccini requires is impossible for Ruggiero, however; such acknowledgment would threaten his successful passage into masculine adulthood, a condition that the gender ideology of his time defined as including the dominance of self-control over pleasure, reason over sensuality, men over women (and over the meaning assigned to women). As a late-Renaissance political man he cannot acknowledge Alcina, either, for both her coherent, continuous selfhood and her ideal of the power balance in a good relationship challenge the foundations of the monarchy-courtiership polis.[27] Medusa-like, Caccini's Alcina represents all that must be repressed for the stability of the world her creator knew. No matter how beautiful or memorable Alcina's song, it must be rejected if the institutions the masterplot supports are to survive. Not only must Alcina's song fail to restore her paradise of egalitarian pleasures, but both she and her influence must be purged from the stage, as they are when she and the monsters who remain faithful to her fly from the sea of fire that consumes her island at the end of Scene 3, leaving a dry, masculinized landscape as the scene for Melissa's triumphant liberation of the enchanted plants (figs. 1 and 2).[28]

A Tale of Two Worlds, a Tale of Two Women

If Caccini's Melissa could be read as resolving the conflict between female identity and successful monarchical power, her Alcina can be read as representing, in her defeat, the feminization and consequent defeat of Renaissance civic humanism. Thus, Alcina's defeat by Melissa's magic of gender deceit and asserted dominance represents a successful resolution

---

remaining in some sense the mirror of her man. Her containment in the discourse of marriage—and therefore of patriarchal projections about women—is symbolically reinforced by the framing of her lament with interjections of a chorus of male fishermen (as distinct from Alcina's chorus of *damigelle*), and it is fully realized when the gods provide her with an alternative husband. On musical references to Teseo in Arianna's lament, see Gary Tomlinson, *Monteverdi and the End of the Renaissance* (Berkeley, 1987), pp. 125–31.

27. This reading is indebted to Joan Kelly's notion that Castiglione's theory of courtly love, as elaborated in *The Book of the Courtier*, is a metaphor for the proper relationship of courtier to king. See her classic essay "Did Women Have a Renaissance?" in *Women, History, and Theory: The Essays of Joan Kelly* (Chicago, 1984), pp. 19–50.

28. According to the multilayered symbolic representations of gender that Renaissance culture inherited from Aristotle, the purging of all evidence of water from the scene represented a purging of the female element by the male—for one of the salient biological differences between women and men was thought to be that women were cool and wet, men hot and dry. Thus the nearly barren landscape of the final scene (shown in Alfonso Parigi's extant drawings) was meant to be seen as a landscape healed of undue feminine influence. On the temperature and relative humidity of the sexes in Renaissance medical thought, see Ian Maclean, *The Renaissance Notion of Woman: A Study in the Fortunes of Scholasticism and Medieval Science in European Intellectual Life* (Cambridge, 1980), pp. 33–35.

ISOLA D' ALCINA ARDENTE TERZA MVTA DELLE SCENE

Figure 1. Alcina's island consumed by flames in *La liberazione*. Drawing by Alfonso Parigi. Courtesy Gabinetto Fotografico, Soprintendenza per i Beni Artistici e Storici, Florence.

of one power struggle implicit in all court operas—the struggle between mortals and gods, or citizens and rulers, for control over events. In terms of late-Renaissance political allegory, the alignment in the opera of a belief in relationships based on mutual responsibility with Alcina's indulgence in fleshly pleasures, faith in sensory evidence, and uncontrollable femaleness robs civic humanism of its legitimacy, showing it to be a threat to social order even while acknowledging its seductive appeal. Alcina's exile in the company of other monstrous creatures still in her thrall successfully feminizes, and thus marginalizes, the once-proud Florentine tradition of oppositional exile by stripping it of its *virtù*, its virility.[29] That is, Caccini's opera assigns meanings to Alcina that match the ruling family's view of her own social and political class; Alcina's defeat by Melissa is the symbolic defeat of civic humanism by the Medici.

29. The Italian word *virtù*, which can mean virtue in a variety of senses, derives from the Latin *vir*, meaning male. In the political theory of Renaissance Florence, *virtù* meant a civic virtue based on Roman republican models, in which all of a citizen's private interests were subordinated to the well-being of his country. Brutus's murder of Julius Caesar, for example, was seen as an act of *virtù* because it was an attempt to preserve the Roman republic

QVARTA MVTA DOVE ESCONO DELLE GROTT I CAVALIERI E DAME.
DOPO ESCONO I CAVALIERI A CAVALLO   Alfonso Parigi I. et F

Figure 2. The "purged" landscape of *La liberazione*. Drawing by Alfonso Parigi. Courtesy Gabinetto Fotografico, Soprintendenza per i Beni Artistici e Storici, Florence.

Furthermore, Alcina's failure to prevail over Melissa and Ruggiero completes the opera's allegorical exploration of women's relationship to power in a patriarchal world. Alcina's understanding of herself, of possible relationships between women and men, indeed of reality itself, is too firmly gynocentric (and thus too different from Ruggiero's understanding of the world) for her ever to have wielded even the limited power of petition granted to skilled artist/citizens in the court opera masterplot. The musical beauty of her petition serves only to emphasize her female-

from Caesar's monarchical ambitions. To Florentine humanists Brutus was a hero, as were the generations of *fuorusciti* (exiles) who contested the hegemony of rival groups when Florence was still a republic. For the origins of the Florentine tradition of civic *virtù*, see Hans Baron, *The Crisis of the Early Italian Renaissance: Civic Humanism and Republican Liberty in an Age of Classicism and Tyranny* (Princeton, 1966). On the systematic dismantling of *virtù* by the Medici dukes, see Furio Diaz, "Cosimo I e il consolidarsi dello Stato assoluto," in Elena Fasano Guarini, ed., *Potere e società negli stati regionali italiani del '500 e '600* (Bologna, 1978), pp. 75–97; and R. Burr Litchfield, "Ufficiali ed uffici a Firenze sotto il granducato medico," in Fasano Guarini, ed., *Potere e società*, pp. 133–49.

ness and to suggest that hers is a sexuality beyond male control. Her failure completes the binary opposition needed to confirm Melissa's success and becomes a warning to all women who would wield power that they must do as Melissa does: they can succeed in enacting their will only if they speak and act from within the androcentric discourse of patriarchy, repressing what is feminine within them. Caccini's opera thus affirms both the dynastic and the personal political agenda of its patron, Archduchess Maria Maddalena.

Yet the sheer beauty and memorability of Alcina's scene of failed persuasion threatens to subvert this apparent affirmation. This scene alone is melodically and harmonically organized so as to remain in the mind's ear long after it is heard—a haunting and brilliant creation which reminds its hearers of both the dangers of sensuous beauty and the dangerous principles for which this sensuous beauty stands. As it lingers in the ear and the imagination, it reminds its listeners, too, that the assertion of difference is not permissible in the masterplot of early opera: the authorities are moved to pity only those whom they can completely control, the creatures of their own imaginative or political power. And it reminds its listeners that control over the meanings assigned to a persona or to an action is essential to the successful exercise of power, while suggesting that such control is deceptive in both the patriarchal and the monarchical world. That is, as this music lingers seductively in the mind's ear it exposes the deceit and the symbolic violence essential to the political and gender systems Melissa's triumph was intended to affirm.

Alcina's transcendence of her plot failure by the beauty of her song points to her composer's power to transcend the limits imposed by both patronage and the genre norms of court opera. Caccini has succeeded where her character Alcina failed, for the composer's power to control her listeners' aural pleasure and aural memory allows her to impose on them an unsettling, deconstructive view of both monarchy and patriarchy. Refusing to follow Melissa's example by creating the same old story from androcentric premises, and refusing to follow Alcina's by insisting on the creation of an entirely different tale from purely gynocentric premises, Caccini charts a delicate course between them. This strategy allows her to expose the unresolvable paradox of female power within patriarchy and to affirm her own power to create an oppositional discourse that can haunt, and perhaps empower, the imaginations of those trapped in the political *aporiae* of her world.

Carnaval, Cross-Dressing, and the Woman in the Mirror

Lawrence Kramer

The "poetic" dimension of Robert Schumann's *Carnaval* (1834–1835) has rarely been taken seriously by modern critics. Both Carl Dahlhaus and Charles Rosen, for example, brusquely set aside Schumann's claim to be engaged on significant terms with the social and psychological dimensions of carnival festivity. What is significant about this music, they argue, is the structural force of its motivic transformations (Dahlhaus) or its cumulative rhythmic vitality (Rosen).[1]

We need not undervalue motivic or rhythmic interest to find this critical approach problematic. Dahlhaus and Rosen are both interested in culture, yet in their concentration on purely formal processes they forgo the opportunity to consider Schumann's music as a dynamic part of culture, an instance of cultural practice. They forgo, in particular, the possibility of understanding a musical work as a concrete effort to affect the cultural forces, both material and ideological, amid which it is produced and received. To some degree this abstention serves as a way to protect the music from the disruptive effects of its own meanings—in the case of *Carnaval*, meanings that challenge established forms of social, intellectual, and sexual authority.

My own critical approach to *Carnaval* is meant to bring these meanings to the fore. Schumann uses the famous design of the work, the quasi-improvisatory grouping of twenty-one short, sometimes fragmentary pieces, as a presiding metaphor of carnival festivity. My aim is to show in detail how the compositional procedures of the music ramify this met-

---

1. Carl Dahlhaus, *Nineteenth-Century Music*, trans. J. Bradford Robinson (Berkeley, 1989), pp. 145–47; Charles Rosen, sleeve notes to his 1963 recording of Schumann's *Carnaval* and *Davidsbundlertänze*, Epic 1269.

aphor, continually inviting the listener to think about the interrelations of festivity, art, and gender. The argument will cover three primary areas.

1. The disunity of the socially constructed self. As conceptualized by Mikhail Bakhtin, carnival is "a minimally ritualized antiritual, a festive celebration of the . . . gaps and holes in all the mappings of the world laid out in systematic theologies, legal codes, normative poetics, and class hierarchies."[2] Carnival festivity frees its participants from the demand that they organize their physical and emotional lives into a coherent (and restrained) totality. The general outbreak of buffoonery, playacting, and masquerade splinters this normative self; its component parts assume the guise of separate characters, or, more exactly, caricatures, personifications of excess or impulse. Caught up in the anarchic scene, the reveler is free to identify with any or all of these figures. *Carnaval* utilizes highly stylized musical textures and motivic/harmonic cross-references to project this free play of identification and to comment on it.

2. Cross-dressing and the mobility of gender. Carnival free play, particularly in masquerade, invites the free crossing of gender boundaries. Cross-dressing by both men and women allows each gender to appropriate the qualities culturally ascribed to the other—forbidden qualities, which in the case of the male masker would normatively be shunned as degrading. *Carnaval* utilizes structural interplay among its masculine and feminine character sketches to recreate and reinterpret the gender-crossing of masquerade.

3. The woman in the mirror. *Carnaval* combines its concerns with gender and identity by forming a network of musical mirror-images. Technically, each image consists of a symmetrical grouping in which a structural unit, large or small, receives a suggestively placed and expressively heightened repetition. Culturally, the proliferating network of images serves to release and empower feminine energies, in keeping with nineteenth-century representations of the mirror as the sphere of feminine privilege. Before the mirror, women may do for themselves affirmatively what men do to women appropriatively: they may gaze with a pleasure that constructs the thing it sees.

As my account of these three areas suggests, the linking element among them, and the ultimate cultural term of *Carnaval*, is gender. In constructing a piece out of miniatures—*scènes mignonnes* he calls them, tiny scenes, cute scenes—Schumann follows a traditionally "feminine" paradigm. For, as Naomi Schor has shown, modern European culture has consistently encoded the art of the miniature, the art of the detail, as

2. Statement by Katerina Clark and Michael Holquist, *Mikhail Bakhtin* (Cambridge, Mass., 1984), p. 300.

feminine.[3] In constructing most of the *scènes mignonnes* themselves out of the repetition of small details—a melodic phrase, a mode of attack or articulation, a rhythmic effect—Schumann follows the same paradigm again. Yet in linking his miniatures through the motivic transformations cited by Dahlhaus, and in closing the cycle of miniatures with a recapitulation, in quasi-sonata style, of its opening themes, Schumann also follows a traditionally "masculine" paradigm: the paradigm of mastery in which variegated details are structured into a unified whole. This "bisexuality" in Schumann's role as the composer of *Carnaval* is the mainspring of musical action within the cycle. The music constitutes an effort—although not, finally, a sustainable effort—to affirm unrestricted gender mobility as a source of social and artistic value.[4] Before examining this effort in *Carnaval* itself, we need to examine its motives, which are both personal—that is, psychosexual—and cultural.

Male artists in nineteenth-century Europe increasingly found their masculinity at odds with their calling. The role of artist, traditionally marked by the achievement of virile mastery within a limited, quasi-artisanal sphere, was changing in dramatic and contradictory ways. Mastery now required the charismatic, hypertrophied virility of a Dickens, a Liszt, a Wagner, as the artist was asked to become a star, a cult figure who miraculously surmounted the fragmentation of modern society. At the same time, the artist's creativity, the modern version of his artisanal skill, was understood to derive from a volatility of emotion and a responsiveness to sensation that were markedly feminine in character. With growing transparency, the artist's public masculinity was understood to be the product of a private femininity embodied in his art.[5]

A brief comparison of two famous poems can serve to measure the extent of this feminization. In the fifth of his *Roman Elegies*, written in

3. Naomi Schor, *Reading in Detail: Aesthetics and the Feminine* (New York, 1987).

4. It is worth pausing to reflect on one further aspect of musical gender mobility. As we will see in connection with *Dichterliebe*, circularity at the end of a composition is by no means invariably coded as masculine. Circularity was a contested term in nineteenth-century discourse; its gender affiliation derives from the work it does. Musical circularity is masculine when it projects analogues to, and so annexes the authority of, sonata form. The same circularity is feminine when it projects an image of self-enfoldedness or the cyclicity of nature. Many other terms were subject to similar contestation during the period; for a discussion of contestatory representations of sexual desire, see my *Music as Cultural Practice: 1800–1900* (Berkeley, 1990), pp. 137–45.

5. On the artist as cult figure, see Jochen Schulte-Sasse, "The Prestige of the Artist Under Conditions of Modernity," *Cultural Critique* 12 (1989): 83–100, and the discussion of the star in Jacques Attali's excessive, problematical, but suggestive *Noise: The Political Economy of Music* (1977), trans. Brian Massumi (Minneapolis, 1985), pp. 68–81. On the feminization of art, see Carol Christ, "The Feminine Subject in Victorian Poetry," *ELH* 54 (1987): 385–401, and my "Culture and Musical Hermeneutics: The Salome Complex," *Cambridge Opera Journal* 2 (1990): 269–94.

1790, Goethe identifies artistic with erotic mastery. Referring to his mistress, Christiane Vulpius, he writes:

> Oftmals hab ich auch schon in ihren Armen gedichtet
> Und das Hexameters Maß leise mit fingernder Hand
> Ihr auf die Rücken gezählt.[6]
>
> (15–17)

> Often I have even made poetry in her arms, and the hexameter's measure
> softly, with fingering hand, counted on her back.

Goethe is only joking, of course, but among men this sort of joke makes a serious claim: the fingering hand, the artist's hand, acts with the power and pleasure of the phallus. Quite a different claim informs Yeats's *Adam's Curse*, written in 1902. The subject is poetry:

> I said, "A line will take us hours maybe;
> Yet if it does not seem a moment's thought,
> Our stitching and unstitching has been naught."
>
> (4–6)

> That beautiful mild woman . . .
>
> . . . .
> Replied, "To be born woman is to know—
> Although they do not talk of it at school—
> That we must labour to be beautiful."
>
> (15, 18–20)[7]

Art here comes, not from working on women, but from women's work: the quintessential women's work of needlepoint and self-adornment. Yeats's image of stitching and unstitching even suggests a parallel to the work of the paradigmatic female artist, Penelope, who continually weaves and unweaves a hero's shroud, thus articulating, in her own terms, the plot of the *Odyssey*.

Inevitably, the feminization of art provoked a defensive reaction. Most male artists sought to recuperate the masculinity of their calling; to that end, they began to take the control or repudiation of femininity as a primary cultural mission. Any man, wrote Nietzsche, who denies "the abysmal antagonism, the necessity of a forever hostile tension" between gender principles, "will probably prove too 'short' for all the basic questions of life . . . unable to penetrate *any* depth."[8]

---

6. Text from Johann Wolfgang von Goethe, *Werke: Hamburger Ausgabe in 14 Banden*, vol. 1 (Hamburg, 1948).

7. Text from William Butler Yeats, *Collected Poems*, 2d ed. (London, 1950).

8. Friedrich Nietzsche, *Beyond Good and Evil*, trans. Marianne Cowan (Chicago, 1955), section 238.

The depiction of predatory women—from Carmen, Delilah, Kundry, Salome, and Electra to Turandot and Lulu, to name only operatic figures—emerged as a popular means of "penetrating" life's questions by "acknowledging," that is, constructing and mastering, the antagonism of gender. This fatal-attraction syndrome is anything but played out, even in opera; Siegfried Matthus's recent *Judith* ends with the spectacle of its biblical castrator being murderously gang-raped.

In this context *Carnaval* figures as a highly radical work, perhaps composed as much to advance as to comply with the process of feminization, which was still nascent in 1834. Certainly, Schumann was predisposed to welcome this trend. He seemed strongly drawn to fantasies of gender mobility and feminine identification, which first crystallized in his early literary efforts. A poem written at the end of 1828 provides a telling example of what Peter Ostwald calls "the flavor of bisexual fantasy":

> Und wie den Jüngling wild der Jüngling liebt,
> Und wie er ihn umarmt, und wie er mit ihm weint,
> So bist Du jetzt; einst warst du mir Geliebte,
> Jetzt bist Du mir Geliebter.
> Und aus den Blüthen deiner Liebe
> Wand sich die Freundschaft sanft hervor.

And as one youth wildly loves the other youth, and as he embraces him, and as they weep together, so are you now; once you were my feminine beloved, now you are my masculine beloved. And from the blossoms of your love, friendship wafts forth softly.[9]

Even more to the point, Schumann clearly identified his creativity with a feminine principle that he acknowledged or desired within himself. A brief sampler of his remarks on the subject leaves little room for doubt:

It's amazing that there are no female composers. . . . Women could perhaps be regarded as the frozen, firm embodiments of music. (1828, *S*, p. 87)

Music is the feminine friend who can best communicate everything that we feel internally. (1838, *S*, p. 138)

I've put on my frilly dress and composed 30 cute little things from which I've selected about twelve and called them "Scenes from Childhood." (1838, *S*, p. 140)

[After orchestrating the Spring Symphony:] I feel like a young woman who has just given birth—so relieved and happy, but also sick and sore. (1841, *S*, p. 169)

9. Peter Ostwald, *Schumann: The Inner Voices of a Musical Genius* (Boston, 1985), p. 42, my translation. This work will subsequently be cited in the text as *S* (translations Ostwald's).

Recognition of Schumann's feminine personae can offer new insight into several of his works. *Dichterliebe*, for example, famously ends with a contradiction. In the last song, *Die alte bösen Lieder*, the jilted poet assumes a hypervirile posture and repudiates both femininity and art. The song, however, dissolves into the lyrical, feminine-identified piano postlude of the earlier *Am leuchtenden Sommermorgen*. On the most obvious reading, the dissolve indicates that the poet is still in love, more in sorrow than anger. Perhaps, though, we should take this dissolve to suggest that the creative imperative, associated with the whispering and talking flowers of the summer morning, is stronger than any erotic imperative. What must be repudiated is precisely the exaggerated masculinity that forms an impediment to art.

Along similar lines, the notorious *Frauenliebe und -leben* might be understood not only as a patriarchal dream of feminine worshipfulness but also as a fantasy of feminine identification that courts the extremes of dependency, passivity, and masochism.[10] As for *Carnaval*, its prominent feminine role-playing can be taken to enact a celebration of Schumann's own creative energies in their most innovative and unorthodox vein. We might even speculate that the music incorporates an attempt to vindicate or sublimate a week-long adventure in debauchery undertaken at the end of February 1830—an adventure that culminated in Schumann's going to a masked ball dressed as a woman (*S*, p. 61).

The miniatures of *Carnaval* are largely of two types: dances or marches, and character sketches. As representations of carnival, these musical types correspond to what Bakhtin identifies as two primary traits of popular festivity.[11] The dances and marches, all of them vigorous, suggest the release of pent-up bodily energies; the character sketches, mercurial and caricaturelike, suggest the collapse of social and psychological boundaries at the prompting of masquerade. Schumann's musical free-for-all encourages the types to mix, but in general the dances and marches serve as a horizon of possibility against which the character sketches crystallize and dissipate in quick succession.

Above all else, these sketches constitute musical skits, impersonations, take-offs of one person by another. Schumann underlines the point by freely taking his sketch subjects both from life and from the *commedia dell'arte*. All the sketches are equally ventriloquistic, even—or especially— when Schumann himself is the subject. All the sketches project a persona that belongs to both the self and the Other. As a series, moreover, the

---

10. For an account of the patriarchal side of *Frauenliebe*, see Ruth A. Solie, "Whose Life? The Gendered Self in Schumann's *Frauenliebe* Songs," in Steven Paul Scher, ed., *Music and Text: Critical Inquiries* (Cambridge, 1991), pp. 219–40.

11. See Mikhail Bakhtin, *Rabelais and His World*, trans. Helene Iswolsky (Bloomington, 1984), pp. 1–58.

sketches in their crazy-quilt diversity challenge the notion that there is a single self behind all the masks. This challenge is particularly important to eighteenth-century masquerade, which, as Terry Castle observes, embodies a "devaluation of unitary notions of the self, as radical in its own way as the more abstract demystifications in the writings of Hume."[12] Eighteenth-century festive practices and their survivals in nineteenth-century German university life are probably Schumann's models in *Carnaval*, as they had been already in *Papillons*, the close of which corresponds to the closing episode of Jean-Paul Richter's novel *Die Flegeljahre* (*Adolescent Years*): a masked ball.

In affirming the nonunitary self, Schumann gives his "own" self an exemplary volatility. Both his musical signature and his poetic projection as the alter egos Florestan and Eusebius come to the fore in *Carnaval*, but only in the most elusive, most imponderable of terms.

Carnaval is famously based on a group of motives printed in the score in double whole notes under the title *Sphinxes*. Each motive contains all the German musical letters found in Schumann's name: S. C. H. A. (E♭-C-B-A), the signature motive; A. S. C. H. (A-E♭-C-B); and As. C. H. (A♭-C-B). The two motives that spell "Asch" refer to the town of that name, the home of Ernestine von Fricken, Schumann's fiancée and, as "Estrella," a character in *Carnaval*. These "Asch" motives, anagrammatical masks for the supposedly primary signature motive, dominate the cycle; the signature motive itself can be felt only as something missing, a lost or perhaps imaginary origin. It surfaces only in one piece, *Eusebius*, which does place it near the core of Schumann's creativity. Yet the signature in *Eusebius* is at best indistinct, almost a mirage, in telling contrast to the "Asch" motives, which are always perfectly clear. Example 1 shows how the signature can be heard radiating faintly (if we listen for it) from the melodic fulcrum of the first measure.

Even more chimerical is the role of the signature motive in the skittish piece entitled *A. S. C. H. S. C. H. A. (Lettres Dansantes)*. The title acts as a riddle, for neither of the motives it names appears in the piece. What does appear, by way of solution, is a teasing "dance" between fragmentary, punning substitutes for these motives: the key of S (E♭) and the minor chord of As (A♭), which alludes to the "Asch" motive *not* named in the title. Neither of these terms is strongly profiled. The E♭ tonality continually "dances" between its dominant seventh and tonic six-four chords without finding—or seeking—a cadence; the A♭ minor triad, its expressiveness

12. Terry Castle, *Masquerade and Civilization: The Carnivalesque in Eighteenth-Century English Culture and Fiction* (Stanford, 1986), p. 4; see pp. 2–6, 26–51, for a general discussion. For a discussion of *Carnaval* in relation to unitary notions of the self, see my *Music as Cultural Practice*, pp. 210–13; several of the technical points raised in that book also appear below for reconsideration in relation to gender.

EXAMPLE 1   Each "letter" of the signature-motive is subtly emphasized within the texture: S by the leap of a fourth, C by semitone voice-leading, H and A by irregular rhythmic grouping.

and a prominent linear projection notwithstanding, is no more than a voice-leading chord. Like the nonunitary self, the dancing letters have no fixed abode.

Schumann's most definite presence in *Carnaval* emerges in the paired pieces named for his alter egos, Eusebius the dreamer and Florestan the man of action. "Definite" in this context, however, is a decidedly relative term. Like *Lettres Dansantes*, though in a limpid, lyrical vein, *Eusebius* is oriented around the six-four chord of E♭, on which it ends. The only cadence comes at the close of the middle section, which consists of a recapitulation, with continuous pedal, of the unpedaled measures 9–16. Thus the "final" cadence is displaced to the middle, where it is blurred into the harmonies that precede it, while the precadential six-four chord is displaced to the end, which it robs of finality.

Florestan, in case we were expecting its virile persona to relieve us of mirages, is even more vertiginous. Agitated and passionate, the piece begins with a dominant minor-ninth chord that once again "resolves" to the tonic six-four; the same dominant, this time without pretense of resolution, returns to supply the end. In between, two interpolations suggest that this open-endedness is the least of Florestan's volatility. The first interpolation tentatively alludes to a theme from the first number of Schumann's *Papillons*; the second interpolation quotes the theme, which is also identified in the score. As the theme crystallizes, we are invited to remember that *Papillons* impersonates the main characters of Jean-Paul Richter's *Die Flegeljahre*, Walt and Vult, whose relationship parallels that of Eusebius and Florestan. Florestan can thus be said to contain Vult, and Schumann Jean-Paul, as an inner double. Nor is that all. The interpolated theme is played, not at its original tempo, but at the tempo we have just heard in *Eusebius*. The effect is introspective, almost dreamy; it suggests that Florestan may also be said to contain Eusebius as an inner double.

That Eusebius is decentered, open-ended, and himself doubled between pedaled and unpedaled musical images carries the whirligig of identities to a giddy extreme, the more so if one connects the "Eusebian" aspect of Schumann's Florestan to the brooding of his counterpart in Beethoven's *Fidelio*. Far from encapsulating and stabilizing Schumann's identity, *Eusebius* and *Florestan* propose that identity is a delusion. There are no selves, only impersonations.

The subjective mobility and lack of boundaries projected by *Eusebius* and *Florestan* have a decidedly feminine association in nineteenth-century culture, though one more often dreaded than courted.[13] Schumann's "Asch" motives, with their implicit feminine persona and anagrammatical play with the absent signature motive, extend the same association over *Carnaval* as a whole. If masquerade is the ruling image of the cycle, then cross-dressing is the ruling form of masquerade, the symbolic means of gaining access to the feminine powers of metamorphosis and creativity.

Two episodes in *Carnaval* make musical cross-dressing especially prominent. The first of these centers on *Coquette*, the piece that follows the pairing of *Eusebius* and *Florestan*. *Coquette* mingles a "flirtatious" figure with broad lyrical gestures; its texture is as stereotypically feminine as that of *Florestan* is masculine. The texture, however, also signals the play of a female impersonator. *Coquette* features prominent registral leaps that connect it to both *Florestan* and the earlier *Arlequin*; its characteristic rhythm, ♪ ♫ , states the characteristic rhythm of *Arlequin* in reverse (ex. 2). What is more, *Coquette* begins by partly resolving the open-ended harmonies of *Eusebius* and *Florestan*. Picking up the dominant that ends *Florestan*, *Coquette* quells it with a V–VI deceptive cadence, then proceeds to cadence on its own tonic, B♭, the very sonority to which the final E♭ six-four of *Eusebius* failed to progress (ex. 2c).

Schumann's masculine personae thus coalesce under a feminine sign. More, they coalesce under a misogynist sign, or at least a satirical one; coquettishness implies vanity, sexual teasing, triviality. These qualities, however, are revalued in the context of carnival, which invites us to understand the coquette as a quintessential impersonator, an unrivaled role-player as acrobatic with her identity as Arlequin is with his body.

The second episode of musical cross-dressing involves a trio of pieces, *Chiarina* (Clara Wieck), *Chopin*, and *Estrella*. In this instance, the feminine character sketches are strikingly virile and Florestan-like. *Chiarina* is impassioned, shot through with *agitato* rhythms; *Estrella* is vigorous and

---

13. On this subject see Nina Auerbach, *Woman and the Demon: The Life of a Victorian Myth* (Cambridge, Mass., 1982); Terry Castle, "The Female Thermometer," *Representations* 17 (1987): 1–27; and my *Music as Cultural Practice*, pp. 117–24.

EXAMPLE 2

a.

b.

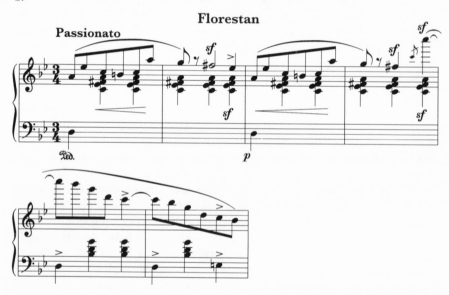

striding, almost swaggering. To a psychoanalytically inclined listener, these pieces might suggest a typical transvestite fantasy in which phallic vitality serves as the hidden core of an enhanced femininity.[14] Such a core or inner double may be represented by *Chopin*, which mediates between *Chiarina* and *Estrella* both expressively and structurally. *Chiarina* empha-

14. See Robert J. Stoller, *Sex and Gender: On the Development of Masculinity and Femininity*, 2 vols. (New York, 1975), vol. 1, pp. 177.

EXAMPLE 2   (*continued*)

c.

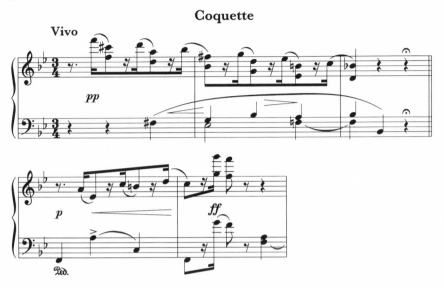

sizes harmonic progression from a subdominant F Minor to a tonic C
Minor; *Estrella* complements this gesture by emphasizing progression
from a dominant C Major to a tonic F Minor (ex. 3). This complementary
progression is anticipated near the end of *Chopin*, but only to tonicize F
Minor briefly within its relative major, A♭. We are free to read this
anticipation as suggesting either that *Estrella* must borrow structural
impetus from a masculine inner double or that the structural impetus
latent in *Chopin* can be realized only through a feminine outer double—or
a pair of them.

The structural relationship between *Chiarina* and *Estrella* also suggests
a mirror-image, which leads us to the third term of my argument. In the
nineteenth century the mirror increasingly becomes the space reserved
for women's subjectivity rather than, as was traditional, the sign of their
vanity. By gazing into the depths of the mirror a woman can enjoy,
explore, and to some degree construct her own identity.[15] Not that this
is an unmixed blessing. The association of feminine identity with visual
pleasure is a masculine convention. The mirror preserves rather than

15. On this subject see Jenijoy La Belle, *Herself Beheld: The Literature of the Looking Glass*
(Ithaca, 1988).

EXAMPLE 3   The harmonic mirroring illustrated here has a melodic counterpart. The melodic figure in m. 1 of *Estrella* is an inversion and approximate augmentation of the upbeat to *Chiarina* (brackets); the quasi-sequential figure at mm. 3–41 of *Estrella* supplies both a more exact augmentation of the *Chiarina* upbeat and an approximate inversion of the repercussive effect to which the upbeat leads.

a.

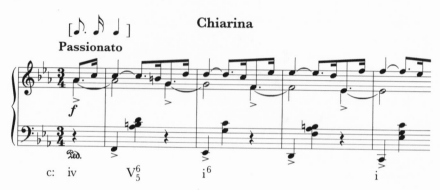

b.

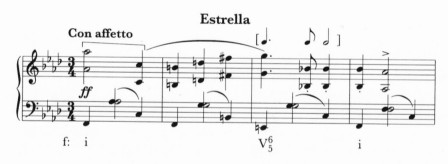

resists male control unless the reflected image becomes too absorbing, in which case the mirror arouses male hostility—and desire—by making the woman psychologically and sexually impenetrable. The speaker of Arthur Symons's poem *Laus Virginitatis* (1887), murmuring "I to myself suffice" to her mirror-image, is a woman self-enclosed in just these terms:

> The mirror of men's eyes delights me less,
> O mirror, than the friend I find in thee.[16]

16. Text from *The Collected Works of Arthur Symons*. Vol. 2: *Poems* (London, 1929), p. 72.

Nevertheless, male artists do sometimes acknowledge the authority of the woman in the mirror; Wagner, for one, gives heroic dignity to the newly awakened Brunnhilde as she defers being caught up by Siegfried's desire:

> Sah'st du dein Bild im klaren Bach?
> Hat es dich Frohen erfreut?
> Rührtest zur Woge das Wasser du auf;
> zerflösse die klare Fläche des Bachs:
> dein Bild säh'st du nicht mehr.
>
> (Siegfried, Act III)

Have you seen your image in the clear stream? Joyous one, has it rejoiced you? Had you stirred the water to waves, the stream's clear surface would have broken up, you would no more have seen your image.

What is more, women artists can take up the mirror appropriatively. Lucy Snowe, the protagonist of Charlotte Brontë's novel *Villette* (1853), negotiates with mirrors repeatedly. At the turning point of her story, and amid the confusions of an outdoor masquerade, she "secretly and chiefly long[s] to come on [a] circular mirror of crystal, and surprise the moon glassing therein her pearly front." At the end, when Lucy attains a Woolfian room of her own, its centerpiece is precisely "[a] small round table [that] shone like the mirror over [the] hearth."[17] Mary Cassatt's painting *Mother and Child* (ca. 1905; Figure 1) interprets the mirror as the means by which feminine identity is passed from mother to daughter; the affectionate scene offers a tacit alternative to the oedipal rivalry typical of male models of cultural transmission. The sunflower at the mother's breast unites nurture with both procreative power and adornment, that is, with both nature and art. The mirrors, large and small, model Cassatt's own art of figure painting, which becomes a cultural projection of the feminine reproductive power also symbolized by the position of the naked child on her mother's lap.

Writing to Clara Wieck in 1836, Schumann adumbrates his own version of the scene in Cassatt's painting. "My future," he tells her, "seems more secure now . . . but I still have to accomplish a great deal just to achieve what you can see anytime you happen to step in front of a mirror—in the meantime you too will want to remain an artist. . . . You will carry your own weight, work with me, and share my joys and sorrows" (*S*, 122). Addressing Clara with the intimate "du" for the first time in their correspondence, as if the term had been vacated by the recent event of his mother's death, Schumann takes the woman/artist in the mirror as the model for the construction of his own subjectivity.

17. Charlotte Brontë, *Villette* (Harmondsworth, 1979), pp. 551, 584.

Figure 1. Mary Cassatt, *Mother and Child* (ca. 1905). National Gallery of Art, Washington; Chester Dale Collection.

Carnaval proposes the same model by compositional means. Both within and between pieces, the cycle is a musical hall of mirrors, a sound-space of feminine pleasure and liberty. Reflection proliferates: in several cases the mirror effect is overdetermined, with a larger symmetry enclosing a smaller. On the largest scale, *Carnaval* as a whole projects a mirror-image, its first half being ruled by the A. S. C. H. motive and its second half by the As. C. H. motive, with *Lettres Dansantes* effecting the transition. *Eusebius*, as we have seen, contains an internal mirror-image created by using the pedal to repeat, enhance, and render more fluid an unpedaled passage. *Reconaissance* does the same thing in heightened form, thereby mirroring both *Eusebius* and itself. The A♭ Major outer sections, with a rhythmically regular inner-voice *staccato*, are recapitulated and developed by a B Major middle section with syncopated inner-voice *legato*. The middle section also creates mirror-images between its own outer voices, repeating in the bass the theme stated in the treble. The title *Reconaissance* suggests recognition, acknowledgment, exploration, the object of which, we may surmise, is the feminine depth of the mirror itself.

Perhaps the most radical mirror piece in *Carnaval* is *Replique*, an abbreviated variant of *Coquette*, which it follows like a stray coda. Like *Chiarina* and *Estrella*, but more explicitly, *Coquette* and *Replique* mirror each other; like *Reconaissance*, *Replique* also redoubles the mirroring process within itself. In this case the internal mirroring involves thematic repetition between upper and inner voices. *Replique* begins by mirroring in the upper voice a short figure first heard as an inner voice at the opening of *Coquette*. A reprise of that opening follows immediately, re-mirroring the figure in its original position (X, ex. 4a). Next we hear the figure assume a new form (Y, ex. 4a), embroidering lightly on what now becomes recognizable as an intervallic cell (P, ex. 4b). This variant, too, first appears in the upper voice to be mirrored immediately as an inner voice. Then a metamorphosis happens: the figure expands into a lyrical melody (Z, ex. 4a) that also varies and inverts the cell (Q, ex. 4b). Like the figures before it, the melody first appears in the upper voice to be mirrored immediately as an inner voice. And that, but for a repeat of the whole process, is that. In *Replique*, mirroring becomes an explicitly creative activity: three mirror-images make up the whole of the piece, itself a mirror-image. In this creative or generative aspect, mirroring claims cultural power for the "feminine" artistry—the metamorphoses, changes of mask, changes of costume—embodied in the sequence of themes. Concurrently, by always moving from upper to inner voices, the mirroring of *Replique* evokes the peculiar sense of enchanted remoteness by which the mirror creates an alternative to the world of men. *Replique*, too, envisions a room of one's own.

In the ideal world, Schumann would have been able to sustain the impetus of *Replique* indefinitely. In the real world, probably no nineteenth-century man could contemplate the feminine with complete equanimity, not even the Schumann of *Carnaval*. Late in the cycle, the free play

EXAMPLE 4   Section b is arranged to suggest that even cells P and Q may be taken as mirror images of one another.

a.

b.

of gender that animates masquerade is arrested; *Pantalon et Columbine* sets masculine and feminine roles in drastic opposition, under the goad of sexual desire. The Pantaloon of Italian pantomime is literally a skirt-chaser, old, greedy, lecherous, and cuckolded; his costume usually includes a prominent phallus. Columbine is saucy, pretty, and intent on escaping Pantaloon's clutches. In what amounts to a parody of *Reconaissance*, which precedes it, *Pantalon et Columbine* evokes the lecher's pursuit with a frenetic, exaggerated *staccato*, and his prey's escape with a slower, exaggerated *legato*. The piece ends with Columbine's articulation gradually overtaking and retarding Pantaloon's (ex. 5a), as if, in a fulfillment of standard-issue male anxieties, she were appropriating his phallus for uses of her own. Columbine, indeed, is always cutting Pantaloon short. Her entrance prevents him from stating the consequent of a 4 + 4–measure period, and her dissolution of his *staccato* not only thwarts the same consequent but derails symmetrical phrasing altogether.

Such a catastrophe cries out for a retort, and Schumann soon provides one in *Paganini*. This appropriately virtuosic piece projects an antithesis to the image of the reflective, feminized artist; it gives us the artist as mesmerizer, the charismatic master of improvisation who possesses the inordinately phallic power of—in Schumann's words—"subjecting the public, of lifting it, sustaining it, and letting it fall again."[18] This phallic bravado is particularly obtrusive because *Paganini* is framed, but in no sense contained, by two renditions of a dance piece, *Valse Allemande*. The waltz seeks to manage the outbreak of sexual anxiety by sublimating the conflict of articulations found in *Pantalon et Columbine*. Columbine's slower *legato* now syncopates the rhythmic motto of *Coquette*, foregrounding both structural and representational continuity within *Carnaval* as a cycle. Pantaloon's faster *staccato* now meshes with social ritual, moving in step with the vigorous waltz rhythm and rounding off the dance with a robust cadence. *Valse Allemande* also couples its *legato* and *staccato* articulations in notably symmetrical periods, as if to rectify or undo the collapse of symmetrical phrasing in *Pantalon et Columbine*. By these means the waltz recasts the sexual as the aesthetic, commotion as custom, contention as balance. *Paganini*, however, rejects these efforts to temporize. With renewed exaggeration it appropriates both the *staccato* and *legato* articulations on behalf of its formidable masculine mystique; it even reverses the earlier collapse of Pantaloon's *staccato* into Columbine's *legato* (ex. 5b). Paganini, in short, retrieves the purloined phallus from Columbine.

Paganini confirms that the sexual opposition of *Pantalon et Columbine* cannot be assimilated to the fluctuations of masquerade. Ripples of unease continue; the second *Valse Allemande* is played faster than the first,

18. Schumann on Paganini and Liszt, in Robert Schumann, *On Music and Musicians*, ed. Konrad Wolff, trans. Paul Rosenfeld (New York, 1969), p. 156.

EXAMPLE 5

a. *Pantalon et Columbine*, mm. 31–38

b. *Paganini*, mm. 15–21

as if its fabric of sublimation were beginning to unravel. (Or is this a disturbance of reflection: "The mirror crack'd from side to side; / 'The curse is come upon me,' cried / The Lady of Shalott"?)[19] Once beset by masculine anxiety, *Carnaval* seems compelled to water down the festive imagery that has guided it so far. Carnival as the scene of masquerade, where subjective unity is cast away or recast in the crucible of gender, dwindles into a sublimated means to *épater les bourgeois*. As I noted earlier, the concluding *Marche des Davidsbündler contre les Philistins* recapitulates the themes of the opening *Preambule* to close the cycle in quasi-sonata style. Free play and radical heterogeneity are thus reduced to an organized procession—a circus parade with Schumann as ringmaster. The music remains rowdy enough to affront any number of Philistines, but it also joins the Philistines by growing deaf to the music of masquerade, of shape-shifting, of gender in free-fall.

Deaf—or almost deaf. The *Marche* also introduces a peculiar new element, a seventeenth-century theme that is labeled as such in the score. At once ironic and nostalgic, the old tune invites us to imagine a social world less rigid than anything the nineteenth century has to offer, a world less privatized, less insulated from wild ruckus. The tune reverts to the utopian dimension of masquerade; it marks the site where the fully radical, radically feminine, dimension of carnival was lost.

In closing, I would like to return to the problems raised by the critical reception of *Carnaval* as exemplified by Dahlhaus and Rosen. When Dahlhaus claims that Schumann's allusions, mottoes, and titles "sometimes appear to mean more than they actually say" or when Rosen writes off the character sketches and motivic signatures as "esoteric" and claims that "the significance of the *Carnaval* for us today lies elsewhere," the critical move being made is not only aesthetically but also politically formalist.[20] Carnival, or at least the idea of carnival, is above all subversive. To ignore the fact makes *Carnaval* far less so. To speak as though rhythmic impetus or motivic versatility were what "really" mattered in this music is to dehistoricize it. To dehistoricize it is to deny its claims to cultural agency. These strictures hold good even amid full descriptions of historical and cultural context, for context in the sense of a background or supplement is not at issue here. At issue are the dynamic, dialogical, and reciprocal transformations worked between different parts of the cultural field.

In the case of *Carnaval*, moreover, and not *Carnaval* alone, the issue is also gender. The formalism of Dahlhaus and Rosen, willingly or not, ignores sexual difference and in so doing insulates Schumann's music

19. Alfred, Lord Tennyson, "The Lady of Shalott" (1832, rev. 1842), lines 115–17; text from *Poems of Tennyson*, ed. Jerome H. Buckley (Boston, 1958).

20. Dahlhaus, *Nineteenth-Century Music*, p. 145; Rosen, sleeve notes to *Carnaval*.

from the force of femininity, even over what we may imagine to be Schumann's vigorous protests. The same insulation extends to Dahlhaus's and Rosen's critical practice itself, which valorizes the "masculine" definiteness of form over the "feminine" suggestiveness of poetic meaning. Precisely by scanting the question of meaning, Dahlhaus and Rosen write a logocentric criticism. Precisely by scanting the question of gender, they write a phallocentric criticism. That the criticism, in its own terms, is of a high order should perhaps add to rather than mitigate our disquiet.[21]

The politics of formalism has strong nineteenth-century roots. For a cautionary tale, consider Camille Saint-Saëns's comments on the piece he intended as the first French tone poem on a Lisztian model, *Omphale's Spinning Wheel* (*Le Rouet d'Omphale*, 1871–1872). Omphale was a Lydian queen who enslaved Hercules, dressed him in women's clothes, and made him sew and spin. Accordingly, as Saint-Saëns tells us in the score, "the subject of this symphonic poem is feminine seduction, the triumphant battle of weakness against strength." But a disclaimer follows immediately—and loudly: "The SPINNING WHEEL is nothing but a pretext, chosen only from the point of view of its rhythm and the general style or pace [*l'allure*] of the piece."[22] Saint-Saëns is stumbling over the fact that musical expressiveness is coded feminine even when what it expresses is misogyny. His need to show off the formal integrity of his music is not so much compelling as compulsory: in the triumphant battle of form against meaning, the composer can win back the masculinity his hero has lost. Nor is it an accident that Saint-Saëns chooses to depreciate the spinning wheel rather than, say, the figure that depicts "Hercules groaning in bondage." For the spinning wheel is associated with feminine creativity, with feminine power in the form of the spinning Fates, and, thanks to Goethe and Schubert, with feminine passion and masculine brutality. The formalization of the spinning wheel is an act of repression.

If the critical stance of Dahlhaus and Rosen has nineteenth-century models, so, too, does the stance I take in this essay. In his long poem *Fifine at the Fair* (1872), Robert Browning presents a married and supposedly domesticated Don Juan trying to justify his sudden infatuation with a gypsy dancer. To find a model for his feelings he turns to nothing other than Schumann's *Carnaval*, which prompts him to see the world at large as a tumultuous, promiscuous masquerade:

> Howe'er it came to pass, I soon was far to fetch—
> Gone off in company with [Schumann's] Music!
> . . . .

21. For a related discussion of the politics of formalism, see Susan McClary, "Terminal Prestige: The Case of Avant-Garde Music Composition," *Cultural Critique* 12 (1989): 57–82.
22. Note to the Durand et Fils edition (Paris, 1872).

And what I gazed upon was a prodigious Fair,
Concourse immense of men and women, crowned or casqued,
Turbaned or tiar'd, wreathed, plumed, hatted or wigged,
  but masked—
Always masked—

. . . .
                              On each hand,
I soon became aware, flocked the infinitude
Of passions, loves and hates, man pampers till his mood
Becomes himself, the whole sole face we name him by.[23]

Browning's version of carnival is seamier than Schumann's, but the community of idea and feeling is evident. Browning also follows Schumann in evoking the appeal of gender mobility, although he reverts to heterosexual norms far sooner than Schumann does. The irresistible Fifine appears first, not as a person, but as a transvestite persona, a "squalid girl" who sheds her petticoats to reveal a "gamesome boy" (section 3). The real Fifine simply reverses the transvestite roles, appearing in a page-boy costume cut down to reveal her breasts (section 15). Like Schumann's Coquette, Browning's Fifine models a creative vitality that is both shameless and limitless, a vitality the composer and the poet themselves cannot quite muster.

Browning's involvement with the poetics of *Carnaval* by no means blinds him to its formal interest. His Don Juan remarks on problems of fingering, on the prevalence of flat keys throughout the cycle, and on the contrast of *staccato* and *legato* in *Pantalon et Columbine* (which he gets backward). Unlike Saint-Saëns, Browning does not use these observations defensively. Rather, his critical practice declines to honor a distinction between formal and poetic elements; it spins the two together on its wheel or loom. Surely the present state of our culture demands that we do the same. The "classical" canon, even a canon no longer limited to the works of white males, is sure to become increasingly marginal unless we can link it to our most vital interests. We can no longer do that as formalists at a time when ideologies of unity are collapsing and the demands of difference and diversity are rightly being heard on all sides. We must learn to spin.

23. Excerpts from sections 93, 95, 96; text from *The Complete Poetic and Dramatic Works of Robert Browning* (Boston, 1895).

Narrative Agendas in "Absolute" Music: Identity and Difference in Brahms's Third Symphony

Susan McClary

The proper object of musical criticism may be music, but only if what we mean by "object" is a goal and not a possession. Music is all too easy to treat as an Abstract Entity, something in but not of culture and history. Perhaps the impulse to idealize music in these terms betrays a need to establish a preserve, a protected area where the compromises and brutalities of the world cannot encroach. Freud once compared our conscious fantasies—daydreams—to preserves like Yellowstone Park; perhaps the compositions we idealize are the national parks of high culture.[1]

Of all the sacrosanct preserves of art music today, the most prestigious, the most carefully protected is a domain known as "Absolute Music": music purported to operate on the basis of pure configurations, untainted by words, stories, or even affect.[2] This category first appeared in the nineteenth century for the purpose of distinguishing presumably autonomous instrumental music from opera, song, and programmatic music. Musicologists have tended to practice different modes of criticism for these various repertories, addressing texted or programmatic music according to the terms set by the verbal or referential components but restricting their observations of string quartets or symphonies to whatever can be discerned through formal analysis alone.

An earlier version of this essay was written for a colloquium on narrative theory at the Wesleyan University Center for the Humanities. I have benefited from the comments of Nancy Armstrong, Christine Bezat, Michael Cherlin, Michael Harris, Lawrence Kramer, Andrew Jones, Bruce Lincoln, Thomas Nelson, Nancy Newman, Richard Ohmann, Jann Pasler, Sanna Pederson, Peter Rabinowitz, Jane Stevens, David Sylvan, Leonard Tennenhouse, Gary Thomas, Robert Walser, and Winifred Woodhull.

1. Lawrence Kramer, "Dangerous Liaisons: The Literary Text in Musical Criticism," *19th-Century Music* 13 (1989): 165.

2. See the critical overview in Roger Scruton, "Absolute Music," *The New Grove Dictionary of Music and Musicians*, ed. Stanley Sadie (New York, 1980), vol. 1, pp. 26–27.

In *The Idea of Absolute Music* Carl Dahlhaus traces the history of this notion that some instrumental music is self-contained, innocent of social or other referential meanings.[3] The concept of Absolute Music arose with the beginnings of German romanticism, in the writings of E. T. A. Hoffmann, Ludwig Tieck, Wilhelm Heinrich Wackenroder, and others, although it was not called by this term until the midcentury debates of Richard Wagner and Eduard Hanslick over texted versus untexted music.[4] Dahlhaus reveals how and for what ideological purposes music was withdrawn from the public sphere of the eighteenth-century Enlightenment and reassigned to the domain of metaphysics. Along the way he observes that this new, nonreferential ideal of wordless music was closely related to the phenomenon of German pietism, that the cult of Absolute Music took on the trappings of religious spirituality.[5] In Hoffmann's words, instrumental music "leads us forth out of life into the realm of the infinite."[6] The early romantics sought in symphonies and quartets the subjective, transcendent experience of mystical union that formerly had been available principally through pietistic devotion. And they sought universal domination for German culture by means of this textless music that does not betray its place of origin.

A subsequent generation (around midcentury) took the autonomous concept of instrumental music from this crypto-sacred, nationalistic context and reclothed it in "objectivity." As Hanslick, the chief polemicist for the absolutists, wrote in 1854: "To the question: What is to be expressed with this musical material? the answer is: Musical ideas. A fully realized musical idea, however, is already something beautiful by itself, is its own purpose, and is in no way merely means or material for the representation of feelings and thoughts. . . . Tonally moving forms are the sole content and object of music."[7] This philosophy still regulates much of musicology, blocking all but the most formalistic approaches to criticism. Indeed, even though Dahlhaus painstakingly delineates this history whereby a social discourse was appropriated and redefined first by romantic mystics and then by objectivists, he continues to respect the prohibitions of that

3. Carl Dahlhaus, *The Idea of Absolute Music*, trans. Roger Lustig (Chicago, 1989).

4. See Carl Dahlhaus, "The History of the Term and Its Vicissitudes," in his *The Idea*, pp. 18–41.

5. Ibid., pp. 5, 86, and 90.

6. As quoted in ibid., p. 67.

7. *On the Beautiful in Music* (Leipzig, 1854); as translated in Dahlhaus, *The Idea*, p. 109. Compare this statement concerning "absolute" art with one by Charles Baudelaire: "Into this horrible book I have put all my *heart*, all my *tenderness*, all my (travestied) religion, all my *hatred*, all my *bad luck*. It is true I will write the contrary, I will swear up and down that it is a book of *pure art*, of mummery and acrobatics, and I will be lying like a con man." Letter to Narcisse Ancelle, 18 February 1866, as quoted in Jerrold Seigel, *Bohemian Paris: Culture, Politics, and the Boundaries of Bourgeois Life, 1830–1930* (New York, 1986), p. 122.

tradition of objectivity. In his *Nineteenth-Century Music* he practices only structural analysis on instrumental music, and he scorns those who would venture into hermeneutic studies of symphonies.[8]

Yet despite—and perhaps because of—Dahlhaus's warning, I find it necessary to rush in where he, among others, feared to tread, into what Lawrence Kramer calls this "protected area where the compromises and brutalities of the world cannot encroach." Nor am I am alone in this venture. One of the most important trends in recent musicology has been the demystification of Absolute Music, the demonstration that those compositions long exalted as autonomous rely—no less than operas or tone poems—on codes of social signification such as affective vocabularies and narrative schemata.[9] The treasured distinction between the musical and the so-called extramusical is starting to dissolve, allowing hermeneutic readings of compositions traditionally held to be exempt from interpretation.

My own interest in Absolute Music extends beyond hermeneutics, although I rely heavily on the kinds of insights offered by studies of narrative and semiotics. I wish to understand what this music apparently intends to convey through its use of publicly shared signs, but I also want to subject it to social critique.[10] For Absolute Music articulates the same dominant social beliefs and tensions as other cultural artifacts of the nineteenth century; indeed, its patterns represent habits of thought so fundamental that they can even be transmitted without verbal cues. Given

8. Carl Dahlhaus, *Nineteenth-Century Music*, trans. J. Bradford Robinson (Berkeley, 1989), pp. 11, 94. See also his *The Idea*, p. 37. It is illuminating to read Dahlhaus in tandem with Terry Eagleton, *The Ideology of the Aesthetic* (Oxford, 1990), and the nineteenth-century segments of Denis Hollier, ed., *The History of French Literature* (Cambridge, Mass., 1989). All three projects investigate the history of "autonomous" art, but only Dahlhaus attempts to preserve intact what he has himself helped to demystify.

9. See Anthony Newcomb, "Once More 'Between Absolute and Program Music': Schumann's Second Symphony," *19th-Century Music* 7 (1984): 233–50; "Schumann and Late Eighteenth-Century Narrative Strategies," *19th-Century Music* 11 (1987): 164–74; and "Sound and Feeling," *Critical Inquiry* 10 (1984): 614–43. See also Lawrence Kramer, *Music as Cultural Practice, 1800–1900* (Berkeley, 1990); Fred Maus, "Music as Drama," *Music Theory Spectrum* 10 (1988): 65–72; and Jann Pasler, "Narrative and Narrativity in Music," in J. T. Fraser, *Time and Mind: Interdisciplinary Issues* (Madison, Conn., 1989), pp. 233–57. Carolyn Abbate, in her *Unsung Voices: Opera and Musical Narrative in the Nineteenth Century* (Princeton, 1991), has raised some important questions concerning narrative readings of instrumental music. I hope to respond at length elsewhere to her arguments.

10. I have written elsewhere about music as social discourse. See, for example, "The Blasphemy of Talking Politics During Bach Year," in Richard Leppert and Susan McClary, eds., *Music and Society: The Politics of Composition, Performance and Reception* (Cambridge, 1987), pp. 13–62; "A Musical Dialectic from the Enlightenment: Mozart's Piano Concerto in G Major, K. 453, Movement 2," *Cultural Critique* 4 (1986): 129–69; and the methodological discussion in the first chapter of my *Feminine Endings: Music, Gender, and Sexuality* (Minneapolis, 1991).

that these covert patterns have managed to operate successfully for two centuries, they stand very much in need of interrogation.[11]

This project owes a great deal to the music criticism of Theodor W. Adorno, who traced the history of bourgeois subjectivity and its contradictions through the same instrumental music that seems so impervious to such analyses. Much of this essay stands as a particularized elucidation of a few extraordinarily provocative pages by Adorno concerning late nineteenth-century Absolute Music:[12] it attempts to make explicit the kinds of mediating steps that enabled Adorno to link musical procedures with society. But my analysis differs from his in that it also addresses issues such as gender and race—issues which were not among Adorno's priorities.

The viability of apparently autonomous instrumental music depends on the powerful affective codes that have developed within the referential domains of vocal music.[13] Familiarity with this network of cultural associations permits us to recognize even in textless music traditional signs for grief, joy, or the heroic. But signification extends far beyond the surface in instrumental music: its formal conventions—often held to be neutral with respect to meaning—are likewise socially encoded. Stuart Hall has written, with respect to narrative, that

> meanings are already concealed or held within the forms of the stories themselves. Form is much more important than the old distinction between form and content. We used to think form was like an empty box, and it's really what you put into it that matters. But we are aware now that the form is actually part of the content of what it is that you are saying. So then one

11. See Stuart Hall, "The Narrative Construction of Reality," *Southern Review* [Adelaide] 17 (1984): 3–17, for a theoretical discussion of the ways narrative conventions permeate virtually all cultural constructs. "In any society we all constantly make use of a whole set of frameworks of interpretation and understanding, often in a very practical unconscious way, and those things alone enable us to make sense of what is going on around us, what our position is, and what we are likely to do. . . . What is it that is secured, put in place, by those being the ways in which we talk to ourselves about life, experience, emotions, new situations? . . . Who is it that benefits? . . . Why do [these stories] take that shape? . . . What are the stories we don't tell ourselves?" (pp. 7–12).

12. See Theodor W. Adorno, "Class and Strata," *Introduction to the Sociology of Music*, trans. E. B. Ashton (New York, 1976), pp. 55–70. See also Rose Rosengard Subotnik, "The Historical Structure: Adorno's 'French' Model for the Criticism of Nineteenth-Century Music," *19th-Century Music* 2 (1978): 36–60.

13. These codes emerged self-consciously in seventeenth-century music and were theorized during the eighteenth century as the *Affektenlehre*, by writers such as Johann Mattheson and Johann David Heinichen. Even though these social codes of signification were no longer acknowledged by most nineteenth-century aestheticians, they are no less operative in the music. Traditional semiotics had been so thoroughly absorbed that they had become transparent or "natural." See the references in note 10.

has to ask why it is that certain events seem to be handled, predominantly in our culture, in certain forms.[14]

What, then, of the forms that guarantee and sustain Absolute Music? Classical instrumental music depends on two interlocking narrative schemata, tonality and sonata. I am referring here to tonality, not in the broad sense of pitch-centeredness (which would include most of Western music), but in the more specific sense of the grammatical and structural syntax of eighteenth- and nineteenth-century European musics. I have written elsewhere about the early history and also the decline of tonal procedures.[15] For our present purposes it is sufficient to recognize that the history of tonality was shaped by its social contexts and that tonality operates according to a standard sequence of dynamic events, giving the music it organizes a distinctly narrative cast.

Tonality emerged as a way of arousing and channeling desire in early opera,[16] although instrumentalists quickly adopted its procedures for their own repertories. In fact, Tieck, one of the early theorists of Absolute Music, described instrumental music as "insatiate desire forever hieing forth and turning back into itself."[17] On both local and global levels, tonality is intensely teleological; it works through the simple mechanism of suggesting a particular pitch for purposes of release, but then withholding that pitch while continuing to imply (through a particular brand of harmonic syntax) that the goal is nearly within reach. The surface of the tonal piece thus alternates between carefully sustained tension or protracted longing and periodic moments of relief.

The tonal composition (with a few idiosyncratic exceptions) ends in the same key in which it began. Consequently, from the very outset of the composition listeners know its probable ultimate goal. Yet that goal can be truly meaningful only if it is called into question. It therefore becomes necessary for the piece to leave the tonic key area and to enact an adventure in which other key areas are encountered and tonal identity is at least temporarily suspended. Regardless of the twists and turns of the composition's particular chain of events, however, the outcome—the inevitable return to the tonic—is always known in advance. To the extent that "Other" keys stand in the way of unitary identity, they register as dissonances and must finally be subdued for the sake of narrative closure.

---

14. Hall, "The Narrative Construction," p. 7.

15. See, for instance, my "The Transition from Modal to Tonal Organization in the Works of Monteverdi," Ph.D. diss., Harvard University, 1976; and *Feminine Endings*.

16. See my "Constructions of Gender in Monteverdi's Dramatic Music," *Cambridge Opera Journal* 1 (1989): 202–23. I am at present writing a book titled *Power and Desire in Seventeenth-Century Music*, to be published by Princeton University Press.

17. As quoted in Dahlhaus, *The Idea*, p. 18.

Difference is thus not coincidental to this schema. Without dissonance, without excursions into other keys, there would be no plot, no long-term dynamic tension. Yet those dissonances and other keys must eventually be purged—sometimes violently—if the composition is to end satisfactorily. The schema thus outlines a kind of narrative based on identity and certainty on the one hand, and difference and excitement (with at least the illusion of risk) on the other. Each individual piece of tonal music fleshes out the paradigm in its own way, principally through its choice of key relationships, its affective vocabulary, and its strategies for manipulating desire. But all of these choices are socially based and socially intelligible insofar as they draw on the powerful social conventions of normative tonality.

My account of tonality differs from most in that it regards as ideologically significant these oppositions between self and Other and the predetermined terms of resolution. But a few other music theorists have also noticed the political implications of the tonal schema, most explicitly Arnold Schoenberg, who writes in his *Theory of Harmony*:

> For [our forebears] the comedy concluded with marriage, the tragedy with expiation or retribution, and the musical work "in the same key." Hence, for them the choice of scale brought the obligation to treat the first tone of that scale as the fundamental, and to present it as Alpha and Omega of all that took place in the work, as the patriarchal ruler over the domain defined by its might and its will: its coat of arms was displayed at the most conspicuous points, especially at the beginning and ending. And thus they had a possibility for closing that in effect resembled a necessity.[18]

In other words, Absolute Music enacts a kind of absolutist political narrative merely by virtue of assuming tonality as a natural imperative.[19]

An additional stratum of narrative convention makes possible the nineteenth-century symphony: namely, sonata procedure—a particular schematic arrangement within tonality. The sonata exposition typically articulates the two initial key areas (tonic and its primary Other) with distinctive themes. In the eighteenth century, composers often replicated the opening theme at the level of the secondary key, thereby maintaining the identity of the implied protagonist throughout the tonal adventure; but in the nineteenth, thematic contrast became central to the paradigm. Thus the tension between identity and difference with respect to keys, which is already fundamental in tonality, is thrown into high dramatic relief by the additional tension between the two thematic types.

18. Arnold Schoenberg, *Theory of Harmony*, trans. Roy E. Carter (Berkeley, 1978), p. 129.

19. In fact, when Wagner coined the term *Absolute Music*, he intended it as a taunt. It is ironic that the term was quickly adopted by those he meant to parody.

James Webster's article in *The New Grove Dictionary of Music* offers the following, presumably neutral, description of this tension and its narrative consequences:

> The second group in the exposition presents important material and closes with a sense of finality, but it is not in the tonic. This dichotomy creates a "large-scale dissonance" that must be resolved. The "sonata principle" requires that the most important ideas and the strongest cadential passages from the second group reappear in the recapitulation, but now transposed to the tonic. The subtle tension of stating important material in another key is thus "grounded," and the movement can end.[20]

Later in this article Webster mentions that mid-nineteenth-century theorists began referring to these themes respectively as "masculine" (the opening material identified with what Schoenberg calls the "patriarchal" tonic) and "feminine" (the theme predestined to be "grounded" in the key of the first). For instance, in 1845 theorist A. B. Marx wrote: "The second theme, on the other hand, serves as contrast to the first, energetic statement, though dependent on and determined by it. It is of a more tender nature, flexibly rather than emphatically constructed—in a way, the feminine as opposed to the preceding masculine."[21]

This convention of designating themes as "masculine" and "feminine" was still common in pedagogy and criticism of the 1960s,[22] although musicology has since repudiated it and has attempted to expunge the memory that such gender-typing ever occurred or, in any event, that it ever truly meant anything. However, eliminating this terminology does not erase the issue of gender from the musical structures of this period: because many of the themes in question draw on the semiotics of "masculinity" and "femininity" as they were constructed in opera or tone poems, they are easily recognized in their respective positions within these musical narratives. We do not need to express verbal confirmation, such as A. B. Marx offers, in order to proceed.

Nor is this a trivial matter of labeling. We have already seen that these "masculine" and "feminine" themes are located in particular slots in the conventional schemata of tonality and sonata, that their respective fates are already cast before the composition begins. The "masculine" tonic is predestined to triumph, the "feminine" Other to be (in Webster's words) "grounded" or "resolved." In this respect, sonata replicates with uncanny

---

20. James Webster, "Sonata Form," *The New Grove Dictionary*, vol. 17, p. 498.

21. As cited and translated in a communication from Peter Bloom to *Journal of the American Musicological Society* 27 (1974): 162.

22. Not only are themes gendered in this way, but also cadences and, occasionally, triads. The underlying rationale always involves relative strength and "naturalness." See my discussion in chapter 1 of *Feminine Endings*.

accuracy the narrative paradigms of myth delineated by narratologists such as Vladimir Propp and Jurij Lotman.[23] As Teresa de Lauretis observes with respect to Lotman's schema:

> The hero must be male, regardless of the gender of the text-image, because the obstacle, whatever its personification, is morphologically female. . . . If the work of the mythical structuration is to establish distinctions, the primary distinction on which all others depend is . . . sexual difference. . . . The hero, the mythical subject, is constructed as human being and as male; he is the active principle of culture, the establisher of distinction, the creator of differences. Female is what is not susceptible to transformation, to life or death; she (it) is an element of plot-space, a topos, a resistance, matrix and matter.[24]

The reason, then, that Absolute Music appears to make itself up without reference to the outside social world is that it adheres so thoroughly to the most common plot outline and the most fundamental ideological tensions available within Western culture: the story of a hero who ventures forth, encounters an Other, fights it out, and finally reestablishes secure identity. So long as composers agreed to stick to the standard narrative, they and their audiences could pretend to be listening in on the utterances of Hegel's *Geist* or Schopenhauer's *Will*: an illusion always heavily circumscribed by convention, always ideologically saturated.

Instrumental composers who wanted to tell other stories risked unintelligibility. One popular solution was to provide listeners with alternative metaphorical grids, conveyed in titles or programs, through which to understand unorthodox formulations—a solution that also offered composers a potentially infinite range of idiosyncratic formal designs.[25]

23. Vladimir Propp, *Morphology of the Folktale*, ed. Louis A. Wagner (Austin, 1968); and Jurij M. Lotman, "The Origin of Plot in the Light of Typology," trans. Julian Graffy, *Poetics Today* 1 (1979): 161–84.

24. Teresa de Lauretis, "Desire in Narrative," in *Alice Doesn't: Feminism, Semiotics, Cinema* (Bloomington, 1984), pp. 118–19.

25. Richard Strauss states this explicitly in a letter to Hans von Bülow in 1888: "I have found myself in a gradually ever increasing contradiction between the musical-poetic content that I want to convey a[nd] the ternary sonata form that has come down to us from the classical composers. . . . Now, what was for Beethoven a 'form' absolutely in congruity with the highest, most glorious content, is now, after 60 years, used as a formula inseparable from our instrumental music. . . . If one wants to create a work of art which is unified in its mood and consistent in its structure . . . this is made possible only by inspiration through a poetic idea, whether it is introduced as a programme or not. I consider it a legitimate artistic method to create an appropriate new form for each subject." As translated in James Hepokoski, "Fiery-Pulsed Libertine or Domestic Hero? Strauss's Don Juan Reinvestigated" (unpublished typescript, 1990). I wish to thank Professor Hepokoski for permitting me to see a copy of this paper.

Critics such as Hanslick condemned the verbal cues of programs for sullying music's purity. But there was even more at stake: programs threatened to blow the lid off the metaphysical claims of the absolutists, for tone poems employed the same codes, the same gestural vocabulary, the same structural impulses—although always acknowledging (at least in part) what they signified.[26]

The schemata of tonality and sonata persisted in organizing European music for about two centuries, but they were anything but static.[27] Some of the transformations resulted from the prevalent anti-authoritarianism of romanticism, for no sooner had tonal or sonata conventions crystallized than composers began rebelling against their constraints; if these paradigms continued to underwrite composition and interpretation, they also provided the terms for resistance. But other shifts were the products of changing social attitudes toward questions of identity and difference, especially as they related to gender.[28] Consequently, no composition can be reduced simply to the narrative conventions that informed it: its historical moment and its particular strategies must also be taken into account. But the specific details of any given piece are intelligible only insofar as they engage dialectically with those conventions.

Thus I would now like to examine a work by a composer who represents the Old Faithful within the Yellowstone Park of Absolute Music, Johannes Brahms's Third Symphony (1883). When Brahms was a mere twenty years old, Robert Schumann hailed him as the hope for German music, the defense against the corruption of programmatic excess, the

26. Some programs, of course, do not fully divulge their agendas. For instance, the last movement of Debussy's *La Mer* ("Dialogue Between the Wind and the Sea") articulates in sound an extremely violent encounter between what are semiotically marked as a "masculine" force (the wind) and a "feminine" one (*la mer/la mère*), even though it does not acknowledge verbally that this is the case. See also Hepokoski, "Fiery-Pulsed Libertine." This rereading of Strauss's *Don Juan* observes much more about this tone poem's sexual narrative than the program admits explicitly.

27. Jay Clayton has recently criticized literary narratologists for the ahistoricity of their structures and analyses. See his "Narrative and Theories of Desire," *Critical Inquiry* 16 (1989): 33–53.

28. Eighteenth-century cultural artifacts typically reach closure in ways that seem unforced, as though the preordained hierarchies of class and gender are simply natural. During the nineteenth century, however, as such hierarchies were destabilized (in part by women who refused to assume subordinate positions), conflicts and attempts at closure became far more violent. This trajectory in literature has been traced by Nancy Armstrong, *Desire and Domestic Fiction: A Political History of the Novel* (Oxford, 1987); Peter Gay, *The Bourgeois Experience, Victoria to Freud.* Vol. 1: *The Education of the Senses* (Oxford, 1984); and Sander L. Gilman, *Difference and Pathology: Stereotypes of Sexuality, Race, and Madness* (Ithaca, 1985). It would be possible to do the same for the history of Absolute Music. This essay attempts to examine one moment; *Feminine Endings* addresses other repertories.

rightful heir to Beethoven, who represented the cornerstone of Absolute Music.[29] Through his rhetoric Schumann deliberately positioned himself as John the Baptist heralding the advent of Christ. Predictably, the young Brahms was almost paralyzed by Schumann's excess and the inflated expectations it raised; he was not to premiere a symphony until twenty-three years later.

When he did finally begin releasing symphonies, they were cast self-consciously in Beethovenian molds and were received in that spirit as well. The first of them was compared to Beethoven's Ninth, the second to the "Pastoral" Symphony.[30] And both stood as evidence that the metaphysical spirit of Absolute Music still smiled on Germany. Brahms's Third Symphony was, like Beethoven's Third, referred to as the "Eroica" or heroic— even by upholders of the absolutist faith, such as Hanslick.[31] The presumed "heroic" quality of the symphony might be denied by today's latterday objectivists, although most listeners can easily recognize the opening gesture of the symphony as belonging to a family that would also include Richard Strauss's Don Juan, Franz Liszt's triumphant Faust, or John Williams's Indiana Jones (mm. 1–3). The opening motto is loud, forcefully played by a band of brasses and winds, and it shoves up by means of apparently herculean effort to a point of release that hurls us into the first movement's narrative. Its sonority, volume, aggression, and rocketlike gesture mark it semiotically as "masculine."[32] Thus the symphony earns its heroic label right off the bat. But the symphony's claim to heroicism extends far beyond mere thematic character: like Beethoven's "Eroica," Brahms's narrative unfolding illustrates how heroic behavior is constituted, but it also revisits and critiques the formal terms of Beethovenian heroicism.

29. Robert Schumann, "New Paths," *Schumann on Music: A Selection from the Writings*, ed. and trans. Henry Pleasants (New York, 1988), pp. 199–200.

30. Eduard Hanslick, *Music Criticisms 1846–99*, ed. and trans. Henry Pleasants (Baltimore, 1950), p. 211.

31. Ibid., pp. 210–13.

32. Tradition has it that this motto—F-A♭-F—was a private sign between Brahms and his friend Joseph Joachim that meant "frei aber froh" (free but glad). This was supposed to have been Brahms's response to Joachim's motto, F-A-E, or "frei aber einsam" (free but lonely), by which he expressed his dissatisfaction with bachelor life. By contrast, the version ascribed to Brahms celebrates bachelorhood, the absence of entanglements with women. See the original anecdote in Max Kalbeck, *Johannes Brahms*, 2d ed. (Berlin, 1908–1914), vol. 1, p. 98.

Michael Musgrave has called this tradition into question because its authenticity cannot be substantiated. See "Frei aber Froh: A Reconsideration," *19th-Century Music* 3 (1980): 251–58. Yet this symphony (the principal composition that utilizes this motto) resonates powerfully with the gist of that "free but glad" slogan, struggling as it always is to throw off "feminine" influence. It is easy to see how this tradition may have arisen from the narrative tensions of the Third Symphony itself.

For although Brahms follows carefully in Beethoven's footsteps, some of the tensions that were audible even in Beethoven's own music had become almost unworkable by the time Brahms received them.[33] In the eighteenth century Haydn found it relatively unproblematic to enact the dynamic processes of tonality and sonata and to make the reconciliation between themes and forms sound natural, rational, unforced. But Beethoven began to question what it would mean for his protagonist— regardless of its individuating idiosyncrasies—to go through the same tonal and formal paces as every other composition. Beginning with his "Eroica," he began trying to make it seem that the protagonist was inventing itself and determining from its own quirks its own tailor-made succession of narrative events, while still holding on to the norms of tonality and sonata that guaranteed intelligibility.[34] Therein lies the revolutionary heroism of that symphony. But this tension between individual expression and social convention became exacerbated over the course of the nineteenth century, so that Brahms inherited both a desire to emulate the classical narrative model and, at the same time, a profound distrust of its strictures—including even what it means to be in a key or to achieve closure.

I introduced the initial gesture of Brahms's symphony as though it were a straightforward sign of heroic swagger. But that opening motto is, in fact, extremely complex. The symphony is ostensibly in F Major, characterized by a bright, sunny A♮. But the motto presents as its second sonority A♭, in direct opposition to the key's fundamental triad. Although the third sonority in the motto sets the mode "right" again with the return of A♮ in the harmony, this confusion over the proper mediant poses the terms of the entire symphony.

For the motto's identity is not reconcilable with the demands of tonality itself, and the symphony vacillates throughout between adhering to the thorny idiosyncrasy that spells this particular self and surrendering to the security, the false consciousness, the law of convention. The placid terrain of plain old F Major, with its consistent A♮, and keys that themselves highlight A♮ stand for enticements to abandon the struggle, while A♭ (which typically veers away from the affirmative into rage or melancholy) represents the attempt to hold on to the anomaly that gives this piece its identity. Yet despite all this individuation, we know that, according to the premises of musical narrative, tonal pieces cannot end in a key other than the one that opened the piece—especially not if the trajectory moves from

33. See Adorno, "Class and Strata," pp. 63–65; and Subotnik, "The Historical Structure."

34. For a narratological reading of the "Eroica," see Philip G. Downes, "Beethoven's 'New Way' and the Eroica," in Paul Henry Lang, ed., *The Creative World of Beethoven* (New York, 1970), pp. 83–102.

triumphant major into dismal minor.[35] If Beethoven first called the narrative model into question, Brahms plunged headlong into the fissures that had opened up in the aftermath of Beethoven's critique.

In the first section of his exposition Brahms's idiosyncratic motto, rather than selling out to the banality of tonal syntax, attempts to blaze its own harmonic path. Underneath the theme, the motto replicates itself end to end like Tinker Toys or a strand of DNA. The result is a sequence of chords that swing among distantly related keys as though arbitrarily, cut loose from the garden-variety tonal syntax that gives the music of this period its illusion of rationality. By avoiding convention the motto may succeed in devising its own solipsistic process, but it is a process that verges on the socially unintelligible.

Moreover, after a mere fourteen bars the motto seems to have run its course: the contradiction apparently cannot be sustained indefinitely. What follows is a serene little tune from which all evidence of A♭ has been expunged (mm. 15–19). In the wake of the heroic flailing that precedes it, however, this theme sounds almost lobotomized. The motto comes back (m. 19), first disguised in a diatonic transformation and then in earnest. When the little tune returns (m. 23), it has been flipped around to D♭ Major, in accordance with the dictates of the motto and in defiance of convention.

We now begin to approach the second key area. Ordinarily, the second key would be on the fifth scale-step. But given the specific tensions of this piece, such a choice could only mean blind adherence to convention. Thus Brahms makes the second key relevant to this particular narrative. It is A Major; the A♮ that has been so problematized as the option spelling loss of identity here asserts itself as a rival key center. We arrive at A Major, moreover, through a sleight-of-hand (mm. 29–35) in which the treasured A♭ is gradually reinterpreted as G♯ resolving dutifully into A. David Brodbeck has argued that these measures refer explicitly to the moment from the Venusburg scene in Wagner's *Tannhäuser* in which sirens seductively beckon "Naht euch dem Strande."[36] And as our sign of heroic resistance loses its vitality, we are delivered over to the second theme.

Let's pretend we have no idea that second themes were sometimes called "feminine." The score marks this one as *grazioso* (in contrast to the opening theme's *passionato*). A dancelike meter emerges, with an ara-

35. Among the few tonal pieces that progress from major to minor is the last of Schubert's Impromptus, Op. 90. This piece is so odd that theorist Edward T. Cone was compelled to write a narrative account of it. See his "Schubert's Promissory Note," *19th-Century Music* 5 (1982): 233–41.

36. David Brodbeck, "Brahms, the Third Symphony, and the New German School," in Walter Frisch, ed., *Brahms and His World* (Princeton, 1990), pp. 67–68. Brodbeck interprets the principal tension in the movement in terms of Brahms's ambivalence toward Wagner.

besque tune in the clarinet that weaves around teasingly over a static, nonprogressing bass. This bass drone contributes what Brodbeck describes as a "pastoral atmosphere," especially after the intellectual torments of the opening (mm. 36–49).[37] Its alignment with "nature," stasis, seduction, and the physicality of the dance indicates that this theme already occupies a position on the "feminine" side of nineteenth-century cultural semiotics.

But it is possible to go further. Hermann Kretzschmar, a critic from the turn of the century who broke rank by writing in hermeneutic terms about the Absolute Music of his day, refers to this theme as Delilah, pointing to the Oriental exoticism, the dizzying rhythms, and the seductive sensuality of this section.[38] Indeed, this theme serves to rob the movement's implied trajectory of its energy, "to lull the powerful elements of the composition to sleep with gentle feelings."[39] It shears off the crucial A♭ that is the secret of the hero's strength and domesticates that pitch for its own purposes—as the G♯ that leads back inevitably to A♮.

However, like Samson after his first encounters with Delilah or like Tannhäuser after Venus, the motto gradually awakens (beginning in m. 49) and throws off the influence of this second theme. It reestablishes its original meter and aggressiveness; and although it is temporarily stuck with A as tonic, its heroic move is to cancel out the affirmative, alluring quality of that key by ending the exposition forcefully in a stoic A Minor. This leads to a return to the explosive beginning of the exposition for a second presentation of self, seduction, and resistance—a dramatic sequence that now threatens to become cyclic rather than resolvable.

I should mention at this point that the story of Samson and Delilah was especially popular in the late nineteenth century, when this symphony was written. Saint-Saëns's opera of that name had appeared six years earlier, in 1877; other operas with vampirish, treacherous women (often marked as racially Other) and victimized heroes were becoming prevalent, *Carmen* being the best known of them.[40] As Peter Gay and Sander Gilman have demonstrated, the story of a white male protagonist ren-

37. Ibid., p. 69.

38. Hermann Kretzschmar, *Führer durch den Konzertsaal: Sinfonie und Suite*, vol. 2, ed. Hugo Botstiber, 7th ed. (Leipzig, 1932), pp. 95–100. The subordinate theme in this symphony may not sound Oriental to our ears, for we are far better acquainted with actual Asian music than was Brahms. Kretzschmar's testimony is helpful because it points up for us what would have been conceived and perceived as "Oriental" within the codes of that time. Tchaikovsky's Symphony No. 4 has a similarly Orientalist "feminine" second theme. See my discussion in "Sexual Politics."

39. Kretzschmar, "The Brahms Symphonies," trans. Susan Gillespie, in Frisch, ed., *Brahms and His World*, p. 136.

40. See my discussion of *Carmen* in "Sexual Politics," and also my *Georges Bizet's Carmen* (Cambridge, 1992).

dered impotent by an exotic temptress appealed enormously to Europeans in the last third of the nineteenth century.[41] And Brahms the absolutist was not oblivious to these trends: when *Carmen* was first produced in Vienna in 1876, he went twenty times to see it.[42]

The development section of the symphony (from m. 71) presents a knock-down-drag-out confrontation between the two forces. It opens with the heroic materials in both low and high instruments, both rightside up and upside down. The protagonist has consolidated its forces and militance, yet its accents are all rhythmically displaced, rendering it unstable. And as soon as it reaches temporary closure, the second theme enters in a savage transformation (m. 77). No longer enticing, it now matches the aggression of the first theme. Our contemporary witness Kretzschmar hears this as wrathful, hysterical, distorted with rage, and he describes the scene with a virtuosity of alliteration that would give Wagner pause.[43]

Gradually, however, its energy dissipates, and we are led into the development's other surprise: the heroic motto transformed into a serene, lyrical melody (m. 101). It is tender, yearning, rather than striving; and although it still twists around harmonically to irrationally related keys in a kind of infinite regress of its idiosyncrasy, it does so without force. We get a glimpse here of the hero's privatized subjectivity. Kretzschmar, in keeping with his Samson trope, refers to it as a dreamer or sleeper and says that it sounds like a nocturne, a genre strongly associated with women and femininity.[44] This passage occupies flat keys: the hero's identification with flats remains intact, but without the antagonism of the other side of the dialectic it lacks vitality. We also seem very far away from the determining tonic.

The heroic theme then enters haltingly in m. 112, divorced from the motto that had always animated it. It sinks down without resistance in

---

41. Gay, "Offensive Women and Defensive Men," in *Education of the Senses*, pp. 169–225; and Gilman, *Difference and Pathology*. See also Mieke Bal, "Delilah Decomposed: Samson's Talking Cure and the Rhetoric of Subjectivity," in her *Lethal Love: Feminist Literary Readings of Biblical Love Stories* (Bloomington, 1987), pp. 37–67.

42. Mina Curtiss, *Bizet and His World* (New York, 1958), p. 426. Brahms presented the *Carmen* score to Clara Schumann. Tchaikovsky likewise was enamoured of *Carmen*, as were Wagner and Nietzsche. For more on Brahms's ambivalence toward women, see Peter F. Ostwald, "Johannes Brahms, Solitary Altruist," in Frisch, ed., *Brahms and His World*, esp. pp. 28–31.

43. Kretzschmar, *Führer*, p. 97: "Ganz unversehens tritt da das zweite Thema herein, aber es ist hier ganz anders gemeint als in der Themengruppe: . . . es kommt in Moll grollend, grimmig abweisend, hoch erregt, mit Zusätzen, die es verzerren und verhöhnen, es wird mit einem schliesslich komischen Eifer abgelehnt under zurückgewiesen."

44. Ibid., p. 97. See Jeffrey Kallberg, "The Harmony of the Tea Table: Gender and Ideology in the Piano Nocturne," *Representations* 39 (1992): 102–33.

what seems like free-fall, its major mediant converting to minor but otherwise without any semblance of its original gritty identity. But at what seems like the last moment before irreversible catatonia, the bass catches on F, the tonic pitch (m. 118). With a gigantic effort requiring that it redouble itself, the motto launches back into the original key, the opening theme complex, and the formal recapitulation (m. 120).

The development thus presents an inversion in power between the first and the second theme, as the "feminine" theme betrays its latent ferocity and the heroic theme lies impotent, effeminized, and helpless, summoning up the strength to escape only at the last moment. The purpose of the recapitulation is to reestablish the rightful relationship and begin the push toward closure. Yet, oddly enough, it is at this moment of apparent narrative triumph that the constraints of sonata itself begin to chafe. Sonata had its beginnings in the Enlightenment and so was originally concerned with formal balance. In Haydn, when the recapitulation repeated the events of the exposition, it served to celebrate the reconciliation of social order with individual will. But in the nineteenth century, when the quality of "becoming" was the ideal, the recapitulation constituted an awkward holdover from that earlier time: a section of the piece where narrative progression suddenly gives way to formal reiteration.

As is typical, Brahms's recapitulation goes through the paces of the exposition once again, restating the themes in their original guises. The second theme, which had threatened to usurp agency in the development, now reappears as it was at the outset, but transposed—not to the tonic, but to D Major, a key that balances symmetrically with its original key (m. 149). By thus presenting the second theme symmetrically and in its initial version, it may be that Brahms reduces it to a mere vestige of the Enlightenment's demand for structural balance. But in withholding the second theme from the control of the "patriarchal" tonic, Brahms also suggests that it remains ungrounded and unresolved, especially since the recapitulation ends with its final (D Minor) rather than with the movement's tonic.

However, it might best be argued that the "feminine" theme is less a threat in and of itself than it is a projection of the hero's own ambivalence. In a sense, the "feminine" Other here is gratuitous, a mere narrative pretext. For the principal dilemma in the symphony is finally oedipal: the archetypal struggle of the rebellious son against the conventional Law of the Father, the struggle that underlies so many Western narratives.[45] As Jessica Benjamin has written of this paradigm, "The struggle for power takes place between father and son; woman plays no part in it, except as prize or temptation to regression, or as the third point of a triangle. There

45. See Ostwald, "Johannes Brahms," pp. 25–28.

is no struggle between man and woman in this story; indeed, woman's subordination to man is taken for granted."[46]

In this movement the principal tension is not between first and second theme (a tension resolved with little difficulty), but, rather, between a first theme that is dissonant with respect to the conventions that sustain its narrative procedures and those conventions themselves. To the extent that the heroic theme bears marks of Otherness with respect to "patriarchal" tonal custom, it itself stands in danger of being purged for the sake of tonal propriety. The remainder of the movement focuses on the resolution of the composition's real dilemma: how to define closure in a piece in F Major that insists on maintaining a defiant A♭ for purposes of identity.

The movement's coda (from m. 183) proceeds with saber-rattling triumph for a while; yet although this enacts a return to the original heroic affect and key, it does little toward solving the A♭/A♮ dilemma. Commentators from Kretzschmar to objectivists such as Hanslick have remarked on the strangeness of the ending. The energy of the movement simply subsides: the motto gives one last appearance (mm. 216–20), and then the heroic theme drifts downward without resistance to resigned acceptance of closure in standard F Major. At the conclusion of what is otherwise an austere formal analysis, Dahlhaus himself grasps at a quasi-programmatic explanation, writing of this ending, "The subject immures itself to the world and turns ultimately to silence."[47]

The remaining movements of the symphony extend these narrative tensions further, first by moving to a serene choralelike movement (recalling the connections of Absolute Music with Lutheran pietism), but then making increasing forays onto the dark side until the final movement returns us, not to the expected F Major, but to F Minor, with its four flats. The struggles for identity that characterized the first movement become even more militant in this finale, which presses relentlessly against any surrender to convention. Yet its conclusion parallels that of the first movement: the minor evaporates, yielding to a replay of the earlier movement's last-minute capitulation, now enhanced with prayerlike chorales.

This conclusion may be read in a number of ways. The unsettling compromise at the end of each of the two critical movements may indicate defeat: the inability either to maintain indefinitely or to solve the contradictions that had initially hurled the symphony into motion. Or the chorale references at the end (also characteristic of transfiguring

46. Jessica Benjamin, *The Bonds of Love: Psychoanalysis, Feminism, and the Problem of Domination* (New York, 1988), pp. 6–7. See also Eve Kosofsky Sedgwick, *Between Men: English Literature and Male Homosocial Desire* (New York, 1985).

47. Dahlhaus, *Nineteenth-Century Music*, p. 269.

encounters with the sublime in Beethoven)[48] may imply apotheosis rather than defeat, a transcendence of the struggle. Yet the fact that tonal banality is the only form of closure available at the end of this and every other composition in the tonal repertory means that the normative term of the dilemma, the conventional A♮, is allowed to prevail after all—that, in some important sense, the struggle was always just an illusion.[49]

Thus if Brahms's symphony is intelligible by virtue of his adherence to his inherited narrative paradigms, its principal conflict involves not so much its own internal thematic elements as the restrictiveness of tonal procedures and of nineteenth-century formal conventions themselves: conventions concerning what it means to be in a key, to undergo recapitulation, to acquiesce to closure in keeping with classical models. Adorno writes: "The ideological side of Brahms also turns musically wrong when the standpoint of the subject's pure being-for-itself keeps compromising with the traditional collective formal language of music, which is not that subject's language any more."[50] Schoenberg's radical solution was, of course, to scrap intelligibility along with the social contracts upon which it had depended.[51]

I have not invaded the Yellowstone Park of Absolute Music to vandalize it. Part of my motivation is to examine the paranoid agendas relating to gender and even to race (in the guise of the treacherous, Oriental temptress) that show up regularly in this music that wants to resist any and all critiques. I hasten to add that Brahms was no guiltier of such narratives and constructions than were most of his contemporaries: the point is not to single him out for castigation, but, rather, to indicate that these mod-

48. For a discussion of musical representations of the sublime in Beethoven and Schubert, see my "Pitches, Expression, Ideology: An Exercise in Mediation," *Enclitic* 7 (1983): 76–86.

49. For a similar reading of another composition by Brahms, see Christine Bezat, Andrew Jones, Thomas Nelson, and Nancy Newman, "Brahms' Intermezzo, Op. 116, no. 4" (unpublished paper, 1990). I wish to thank the four of them for stimulating discussions of these issues. See also Thomas Nelson, "A Sublime Object of Ideology: Case Study #116/4" (unpublished paper, 1990). I am also grateful to Sanna Pederson for permitting me to read her "The German Symphony After Beethoven" (unpublished paper, 1990).

50. Adorno, "Class and Strata," p. 65.

51. See Schoenberg, *Style and Idea*, trans. Leo Black (Berkeley, 1975), and his *Theory of Harmony*. See also Adorno, "Arnold Schoenberg, 1874–1951," in *Prisms*, trans. Samuel and Shierry Weber (Cambridge, Mass., 1981), pp. 147–72. Again Jessica Benjamin's analysis proves insightful, as we consider the serial aftermath of Schoenberg's revolution: "The sons who overthrow the father's authority become afraid of their own aggression and lawlessness and regret the loss of his wonderful power; and so they reinstate law and authority in the father's image" (*The Bonds of Love*, p. 6).

els were so pervasive that they informed even Brahms's presumably abstract compositions. Moreover, such narratives still prevail in Western society, reproduced and transmitted in part by prestigious public texts such as symphonies. Thus we cannot afford to let Absolute Music pass unexamined: even those of us who would like to get beyond issues of gender difference can do so only if we perceive the extent to which culture—even High Culture—traffics in such images and stories.

Far from dismissing this symphony, however, I want to take it seriously as a cultural artifact, an object that tells us something about the values of the historical moment from which it emerged and of subsequent generations who have found meaning in such works—a document that speaks of heroism, adventure, conflict, conquest, the constitution of the self, the threat of the Other, and late-nineteenth-century pessimism. If the Enlightenment wished to maintain that individual will and social contract were mutually compatible, by the late nineteenth century this belief was seen by many as an untenable fairytale.[52] But the formal processes of classical music, which were developed during the Enlightenment, continued, regardless of the composer's intentions, to transmit something of that story. Brahms's Third Symphony presents tonality and sonata in a state of narrative crisis. It takes on and attempts to derail those Enlightenment assumptions, thus giving voice to the increasing self-alienation of the late-nineteenth-century individual (usually assumed to be male) and his feelings of impotence in a totalizing world that always defeats in advance his challenges to its absolute authority.

To be sure, the blame for these feelings of impotence was all too often displaced onto feminine and ethnic Others, as it is in the second-theme subplot of this symphony. But we do not have to agree with Brahms's particular narrative arrangements in order to admire the integrity with which he articulated and grappled with the problems. We need to be able to understand him not as a universal oracle but, rather, as a witness to and participant in a cluster of tensions specific to late-nineteenth-century Austro-Germany.[53] And if we do not want to accept his solutions, we must find other ones—without, however, losing sight of the complex moment in our cultural history about which he testifies so eloquently.

Ironically, perhaps, in this process of excavating the suppressed narrative strategies of composers such as Brahms, we can learn a great deal about the music itself—not just its formal intricacies, but its human and

52. For instance, see again the quotation in the text, from Schoenberg, and in note 25, from Richard Strauss.

53. See Leon Botstein, "Time and Memory: Concert Life, Science, and Music in Brahms's Vienna," in Frisch, ed., *Brahms and His World*, pp. 3–22.

historical dimensions as well. For we have long stifled the violence, the anxieties, the pain, the ideological contradictions of this music so as to exalt it as manifesting pure order. If removing Brahms's Third Symphony from the Yellowstone Park of Absolute Music opens it to critique, this same critique permits it to live and speak again.

Contributors

Carolyn Abbate is professor of music at Princeton. With Roger Parker, she has co-edited *Analyzing Opera: Verdi and Wagner* (1988), and she is the author of *Unsung Voices* (1991). She has extensively utilized literary theory and postmodern philosophical and critical orientations in her work.

Philip Brett is professor of music at the University of California, Riverside. He is general editor of *The Byrd Edition* and compiler of the Cambridge Opera Handbook on *Peter Grimes* (1983), and he has published articles on other areas of English music as well as on the theory of textual criticism. He has recently founded a Gay and Lesbian Study Group within the American Musicological Society.

Suzanne G. Cusick has taught music and women's studies at several institutions, including Wells College, the State University of New York at Oswego, and Oberlin College, and she has done nonacademic work as a consultant in gender equity. She is currently teaching at the University of Virginia. She is the author of *Valerio Dorico, Music Printer in Sixteenth-Century Rome* (1981), and she has written on Francesca Caccini, gender in early opera, and parlor music in nineteenth-century America.

Barbara Engh is a Ph.D. candidate in the program in Cultural Studies and Comparative Literature at the University of Minnesota. Her dissertation will explore the question of phonography and of musicality in critical theory.

Ellen Koskoff is an ethnomusicologist who is currently associate professor of musicology at the Eastman School of Music. She is the editor of *Women and Music in Cross-Cultural Perspective* (1987) and the author of "Thoughts

on Universals in Music," in *World of Music* (1984), and of many articles on
Hasidic music and on various aspects of gender and music, and particularly on women's roles in ritual and performance.

Lawrence Kramer, professor of English and comparative literature at
Fordham University, works as a musicologist, composer, and literary
critic. He is the author of *Music and Poetry: The Nineteenth Century and After*
(1984) and *Music as Cultural Practice, 1800–1900* (1990), as well as numerous articles.

Susan McClary is professor of music in the Faculty of Music at McGill
University. Her publications include articles on seventeenth-century
style, ideological dimensions of music by Bach and others, problems in the
reception of new music, current popular music, and feminist music criticism. She is co-editor with Richard Leppert of *Music and Society* (1987)
and author of *Feminine Endings: Music, Gender, and Sexuality* (1991) and
Georges Bizet: Carmen (1992).

Mitchell Morris teaches at the University of California, San Diego. His
research interests include music, particularly Russian and American, of
the late nineteenth and the twentieth century, and issues of music criticism. He is currently at work on his dissertation, "Musical Eroticism and
the Transcendent Strain: The Music of Alexander Skryabin 1900–09."

Nancy B. Reich is the author of *Clara Schumann: The Artist and the Woman*
(1985) and of articles and reviews in *Notes, The Musical Quarterly, 19th-
Century Music,* and other publications. Her interests include nineteenth-
century European music history and women in music. She has taught at
Queens and Lehman colleges of the City University of New York, at New
York University, at Manhattanville College, and at Bard College, and she
has been a visiting scholar at the Center for Research on Women at
Stanford University. She has been appointed Arnold Bernhardt Visiting
Professor of Music at Williams College for Spring 1993.

Carol E. (Carolina) Robertson was raised in Andean Argentina. Since
1969 she has done field research on music, gender, and the performance
of healing among Tzeltal (southern Mexico), Mapuche (Andean Argentina), Kassena-Nankani (Ghana/Burkina Faso), and Hawaiians (Polynesia). She is a former president of the Society for Ethnomusicology and is
currently an associate professor at the University of Maryland. She edited
Musical Repercussions of 1492: Explorations, Encounters and Identities (1992)
and is completing a book entitled *Spirit, Gender, and Musical Performance.*

John Shepherd is professor of music and sociology at Carleton University, Ottawa, where he is director of the School for Studies in Art and Culture. He is a co-author of *Whose Music? A Sociology of Musical Languages* (1977), the author of *Tin Pan Alley* (1982), *La musica come sapere sociale* (1988), and *Music as Social Text* (1991), the editor of *Alternative Musicologies* (1990), a special issue of the *Canadian University Music Review*, and the co-editor, with Will Straw, of *The Music Industry in a Changing World* (1991), a special issue of *Cultural Studies*. Professor Shepherd has written many articles on the sociology and aesthetics of music, the sociology of music education, and popular music, and was from 1983 to 1987 the general secretary of the International Association for the Study of Popular Music.

Ruth A. Solie is professor of music at Smith College and a participant in the women's studies program there. She is an associate editor of *19th-Century Music*, co-editor, with Eugene Narmour, of *Explorations in Music, the Arts, and Ideas: Essays in Honor of Leonard B. Meyer* (1988), and author of articles on nineteenth-century music and its cultural and intellectual history, some from a feminist perspective.

Judith Tick is professor of music at Northeastern University. She is the co-editor, with Jane Bowers, of *Women Making Music: The Western Art Tradition* (1986) and the author of *American Women Composers Before 1870* (1983). She is currently at work on a biography of Ruth Crawford Seeger, to be published by Oxford University Press.

Leo Treitler is Distinguished Professor of Music at the City University of New York Graduate Center. A specialist in music of the Middle Ages, especially in regard to questions of orality and literacy, he has published many critical essays and essays on the historiography and epistemology of musical studies, several of which have recently been collected under the title *Music and the Historical Imagination* (1989).

Gretchen A. Wheelock is associate professor of musicology at the Eastman School of Music. She specializes in music of the Classical period and has recently completed a book on wit and humor in Haydn's instrumental music. Her scholarly work has focused on issues of aesthetics, reception history, and performance practice, with a particular interest in the transition from private to public patronage and its impact on style, genre, and venues of music-making in the late eighteenth century.

Elizabeth Wood is a musicologist and novelist who teaches feminist theory and lesbian literary traditions at Sarah Lawrence College. She has published essays and reviews of nineteenth- and twentieth-century women's musical production and auto/biography, British and Australian music and opera, and musical representations of gender and sexuality. She is completing a study of the English composer Ethel Smyth, to be published by Bloomsbury Publishing of London.

Index

Abbate, Carolyn, 18
Abraham, Julie, 173
Absolute music, 326–35, 338, 341, 342–44; assumed superiority of, 259; meaning in, 12
Accomplishment, female, music as, 90–91, 98, 132
Adams, Parveen, 12
Adorno, Theodor W., 329, 342
Aesthetics of music, 38; gay, 185; gendered, 9, 83; ideology of, 186, 327
Amateur, in Barthes, 75–76
American Musicological Society, 260
Analysis, of music, 73; ideology of, 30, 324; including gender and race, 329
Anderson, Bonnie, 130
Anthropology, discourse of, 149–63
Anti-modernism, 88, 98
Apel, Willi, 29–30, 33
Ariosto, Lodovico: *Orlando furioso*, 285
Artist-musician class, 125
Auden, W. H., 265, 266, 276
Auerbach, Nina, 14
Author: in Barthes, 231; death of, 42, 229–32, 234; female, 237
Authorial voice, 19, 229, 230n.11; dispersion of, 242, 252, 255; female, 228, 229, 233, 236, 252; male, 232, 247; usurpation by performer, 234, 255
Authority: of the European musical tradition, 99–100; of experience, 185; in performances, 234–36, 255

Autobiography, 168–69; lesbian, 164–65; in music, 177

Babbitt, Irving, 88
Bach, Johann Sebastian: *The Art of Fugue*, 168
Bakhtin, Mikhail, 306, 310
Barber, C. L., 268
Barnett, Clara Kathleen. *See* Rogers, Clara Barnett
Barrow, Tui Terrence, 116
Barthes, Roland, 14, 19, 200, 229–34, 252; and music, 66–79
Basedow, Johann Bernhard, 133
Battersby, Christine, 9
Beethoven, Ludwig van, 76; Brahms as heir to, 335–37; as epitome of European music, 35; Symphony no. 9, 36, 38–39, 41–43, 133
Bel canto, 190, 197, 199
Benjamin, Jessica, 340
Bernal, Martin, 31–33
Bernard, Sam, 120
Besseler, Heinrich, 34
Binaries. *See* Dualities
Biological determinism. *See* Essentialism
Biology, as a ground of difference, 4
Body, as music's referent, 73
Boethius, 23
Brahms, Johannes, 178; Symphony no. 3, 12, 334–44
Brecht, Bertolt, 78

Compositor: Braun-Brumfield, Inc.
Music setter: Dennis Riley
Text: 10/12 Baskerville
Display: Baskerville
Printer: Braun-Brumfield, Inc.
Binder: Braun-Brumfield, Inc.